Qualitative Reading Inventory-7

Lauren Leslie
Marquette University

JoAnne Schudt Caldwell
Cardinal Stritch University

Pearson

Cataloging-in-Publication Data is available on file at the Library of Congress.

1R_2021

ISBN-10:   0-13-756087-7
ISBN-13: 978-0-13-756087-5

Access Code Card
ISBN-10:   0-13-577510-8
ISBN-13: 978-0-13-577510-3

Instructor's Review Copy
ISBN-10:   0-13-670685-1
ISBN-13: 978-0-13-670685-4

Brief Contents

Section 1 Introduction to Basic Concepts of Reading Assessment   1

Section 2 Research Guiding the Development of the *Qualitative Reading Inventory*   9

Administration and Scoring of the *QRI-7*

Section 3 Purposes and Basic Steps for Administering the *Qualitative Reading Inventory-7*   25

Section 4 Determining Reading Levels   32

Section 5 Using the Word Lists   39

Section 6 Assessing Word Identification in Context, Automaticity, and Prosody   49

Section 7 Assessing Comprehension: Questions and Retellings   59

Section 8 Assessing Strategic Reading: Think-Alouds   70

Section 9 Recording, Analyzing, and Using Results of the *QRI-7*   79

Word Lists and Elementary Grades: Level-Diagnostic Passages

Middle School and High School: Level-Diagnostic Passages

Section 10 *QRI-7* Test Materials: Word Lists and Level-Diagnostic Passages   91

Administering and Scoring the Inference-Diagnostic Passages

Section 11 Administering and Scoring the Inference-Diagnostic Passages   379

Inference-Diagnostic Passages: Grades 4–High School

Section 12 Inference-Diagnostic Materials   389

Section 13 Technical Development of the *Qualitative Reading Inventory-7*   503

Appendix: Videos for Extra Practice (Pearson eText)   522
References   528
Index   533

Contents

Preface   ix

Section 1   Introduction to Basic Concepts of Reading Assessment   1

What is reading?   1
Implications for Assessment   3
Introduction to Informal Reading Inventories   3
Measures of Difficulty   4

Section 2   Research Guiding the Development of the *Qualitative Reading Inventory*   9

How the *QRI* Is Different from Other IRIs   9
Factors Related to Reading Comprehension   10
    Word Recognition and Identification   10
    Oral Reading   11
    Fluency, Automaticity, and Prosody   14
    Content Knowledge   16
    Text Structure   16
    Methods of Assessment of Reading Comprehension   17
    Interactive Strategies to Assess Reading Comprehension   22
Summary   23

Administration and Scoring of the *QRI-7*

Section 3   Purposes and Basic Steps for Administering the *Qualitative Reading Inventory-7*   25

Purposes for Administering *QRI-7*   25
    Determine a Student's Instructional Reading Level   25
    Assessment of Prior Knowledge   27
    Assessment of Word Pronunciation Errors, Fluency, and Prosody   27
    Assessment of Comprehension: Retelling and Answering Questions   27
    Assessment of Comprehension through Look-Backs and Think-Alouds   28
    Assessment of Reading Growth   28
Steps in Administering the *QRI-7*   28
    Gather Materials and Put Students at Ease   28
    Administer the Word Identification Lists   29

    Administer an Initial Passage   29
    Administer Additional Passages   30
Frequently Asked Questions   30

Section 4   Determining Reading Levels   32

How are Reading Levels Determined?   32
    The Independent Level   33
    The Instructional Level   33
    The Frustration Level   33
Factors Affecting Reading Levels   34
    Prior Knowledge of the Topic   34
    Text Structure: Narrative and Expository   34
    Mode of Reading: Oral and Silent   35
    Questions: Literal and Inferential   35
    Look-Backs   35
Finding an Instructional Reading Level   36
    Order of Administration   36
    Finding an Instructional Reading Level for Narrative and Expository Text   36
    Using Scores to Determine Passage Level   38

Section 5   Using the Word Lists   39

Purposes for Administering the Word Lists   39
    Estimating Automatic Word Recognition and Word Identification   39
    Estimating the Starting Point for Passage Administration   40
    Estimating Automaticity of Word Recognition   40
    Analyzing the Differences Between Word Identification in Isolation and in Context   41
    Estimating Knowledge of Letter–Sound Matches   41
    Examining Knowledge of Vowel Patterns   41
Procedures for Administering the Word Lists   41
    Instructions to the Student   42
    Choosing a Starting Point   42
    Recording Student Responses: Accuracy and Automaticity   42
Using the Word List Scores   43
    Estimating the Starting Point for Passage Administration   43
    Interpreting Word Identification and Word Recognition Scores   45
    When the Word Lists Do Not Predict Reading Level   45

Reading by Analogy   45
  Using the Reading by Analogy Test   46
Additional Uses of the Word Lists   47
Development and Analysis of the
Word-Identification Tests   47

Section 6 Assessing Word Identification in Context, Automaticity, and Prosody   49

Identifying Oral Reading Miscues   49
Scoring Oral Reading Miscues: Total Accuracy   51
Scoring Oral Reading Miscues: Total Acceptability   53
  Semantic Acceptability   53
  Syntactic Acceptability   53
Analyzing Oral Reading Miscues: Miscue Analysis   55
  Analysis of Freddie's Miscues   56
Evaluating Automaticity   56
Evaluating Prosody   58
  Prosody Rating Scale   58

Section 7 Assessing Comprehension: Questions and Retellings   59

General Procedures   59
  Scoring Explicit Questions   60
  Scoring Implicit Questions   60
Criteria for Determining Reading Levels   61
  Use of Explicit and Implicit Questions to
  Gather Information About Comprehension   61
Analysis of Retelling: Elementary and Middle School   62
  General Procedures   62
  Scoring Retelling   62
Retelling Examples   63
  Narrative Text   63
  Expository Text   66
Retelling: Upper Middle School and High School   68
Using Look-backs   68

Section 8 Assessing Strategic Reading: Think-Alouds   70

Definition of Think-Alouds   70
Modeling Think-Alouds   71
Examples of Think-Alouds   73
  Emory's Think-Aloud Comments   73
  Stella's Think-Aloud Comments   75
  Carol's Think-Aloud Comments   77

Section 9 Recording, Analyzing, and Using Results of the *QRI-7*   79

Reviewing the Purposes of the *QRI-7*   79
Completing the Student Summary Form   80
Using the Student Summary Form to Plan
Intervention Instruction   80
Selecting Materials for Intervention Instruction   85
Selecting Instructional Strategies for Intervention
Instruction   86
Using the *QRI-7* to Indicate Growth and
Monitor Progress   87
Reading Performance Case Studies   88

Word Lists and Elementary Grades: Level-Diagnostic Passages

Section 10 *QRI-7* Test Materials: Word Lists and Level-Diagnostic Passages   91

Student Word Lists   92
Student Reading by Analogy Lists   96
Examiner Word Lists   97
  Reading by Analogy Examiner Lists   103
Pre-Primer 1 Passages   104
  "I Can" (Narrative/Pictures)   104
  "I See" (Narrative/Pictures)   110
Pre-Primer 2 Passages   115
  "Just Like Mom" (Narrative/Pictures)   115
  "People at Work" (Expository/Pictures)   120
Pre-Primer 3 Passages   123
  "Lost and Found" (Narrative)   123
  "Spring and Fall" (Narrative)   124
Examiner Copies   125
Primer Passages   137
  "A Night in the City" (Narrative/Pictures)   137
  "Fox and Mouse" (Narrative/Pictures)   141
  "The Pig Who Learned to Read" (Narrative/
  Pictures)   145
  "Who Lives Near Lakes?" (Expository/Pictures)   148
  "Living and Not Living" (Expository)   149
Examiner Copies   150
Level 1 Passages
  "The Surprise" (Narrative/Pictures)   160
  "Marva Finds a Friend" (Narrative/Pictures)   164
  "The Bear and the Rabbit" (Narrative/Pictures)   167

"Air" (Expository) 170

"The Brain and the Five Senses" (Expository/Pictures) 171

Examiner Copies 172

Level 2 Passages

"The Family's First Trip" (Narrative) 185

"The Lucky Cricket" (Narrative/Pictures) 186

"Father's New Game" (Narrative/Pictures) 190

"Whales and Fish" (Expository) 193

"Seasons" (Expository) 194

Examiner Copies 195

Level 3 Passages

"A Special Birthday for Rosa" (Narrative) 210

"The Friend" (Narrative) 212

"A New Friend from Europe" (Narrative) 214

"Cats: Lions and Tigers in Your House" (Expository) 217

"Where Do People Live?" (Expository) 218

"Wool: From Sheep to You" (Expository) 219

Examiner Copies 220

Level 4 Passages

"Amelia Earhart" (Narrative) 240

"Tomie dePaola" (Narrative) 241

"Early Railroads" (Expository/Pictures) 242

"Plant Structures for Survival" (Expository/Pictures) 243

Examiner Copies 244

Level 5 Passages

"Margaret Mead" (Narrative) 256

"Patricia McKissack" (Narrative) 257

"Farming on the Great Plains" (Expository/Pictures) 258

"How Does Your Body Take in Oxygen?" (Expository/Pictures) 259

Examiner Copies 260

Middle School and High School: Level-Diagnostic Passages

Level 6 Passages

"Abraham Lincoln" (Biography) 277

"The Early Life of Lois Lowry" (Biography/Think-Aloud) 278

"The Lifeline of the Nile" (Social Studies/Pictures) 279

"Building Pyramids (Social Studies/Pictures/Think-Aloud) 280

"Temperature and Humidity" (Science/Pictures) 281

"Clouds and Precipitation" (Science/Pictures/Think-Aloud) 282

Examiner Copies 284

Upper Middle School Passages: Literature

"Jaime Escalanté: Teacher Extraordinaire" (Biography/Think-Aloud) 311

Upper Middle School Passages: Social Studies

"Immigration—Part 1" (Social Studies/Pictures) 313

"Immigration—Part 2" (Social Studies/Pictures/Think-Aloud) 315

Upper Middle School Passages: Science

"Life Cycles of Stars—Part 1" (Science/Pictures) 317

"Life Cycles of Stars—Part 2" (Science/Pictures/Think-Aloud) 319

Examiner Copies 321

High School Passages: Social Studies

"World War I—Part 1" (Social Studies/Pictures) 345

"World War I—Part 2" (Social Studies/Pictures/Think-Aloud) 348

High School Passages: Science

"Characteristics of Viruses—Part 1" (Science/Pictures) 351

"Characteristics of Viruses—Part 2" (Science/Pictures/Think-Aloud) 354

Examiner Copies 356

Administering and Scoring the Inference-Diagnostic Passages

Section 11   Administering and Scoring the Inference-Diagnostic Passages 379

Purpose of the Inference-Diagnostic Passages 379

Differences Between Level-Diagnostic and Inference-Diagnostic Passages 380

Choosing an Inference-Diagnostic Passage 381

Mode of Reading: Oral or Silent? 381

Mode of Answering Questions 381

Questions for Inference-Diagnostic Passages 381

Guidelines for Determining the Acceptability of Answers 382

Recording Results and Identifying a Focus for Instruction 382

Evaluating Summaries 383

Scoring and Analysis of Narrative/Biographies Summaries 384

Scoring and Analysis of Expository Summaries 385

Guidelines for Scoring Summaries 387

Summary 387

Inference-Diagnostic Passages: Grades 4–High School

Section 12   Inference-Diagnostic Materials   389

Grade 4   390

Cynthia Rylant: The Development of an Author (Biography)   390

Linking East and West (Social Studies/Picture)   392

How Do Organisms Compete for Resources? (Science/Picture)   395

Examiner Copies   398

Grade 5   410

Jane Goodall, Goddess of the Apes (Biography)   410

The Rise of Cattle Drives (Social Studies/Picture)   412

The Body's Transportation System (Science/Picture)   415

Examiner Copies   418

Grade 6   430

The Legacy of Jim Thorpe (Biography)   430

From Dynasty to Dynasty (Social Studies/Picture)   433

What Causes Weather? (Science/Picture)   436

Examiner Copies   439

Middle School   452

Malcolm X: The Development of a Separatist (Biography)   452

A Wave of Nativism (Social Studies/Picture)   456

What Is a Comet? (Science/Picture)   459

Examiner Copies   462

High School   477

The Life of Georgia O'Keeffe: The Artist and the Woman (Biography)   477

America Adjusts to Peace (Social Studies/Picture)   481

The Kingdoms of Life (Science/Picture)   484

Examiner Copies   487

Section 13   Technical Development of the Qualitative Reading Inventory-7   503

Piloting Materials for the QRI   504

Piloting the Sixth Edition   504

Piloting the Fifth Edition   505

Analysis of the Word List Data   505

Development and Analysis of the Prior-Knowledge Assessments   506

Identification of Concepts   506

Analyses of Correlations Between Prior Knowledge and Other Test Components   506

Development of the Measures of Comprehension: Level-Diagnostic Materials   507

Analyses of the Measures of Comprehension on Level-Diagnostic Passages   507

Development of the Think-Aloud Procedure   509

Development and Analysis of the Measures of Comprehension: Inference-Diagnostic Materials   510

Comparing the Difficulty of the Inference-Diagnostic Materials to the Difficulty of the Level-Diagnostic Materials   510

The Pillars of Excellence in Educational Assessment   511

Reliability and Validity   511

Issues of Validity of an Informal Reading Inventory   511

Issues of Reliability of an Informal Reading Inventory   516

Cautions in Interpretation   519

Test-Retest and Alternate Form Reliability   520

Appendix: Videos for Extra Practice (Pearson eText)   522

References   528

Index   533

Preface

The seventh edition of *Qualitative Reading Inventory* continues the emphasis on authentic assessment of children's reading abilities, from the earliest emergent readers (pre-primer/primer) to advanced readers (upper middle school/high school). The *QRI-7* contains several unique features. Prior to reading, knowledge of concepts important to an understanding of the passage is assessed. This allows the examiner to label a passage as familiar or unfamiliar to each student. The *QRI-7* measures comprehension in several ways: through an analysis of the student's retelling or summary; through the student's answers to explicit and implicit comprehension questions; and through the use of look-backs. Look-backs separate what readers remembered after reading from what they comprehended during reading. The *QRI-7* provides the use of think-alouds at the sixth-grade level and above to analyze the student's thoughts during reading.

Like other informal reading inventories, *QRI-7* provides graded word lists and passages designed to assess a student's oral reading accuracy, rate of reading, and comprehension of passages read orally and silently. The *QRI-7* contains narrative and expository passages at each level. All are self-contained selections highly representative of the structure and topics of materials found in basal readers and content-area textbooks. For example, passages at the pre-primer through second-grade levels are presented with pictures. Maps and illustrations are part of expository selections at fourth grade through high school levels.

New to this Edition

- **Pearson eText**—One of the most visible changes in *QRI-7*, also one of the most significant, is the expansion of the digital learning and assessment resources embedded in the Pearson eText. The following features are designed to: 1) provide you with authentic practice scoring and analyzing *QRI-7* results, and 2) make it easier to print materials for *QRI-7* administration.

- **Video Examples**—19 all-new video clips have been included in the new edition. Video clips in Sections 3–8 provide a model for how to introduce, administer, and score different parts of *QRI-7*. Many of these videos include a split-screen view so you can observe the examiner's scoring marks in real time. The Appendix includes videos of full sessions with six different students, and allows you to practice scoring word lists and passages. The Appendix also includes links to author-scored versions of these sessions for you to check your work.

- **Application Exercises**—32 application exercises have been added in eight different sections to provide you with additional practice scoring and analyzing *QRI-7* results, and making instructional decisions. Many of these exercises include linked forms and artifacts as the basis for the practice. The questions in these exercises are usually constructed-response. Once learners provide their own answers to the questions, they receive feedback in the form of model answers written by the authors.

- **Teacher Resources**—The opening outlines of Sections 10 and 12 provide quick links to printable PDF versions of all testing materials in those sections. Additional resources like the Window Card Template (Section 5) and blank Student Summary Form (Section 9) are also linked for easy printing or downloading.

Key Content Changes

- *QRI-7* has been rewritten and reorganized for clarity:

  - Section 1 defines reading and challenges simplistic views of reading comprehension. It also explains informal reading inventory (IRI) assessment and discusses the issue of text complexity. Difficulty ratings of passages included in the *QRI–7* are presented in tabular form.

  - Section 2 explains how the *QRI-7* is different from other published IRIs, and explains the research that guided the development of the *QRI-7*.

  - Section 3 clearly describes the different purposes for administering *QRI-7*, and outlines the basic steps for conducting the assessments. Sections 4–8 provide detailed descriptions of how to administer *QRI-7* for its various purposes.

  - Section 9 now focuses on recording, analyzing, and using the results of *QRI-7*. This includes using the Student Summary Form to select materials and instructional strategies for intervention instruction. We have also included information about how to use *QRI-7* to indicate growth and monitor progress.

  - Section 10 includes the testing materials (word lists and Level-Diagnostic passages) that were previously found in Section 12.

  - An all-new Section 11 provides greater detail on how to administer, score, and analyze results for the Inference-Diagnostic passages. Testing materials for Inference-Diagnostic passages are now included in Section 12.

  - Section 13 describes the extensive piloting of testing materials found in *QRI-7*, and includes reliability and validity data for the overall test.

- Two additional middle school narrative texts (Lois Lowry and Jaime Escalante) have been formatted for use as think-alouds. The *QRI-7* now includes eight think-aloud passages that provide information about students' thinking process while reading.

- The high school passages *Where the Ashes Are* Parts 1 and 2 were removed because copyright permission was not extended. This notification came too late for us to substitute a new passage. Users are asked to contact lauren.leslie@marquette.edu if this presents a burden to them so that we may develop a new high school literature text in the future.

- All sections of the book have been rewritten to make it easier for all teachers to use *QRI-7* to assess students' reading abilities. Additional figures, tables, and boxes have been included in all sections to allow users to more quickly scan for information.

Acknowledgments

We extend our heartfelt appreciation to Linda Simmons, Associate Professor (Retired), Cardinal Stritch University, for her technological expertise with changes required of the *QRI-7.* Without her expertise the revision would have been far more difficult. We also wish to thank our editor, Drew Bennett, for his suggestions on improving the eText. Special thanks go to Heather M. Pauly, Ph.D., Cardinal Stritch University, for her role in the development of the new videos and to the students and faculty of Étude Elementary School in Sheboygan, Wisconsin, for allowing the videotaping.

We would like to thank the reviewers of this edition for their valuable input:

Gwyenne Ellen Ash, *Texas State University*
Joyce C. Fine, *Florida International University*
Jon Wargo, *Boston College*
Kathie M. Carwile, *Liberty University*
Linda Impecoren-Lind, *Iowa State University*
Michelle Lia, *Loyola University Chicago*
Stacey Bose, *Liberty University*

Section 1

Introduction to Basic Concepts of Reading Assessment

∨	Chapter Outline

What is Reading?

Implications for Assessment

Introduction to Informal Reading Inventories

Measures of Difficulty

WHAT IS READING?

Reading has been defined as the process of constructing or gaining meaning from text by recognizing or decoding words. Therefore, at its most basic level, reading comprehension is the result of word recognition or decoding and the ability to understand language. This model has been termed the "Simple View of Reading" (Gough & Tunmer, 1986), and while research has provided evidence for it (Vellutino et al., 2007; Hoover & Tunmer, 2018), some studies have challenged its simplicity (Catts, 2018; Kendeou & Rapp, 2009; La Russo et al., 2016; Tilstra et al., 2009; Snow, 2018).

The Simple View of Reading

Comprehension = word recognition/decoding × ability to understand language

---

In many research studies, especially those using an elementary grade population, a large part of students' variability in reading comprehension can be explained by word recognition or decoding and measures of oral language, often measured as listening comprehension. However, the importance of these two factors to comprehension varies with the stage of reading development. In beginning readers, word recognition plays a larger part in explaining reading comprehension because word learning is still developing, and materials written for beginning readers are conceptually simple. That is, the materials for beginning readers contain frequently used words, short sentences, and content that is familiar to them.

As students get older, their word recognition and decoding abilities improve to a point where there is little variance among students, and language ability plays a larger role in explaining comprehension. Older students' word recognition and decoding abilities become quite similar, so the differences in comprehension must be due to another factor, which, in the Simple View, is understanding language. In the past decade, research has examined whether the Simple View is sufficient to explain reading comprehension, or whether other abilities are involved. Tilstra and colleagues (2009) found that two factors (in addition to decoding and listening comprehension) predicted reading comprehension for students in grades 4, 7, and 9:

- verbal proficiency (measured by an expressive measure of vocabulary knowledge), and
- reading fluency (i.e., the number of words read correctly in one minute).

These four measures—decoding, listenting comprehension, verbal proficiency, and reading fluency—predicted silent reading comprehension at all grade levels and explained decreasing amounts of variability as students' grade level increased. Specifically, 61% of the variance in reading comprehension was explained in fourth grade, 48% in seventh grade, and 38% in ninth grade (Tilstra et al., 2009). In other words, measuring these four factors was less effective at predicting comprehension in the upper grades compared to fourth grade. As expected, decoding accounted for more variance in reading comprehension for fourth-graders than for the older groups. Verbal proficiency, on the other hand, contributed an additional 12% of the variance in comprehension for ninth-graders, but only 5% for fourth-graders and 8% for seventh-graders. These results suggest that the Simple View of Reading is a powerful but incomplete model of reading, especially for students in middle school and high school (Snow, 2018).

A recent article acknowledges that although the Simple View of Reading (SVR) has provided a useful framework for understanding basic factors influencing reading comprehension, the model has led us to assume that comprehension (listening or reading) is simpler than it is (Catts, 2018). Although the complexity of reading comprehension has been acknowledged (Gough, Hoover, & Peterson,1996; Willingham, 2006), complex measures of it are few and far between. A review of the SVR model in the September 2018 issue of *Remedial and Special Education* concludes that although the SVR model has been useful in promoting research into factors that underly reading comprehension, many factors such as content knowledge, text structure, and demanding comprehension tasks have not been considered by SVR. The model works well for students in the primary grades but is lacking in the explanation of higher-order comprehension in the upper grades (Snow, 2018; Catts, 2018).

A recent study using a more complex measure of comprehension illustrates how factors beyond word recognition and language comprehension contribute to reading comprehension (La Russo et al., 2016). Students in grades 4 through 7 were given tasks that measured academic language, perspective taking, complex reasoning, and deep reading comprehension. Students were asked to make real-world decisions and were given a variety of resources (e.g., blog, website, news article, email, textbook excerpt) to use to decide, for example, whether a wind farm is good for their community. The resources were thematic, sequenced with regard to difficulty, and they allowed the students to "apply what they read to different contexts, situations and perspectives" (La Russo et al., 2016, p. 209). The final model, which included all three predictors of reading comprehension (perspective taking, academic language, and complex reasoning) and their covariates, explained 52% of the total variance in deep comprehension. This initial study provides a promising new method for examining the deep comprehension demanded by state and local agencies. But how does the model specifically apply to reading assessment and instruction?

IMPLICATIONS FOR ASSESSMENT

We accept a more complex view of reading comprehension that includes not only word recognition and language comprehension, but also fluency, student content knowledge, student knowledge of the structures of narrative and expository text, vocabulary, and complex reasoning. Therefore, we believe reading assessment should measure:

- Word recognition/identification
- Fluency
- Vocabulary and/or content knowledge
- Text structure knowledge
- Literal comprehension
- Inferential comprehension of various types

Measuring these factors allows for diagnoses of several types of reading difficulties. At the simplest level, oral reading of a grade-level text can determine whether the student has sufficient word recognition abilities to successfully comprehend that text. If the student cannot read the text with at least 90% accuracy, it is likely that problems with word recognition will contribute to a low comprehension score. On the other hand, if a student can read the text with 95% accuracy, but his or her oral language understanding and reading comprehension are below average, we can infer that the student's reading comprehension difficulty is caused, at least in part, by a lack of language understanding. The *QRI-II* (Leslie & Caldwell, 1995) was used to examine the diagnostic profiles of fourth-grade students who failed a state proficiency exam (Valencia & Buly, 2004). They detected six clusters of students that varied in three abilities—word recognition, fluency, and comprehension—with only 9% being low in all areas. This study documented the usefulness of the *QRI-II* to diagnose reading difficulties. Given the strong similarity between the *QRI-II* and the present edition, we can assume that the present edition will be as useful.

In addition to word recognition and fluency, the *QRI* measures comprehension in both narrative and expository text; this is because research demonstrates greater difficulties in comprehending expository text. The passages in the *QRI* can also be used to measure listening comprehension by reading passages to the student.

An example will be illustrative. José, a third-grade student whose native language was Spanish, was referred by his classroom teacher to a reading specialist for assessment. The teacher was concerned that José did not understand the stories being read in his reading group. The assessment showed that his word recognition ability was within the average range for a third-grader, and he read with appropriate phrasing and expression. However, his reading comprehension was below grade level. To determine whether José's comprehension problem was at least partially an oral language problem, the reading specialist read a grade-level text to him. She found that he still did not understand it. She concluded that José needed instruction in understanding the English language. The *QRI-7* was designed to assess students with a range of abilities, José's being only one type, and six profiles were identified by Valencia and Buly (2004). The addition of more complex passages at Grades 4–high school requiring more in depth understanding, and summarization of text, expanded the use of the *QRI-6* beyond previous editions. The *QRI* is one type of informal reading inventory (IRI) assessment, which has a long history of use in the classroom and clinic.

INTRODUCTION TO INFORMAL READING INVENTORIES

An IRI is an individually administered reading assessment composed of graded word lists and passages of increasing difficulty.

IRIs vary in the levels of materials provided for the student to read. Some include short, simple selections (less than 50 words) for beginning readers. Some include pictures. The purpose of these materials is to identify words that the child can read and those he or she cannot read without the aid of pictures. The materials also provide an opportunity to observe strategies the child uses when faced with unknown words. IRIs contain word lists and passages that increase in difficulty paralleling the grade levels they represent. As the levels of passages increase, materials become more complex, sentences get longer and more complex, words are less frequent, and ideas are more abstract. All IRIs include fiction and nonfiction materials for use with students reading from kindergarten through eighth grade. Some inventories stop at eighth grade (e.g., Morris, 2014), but many others continue through high school (e.g., Roe & Burns, 2010; Johns & Johns, 2016; Woods & Moe, 2014; *Qualitative Reading Inventory-6*).

Using the *QRI-7* graded materials, teachers can identify the level of text that students can read with:

- 98%+ oral reading accuracy and a minimum of 90% comprehension. This is called the student's independent level because students can read this level of material without assistance.

- 90–97% oral reading accuracy and a minimum of 70% comprehension. This is called the student's instructional level. Students should be instructed in using material at this level as there are unfamiliar words and ideas to learn.

- Less than 90% oral reading accuracy and less than 70% comprehension. This is called the student's frustration level. It is believed that students will become frustrated when reading material at this level.

These materials can also be used to analyze a student's strengths and weaknesses in reading, as illustrated in the example of José.

MEASURES OF DIFFICULTY

Fiction and nonfiction materials on IRIs vary in difficulty from the simplest to very complex. Almost 100 years of research has examined what makes text difficult to read. A review of that literature is beyond the scope of this book; however, we will provide a summary of relevant literature. A common method of describing text difficulty is the use of readability formulas. Readability formulas are based on two components. One is word difficulty, estimated by the frequency of the word or its length. For example, "matriarch" is much less frequent in our language than "mother," so a text containing "matriarch" would likely have a higher readability level. Similarly, "received" is a longer word than "got," and its inclusion in a text would probably increase the readability estimate. Another readability component is sentence complexity, often measured by sentence length. Thus, "Because she needed sugar, Mary jumped in the car and quickly drove to the store" would increase a text readability estimate more than "Mary needed sugar. She jumped in the car. She quickly drove to the store." However, it is worth noting that attempts to lower readability by deleting signal words and transitional phrases such as *because, therefore,* and *in order to* may inadvertently make the text more difficult because removing such connectives obscures syntactic relationships (Hiebert & Mesmer, 2013) and increases the inference demand on the reader.

Readability formulas provide only a general and very rough estimate of text difficulty level because many other components contribute to the complexity of a text. Readability scores overlook "the qualitative and reader-specific factors that should be considered" (Fisher, Frey, & Lapp, 2012, p. 31). Is the text coherent and well written? Does it include supportive pictures and/or diagrams? Do headings and central idea statements accurately indicate content? Is it on a familiar topic? Is the topic interesting to the reader? Is the structure of the text clearly signaled? To what extent does the language of the text parallel spoken language, or does the language represent a stylized and formal form of writing?

A popular measure, the Lexile scale provides two readability levels, a text level and a reader level. Like other readability formulas, the text level is based on word familiarity and sentence length. Reader levels are based on administration of short passages with one question that determine a reader's score in Lexile units. The reader is then expected to comprehend approximately 75% of text with the same Lexile level (MetaMetrics, 2013).

Like other readability formulas, the Lexile scale does not address the role of predictable text, pictures, and other graphic features, which makes it an inappropriate measure for pre-primer and primer text. Fountas and Pinnell (2006) have grouped texts according to characteristics that move beyond traditional readability components. These include length, print size, layout, difficulty of vocabulary and concepts, language structure, genre, text structure, predictable language, and support offered by illustrations. They used these characteristics to describe 16 guided reading levels crossing kindergarten through third grade: nine levels for kindergarten and first-grade text, four levels for grade 2, and three levels for grade 3. Although the Fountas and Pinnell system has achieved wide recognition and usage among teachers, it provides only a moderate amount of support for word recognition instruction and almost no support for decoding instruction in the use of onsets and rimes. In addition, books leveled for use in Reading Recovery do not consistently increase in word-level demands as their levels increase (Cunningham et al., 2005).

Hiebert (2013) suggests that determination of text complexity should move beyond word frequency and sentence length to consider four additional components: levels of meaning, knowledge demands, language conventions/clarity, and structure. These can make a text manageable or difficult despite its readability score. Levels of meaning in a text can range from a focus on relatively straightforward and concrete topics to more complex issues. Knowledge demands refer to the inclusion or lack of concepts familiar to the reader. For example, science and social studies texts often focus on unfamiliar content, such as the continental drift theory and post–World War I nativism. Language conventions/clarity refers to the style and structure of the text, as well as the inclusion and/or absence of definitions or explanations for unfamiliar words and concepts. Content area texts often "receive inflated readability scores since key concepts that are rare (e.g., *photosynthesis, inflation*) are often repeated which increases vocabulary load, even though repetition of content words can support student learning" (Hiebert & Mesmer, 2013, p. 46). Structure focuses on the existence and clarity of topic headings and central idea/theme statements, as well as the overall structure of the text and how it is signaled by the author. A summary of the qualitative components of text complexity and its relationship to the *QRI-7* is presented below.

Relationship between Hiebert's Qualitative Components of Text Complexity and the *QRI-7*

Component	Definition	QRI-7 component
Levels of Meaning	Concrete to abstract	Increasingly more complex topics and concepts are included as grade level increases
Knowledge Demands	Familiar vs. unfamiliar	Provides prereading concept questions to measure subject familiarity
Language Conventions & Clarity	Definitions of unknown words	Unfamiliar words are either defined or clues to meaning are given
Structure	Signals of text structure are provided	Main ideas of expository text are provided; main ideas are stated explicitly, and narratives explicitly follow narrative structure

The nature of the above components may allow a student to read text at a higher readability level than might be anticipated. The opposite is also true. Despite a readability level appropriate for a specific grade, a student may find the text impossibly difficult. We have chosen *QRI* texts with appropriate reading levels according to readability formulas. However, a student's performance should always be examined in relation to components that are not addressed by such formulas. If, for example, a sixth-grader meets frustration in the grade-level text, the student's familiarity with the topic should be examined by using his or her responses to the concept questions included in the *QRI-7*. The teacher should also consider the conceptual difficulty of the passages. A description may be easier to comprehend than an explanation of a process. For example, an explanation of temperature and humidity at the sixth-grade level probably represents more difficult concepts than an account of pyramid building at the same level. The structure of the passage may also play a part. A narrative structure is generally more familiar than the structure of expository text, which can employ several different structures within the same selection.

To assign levels to passages for the editions of the *QRI*, we have subjected each passage to a variety of readability formulas at every level and found wide fluctuations in the grade levels assigned by different formulas. We chose the level agreed on by at least two out of three formulas in the lower grades. For grades 5 through high school, we averaged the scores of three formulas to obtain a more reliable estimate, and then tested the appropriateness of the level through piloting. Because of the popularity of the Lexile scale, we chose the Inference-Diagnostic Passages with Lexile levels appropriate to their grade level and also assessed readability through a consensus among seven formula estimates (http://www.readabilityformulas.com/free-readability-formula-tests.php).

Table 1.1, Table 1.2, and Table 1.3 present the quantitative measures of difficulty of the Level Diagnostic Passages, and Table 1.4 presents the mean Lexile values on the Inference Diagnostic Passages.

A comparison of the Lexile levels of the Level Diagnostic and the Inference Diagnostic materials showed no significant differences at grades 4 through upper middle school, but at the high school level the Inference Diagnostic materials had higher Lexiles than the Level Diagnostic materials. Details of these analyses are discussed in Section 13.

Table 1.1   Leveling *QRI-7* Text: Comparing Two Raters' Use of Fountas and Pinnell (2006), Harris-Jacobson Readability Levels, and Gunning Classifications on Pre-Primer through Grade 1 Passages

	RR Level Rater		HJ Readability	Gunning
Pre-Primer: C-D-E	**1**	**2**		
Narrative: "I Can" (P)[a]	A	A	1.0	Easy Sight
Narrative: "I See"[b] (P)	B	B	1.4	Easy Sight
Narrative: "Just Like Mom" (P)	C	C	1.0	Easy Sight
Narrative: "Spring and Fall"	E	E	1.3	Easy Sight
Narrative: "Lost and Found"	F	F	1.0	Easy Sight
Expository: "People at Work" (P)	E	E	1.1	Easy Sight
Primer: F and G				
Narrative: "A Night in the City" (P)	G	G	1.5	1.65
Narrative: "Fox and Mouse" (P)	F	F	1.4	1.40
Narrative: "The Pig Who Learned to Read" (P)	G	G	1.7	1.50
Expository: "Who Lives Near Lakes?" (P)	F	G	1.3	1.3
Expository: "Living and Not Living"	G	F	1.1	1.2
First: H and I				
Narrative: "The Surprise" (P)	I	I	1.8	1.75
Narrative: "Marva Finds a Friend" (P)	H	I	1.8	2.30[*]
Narrative: "The Bear and the Rabbit" (P)	I	H	1.7	1.8
Expository: "Air"	I	H	1.5	1.5
Expository: "The Brain and the Five Senses" (P)	H	H	1.5	1.6

Note: Two people unknown to each other independently rated the pre-primer, primer, and first-grade materials using the Fountas and Pinnell leveling system, and the ratings were identical or within one level.

[*]Gunning has a more restrictive word list than does the Harris-Jacobson.

[a](P) indicates a pictured passage.

[b]The rhyming pattern of this story makes it easier than the readability estimate indicates.

Table 1.2 Difficulty Levels of *QRI-7* Text: Comparing Fountas and Pinnell Levels, Harris-Jacobson Readability Levels, and Lexiles for Grades 2–4

	Level	HJ	Lexile (without Graphics)
Second: J–M			
Narrative: "The Lucky Cricket" (P)	L	2.1	510
Narrative: "Father's New Game" (P)	M	2.7	480
Narrative: "The Family's First Trip"	M	2.3	560
Expository: "Whales and Fish"	L	2.9	590
Expository: "Seasons"	M	2.4	480
Third: N–P			
Narrative: "A Special Birthday for Rosa"	O	3.2	750
Narrative: "The Friend"	P	3.9	710
Narrative: "A New Friend from Europe"	Q	3.8	770
Expository: "Cats: Lions and Tigers in Your House"	N	2.7	750
Expository: "Where Do People Live?"	O	2.6	500
Expository: "Wool: From Sheep to You"	P	4.6	700
Fourth: Q-T			
Narrative: "Amelia Earhart"	R	3.3	500
Narrative: "Tomie dePaola"	T	4.4	910
Expository: "Early Railroads"	Q	3.8	810
Expository: "Plant Structures for Survival" (G)	T	4.6	930

Note: (P) indicates a pictured passage, and (G) indicates a passage with a graphic.

The Lexile system removes all graphics, headings, bolded words, and so on when estimating a level. Therefore, to the extent that the graphics enhance comprehension, the Lexile may overestimate the difficulty of a selection. In addition, readability formulae and Lexiles do not consider the effects of prior knowledge on comprehension.

SEM of Lexiles is estimated to be 64 divided by the square root of the number of slices of 125 words (Stenner et al., 2006). Therefore, passages around 250 words would be composed of two slices of 125 words each, and the square root of 2 = 1.41, so 64/1.41 = 45.39. Most of the second-grade through fourth-grade passages are around 250 words. Passages of 350 words would have a SEM of 38.32.

Table 1.3 Difficulty Levels of *QRI-7* Text: Mean of Three Readability Formula Estimates and Lexiles Grade 5 through HS

	Average of Three*	Lexile (without Graphics)
Fifth		
Narrative: "Margaret Mead"	5.0	660
Narrative: "Patricia McKissack"	7.5	970
Expository: "Farming on the Great Plains"	5.4	810
Expository: "How Does Your Body Take in Oxygen?" (G)	5.6	900
Sixth		
Literature: "Abraham Lincoln"	5.7	760
Literature: "The Early Life of Lois Lowry"	6.6	980
Social Studies: "The Lifeline of the Nile" (G)	6.9	850
Social Studies: "Building Pyramids" (G)	6.6	850
Science: "Temperature and Humidity"	7.5	1,030
Science: "Clouds and Precipitation" (G)	6.2	1,000
Upper Middle School		
Literature: "Jaime Escalanté: Teacher Extraordinaire"	7.8	950

(*continued*)

Table 1.3 (*Continued*)

	Average of Three[*]	Lexile (without Graphics)
Social Studies: "Immigration—Part 1"	9.5	1,000
Social Studies: "Immigration—Part 2"	7.8	870
Science: "Life Cycles of Stars—Part 1"	7.5	820
Science: "Life Cycles of Stars—Part 2"	7.5	840
High School	**Average of 7[**]**	
"World War I—Part 1"	11.2	1,130
"World War I—Part 2"	9.0	1,020
"Characteristics of Viruses—Part 1"	9.0	970
"Characteristics of Viruses—Part 2"	9.0	950

[*]Because of the variability among the New Dale-Chall readability formula, the Fry Readability graph, and Flesch Grade Level estimates, we averaged the three to obtain a more reliable estimate.

[**] The high school material was evaluated by readabilityformulas.com, which calculates a consensus estimate based on seven formulas.

Note: The Lexile system removes all graphics, headings, bolded words, and so on when estimating a level. Therefore, to the extent that the graphics enhance comprehension, the Lexile may overestimate the difficulty of a selection. In addition, neither Lexiles nor readability formulae consider the effects of prior knowledge on comprehension.

SEM of Lexiles is estimated to be 64 divided by the square root of the number of slices of 125 words (Stenner et al., 2006). Therefore, passages around 375 words would be composed of three slices of 125 words each, and the square root of 3 = 1.73, so 64/1.73 = 46.99. Passages at the fifth-grade and sixth-grade level range in length from 254 to 591 words. Passages at the upper middle school level range from 382 to 786 words. Passages at the high school level range from 354 to 1,224 words. SEM of Lexiles of passages around 500 words is 32L (Stenner et al., 2006).

Table 1.4 Difficulty Estimates of the Inference Diagnostic Passages Using the Mean of Seven Readability Formula Estimates and Lexiles in Grade 4 through HS

	Average of Seven	Lexile (without Graphics)
Fourth		
"Cynthia Rylant—The Development of an Author" (Biography)	6th	810
"Linking East and West" (Social Studies)	8th	970
"How Do Organisms Compete for Resources?" (Science)	8th	790
Fifth		
"Jane Goodall, Goddess of the Apes" (Biography)	7th	850
"The Rise of Cattle Drives" (Social Studies)	7th	970
"The Body's Transportation System" (Science)	6th	850
Sixth		
"The Legacy of Jim Thorpe" (Biography)	7th	930
"From Dynasty to Dynasty" (Social Studies)	7th	970
"What Causes Weather?" (Science)	8th	880
Middle School		
"Malcolm X: The Development of a Separatist" (Biography)	9th	1080
"A Wave of Nativism" (Social Studies)	9th	920
"What Is a Comet?" (Science)	7th	890
High School		
"Georgia O'Keeffe" (Biography)	10th	1110
"America Adjusts to Peace" (Social Studies)	10th	1130
"The Kingdoms of Life" (Science)	12th	1070

Pearson Education; http://www.readabilityformulas.com/free-readability-formula-tests.php. The seven formulas used to determine the average were Flesch Reading Ease, Flesh-Kincaid, Fog, Smog, Coleman-Liau, Automated Reading Index, and Linear Write Formula.

Section 2
Research Guiding the Development of the *Qualitative Reading Inventory*

 ## Chapter Outline

How the *QRI* Is Different from Other IRIs

Factors Related to Reading Comprehension
> Word Recognition and Identification
> Oral Reading
> Fluency, Automaticity, and Prosody
> Content Knowledge
> Text Structure
> Methods of Assessment of Reading Comprehension

HOW THE *QRI* IS DIFFERENT FROM OTHER IRIs

The *QRI* (1990) was the first informal reading inventory (IRI) to explain the research base for its development. Research indicated that reading comprehension was affected by five factors:

1. Word identification/recognition
2. Fluency
3. Content knowledge of the reader that related to text content
4. The genre and structure of the text
5. The method of assessment used to measure reading comprehension

We believe that assessment should mirror research, so based on the areas listed above, the *QRI* includes:

- Word lists and passages of varying difficulty
- Measures of fluency and prosody
- Prior knowledge assessment to be administered before the student reads the passage
- Narrative and expository passages from pre-primer through high school
- Three measures of comprehension: retelling, questions, and think-alouds

In addition, we provided data analysis from students who were given the *QRI* (see Section 13). These data documented the increasing difficulty of the word lists and passages, interscorer reliability, item reliability, and many types of validity. These analyses were far more extensive than previous informal reading inventories had provided. We wanted the *QRI* to be research-based to the extent possible with an informal reading inventory.

FACTORS RELATED TO READING COMPREHENSION

Word Recognition and Identification

As explained in Section 1, reading comprehension is the generation of meaning based on the recognition of words in a text. Put another way, a beginning reader looks at print and attempts to make sense of it. As the Simple View of Reading describes (see Section 1), reading comprehension is equal to the product of word recognition and oral language comprehension, or $RC = WR \times LC$. It is a multiplicative relationship, not an additive one. Therefore, $RC = 0$ if the student cannot recognize or decode any words, or if the student does not understand the language (Hoover, & Tunmer, 2018).

Students' ability to recognize words is based, in part, on the word's frequency of occurrence in the written language being read (Seidenberg & McClelland, 1989). The word *the* has the highest standard frequency index (SFI) in English (Zeno et al., 1995), but probably is not the first word children learn to read. The first word read is likely to be idiosyncratic based on the child's environment. Nouns are typically learned first because they are labels for things, such as the child's name, or a label on a favorite toy.

Students' ability to decode words, often referred to as *sounding out*, is based (in part) on the regularity of letter–sound relationships known to the child and their frequency in the words the child attempts to read. For example, if a child knows the letter–sound relationships for all consonants, and that the vowel *a* can sound like ă, then the child may be able to decode the words *can, cat, mat, fan, cap,* etc. We say *may be able to decode* because many children who know letter–sound relationships do not necessarily know how to use this knowledge to decode a word. This is a common result of teaching letter–sound relationships without teaching how they are used to read words.

Accuracy of reading words is also affected by the regularity of vowel pronunciation in words. Research has found that the vowel's pronunciation is more regular if the final consonant in the syllable is considered (Kessler & Treiman, 2001). In a word such as *flag,* the first two letters are the onset, and the vowel and final consonant (*-ag*) are referred to as the *rime*, or spelling pattern. In addition to word frequency, the frequency of the rime is a powerful predictor of children's word recognition and decoding (Leslie & Calhoun, 1995). Practically, this means that words with high-frequency rimes will be recognized more often than words with low-frequency rimes, even if the words have equal standard frequency indexes. For example, *vain* will be read correctly more frequently than *foul.* Although they have similar SFIs (48.8 vs. 47.8, respectively), the spelling pattern *-ain* is more common than *-oul.* The process of using a known word to read an unknown word with the same spelling pattern is called *reading by analogy* (Goswami, 1986).

Implications for the Development of the QRI.   The *QRI* word lists were developed by choosing the most common words from our passages, that is, words with the highest SFI (Zeno et al., 1995). For example, the first-grade word list includes "thought" and "knew," which are in the stories "The Bear and the Rabbit" and "Marva Finds a Friend," respectively. These words are found in many stories that children read. In contrast, we did not include words such as "softly" and "newspaper," because although they are also in these stories, they are less likely to be found in children's reading materials.

We also separated the most frequent words included on the pre-primer passages. The most common words became the pre-primer 1 (PP1) list. The mean SFI of the words on the PP1 list is 77.91. It includes many of the most frequent words in written English (e.g., "the," "a," "in," "of," "to"). The pre-primer 2/3 list also includes words from the pre-primer stories (e.g., "make," "my," "some," "people"), but these words are

Table 2.1 Mean Standard Frequency Index for *QRI-7* Word Lists

Pre-Primer 1	Pre-Primer 2/3	Primer	First	Second	Third	Fourth	Fifth	Sixth	MS	HS
77.91	70.25	67.95	64.93	59.4	56.5	51.95	49.38	45.90	43.50	37.76

Note: The SFI for all words was determined based on Zeno et al., 1995.

less frequent than those on the PP1 list. This list has a mean SFI of 70.25. The average SFI of each word list is presented in Table 2.1.

Reading by analogy is using a known word to read an unknown one. To measure students' ability to read by analogy, the *QRI-7* includes a list of low-frequency words that contain 18 frequent spelling patterns (Beck, 2006; Fry, 1998; Gaskins, Downer, & the Teachers of the Benchmark School, 1997). The high frequency words are on the word lists and occur in passages at the pre-primer through first-grade levels. A comparison between the student's ability to read the high-frequency words with the spelling pattern (e.g., *can*) and his or her ability to read a low-frequency word with the same spelling pattern (e.g., *pan*) provides evidence of the student's ability to use a known spelling pattern to read an unknown word—that is, reading by analogy.

Analyses were conducted using our data on a student's ability to read a low-frequency word given that the student correctly read a high-frequency word with the same spelling pattern. Each analysis was conducted within a range of student reading instructional levels. For example, the first analysis used data from first-grade students with instructional reading levels of less than or equal to pre-primer. Their performance on the PP1 and PP2/3 lists showed that the easiest patterns (those on which students were most likely to read the low-frequency word correctly) were "-ook," "-eed," "-an," and "-in," which are high-frequency rimes. The most difficult patterns on the pre-primer lists were all words with the consonant vowel/consonant/e pattern (CVCE). These include "-ame," "-ace," "-ike," and "-ake." The same pattern of difficulty was found for second-graders with the same reading levels. We infer that the students had not yet learned to generalize the CVCE spelling pattern. Details on administering and scoring the word lists can be found in Section 5.

Pearson eText Application Exercise 2.1: Understanding Word Recognition and Identification

---

Oral Reading

The growth in a student's word recognition ability can also be measured by their accuracy in oral reading of passages of increasing difficulty. Oral reading accuracy can be measured in two ways: by Total Accuracy, which counts all errors that are not self-corrected by the reader, and by Total Acceptability, which counts only errors that change meaning.

Section 1 defines three levels of reading: independent, instructional, and frustration. We use Total Accuracy to determine these levels following the recommendations of Betts (1946), Harris and Sipay (1990), and McKenna and Picard (2006/2007). We recommend counting all oral reading errors during testing because counting all uncorrected miscues takes less time than deciding whether a miscue did or did not substantively change meaning. In addition, counting all uncorrected miscues represents a more reliable practice because examiners vary in their interpretation of what constitutes a meaning-change miscue. For example, while many individuals might not consider the substitution of "a" for "the" as a miscue that changes meaning, others might disagree and distinguish between the indefinite ("a") and definite ("the") articles. In our classes, we have noticed similar disagreements regarding whether meaning is changed by miscues such as the following: "song" for "singing"; "find" for "get"; "special" for "precious"; and "shiny" for "waxy." In Section 6, we offer guidelines for determining whether or not a miscue changes meaning.

Miscue Analysis.   Examining errors for whether they change meaning is part of what is termed *miscue analysis*, which examines the relationship between a student's error and the text (Goodman, 1965, 1967). Goodman referred to word pronunciation errors as miscues influenced by three possible cue systems:

- **Graphophonic (or graphic) cue system**: This refers to relationships between graphemes (letter and letter combinations) and phonemes (units of sound). *Example:* If a reader pronounces "jump" as "junk," one can infer that the reader is utilizing sound cues from the initial consonant and vowel, but is not attending to semantic cues (see below) that signal "junk" did not make sense in the context of the sentence.

- **Syntactic cue system**: This refers to the position of the word within the sentence. If the reader reads "Mary sat on her chair" as "Mary sat on a chair," one can infer that sentence syntax influenced the substitution of an indefinite article (*a*) for a pronoun (*her*), and less attention was paid to graphophonic cues.

- **Semantic cues**: These are meaning cues obtained from the content of what is being read. For example, if a reader reads the sentence "I received six presents for my birthday" as "I got six presents for my birthday," one can infer that the reader is using semantic information in saying "got" for "received," while paying less attention to graphophonic cues (*received* and *got* do not look or sound alike).

Goodman's theory was that a reader's use of context, as exemplified by using semantic and syntactic cue systems, was an important and strong influence in word pronunciation (Goodman, 1965, 1967). He believed that as readers develop word recognition skill and speed, they use less graphophonic cues. Therefore, miscues that indicate context usage are strengths because they indicate developing expertise on the part of the reader and a focus on meaning. On the other hand, Goodman believed that overreliance on letter–sound cues suggested a poor reader.

Research has challenged Goodman's theory of the dominant role of context in efficient word recognition (Tunmer & Nicholson, 2011; Stahl, 2006; Stahl & Hiebert, 2005; Stanovich, 2004). Stanovich argues that word-identification skill does not depend on contextual prediction but rather "the level of word recognition skill determines the extent to which contextual information will be relied on" (Stanovich, 2004, p. 466). To put it another way, as readers develop skill in using the graphophonic cue system, they use context less and less to identify words.

Stanovich's predictions were verified in a year-long study of Reading Recovery® students. The students began the intervention heavily dependent on context for determining unknown words. However, those who finished first-grade reading grade level materials successfully, increased their use of graphic cues. By the end of the intervention year they were using a combination of graphic and contextual cues. These higher-achieving students figured out a word using letter-sounds and word parts, and then used context to determine whether their reading made sense. If it did not, they attempted to self-correct, and were often successful in doing so (McGee et al., 2015). These results support the notion that context becomes a factor in the comprehension process as opposed to the word-identification process (Tunmer & Nicholson, 2011; Stanovich, 1993/1994). Miscue analysis provides the examiner/teacher with a window into the child's understanding of reading, especially at points of difficulty (McGee et al., 2015). It allows teachers to provide effective scaffolding to beginning readers (Rodgers et al., 2016).

Miscue analysis, as traditionally used, describes miscues made during oral reading of passages. However, it may not provide information on a reader's specific needs in decoding because such needs may be "masked by context" (McKenna & Picard, 2006/2007, p. 379). A reader aided by context may be able to read a word correctly in a story but be unable to identify it on a word list. This suggests that word identification must also be evaluated apart from context, as in a word list format. The *QRI-7* provides two ways of analyzing the cue systems used by a reader. All words that appear on the *QRI* word lists also appear in stories at the same level of difficulty or one level lower. This allows the teacher to examine the student's dependence on context by noting words that were read incorrectly on a list but read correctly in the text.

Studies have also examined whether students at different ages and ability levels comprehend better in oral than in silent reading. One study found no differences in comprehension between the modes, but the small numbers of students at each age level prevented the researchers from analyzing a developmental trend (McCallum et al., 2004). A second study examined the developmental patterns of comprehension by having all students read texts orally and silently. This allowed for comparison within individual students, and a developmental pattern was noted. Oral reading was associated with higher comprehension in grades 1–5. No differences in comprehension between modes were seen in sixth grade. In seventh grade, silent reading was associated with higher comprehension than oral reading (Prior et al., 2011). In addition, there was a noticeable drop in comprehension in both modes at fourth grade, likely because of the shift in genre at fourth grade: Student participants read narratives in grades 1–3 but shifted to reading all nonfiction texts in grades 4–7.

A recent study examined the comprehension of middle school students who orally and silently read narrative and expository texts (Dickens & Meisinger, 2017). Sixth- and seventh-grade students read passages from the *QRI-5* and answered comprehension questions. No effect of modality was found at either grade level, although the differences at sixth grade approached significance in favor of oral reading. At both grade levels, comprehension of narrative text was higher than expository text.

Pearson eText Application Exercise 2.2: Understanding Oral Reading and Miscue Analysis

---

Implications for Development of QRI-7.   Users of *QRI-7* can examine word recognition from lists or in oral reading of passages. Data illustrating the increasing difficulty of word lists and stories can be found in Section 13. Users can also count all miscues as well as those that changed meaning. Our pilot data suggested that the best predictor of instructional-level comprehension is 95% for Total Acceptability, the measure of accuracy attained when only uncorrected meaning-change miscues are counted. We encourage qualitative miscue analysis to examine how much attention the reader is paying to the graphic elements of the text and to components of meaning. We also suggest, based on pilot data, that reader self-corrections may indicate whether the reader is paying attention to decoding or to passage meaning. We examined the self-correction strategies of children reading pre-primer through third-grade passages. We distinguished between miscues that changed meaning and were corrected and miscues that did not change meaning but were also corrected. Children with reading levels of pre-primer through grade 2 showed no differences between the correction rates. Children were as likely to correct a miscue that distorted meaning as they were to correct one that did not. However, at the grade 3 level, there was a change; children tended to correct significantly more meaning-change miscues than those that did not change meaning. This suggests that at instructional levels of pre-primer through grade 2, children are still focused on pronouncing words and, as a result, little distinction is made between meaning-change or non-meaning-change correction attempts. However, at the third-grade instructional level, developing word-pronunciation skill and increased fluency allows them to focus more on overall passage meaning. The result is that they correct more meaning-change miscues. Our miscue analysis worksheet in Section 6 reflects this alternative interpretation.

Fluency, Automaticity, and Prosody

Other researchers have examined the relationship between oral reading fluency and reading comprehension. This area of research has increased since the development of curriculum-based measures (CBM) of fluency (Fuchs et al., 2001; Good & Kaminski, 2002). The research surrounding the development of CBM is beyond the scope of this book; however, we will briefly review the areas that provided the groundwork upon which the measures of fluency on the *QRI-7* have been developed. First, what is fluency and what is the relationship of fluency to comprehension? Is fluency more important at some developmental levels than at others? Does the ability of a student to read quickly and accurately lead directly to comprehension, or do fluency and comprehension facilitate each other?

The simplest definition of fluency is the number of words read correctly within one minute. This is termed oral reading fluency (ORF), and it measures the accuracy and speed with which a student can read a piece of text. Because early reading development involves learning to read words automatically, ORF should be assessed in students who are beginning readers as well as pre-readers at risk of learning to read. In fact, growth in ORF during first grade was the best predictor of reading comprehension on the SAT-10 achievement test in first and third grades (Kim et al., 2010). Growth in ORF is particularly important if teachers use it to measure improvement from an intervention plan.

Accuracy and speed are not the only aspects of oral reading that are important to the development of fluent reading. Theoretical analyses of the construct of fluency (Kuhn, Schwanenflugel, & Meisinger, 2010) suggest that fluency should include prosody, which is reading "with appropriate expression or intonation coupled with phrasing that allows for the maintenance of meaning" (Kuhn, Schwanenflugel, & Meisinger, 2010, p. 233). There are several features of prosody:

- pitch (the regulation of the rising or falling of pitch),
- duration (the duration of vowel pronunciation) representing the familiar stress patterns of the language and
- pausing (the frequency and location within or between sentences).

As children become more fluent readers, they make shorter and less variable inter-sentential and intra-sentential pauses, and larger pitch changes. They begin to sound more like the average adult. Changes in prosody are most obvious between first and second grade and predict later fluency (Miller & Schwanenflugel, 2008). This supports the previous finding that ORF growth in first grade predicts later reading achievement. Miller and Schwanenflugel (2008) identified two factors that predicted fluency and comprehension at the end of third grade: pausal intrusions at the end of first grade and the extent to which reading approximates an adult intonation contour at the end of second grade.

The validity of the measurement of prosody is affected by the difficulty of the text compared to the skills of the reader. Measures of prosody from a text that is easy for the reader are less likely to be predictive of comprehension than measures from a more difficult text (Kuhn et al., 2010).

Implications for the Development of the QRI. The most useful measure of prosody is reading from either instructional level or frustration level material. Because examiners are not able to predict the levels for a student, prosody measures must be taken immediately after the student reads aloud. The rating should come before the student is asked to retell the passage so that the examiner does not forget how the reading sounded. After determining the instructional level based on accuracy and comprehension, the examiner should compare the prosody ratings when the student reads at instructional versus frustration levels.

How should fluency be measured in an informal reading inventory? Should accuracy and rate be considered separately, or should accuracy be subsumed within the metric "correct words read per minute"? What measure of prosody should be used? The National Assessment of Educational Progress (NAEP) scale combines several measures of prosody: phrasing, expressiveness, and adherence to author's syntax (Pinnell et al., 1995). But another view of prosody is multidimensional separating of phrasing and expression as one factor, accuracy and smoothness as another, and pacing as the third (Rasinski, Rikli, & Johnston, 2009).

Valencia and colleagues (2010) examined the developmental course of fluency development and its relationship to overall reading comprehension among second-, fourth-, and sixth-grade children. Fluency was measured by oral reading accuracy and rate, at one minute and three minutes, and by the NAEP rating of prosody. They concluded that rate, accuracy, and prosody should be used as separate measures of fluency. This will maximize the prediction of overall reading comprehension and provide the most diagnostic information. For example, students with the same words correct per minute (WCPM) could have very different profiles. A student might read accurately, but slowly. Another might read quickly but make many errors. These suggest different instructional interventions. Not surprisingly, comprehension of a grade-level passage also added to the prediction of overall reading comprehension in the Valencia et al. study. An examination of factors that predicted reading comprehension found that word recognition accuracy was the more powerful predictor of reading comprehension in first- and second-grade students, but beginning in third grade fluency was a better predictor (Language and Reading Research Consortium, 2015).

The *QRI-7* will continue its use of oral reading accuracy, rate, and comprehension to assess students' reading abilities. In the sixth edition we added a prosody rating used by NAEP (Pinnell et al., 1995) at grade levels 1 through 6 (Valencia et al., 2010), which is shown below.

Oral Reading Prosody Scale—QRI-7. **Directions:** Please circle the number below that best represents the student's one-minute oral reading of this passage. It is best to measure this in the middle of the passage because students often are less prosodic when reading the beginning of a text.

4	3	2	1
Reads primarily in larger, meaningful phrase groups. Some or most of the story is read with expression.	Reads primarily in three- or four-word phrase groups. Little or no expressive interpretation is present.	Reads primarily in two-word phrases with some three- or four-word groupings. Word groupings may be awkward.	Reads primarily word-by-word with occasional two-word or three-word phrases.

Because growth in prosody occurs most rapidly in the early primary-grade years, assessing prosody should begin in first-grade-level text (Kim et al., 2010; Miller & Schwanenflugel, 2008). It should continue through sixth grade because prosody is still related to comprehension in fifth and sixth grades (Klauda & Guthrie, 2008; Valencia et al., 2010). More information on the scoring of prosody can be found in Section 6.

In addition to word recognition and fluency, there are three other factors that affect reading comprehension: content knowledge of the ideas in the text, text structure, and the methods of assessment.

Pearson eText Application Exercise 2.3: Understanding Reading Fluency

Content Knowledge

Research on the effects of content knowledge on reading comprehension has been conducted for over 40 years. Initially, studies examined how comprehension differed as a function of adults' cultural or religious perspective (e.g., Lipson, 1983; Steffenson, Joag-Dev, & Anderson, 1979). This was followed by examination of the role of specific content knowledge on students' comprehension of text (Taft & Leslie, 1985; Recht & Leslie, 1988). More recently, content knowledge has been one of several measures used to predict reading comprehension. Studies have examined the relative contribution of content knowledge, strategy use, and word decoding to predict comprehension (Samuelstuen & Bråten, 2005). Because of the consistent power of prior knowledge to predict comprehension, researchers have measured content knowledge and attempted to control for its effects while studying other variables related to comprehension (Taboada & Guthrie, 2006). In a similar vein, domain knowledge (knowledge within a subject area, such as cell biology) has been measured to compare students' use of strategies to regulate their comprehension. Students with domain knowledge plan and monitor their comprehension, but do not engage in note taking or summarizing (Moos & Azevedo, 2008). These strategies are used by those without a domain knowledge base, presumably to build that base.

Another area of research has examined how incorrect knowledge in science (i.e., a misconception) can be changed to scientifically valid knowledge. The question has been: What will it take to change the understanding of a science concept from an everyday understanding to a scientifically valid one? It is not enough to simply explain the scientific perspective, but rather the belief must be refuted by stating the misconception in the text, such as, "If ____ is what you believe, you are mistaken," or some other direct indication that the reader's knowledge is wrong. It is necessary to explicitly state the misconception, refute it, and then present the correct conception for college students to change their beliefs (Braasch, Goldman, & Wiley, 2013). It is unlikely that younger students would need less.

The measurement of prior knowledge has taken many forms, including multiple-choice tests (van Kesteren et al., 2014), oral and written interviews, open-ended questions (e.g., Cordova, Sinatra, & Jones, 2014; Johnson, Ozogult, & Reisslein, 2014; Roelle et al., 2015), oral or written predictions, and "tell me everything you know about ____." Each method is likely measuring something different. For example, students who can articulate a coherent, organized essay about their knowledge of a concept have a depth of knowledge far beyond someone who answered many factual questions on a multiple-choice test.

Implications for Development of the QRI.   Studies of previous editions of the *QRI* have shown that asking students what a word or concept means correlates more highly with text comprehension than general instructions that ask students to tell us what they thought of when they heard a word (Leslie & Cooper, 1993). Therefore, the *QRI-7* continues with a direct questioning method to assess students' knowledge. The purpose of the concept measure is to provide a reason why some students do not understand the material that they read. That is, if a student scores below 70% comprehension on a text, it may be because the student had little to no understanding of important concepts in the text. Details on scoring the prior knowledge task can be found in Section 4.

Text Structure

Reading literature, social studies, or science involves some similar processes. Readers identify both unfamiliar and familiar words, attain automaticity in doing so, and comprehend connected text. However, to comprehend text in different disciplines, additional skills are required. Reading comprehension is "context-dependent and influenced in part by the kind of text that one reads" (Shanahan, 2009, p. 257).

Children's familiarity with the structure of narratives is greater than their familiarity with the structures of expository text. Children have been read more narrative than expository texts. Even now, when teachers are encouraged to include nonfiction in reading and language arts activities, children's experiences with narratives likely predominate. Another reason that narrative text may be easier to comprehend may be related to readers' knowledge of content. Students tend to know more about the topics discussed in narrative writings (people, events) compared to those usually presented in expository texts. A "genuine predictor of reading comprehension is children's narrative reasoning, the ability to understand the elements and relations in goal-directed narratives" (Paris et al., 2005 p. 153).

Differences in text structure have often been described as fiction/nonfiction or narrative/expository. These relatively simplistic categories do not capture the nature of the different text structures present in the disciplines of literature, social studies, and science. For example, literature includes short stories, plays, essays, biographies, poetry, and novels. Social studies contains the disciplines of history and political science, while science embraces biology, chemistry, and physics, to name a few. Each of these subdisciplines has a unique structure and content (Shanahan, 2009).

Children's knowledge of expository structure is less developed than their understanding of narrative structure (Klingner & Vaughn, 2004). History texts, for example, often focus on chronological accounts and cause-effect relationships; science texts emphasize procedures and explanations. Using think-alouds and focus-group discussions, researchers have identified important differences in how disciplinary experts read text in their specific discipline (Shanahan, Shanahan, & Misischia, 2011). Historians paid attention to text authors' point of view and the source of their information, while chemists regarded the author as a possible predictor of quality. When the text was written was another issue. Historians were concerned that this might influence the content, while chemists were concerned with whether the content represented out-of-date material. Finally, the experts' knowledge base was used in interpreting the article. Historians focused on whether the author represented a credible source. Chemists defined text credibility as "plausibility or its congruence with scientific evidence" (Shanahan, Shanahan, & Misischia, 2011, p. 420). A student who demonstrates skill in comprehending stories will not necessarily be as adept when asked to comprehend a play. Similarly, a student who comprehends a history text may or may not be as successful when reading about a science experiment. Recent evidence suggests that comprehension of narrative text is superior to comprehension of expository text even among average students in middle school (Dickens & Meisinger, 2017).

Implications for the Development of the *QRI*.   The *QRI* continues to provide both narrative and expository texts from the pre-primer level through high school. In addition, from third grade through high school, at least one social studies and one science passage is included. These Level Diagnostic materials allow a user to examine whether a student's instructional reading level varies depending on the genre or content area being read.

Pearson eText Application Exercise 2.4: Understanding Text Structure

---

Methods of Assessment of Reading Comprehension

Reading comprehension has been measured by:

* retelling and summarization
* answering questions

Retelling and Summarization.   Retelling and summarizing are two distinct cognitive skills (Kintsch & van Dijk, 1978). Although they are often considered to be interchangeable, they "do not measure equivalent cognitive processes" (Reed & Vaughn, 2012, p. 211).

Like its name suggests, a retelling is usually oral in nature. Because it generally occurs without looking back in the text, memory plays a large part in the amount of text recalled. Because a retelling is often assessed in an oral mode, language production also plays a part (Reed & Vaughn, 2012). A retelling indicates how the student has organized the text in memory and may divulge inferences made during comprehension. Unfortunately, little consensus exists about how retelling quality should be determined. Scoring rubrics can include such components as gist/main idea statements, details/story elements, interpretive ideas, generalizations, retelling coherence, retelling completeness, use of linguistic/language conventions, inclusion of additional information not in the passage, and scorer ratings of effectiveness (Brown et al., 1996; Hall, Markham, & Culatta, 2005; Romero, Paris, & Brem, 2005). However, Reed and Vaughn determined that none of these clearly discriminate between students at different percentiles for reading, and they concluded that "retell scores derived through quantitative methods have not yet demonstrated they function well in monitoring students' reading progress or in determining their understanding of narrative and expository text" (Reed & Vaughn, 2012, p. 198).

In contrast to retelling, a summarization generally focuses on "the most relevant ideas and salient details" (Klingner, Morrison, & Eppolito, 2011, p. 234). Perin (2007) describes the following operations for summary writing: delete unnecessary and redundant material; select general words to replace lists of items or actions; and select or compose a topic sentence. Writing a summary usually involves review of the text and multiple revisions on the part of the author (Helsel & Greenberg, 2007).

The goal of using students' retelling or summarization data is to guide instruction. Retelling and/or summarizing are important skills. Not only are they important for success in school, they represent tasks that individuals engage in every day as they describe a sequence of events or summarize the contents of a newspaper editorial. In addition, acquisition of the skills of retelling and summarizing is often included in national and state educational standards (CCSSO, 2010). However, these scores are not to be used to determine a reading level. Additional information on retelling can be found in Section 7 and on summarization in Section 11.

Implications for the Development of the QRI.   *QRI-6* made changes to the scoring of the retelling. First, instead of listing the propositions in the story, we listed sentences. This change was made because we believed that using the proposition as the unit of analysis was too detailed, and basic research had been using clauses and sentences (Trabasso & Magliano, 1995). We also listed only sentences that were either important to the text or recalled by at least 33% of the students in recent pilot studies. Because adjectives and adverbs are meaningful only in connection to specific nouns or verbs, students receive credit if they identify and/or paraphrase the noun and verb. Finally, recent research has indicated that good and poor readers can correctly answer inference questions when they recall the information necessary to make the inference during retelling (Hua & Keenan, 2014). The implication for the *QRI-7* is that our retelling forms include any information necessary to answer one of our implicit or inference questions.

The Level Diagnostic Passages from pre-primer through high school provide an opportunity to evaluate the completeness and accuracy of oral retellings. After reviewing over 50 studies of retelling as an indicator of comprehension, Reed and Vaughn stated that "little guidance was provided (*by research*) for making conclusions about what a desirable percentage of recalled idea units might be or what percentage might indicate comprehension difficulty" (Reed & Vaughn, 2012). Therefore, we do not suggest that you derive a numerical score for retellings but instead analyze the quality of the retelling. Did it include the components of narrative structure? Did informational recall focus on main ideas with some supporting details?

We also developed Inference Diagnostic Passages from fourth grade through high school. There is one biography, one social studies, and one science text at each level. These texts are longer than the Level Diagnostic Passages. They can be administered in groups, with written responses required of the students, or individually in an oral format.

> **Pearson eText Application Exercise 2.5:** Understanding Retelling and Summarization

Asking Questions.   Questions used to assess comprehension have traditionally been divided into two categories: literal and inferential.

- Literal questions ask what was explicitly stated in the text and usually begin with such words as "who," "what," "where," and "when."
- Inferential questions are defined as those requiring an inference to answer.

Taxonomies of question forms have identified different types of inferential questions (Applegate, Quinn, & Applegate, 2002; Bloom & Krathwohl, 1956; Ciardiello, 1998; Graesser, Ozuru, & Sullins, 2010; Mosenthal, 1996; Raphael, 1982, 1986). These taxonomies suggest that inferential questions vary considerably in what students must do to answer the questions. Drawing an inference is not a unitary concept, and there are different types of inferences, with some demanding a higher level of comprehension than others. Such taxonomies also suggest that the ability to answer one form of inference may not transfer to a different form.

Perhaps the most well-known taxonomy of question types is that of Bloom's six categories: knowledge, comprehension, application, analysis, synthesis, and evaluation (Bloom & Krathwohl, 1956). A revision of Bloom's original work (Anderson & Krathwohl, 2001) offered the following levels: remembering, understanding, applying, analyzing, evaluating, and creating. Other question taxonomies followed; like Bloom, they based questions types on the cognitive processes believed to be needed to answer different kinds of questions.

Davis (1968, 1972), one of the first to conceptualize comprehension as involving different processes, proposed nine logically distinct comprehension skills: remembering word meaning; determining word meaning from context; understanding explicitly stated content; weaving together ideas in the text; drawing inferences; formulating the main thought of a text; recognizing the author's purpose, mood, and/or tone and point of view; identifying literary techniques; and following the structure of the text. Although he believed these cognitive processes would be independent, the data showed that only two factors accounted for differences in comprehension: memory for word meanings and the ability to make inferences from the content.

More recent attempts to develop question taxonomies have been based on the information being sought in a good answer and have reduced the number of categories to three or four. For example, Graesser and Person (1994) based their taxonomy on "the nature of the information being sought in a good answer to the question" (Graesser, Ozuru, & Sullins, 2010) and categorized question types in three ways:

- Shallow: provide an example, state whether something occurred or did not occur
- Intermediate: definitions, comparisons, determining the value of something
- Complex: interpretations of data; causes or consequences; goals and resources; goals, instruments, and procedures (in science)

Mosenthal also differentiated questions in terms of the type of information needed to provide an acceptable answer but added that questions also varied "on how concrete or abstract different types of requested information are" (1996, p. 323). Like Graesser and Person (1994), Applegate, Quinn, and Applegate (2002) divided inferential question types into three levels: low, high, and response. "While high level inferences are directed toward a specific element or problem in the passage, response items require a reader to discuss and react to the underlying meaning of the passage as a whole" (Applegate, Quinn, & Applegate, 2002, p. 176). Although the authors rated the questions on the *QRI* as the most difficult, they criticized existing informal reading inventories for not differentiating or controlling for the type of inference questions used to determine student understanding of a text.

Figure 2.1 illustrates a classification schema for inference questions when all the taxonomies are considered.

Despite differences in terminology and number of question categories, all taxonomies recognize that the term "inference" is not a unitary concept; it embodies a variety of different cognitive activities. These various taxonomies suggest that inference questions are generally more difficult to answer than literal questions. In a similar vein, it has often been assumed that poor readers experience more problems in answering them than do good readers. However, Hua and Keenan (2014) found no difference between good and poor readers in answering inference questions when they possessed memory for what was read. Using *QRI* retelling sheets, they first asked readers to retell what they read, and then asked the questions. No difference was noted between good and poor readers' answers to inference questions if their retelling included part of the text necessary for a specific inference. They concluded that "text memory is crucial in distinguishing poor comprehension" (Hua & Keenan, 2014, p. 415). Accordingly, we modified *QRI* retelling forms to include all elements critical for answering inference questions (see Section 7 for details on scoring retellings).

In practice, taxonomy levels are defined by question stems, that is, the words used to describe what a student should do. A question stem can use a question word, such as *who, what, when,* or *where,* or it can include a direction, such as *explain, describe,* or *analyze.* It is assumed that students understand the subtle differences between question stems. For example, does *analyze* differ from *interpret*? Do *compare* and *categorize* carry the same or different meaning? A student's ability to answer a question obviously depends on his or her ability to read the text, but it also depends on the student's understanding of the question stem. The Common Core State Standards Initiative (CCSSO, 2010) uses uniform question stems across grade levels: determine, cite, analyze, assess, interpret, integrate, evaluate, and compare. Figure 2.2 lists commonly used question stems divided into literal and inferential.

Figure 2.1

	Question Types	
Low Level Literal	**Inference Application**	**Inference Analysis**
Basic	**High or Intermediate**	**Highest Level Complex**
Who was involved?	What is an example of ...?	What caused ...?
What happened?	What are qualities of ...?	What are consequences of ...?
When did it happen?	What is the value of ...?	What are motivations/goals?
Where did it happen?	What does ... mean?	How were goals accomplished?
	How are ... similar/different?	

Figure 2.2 Question Stems/Words

Literal Question Stems	Inferential Question Stems
who, what, where, when, list, identify, name	analyze, assess, categorize, classify, compare, connect, conclude, contrast, defend, define, delineate, demonstrate, determine, describe, discuss, evaluate, explain, how, infer, integrate, interpret, judge, justify, predict, provide evidence, recommend, summarize, why

That inferencing ability is not a unitary concept was demonstrated by our research experience with the *Content Area Reading Assessment* (Leslie & Caldwell, 2015) (*CARA*), a group-administered content area assessment. Over 3,000 students in grades 4–9 with wide-ranging differences in achievement revealed consistent weaknesses in certain types of inferential comprehension, depending on the level of the text and the content area. If average-achieving students show such weaknesses, it seems likely that struggling readers will do so as well, even when reading materials are at their instructional level.

Implications for the Development of the *QRI*.   Questions asked on the Inference Diagnostic Passages are all inferential. The stems are designed to be parallel across narrative and expository texts. Figure 2.3 illustrates these question stems. More information on these types of questions can be found in Section 11.

> **Pearson eText Application Exercise 2.6:** Understanding Inferential Questions

Look-Backs.   There are two different forms of look-backs: looking back during reading and looking back after reading. The former is often examined through analysis of eye movements and is beyond the scope of an informal reading inventory assessment. Looking back after reading often occurs in response to a specific need or direction. The reader may be asked a direct question about the text or may wish to review, clarify, or expand on what was read.

Looking back in the text has taken on increased importance in relation to close reading. The Common Core State Standards "focus on students reading closely to draw evidence and knowledge from the text" (Coleman & Pimentel, 2011, p. 1). Students are expected to answer text-dependent questions that focus on ideas and information present in the text (Hinchman & Moore, 2013). This can involve multiple readings (Fisher & Frey, 2014) and multiple occasions for engaging in look-backs.

Figure 2.3 Question Stems for Narrative and Expository Texts on Inference Diagnostic Passages

Narrative Passages	Expository Passages
Support an inference	Support an inference
Determine theme	Determine central idea
Explain why or how	Explain why or how
Determine word meaning	Determine word meaning
Determine point of view	Determine point of view
Determine text structure	

From the viewpoint of literacy assessment, allowing a student to look back in the text differentiates between understanding during reading and memory for what was read and understood. Leslie and Caldwell (2009, 2006, 2001) found that students with reading levels at third grade and above were able to use look-backs effectively; that is, they were able to skim the text, find the location of the answer, and respond with a correct answer that was unavailable to them without looking back. If looking back increases comprehension, it suggests that assessments that do not allow look-backs may underestimate a student's level of comprehension.

The *QRI-7* includes the option of asking students to engage in look-backs to resolve comprehension failures. That is, students first answer questions, then, after all questions are answered, the examiner asks them to look back on questions that were not answered correctly. Examining whether students can look back and correct or add to answers provides valuable information for instruction. If a student is not able to do this, instruction should point out helpful look-back components such as topic headings and signal words. Additional information on look-backs can be found in Section 7 and analysis of our look-back data is in Section 13.

Pearson eText Application Exercise 2.7: Understanding Look Backs

---

Interactive Strategies to Assess Reading Comprehension

Thinking Aloud.   Asking readers to read a selection and think out loud as they do so can provide valuable information about the strategies that readers use as they attempt to comprehend text. It offers the opportunity to gather observations about the thinking that occurs during the reading process.

Over two decades ago, Pressley and Afflerbach (1995) provided a comprehensive summary of studies that examined the think-aloud process and concluded that skilled readers and those with higher levels of prior knowledge employ more and varied think-aloud strategies than poorer readers or those struggling with unfamiliar text. Leslie and Caldwell (2009) summarize research studies on a variety of issues related to think-alouds:

- their relationship to comprehension;
- their use with different forms of text and different age groups;
- the validity and reliability of the system devised for coding reader comments; and
- the amount of text read prior to offering a think-aloud comment.

Traditional assessment measures often have predictive validity; that is, good performance on these measures tends to predict average or above-average classroom performance. However, such measures do not assess process and offer no suggestions for increasing learning. Thinking aloud "captures the process, not just the end product of reading" (Paris & Hamilton, 2009, p. 36). For example, Shanahan, Shanahan, and Misischia (2011) used think-alouds to determine how specialists in history, mathematics, and chemistry read and comprehend text in their disciplines. Think-aloud data can suggest instructional directions; that is, a think-aloud can act as a "method of inquiry and also as a means of facilitating student comprehension of text" (Gavelek & Bresnahan, 2009, p. 158). For example, lack of inferential comments by a student may suggest a need to focus on drawing inferences during instruction.

A series of studies have identified two groups of struggling comprehenders (Kraall et al., 2017; McMaster, Espin, & van den Broek, 2014; McMaster et al., 2012; Rapp et al., 2007). One group, called elaborators, make inferences while thinking-aloud;

however, many of their inferences are invalid or inaccurate. The other group, called paraphrasers, tend to restate what the text says and do not generate causal connections between events in narrative text. McMaster and colleagues (2012) examined whether different instructional conditions would differentially affect the two types of fourth-grade struggling readers. They reasoned that elaborators would benefit from causal questions that prompted them to think of causal relationships among events in the story. In contrast, paraphrasers would benefit more from general questions that asked, "How does the sentence you just read connect with something that happened before in the story?" Their results supported these predictions.

Implications for the Development of the QRI.   We included passages that included locations for think-alouds at the high school level beginning with the third edition. For the fourth edition, we added think-aloud passages to the sixth-grade and upper middle school nonfiction texts, where we estimated the greatest problems in comprehension would occur. New to the seventh edition are two narrative texts with think-aloud formatting, one at the sixth-grade level and one at the upper middle school level. Based on the research cited above, we recommend that users of the *QRI-7* use think-aloud passages to assess to which group a struggling reader belongs and then design intervention based on recommendations by McMaster et al. (2012). An explanation of the development of think-aloud materials and their use can be found in Section 8 and analyses of the think-aloud data can be found in Section 13.

Pearson eText Application Exercise 2.8: Understanding Think Alouds

---

Summary

The *Qualitative Reading Inventory-7* is an informal reading inventory based on a large research base. This section has reviewed that research and described how it guided development of the *QRI*. In addition, our procedures and materials have undergone extensive piloting over the past 25 years, and some of those results are presented in Section 13. The next sections will provide you detailed instructions on how to administer, score and interpret the *QRI*.

Section 3

Purposes and Basic Steps for Administering the *Qualitative Reading Inventory-7*

 ## Chapter Outline

Purposes for Administering *QRI-7*

Determine a Student's Instructional Reading Level

Assessment of Prior Knowledge

Assessment of Word Pronunciation Errors, Fluency, and Prosody

Assessment of Comprehension: Retelling and Answering Questions

Assessment of Comprehension: Look-Backs and Think-Alouds

Assessment of Reading Growth

Steps in Administering *QRI-7*

Gather Materials and Put Students at Ease

Administer the Word Identification Lists

Administer an Initial Passage

Administer Additional Passages

Frequently Asked Questions

PURPOSES FOR ADMINISTERING *QRI-7*

Determine a Student's Instructional Reading Level

The primary purpose for administering the *QRI-7* is to determine a student's instructional reading level. There are three distinct reading levels: independent, instructional, and frustration. Passages at a reader's independent level can be read independently with adequate word identification and comprehension. An instructional-level passage can be read successfully with the support of the teacher. Intervention instruction focuses on passages at this level. Frustration passages are what the name suggests—they are beyond the ability of the reader and are generally avoided in intervention.

Passages in the *QRI-7* include narrative and expository selections from pre-primer through middle school, and expository selections through high school. Expository texts contain examples of both social studies and science passages. This allows the teacher to examine a student's reading ability in three very different kinds of texts: narrative, social studies, and science. Comprehending a text is dependent upon understanding text structure. The structure of a narrative includes the setting, a main character, the character's problem/s, and how the problem is solved. The structure of expository material is very different. It centers on identification of the topic, what the author says about the topic, and identification of the main idea (which may or may not be explicitly stated). An expository text can have a different topic and main idea in succeeding paragraphs. Because of these differences, a reading level for narratives seldom transfers to an expository selection.

Using *QRI-7* to determine an individual's passage level involves two steps. First, a student orally reads a list of words, and the examiner uses the student's performance to determine the level of passage that is appropriate to begin passage administration. Second, the student reads one or more passages orally and/or silently. Oral reading allows you to examine a student's word identification strategies and his/her reading fluency. For students in fourth grade and above, it is important to examine the extent to which a student has transitioned to effective silent reading, so silent reading may be more appropriate. For both oral and silent reading, the examiner evaluates a student's comprehension in two ways: asking the student to retell the text, and then asking the student to answer explicit and implicit questions. See Figure 3.1. Evaluating word recognition on word lists and in stories and evaluating comprehension through retelling and asking questions is described in detail in Sections 5, 6, and 7.

Figure 3.1 Purposes for Administering the *Qualitative Reading Inventory-7*

Goal	Materials	Purpose	Student Reads Orally or Silently?
Determine a Student's Instructional Reading Level	Word Lists	- Determine a starting point (level) for passage administration	Orally
	Level Diagnostic Passages	- Determine instructional level based on two factors: 1) number of miscues (if read orally), and/or 2) number of explicit/implicit questions answered correctly[**]	Orally and/or silently[*]
Assessment of Prior Knowledge	Concept Questions (Located before each Level Diagnostic Passage)	- Evaluate a student's comprehension in relation to their knowledge base (familiar and unfamilar topics)	N/A—Prereading questions to be answered orally
Assessment of Word Pronunciation Errors, Fluency. and Prosody	Word Lists	- Examine a student's word identification strategies (in isolation)	Orally
	Level Diagnostic Passages	- Examine a student's word identification strategies (in context) by counting total miscues - Examine a student's fluency by calculating words correct per minute (WCPM) and using Oral Reading Prosody Scale	Orally
Assessment of Comprehension: Retelling and Answering Questions	Level Diagnostic Passages	- Examine a student's comprehension by asking the student to retell the text - Examine a student's comprehension by asking the student to answer explicit and implicit questions about the text[**]	Orally and/or silently[*]
Assessment of Comprehension: Look-Backs and Think-Alouds	Level Diagnostic Passages	- Examine a student's comprehension by asking the student to answer explicit and implicit questions about the text using look-backs to correct any errors - Observe a student's thought patterns (comprehension) while reading a text using think-alouds	Orally and/or silently[*]
Assessment of Reading Growth	Word Lists and Level Diagnostic Passages	- Measure growth by determining a student's instructional reading level (see above) at different points in the school year. Note: passages used for pre- and post-testing should come from the same type (i.e., both narrative, both social studies, or both science)	Orally and/or silently[*]

[*]For students in fourth grade and above, it is important to examine silent reading ability.

[**]Beginning at the third-grade level, passages include guidelines for scoring with and without look-backs.

Assessment of Prior Knowledge

Each selection is prefaced by three or four concept questions that are scored on a 3-2-1-0 scale of familiarity. Asking these questions prior to reading allows you to determine whether the topic of a selection is familiar to the student. Readers generally do better with text about familiar topics, and often have lower reading levels when reading unfamiliar material.

Many of the passages at the pre-primer through third grade levels focus on familiar topics such as birthday parties, pets, seasons, and family trips. However, at the fourth-grade level and above, they center on topics that may be unfamiliar to the reader. Assessing the level of a student's reading of unfamiliar material can indicate the nature of instruction that is needed, especially for students in grades 4 and above.

We strongly recommend that you administer the concept questions. It does not take long, and it activates student background for the topic of the passage. It also allows you to evaluate comprehension in relation to the student's knowledge base and can suggest a direction for intervention activities. For example, difficulty in reading unfamiliar text below or at a student's chronological grade level suggests that strategies for reading and comprehending such a text should represent a focus for intervention instruction. An explanation of how to score student responses to the concept questions is provided in Section 4.

What if you cannot find a familiar passage? QRI-7 passages at the pre-primer through third-grade levels represent narratives on relatively familiar topics, so this is seldom an issue at those levels. However, if responses to the concept questions suggest unfamiliarity on the part of the student, you have two options: select another passage, or administer the selection but note that performance may have been influenced by a student's lack of prior knowledge.

Assessment of Word Pronunciation Errors, Fluency, and Prosody

There are two ways to assess a student's ability to accurately pronounce words: administering the word lists and administering the passages. The word list requires readers to pronounce words without the support of passage context. Words on the word lists are taken from the passages, which allows you to compare a student's word recognition without and with the support of context. Some readers do better when pronouncing single words; others do better when reading words in the context of a sentence or passage.

Performance on the word list can indicate the level of passage to select for additional assessment. Choose a passage level where the student has attained an independent level ($\geq$ 90%) on the word list at that level. This helps to avoid starting too low or too high. If the passage is too difficult, frustration at the beginning of a testing session can prejudice the student against the entire process. Administering and scoring the word lists is described in Section 5.

As the student orally reads a passage, record all word pronunciation errors or miscues. These include the following: substitution of a word for the word in the passage; omission of a word or words; insertion of a word or words; and reversals of words. The number of oral reading miscues determines the level for word identification in context. Recording and analyzing word pronunciation errors is explained in Section 6.

To examine the student's fluency, time how long it takes the student to orally read a passage and calculate the number of words correct per minute (WCPM). Also consider the student's prosody or expressive reading. Charts for determining WCPM and for rating prosody are part of scoring for each passage.

Assessment of Comprehension: Retelling and Answering Questions

There are two options for assessing whether the student has comprehended the text: retelling and answering questions. After the student has read the text orally or silently, ask the student to retell what was read. Each passage has a retelling scoring sheet that allows you to evaluate retelling in terms of the structure of the text. For narrative materials, the retelling scoring sheet includes the following topics: setting/background, goal, events,

Pearson eText
Video Example 3.1

Using Concept Questions to Assess Prior Knowledge
This video includes an example of how the concept questions are introduced to the student and how they are scored. Pay attention to how the examiner writes what the student says.

and resolution. For expository passages, the retelling scoring sheet focuses on main ideas and details.

After retelling, ask the student to answer the questions that follow each passage without looking back in the text. Selections have five, six, eight, or ten questions depending upon the grade level of the passage. Questions are both literal (explicit) and inferential (implicit) in nature. The number of questions that are answered correctly determines the level of comprehension. It can also indicate differences in the types of questions that a student can answer. For example, students often do well with literal questions for which answers are stated explicitly in the text. But the same students may have difficulty with inferential questions.

Assessment of Comprehension through Look-Backs and Think-Alouds

Asking the student to look back in the text to correct an erroneous answer is most effective at or above the third-grade level. A student who can correct errors probably understood the text at least after rereading. Stopping after the student has read a segment of text and asking the student to say what s/he is thinking about is appropriate for the sixth-grade level and above. It allows you to observe the student's thought patterns as s/he reads the text. Look-backs are explained in Section 7, and think-alouds are explained in Section 8.

Assessment of Reading Growth

As stated in Section 1, the QRI-7 is commonly used to:

1. determine the student's instructional reading level, and
2. determine the student's strengths and weaknesses in reading.

In addition, it can be used to determine how far the student's instructional level is below his or her grade placement. Also, the QRI-7 can be used to assess a student's growth in the level of materials that he or she can read successfully; that is, to determine a change in the student's instructional reading level. The pre-test and post-test passages must be of the same type: narrative, social studies, or science. Do not assume that success in reading narratives will carry over to social studies and science texts. Several published studies have used the QRI to document growth in reading based on a specific type of instructional program or intervention. Some of the studies that used the QRI for research purposes are found in the References and are marked with an asterisk.

The QRI-7 allows you to determine one or more reading levels for an individual student based upon the nature of the text and the reader's prior knowledge. It can also be used to answer the following questions about a student's strengths and needs. At what level and in what type of text (narrative or expository) can a student:

1. identify words accurately and automatically? (Section 5 and 6)
2. read with acceptable fluency or prosody? (Section 6)
3. retell what was read? (Section 7)
4. answer explicit or literal questions? (Section 7)
5. answer implicit or inferential questions? (Section 7)

Figure 3.1 summarizes the purposes for administering the *Qualitative Reading Inventory-7*.

STEPS IN ADMINISTERING THE *QRI-7*

Gather Materials and Put Students at Ease

Administer the QRI-7 in a quiet place that is free from distractions. Before meeting the student, gather all materials: word lists, student passages, and accompanying sheets for your recording. We strongly recommend audio recording the entire session so you can listen to the student later and verify your scoring accuracy. It is often difficult to determine how many scoring sheets to prepare, and it is better to have too many than not enough. If you prepare a kit of scoring sheets for all the passages and organize them according to grade level, this can ensure that the correct passages will be available.

Before beginning the testing, strive to put the student at ease. Engaging in conversation about the student's interests can act as an effective ice-breaker. Some students are concerned about the examiner's use of a timer or recorder. Placing both out of immediate sight can make them less noticeable. Explain that you are recording the session to help you and make certain that you do not make mistakes. This usually relieves anxiety on the part of the student.

Tips for Administering the QRI-7

- Choose a location that is free from distractions.
- Before meeting, gather all materials (word lists, passages, and scoring sheets).
- It is better to have too many materials than not enough. When preparing a kit of passages and scoring sheets, organize by grade level.
- Audio record each session (***strongly recommended***) to allow for scoring verification later.
- Put the student at ease:
  - Engage in conversation about their interests as an ice-breaker.
  - Place your timer and audio recording device out of immediate sight.
  - Explain that you are recording the session to make certain you do not make mistakes.

Administer the Word Identification Lists

The word lists provide a quick estimate of a student's word identification ability. Administer the word-identification lists to estimate a starting point for selecting the passages. Score them immediately to select the first passage. Detailed instructions are provided in Section 5.

Administer an Initial Passage

Select an initial passage at the same level as the highest level where the student scored 90% + on the word lists. If a student does not score at 90% or above for any word list, select a passage at the highest level attained by the reader. Narrative assessment represents a good beginning point. It is generally easier than expository text, and often leads to initial experiences of success for younger students

Each passage is preceded by three to four concept questions. Asking these can determine whether the topic of the passage is familiar to the student. Passages at the pre-primer through third-grade levels generally represent topics that are familiar to most students. This may not be the case for passages at a fourth-grade level and above. If the concept questions suggest that the topic is not familiar, select another more familiar passage for the first passage. Reading about a familiar topic usually represents a student's highest achievement. Although a narrative text is a good starting point for students in fourth grade and above, it is important to also assess their ability to comprehend expository text. (See Sections 6 and 7.)

Administer Additional Passages

There are several reasons for administering additional passages. The initial passage may not clearly indicate a student's instructional level; that is, the student may perform at an independent or frustration level. One or more additional passages may be necessary to determine the student's highest instructional level.

An instructional level in narrative text does not guarantee that the student will read expository texts at that same level. It is particularly important that students in fourth grade be taught how to read and comprehend unfamiliar expository text, as that is what they meet every day in their content classrooms. Also, for students in fourth grade and above, silent reading should be assessed, as older students are often hampered by a slow rate of reading.

FREQUENTLY ASKED QUESTIONS

Do I have to administer the concept questions?   We strongly recommend that you administer the concept questions. It does not take long, and it activates student background for the topic of the passage. It also allows you to evaluate comprehension in relation to the student's knowledge base and can suggest a direction for intervention activities. Difficulty in reading unfamiliar text below or at a student's chronological grade level suggests that strategies for reading unfamiliar text should represent a focus for intervention instruction.

What if I cannot find a familiar passage?   *QRI-7* passages at pre-primer through third-grade levels represent narratives on relatively familiar topics, so this is seldom an issue at those levels. However, if responses to the concept questions suggest unfamiliarity on the part of the student, you have two options: select another passage or administer the selection but note that performance may have been influenced by a student's lack of prior knowledge.

What level of passage should I begin with?   Choose a passage level at which the student has attained an independent level ($\geq$ 90%) on the word list. This helps to avoid starting too low or too high. If the passage is too difficult, frustration at the beginning of a testing session can prejudice the student against the entire process. See Section 5 for more details regarding word list administration and scoring.

How do I find an instructional level?   The instructional level is the level at which a student can read with assistance. Section 4 explains in detail the procedure for determining an instructional level. At the instructional level, oral reading accuracy is 90% if all errors are counted and 95% if only meaning errors are counted, and comprehension is between 70% and 88%. See Section 6 for more details about finding an instructional level for both word identification and comprehension.

What if a reader's total miscues and total number correct on the questions suggest different reading levels (e.g., total miscues indicate instructional level but responses to comprehension questions indicate frustration level)?   Focus on the lowest level when choosing the next passage. For example, if a student reads a third-grade passage and scores at an instructional level for word identification but a frustration level for comprehension, have the student read a second-grade passage. See Section 4 for more information about determining the instructional level.

Must I find independent, instructional, and frustration levels for all types of text, narrative/expository and familiar/unfamiliar?   No. To do so would demand an unrealistic amount of time, and student fatigue would be a concern. Determining an instructional level in narrative text is of primary importance for younger students. For students in fourth grade and above, determining a level in expository material may be more helpful in describing the nature of a student's difficulty.

Which mode should I use: oral or silent?   We suggest that you use an oral reading format with primary-grade children and with older students suspected of reading below the third-grade level. You can estimate this by the word list scores. For students reading at third-grade through fifth-grade levels, use a combination of oral and silent reading. Once you establish an instructional level, you can change to a silent reading mode. It is important to evaluate ability in expository text through silent reading, because most students are expected to read such material silently in school. For students reading at the sixth-grade through high school level, silent reading is the best format because individuals do little oral reading at these levels.

Section 4
Determining Reading Levels

 ## Chapter Outline

How Are Reading Levels Determined?
The Independent Level
The Instructional Level
The Frustration Level

Factors Affecting Reading Levels
Prior Knowledge of the Topic
Text Structure: Narrative and Expository
Mode of Reading: Oral and Silent
Questions: Literal and Inferential
Look-Backs

Finding an Instructional Reading Level
Order of Administration
Finding an Instructional Reading Level for Narrative and Expository Text
Using Scores to Determine Passage Level

HOW ARE READING LEVELS DETERMINED?

A student's reading level is estimated in two ways depending on whether the text is read orally or silently.

Oral Reading
- The number of word pronunciation errors made by the reader (often called miscues)
- The number of questions that the reader answers correctly

Silent Reading
- The number of questions that the reader answers correctly

These scores are used to identify three levels:

- The level at which a student can read independently
- The level at which a student can read with instructional guidance
- The level that causes a student to experience frustration

The Independent Level

This is the level at which a student can read successfully and without any assistance. Oral reading is fluent. The student reads in phrases and with expression. The student comprehends the text and correctly answers most questions. Materials written at this level are appropriate for the student's personal independent reading. Figure 4.1 outlines performance indicators associated with the independent level.

Figure 4.1 The Independent Level

Oral Reading Accuracy:	98% if all errors are counted
Oral Reading Acceptability:	95–97% if only meaning-change errors are counted
Comprehension:	90%

The Instructional Level

This is the level at which a student can read with assistance. Materials written at an instructional level are appropriate for both reading instruction and content-area instruction. You may count student errors in two ways. Count all word identification errors using a criterion of 90% accuracy and/or count word identification errors that change meaning using a norm of 95% accuracy. Details on how to record and count word identification errors are explained in Section 6. The student must also correctly answer at least 70% of the comprehension questions. We recommend that you use total accuracy first, then look at miscues to judge meaning change. Figure 4.2 outlines performance indicators associated with the instructional level.

Figure 4.2 The Instructional Level

Oral Reading Accuracy:	90% if all errors are counted
Oral Reading Acceptability:	95% if only meaning-change errors are counted
Comprehension:	70–88%

The Frustration Level

At the frustration level, the student is not able to read with adequate word identification and/or comprehension. Oral reading lacks fluency and expression, and a word-for-word, halting style is common. Figure 4.3 outlines performance indicators associated with the frustration level.

Can a student have more than one reading level? Yes. It is simplistic to talk about a single independent, instructional, or frustration level for an individual. Reading is a very complex activity, and a variety of factors affect comprehension.

Figure 4.3 The Frustration Level

Oral Reading Accuracy:

Below 90% if all errors are counted
Below 95% if only errors that changed meaning are counted

Comprehension: Below 70%

Pearson eText Application Exercise 4.1: Determining Reading Levels Based on Number of Miscues

Pearson eText
Video Example 4.1

Using Concept Questions to Assess Prior Knowledge This video includes an example of how the concept questions are introduced to the student and how they are scored. Pay attention to how the examiner writes what the student says.

FACTORS AFFECTING READING LEVELS

A variety of factors beyond word identification can affect an individual's reading level. These include the reader's prior knowledge of the subject matter, the structure of the text, the mode of reading, the type of questions used, and whether the student is allowed to use look-backs.

Prior Knowledge of the Topic

When readers possess extensive prior knowledge about a topic, they can read and comprehend at a higher level than when they are faced with unfamiliar content. This is well illustrated by the difficulty that able adult readers might have with an income tax form, the language of an insurance policy, or an article on quantum physics. Students generally have their highest reading level when reading material on familiar topics (e.g., classroom friends, birthday celebrations, famous people, etc.). The *QRI-7* estimates the familiarity of the text by asking three or four concept questions prior to each passage. These allow you to determine whether the topic of the passage is familiar or unfamiliar to the student; scoring examples are provided for each concept. Student responses are scored on a 3-2-1-0 basis. A score of 3 indicates that the student defined the term or gave a synonym or antonym for it. A score of 2 is given when the student provided a correct example of the term, an attribute of the term, or a function of the term. A score of 1 might include a personal association, or the isolation of a prefix, suffix, or root word contained in the word. A score of 0 is given when the response is not related to the term in any way. An example of concept questions is provided in Figure 4.4.

Figure 4.4 An Example of Concept Questions

Narrative Concept Question from "The Family's First Trip," Level 2:

What can children do to keep themselves busy on long rides in a car? *(Note: this concept cannot be defined, so there are no 3-point answers; 2: play games, read, use my iPad, any reasonable example; 1: sleep)*

What does it mean to travel? *(3: to go somewhere far, or go to another country/land; 2: go on vacation, beach 1: fun)*

How does the weather affect what you bring along on a trip? *(3: if it's raining you bring an umbrella/raincoat, if it's cold you bring a coat; 2: bring many types of clothes; 1: bring lots of clothes)*

Pearson eText Application Exercise 4.2: Using Concept Questions to Measure Prior Knowledge

Text Structure: Narrative and Expository

It is common for a reader to perform better while reading narrative texts compared to expository texts. This is because younger students who have been read to on a regular basis often develop a sense of narrative text structure. This can positively affect their comprehension when they begin to read on their own. Narrative text is structured around a goal or problem. In contrast, disciplines such as science and social studies have multiple text structures: description, sequence, cause-effect, problem-solution, and compare-contrast. They also deal with unfamiliar concepts, such as the continental drift theory and the fall of the Roman Empire. These elements make expository texts more difficult to comprehend than narratives. A student may have one grade level for narrative text and a much lower one for expository material.

Which level best estimates the overall reading ability of the student? Because reading a familiar narrative is generally easier than reading expository and unfamiliar text, the familiar narrative level probably represents a reader's highest instructional level. Once a reading level based on narrative text is determined, the assessment process often ends. This is unfortunate because understanding the structure of a narrative seldom transfers to expository texts. Furthermore, ending an assessment session without determining a level for expository material does not help struggling readers in grades 4 and above who encounter expository texts in their classrooms on a regular basis.

We believe that especially for students in grades 4 and above, assessment is not complete without determining a level for expository text. When choosing expository passages to administer, select materials one or two levels below the student's narrative level.

Mode of Reading: Oral and Silent

Whether a student reads orally or silently is another factor that can affect comprehension. Younger and less-fluent readers generally comprehend more when they read orally, which can impact performance. Older readers are more used to silent reading and are often self-conscious when reading orally, which can impact performance.

Questions: Literal and Inferential

The type of questions asked after reading also influences reading level. Higher-level inference questions are generally more difficult than explicit literal questions. Inference questions ask readers to think about sections of the text and draw conclusions from it; the answer is not explicitly stated in the text. Because the ability to draw inferences is critical for comprehension, questions for determining reading level in *QRI-7* contain both explicit (literal) and inferential questions.

Look-Backs

Can a student find the correct answer to a question if he or she is allowed to look back in the text? Skilled readers often engage in looking back to find answers to questions or to clarify their comprehension. Scoring questions without allowing a student to look back may underestimate a student's comprehension, especially in text that is about an unfamiliar topic. For each passage at or above a third-grade level, the *QRI-7* provides a summary table for scoring the number of explicit and implicit questions that are answered with or without look-backs.

> **Pearson eText Application Exercise 4.3:** Using Questions with/without Look-Backs to Determine Reading Level

FINDING AN INSTRUCTIONAL READING LEVEL

Use the following tools and methods to help determine the instructional reading level for a particular student.

Order of Administration

As mentioned previously, an instructional reading level is determined by two factors:

- the number of oral reading errors (often called miscues) and
- the number of correct answers to questions.

You can count errors/miscues in one of two ways. Count all miscues and use this total to determine the student's level. We call this *Total Accuracy*. (See Section 6). You can also only count miscues that change meaning. We call this *Total Acceptability*. (See Section 6). The number of questions that the student answers correctly determines the comprehension level (See Section 7).

If the student scores within the independent or instructional range on the first passage, choose another passage at the next higher level. Continue moving upward until the student reaches a frustration level. If the student reaches a frustration level on the first passage, move downward until the student reaches an instructional level. There may be times when you may not choose to find the highest instructional level. For example, if the student's instructional level is the same as his/her actual grade level, determining levels above grade placement or ascertaining the exact frustration level may have little value. Figure 4.5 provides a basic order for administering the QRI word lists and passages.

Figure 4.5 Order of Administration

Word Lists	Start with list	Find highest list	End with list
	2 levels below grade level	Student reads with 90% accuracy	Student reads at or below 50% of words
Passages	**Start with passage**	**Find highest passage**	**End with passage**
	At highest level where student read 90% of words on word list	Student reads with 90% accuracy and correctly answers 70% + of comprehension questions	Student reads less than 90% accuracy or correctly answers less than 70% of comprehension questions

Finding an Instructional Reading Level for Narrative and Expository Text

As mentioned before, determining a student's reading level for expository text is important, especially for students in fourth grade and above. Expository passages are generally unfamiliar in both content and structure, and a student's performance often falls below his or her instructional level for narrative material. When assessing reading levels for expository text, initial passages should be one or two levels below a student's instructional level for narratives. Figure 4.6 provides a complete flow chart for using *QRI-7* to find an instructional level for both narrative and expository text (See Figure 4.6 on next page).

Figure 4.6 Finding an Instructional Reading Level for Narrative and Expository Text

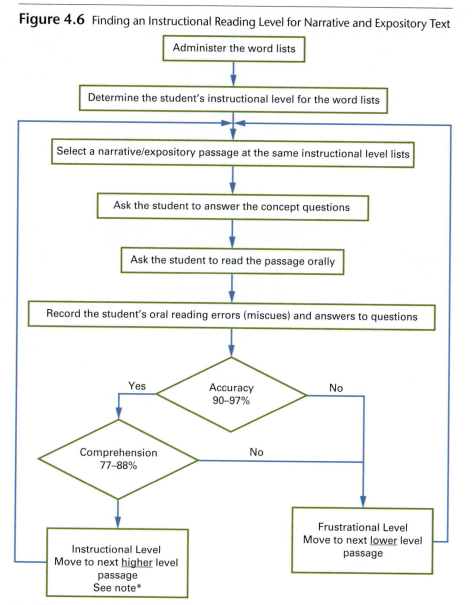

Note: *If the examiner wants the highest instructional level, go to the next highest level. If the examiner only wants to know if the student can read grade level text, then STOP.

Disclaimer: Do not assume the student's level in narrative text will translate to expository text.

Using Scores to Determine Passage Level

Once you have the word identification and comprehension levels, you can determine the total passage level. This is represented by the lower of the two scores. For example, if word identification is at an independent level and comprehension is at an instructional level, then the total passage level is instructional. Similarly, if word identification is at an instructional level and comprehension is at a frustration level, total passage level is frustration. If the student reads silently, determine the total passage level by the comprehension score alone. Figure 4.7 provides guidelines for determining total passage level based on the two scores (See Figure 4.7 below).

Figure 4.7 Guidelines for Determining Total Passage Level

IF	Word Identification Performance =	AND	Comprehension Performance =	THEN	Total Passage Level =
	Independent		Independent		Independent
	Independent		Instructional		Instructional
	Independent		Frustration		Frustration
	Instructional		Independent		Instructional
	Instructional		Instructional		Instructional
	Instructional		Frustration		Frustration
	Frustration		Independent		Frustration
	Frustration		Instructional		Frustration
	Frustration		Frustration		Frustration

Section 5
Using the Word Lists

 ## Chapter Outline

Purposes for Administering the Word Lists
  Estimating Automatic Word Recognition and Word Identification
  Estimating the Starting Point for Passage Administration
  Estimating Automaticity of Word Recognition
  Analyzing the Differences Between Word Identification in Isolation and in Context
  Estimating Knowledge of Letter–Sound Matches
  Examining Knowledge of Vowel Patterns

Procedures for Administering the Word Lists
  Instructions to the Student
  Choosing a Starting Point
  Recording Student Responses: Accuracy and Automaticity

Using the Word List Scores
  Estimating the Starting Point for Passage Administration
  Interpreting Word Identification and Word Recognition Scores
  When the Word Lists Do Not Predict Reading Level

Reading By Analogy
  Using the Reading by Analogy Test

Additional Uses of the Word Lists

Development and Analysis of the Word Identification Tests

PURPOSES FOR ADMINISTERING THE WORD LISTS

The three major purposes for administering the word lists are to determine the:

1. student's ability to recognize words quickly;
2. student's ability to identify words that were not recognized quickly;
3. starting point for passage administration.

Estimating Automatic Word Recognition and Word Identification

The word lists provide a quick estimate of the student's word recognition and identification ability. We use the term *word recognition* when the student pronounces a word within one second of seeing it. We use the term *word identification* when the student takes longer than one second to read it or if the student decodes the word. For example, if a student reads the word *song* as *s-ong*, we infer that the student didn't recognize the word immediately and had to use phonetic cues to decode it.

Word Recognition
- Word is pronounced within one second

Word Identification
- Word is pronounced after one second or after the student decodes it

Estimating the Starting Point for Passage Administration

Word list performance may also help you estimate the level of text passage the student should begin reading. This is because words on the lists appear in the passages at the same readability level. If the student has problems with word identification, his or her performance on the word lists will indicate a realistic beginning point for passage administration.

Words in the passages are underlined if they are present on the word list at the same level or the preceding level. This underlining allows you to compare a student's word recognition in the context of reading a passage with his or her reading of the same word on a list. Words occur on more than one word list because they are common/frequent words. For example, in the primer story "Fox and Mouse," several words were underlined that appeared on the primer word list, including *one, went, every, why,* and *said.* This passage also contains common words in the story that appeared on the pre-primer 1 (PP1) and pre-primer 2/3 (PP2/3) word lists, including *help, they,* and *was.* These words occurred in the primer story because they are commonly used in stories read by beginning readers.

Estimating Automaticity of Word Recognition

You can estimate automaticity of word recognition by silently counting "one thousand one" as the student reads each word. If a student reads a word within one second, you can assume that the student has recognized the word automatically without needing to decode it. The more words that a reader identifies automatically, the more likely it is that he or she will fluently read passages at the same level.

Words that are automatically recognized have often been termed *sight vocabulary.* It was once thought that a direct link occurred between the visual aspects of a word and the word meaning. However, research shows that automatic word recognition involves a strong sound component (Ehri, 1992; Ehri, 2014; Miles, Rubin, Gonzalez-Frey, 2018). Therefore, *sight vocabulary* may be a misnomer, and we prefer to use the term *automatic word recognition.* In other words, the term *sight vocabulary* implies that students recognize the word using only visual clues, but research evidence suggests that a strong sound component is part of automatic word recognition.

Key Points About Word Lists
- Words in lists appear in passages that have the same readability level
- Performance on the word lists indicates a beginning level for passage administration
- Performance on the word lists estimates automaticity of word recognition (i.e. sight vocabulary and reading fluency)

Analyzing the Differences Between Word Identification in Isolation and in Context

Typically, students read more accurately in a story than they do on word lists because the sentence context aids in word identification. Beginning readers often rely on context to determine word pronunciation and, at early levels, this can be regarded as a strength (Stanovich, 2004). However, at Level 3 and above, reliance on context for word identification may be evidence of inadequate decoding and/or inadequate automatic word recognition; readers attempt to compensate for such deficiencies by use of context. If the reader identifies many more words in the stories than on the word list, then instruction on identifying common words may be in order. You can determine whether the reader uses context by examining whether the student can identify words in a passage that she or he could not identify on the word list.

Estimating Knowledge of Letter–Sound Matches

All other words that the student reads correctly beyond a one-second limit are probably decoded; that is, the student is matching letters and sounds to identify the word. You can examine correct and incorrect pronunciations to assess the letter–sound matches that the student knows and those that might need emphasis in an intervention program.

Examining Knowledge of Vowel Patterns

The *QRI-7* also provides examiners with the opportunity to examine the student's knowledge and use of 18 frequently used vowel patterns, often called *spelling patterns* or *phonograms* (Beck, 2006; Fry, 1998; Gaskins et al., 1997). A *spelling pattern* is the vowel and the letters that follow it in a syllable. Examples of spelling patterns are *-an* (can, pan, tan), *-ake,* (make, take, lake), *-ook* (look, book, took), and *-at* (cat, fat, hat). If children learn a vowel pattern in one word, they may transfer this knowledge to other words. For example, if a student knows the word "can," the student may use the vowel pattern *-an* to decode "pan." The student must delete the sound represented by the letter "c" from "can" and replace it with the sound represented by the letter "p." This is called *reading by analogy* (Conrad, 2008), and not all readers do this without instruction. Because of the usefulness of reading by analogy, the *QRI-7* offers examiners insight as to whether a student is using this strategy. Teaching students to recognize and use these common patterns is a useful component of phonics instruction.

PROCEDURES FOR ADMINISTERING THE WORD LISTS

1. Give the student the list of words and ask him or her to pronounce them. You may use a window card, which is a 3 × 5-inch card with a section cut out so that only one word on the word list can be seen. Or you can simply hand the list to the student to read at his or her own pace.

2. While the student is reading, record the answers on the accompanying scoring sheet.

3. Mentally count "one thousand one" to differentiate between words identified automatically and those identified after some delay.

4. Mark words identified automatically in the Recognized Automatically column.

5. If the student has not pronounced the word within one second, mark any attempt, correct or otherwise, in the Identified column.

Pearson eText Teacher Resource: Window Card Template

There are several ways to administer the lists. Each may seem awkward at first, but with practice, you will soon find the method with which you are most comfortable.

As you juggle the word lists and the timing, recording the student's answers may seem difficult at first. Until you become more accustomed to timing, listening, and recording all at once, audio-record the entire session. A recording also helps if you are

Figure 5.3 Reading by Analogy Test

PP 1			
High-Frequency Words from the Word Lists	**Correct**	**Low-Frequency Words**	**Correct**
can	c	pan	c
in	c	pin	c
see	c	bee	c
at	c	rat	c
PP 2/3			
make	c	rake	rag
same		fame	
like	c	bike	c
place	c	race	rat
play		bay	
look	c	book	c

the same vowel spelling patterns. So, we ask the student to read the matching low-frequency words. If the student also correctly identifies the low-frequency words, we can infer that decoding by analogy was probably used. To put it another way, a child who correctly identifies "make" but is unable to read "rake" probably recognized "make" automatically. However, the child who correctly identifies both "make" and "rake" probably decoded "rake" by using the known vowel spelling pattern -*ake*.

Figure 5.3 illustrates an example of the Reading by Analogy Test and its scoring. Notice that the student did not read the common words *same* and *play* correctly, so the examiner did not have him or her attempt to read *fame* and *bay*. The student correctly read the low-frequency words with the following spelling patterns: -*an*, -*in*, -*ee*, -*ake*, -*ike* and -*ook*, which suggests that the student is frequently able to use known spelling patterns to read unknown words.

Using the Reading by Analogy Test

The Reading by Analogy Test can be used in two different ways:

- **As a stand-alone measure that is administered apart from the word list tests**. In this case, ask the child to read both the high-frequency words from the word lists and the 18 low-frequency words. You have the option to administer all four levels (PP1, PP2/3, Primer, and 1st) or to just ask the child to read words matching his or her word identification level. If a child correctly reads *both* the low-frequency and the high-frequency words containing the same vowel pattern, you can assume knowledge and use of vowel spelling patterns in word identification.

- **After the word lists have been administered**. Identify the high-frequency words that were read correctly and ask the child to read the corresponding low-frequency words at the same level. Do not ask the child to read a low-frequency word if the student did not read the high-frequency word with the same spelling pattern correctly.

The value of this test is not in obtaining a score but in identifying characteristics. For example:

- Has the student internalized any letter–sound patterns, or is she or he approaching each unfamiliar word as a completely new phenomenon unrelated to any previously known words?

- Which vowel patterns are known? Which are unknown?

Answers to these questions can offer insights into the type of phonics instruction that will best help the reader. The student can be shown how to use known sound patterns to pronounce new words. Known vowel patterns can be applied to unfamiliar and multisyllabic words, and phonics instruction can focus on teaching students to segment words to find the spelling pattern to use to identify unknown words.

ADDITIONAL USES OF THE WORD LISTS

The word lists can be used to note the accuracy of the student's decoding attempts within the untimed format. For example:

- Are there any consonant or vowel sounds that are missed consistently?
- Does the student attempt to apply phonetic strategies to irregular words?
- Which phonetic principles are applied erroneously?

Word list administration can also provide you with a tool for probing into the student's strategies for pronouncing words. For example, after a student has read a list, you can:

- Direct the student to various parts of unknown words and model word-analysis strategies to see whether she or he can take advantage of them. For example, if the student didn't know the word *morning*, you could cover-up *morn* and ask the student if they can read *-ing*. Then cover up *-ing* and see if the student can figure out *morn*.
- Cover up parts of words and uncover them sequentially for the student to pronounce. For example, on the word *animals*, cover the entire word, then show the *an*, followed by *i*, then *mal*, then *s*.
- Contrast an unknown word with one of similar spelling or pronunciation to see whether the student can transfer knowledge to the unknown word. For example, if the student didn't know the word *trade* on the second-grade list, you could write *made*, and see if the student could read *trade* correctly after identifying *made*.

Any success achieved through your aid should be noted on the scoring sheet, but a student *should not receive credit for it* when you are determining independent, instructional, and frustration levels for word identification in isolation.

Caution: As mentioned earlier, a student's ability to decode words in isolation may be very different from her or his ability to identify words in context (Nicholson, Lillas, & Rzoska, 1988). Therefore, any diagnostic interpretation made on word list reading should be corroborated by the student's performance when identifying words in the context of QRI-7 passages. Thus, if the student misread words with vowels in the middle of the word, such as *heard, afraid, brain,* or *friend,* you cannot make any inference about the student's knowledge of vowel patterns until you first see whether the student could read the same words in the context of the stories (e.g., "The Bear and the Rabbit" includes the words *heard* and *afraid*).

> **Pearson eText Application Exercise 5.2:** Analyzing Word Recognition: Word Lists and Passages

DEVELOPMENT AND ANALYSIS OF THE WORD-IDENTIFICATION TESTS

The word lists were developed by choosing words in our passages that represented the most common words, that is, words with the highest Standard Frequency Index (SFI) from *The Educator's Word Frequency Guide* (Zeno, Ivens, Millard, & Duvvuri, 1995). For example, the first-grade list includes the words *thought* and *knew*, which were in the stories "The Bear and the Rabbit" and "Marva Finds a Friend," respectively. These words are likely to be found in many stories that children read every day. In contrast, we did not include words such as *softly* and *newspaper*, because although they too were in these stories, they are less likely to be found in children's reading materials.

We also separated the most frequent words included on the pre-primer passages. The most common words became the PP1 list. The mean SFI of the words on the PP1 list is 77.91 and includes many of the most frequent words in written English (e.g., *the, a, in, of,* and *to*). The PP2/3 list also includes words from the pre-primer stories (e.g., *make, my, some,* and *people*), but these words are less frequent than those on the PP1 list, with a mean SFI of 70.25. The average SFI of each word list is presented in Table 5.1. Analyses of the word list data can be found in Section 13.

Table 5.1 Mean Standard Frequency Index for *QRI-7* Word Lists

Pre-Primer 1	Pre-Primer 2/3	Primer	1st	2nd	3rd	4th	5th	6th	MS	HS
77.91	70.25	67.95	64.93	59.4	56.5	51.95	49.38	45.90	43.50	37.76

Section 6

Assessing Word Identification in Context, Automaticity, and Prosody

 ## Chapter Outline

Identifying Oral Reading Miscues

Scoring Oral Reading Miscues: Total Accuracy

Scoring Oral Reading Miscues: Total Acceptability
Semantic Acceptability
Syntactic Acceptability

Analyzing Oral Reading Miscues: Miscue Analysis

Evaluating Automaticity

Evaluating Prosody
Prosody Rating Scale

IDENTIFYING ORAL READING MISCUES

As explained in Section 3, a student's independent, instructional, and frustration reading levels are determined by the number of oral reading errors (miscues) and the number of questions that are answered correctly. This section explains how to record and analyze miscues. Section 7 focuses on scoring questions and evaluating retellings.

There are four types of miscues that are scored: substitution of a word, omission of a word, insertion of a word, and reversal in the order of two words. Two additional elements provide further information about a student's word recognition ability: miscues that change text meaning, and self-corrections. Figure 6.1 gives examples of different types of miscues that readers can make.

Use the following system for recording miscues.

- *Substitution:* Write what the student said above the word as it appears in print.
- *Omission:* Circle the omitted word.
- *Insertion:* Write the insertion above the text and mark it with a ^.

Figure 6.1 Types of Miscues and Reader Behaviors

Miscues	Reader Behavior	Example
Substitution	Reader replaces a word	Fox wanted to plant a garden. *Fox went to plant a garden.*
Omission	Reader omits a word	He dug up one of the seeds. *He dug _____ one of the seeds.*
Insertion	Reader inserts a word	Mouse helped him. *Mouse helped him ^ plant.*
Reversal	Reader reverses words.	"It is only one seed," thought Mouse *"It is only one seed," Mouse thought.*
Additional Behaviors		
Meaning Change	Reader makes a miscue that changes meaning.	He wanted to see if it was growing. *He wanted to see if it was good.*
Self-correction	Reader corrects an error.	Fox will not know who ate the seed. *Fox will not care who knows...who ate the seed.*

Note: In each example, the first line is the text and the second is how the student read it.

- *Reversal:* If the student transposes two words or phrases, such as "said John" for "John said," mark the reversal with the following symbol: ⌢.
- *Self-correction:* If a student corrects a miscue, write the miscue and mark it with "C" but do not count it as a miscue.
- *Meaning Change Miscues:* Mark miscues that change meaning as "MC." We suggest that you determine this later as opposed to during the initial administration of a passage. When you are re-examining a student's performance, you will have more time to determine whether a miscue changes meaning.

It is helpful to audio-record a student's oral reading so you can listen to it later and determine whether your initial coding was correct. As you become more skilled in writing and recording student miscues, audio support will become less important. Figure 6.2 provides an example of a written miscue sheet.

Figure 6.2 Who Lives Near Lakes?

<u>Substitutions.</u> The student made the following substitutions: "anmals" for "animals"; "turts" for "turtles"; "the" for "a"; "chicks" for "ducks"; "with" for "behind"; "fishes" for "fish"; "lake" for "water"; "seeing" for "see"; and "fish" for "animals." Write substitutions above the words.

<u>Omissions.</u> In this example, the student omitted two words: "them" and "to." Circle omitted words.

<u>Insertions.</u> The student inserted two words: "there" and "some." Write the insertion above where it occurred and indicate with a ^.

<u>Self-corrections.</u> The student corrected the insertion of "are." Corrections are not counted as miscues.

<u>Reversals.</u> The student reversed "mother duck" to "duck mother." This does not change meaning. If a reversal changes meaning, it should be marked as such.

<u>Meaning change miscues.</u> The student pronounced "animals" as "anmals" and "turtles" as "turts." Nonwords words like "anmals" and "turts" are always counted as meaning change miscues. In the fifth sentence, "chicks" was substituted for "ducks." This represents a meaning change miscue as "chicks" is not a synonym for "ducks." In the sixth sentence, the student substituted "with" for "behind," which also changes meaning and should be marked as such. In the last sentence, the student substituted "fish" for "animals." This changes meaning as "animals" refers to turtles, ducks, and fish.

SCORING ORAL READING MISCUES: TOTAL ACCURACY

You can determine independent, instructional, and frustration levels by counting all miscues that the student makes. We call this Total Accuracy. You can also determine reading levels by only counting miscues that change meaning. This is called Total Acceptability. We will discuss Total Accuracy first. See Figure 6.3.

Figure 6.3 Total Accuracy: Word Identification

Independent Level:	98% accuracy
Instructional Level:	90–97 % accuracy
Frustration Level:	less than 90% accuracy

Pearson eText
Video Example 6.1

Using Passages to Identify Oral Reading Miscues
In this video, you will learn how an oral passage is introduced and how it is scored. Pay attention to how the examiner scores what the student says.

Counting Total Accuracy is easier than determining Total Acceptability. It takes less time to score because you do not have to spend time deciding whether a miscue changes meaning. Count substitutions, omissions, insertions, and reversals as miscues. Do not count repetitions of words, hesitations, or omissions of punctuation. They do not truly represent an error because they do not significantly alter the text. Do not count self-corrections as they also do not change text meaning. Below you will find guidelines for scoring oral miscues for Total Accuracy:

- One common question among examiners is, "Should I assist a student who encounters an unfamiliar word?" We do not recommend this. It is impossible to assess the effect of word identification on comprehension if the student is given the correct pronunciation. If a student is unable to identify a word, gently ask him or her to move on.

- Miscues made on proper names represent a special problem because of the extreme variability in the pronunciation of some names. We recommend the following: If the student pronounces a proper name as a nonsense name—a name you have never heard—and repeatedly calls the character by that name, count it as one miscue. For example, if the student consistently refers to "Joseph" as "Jostep," these deviations count as one miscue. If, however, the student refers to "Joseph" as "Jostep," "Jossy," and "Joseep," each deviation is a separate miscue.

- If a student makes the same miscue on the same word several times in the passage and it does not change the meaning of the passage, count it as one miscue. For example, if a student consistently refers to "puppy" as "pup" or to "planes" as "airplanes," these count as one miscue. If, however, the consistent miscue changes meaning, such as "poppy" for "puppy" or "please" for "planes," each pronunciation counts as a separate miscue. Assign *one* point to several miscues only if the mispronunciation does not change meaning and is consistent across the entire passage.

- Do not count variations in pronunciations due to articulation difficulties or regional dialects as oral reading miscues. Determine speaking patterns through casual conversation with the student before testing.

- When a single word is mispronounced numerous times throughout a passage, students often pronounce it differently each time and then change to another pronunciation. Score each of the mispronunciations as separate miscues. If a student omits an entire line, count it as one miscue because the omission represents a loss of place, not a conscious omission because of inability to identify words. Obviously, in this case, the student is not monitoring his or her comprehension, and counting each omitted word as a separate miscue could distort the final level designation. Figure 6.4 provides a summary of guidelines for counting miscues.

Figure 6.4 Counting Miscues

Repetitions, hesitations	Do not count as a miscue.
Omissions of punctuation	Do not count as a miscue.
Self-corrections	Do not count as a miscue.
Miscues on proper names	Count as one miscue if it is consistently repeated throughout the text. Count as separate miscues if it is pronounced differently throughout the text.
Miscues of words repeated in the text	Count as one miscue if the word is pronounced consistently. Count as separate miscues if the word is pronounced differently.
Omission of an entire line	Count as one miscue.
Variation in pronunciation due to articulation and/or dialect.	Do not count as a miscue.

Count the total number of miscues and use this to determine whether the student's performance reflects an independent, instructional, or frustration level. Each level diagnostic passage in the *QRI-7* lists the number of miscues that determine independent, instructional, and frustration levels. For example, when looking at total accuracy, the passage "Who Lives Near Lakes?" identifies 0–1 miscues as an independent level, 2–6 miscues as an instructional level, and 7+ miscues as a frustration level. See Figure 6.5.

Figure 6.5 Who Lives Near Lakes?

Accuracy		Acceptability
0–1 miscues _____	Independent _____	0–1 miscues
2–6 miscues _____	Instructional _____	2–3 miscues
7+ miscues _____	Frustration _____	4+ miscues

Pearson eText Application Exercise 6.1: Scoring Oral Reading Miscues for Total Accuracy

---

SCORING ORAL READING MISCUES: TOTAL ACCEPTABILITY

You may choose to only count miscues that change the meaning of the passage. We call this Total Acceptability. Acceptable miscues are miscues that do not change or distort passage meaning. For example, If the student says *Fox wanted to have a garden* when the text says *Fox wanted to plant a garden,* the miscue of *have* for *plant* does not change meaning. If you decide to use Total Acceptability, record a student's accuracy for all miscues during administration of the passage and decide which ones to count later. The acceptability of a miscue is not always clear, and having to make an immediate decision about a miscue while the student is still reading is extremely difficult and often leads to inaccurate assessment. Figure 6.6 provides guidelines for determining Total Acceptability.

Figure 6.6 Total Acceptability: Word Identification

Independent Level:	98% acceptability
Instructional Level:	95% to 97% acceptability
Frustration Level:	less than 95% acceptability

Semantic Acceptability

In determining whether a miscue changes meaning, consider both semantic acceptability and syntactic acceptability. Semantic acceptability refers to the meaning of the sentence. Consider the following when reviewing for semantic acceptability:

- Substitutions of nonsense word or words with definitions other than the text word change meaning. Example: A student pronounces "fuzzy" as "fizzy."

- Meaning can also be changed by the omission or addition of a negative marker. Example: "Sam did understand why they were there" is very different from "Sam did not understand why they were there."

- Meaning may or may not be changed by the addition or omission of a plural ending or the substitution of a pronoun for a noun. It all depends on the context of the sentence. Example: Given the sentence "The puppy put his paw on the cage," a miscue of "paws" for "paw" does not change meaning, while the substitution of "in" for "on" does, given the preceding story context.

Syntactic Acceptability

Syntactic acceptability refers to conventions of grammar. Does the sentence follow the grammar rules of oral and written language? Consider the following when reviewing for syntactic acceptability:

- All sentences contain a main noun and a verb. The omission or mispronunciation of one of these changes may distort meaning. Example: "The chases the mouse" is meaningless without a noun describing who did the chasing. Similarly, "the cat the mouse" is meaningless without a verb.

- The omission of an adjective or an adverb may not change meaning. Example: "The big dog barked loudly." "Big" and/or "loudly" may be omitted without changing meaning.

- A change in verb tense may not change meaning. Example: "Ben and Ruth want something to do" or "Ben and Ruth wanted something to do."

- In judging syntactic acceptability, we suggest that you read the sentence to yourself. If a sentence sounds "funny," it probably differs in some way from language conventions followed both in speech and written text. Miscues that violate the linguistic conventions of standard English should be counted as miscues that change or distort passage meaning.

- If a student substitutes a nonword for a proper name ("Rutz" for "Ruth"), it does not necessarily change meaning if the substitution is consistent throughout the passage. However, if the student pronounces the name differently each time it is encountered ("Rutz," "Reth," "Rath"), count each attempt as a meaning-change miscue. Use the same rule for names of cities, states, and countries. Figure 6.7 offers additional examples for meaning change.

- Younger students will occasionally add verb endings (-ed, -ing) in an inappropriate way: sit/sitted; think/thinked/put/putted; did/didded; went/wented; see/seed, etc. It can be argued that this does not represent a significant change in meaning and suggests that the reader understands the function of the -ed ending. However, you may disagree and prefer to mark such words as meaning change miscues. Whatever you decide, be consistent across all passages.

Figure 6.7 Meaning Change Miscues

Miscue	Original	Student
Substitution of a nonsense word	They watered the seeds.	They wittered the seeds.
A miscue that results in an ungrammatical sentence	They were playing together.	They were played together.
A miscue that changes the meaning of a sentence	A man had a horn.	A man had a horse.
Omission or addition of negative markers	He was not like other pigs.	He was like other pigs.
Substitutions of words with inappropriate meanings	Animals are living things.	Animals are loving things.
Omissions/additions of word endings	He wanted to learn to read.	He want to learn to read.
Substitution of a pronoun for a noun	Marva gave the cat some food.	She gave it some food.
A mixture of verb tense in a sentence	Marva went out and picked up the cat.	Marva went out and pick up the cat.

If a student consistently makes a meaning change miscue on the same word throughout the text, we suggest that it be counted each time because each mispronunciation, however consistent, distorts the text in some way. Judge meaning change miscues as strictly as possible. It is better to underestimate a student's level than to overestimate it.

It is impossible to offer specific guidelines for all possible miscues that students will make. Each miscue must be examined within the context of the sentence and, in some cases, the previously read text to determine whether it distorts the meaning or grammar of the text. Figure 6.7 offers some general suggestions.

After counting the meaning change miscues and subtracting the result from the number of words in the passage, divide this by the number of words in the passage, rounding upward to find the percentage of Total Acceptability. Example: A passage has 62 words. A student made a total of 8 miscues. Four of these were meaning change miscues. $62 - 4 = 58$, and $58 \div 62 = 93.5 = 94\%$ Total Acceptability. You may also use the guidelines given at the end of *QRI* passages, which indicate how many meaning change miscues result in an independent, instructional, or frustration reading level. A comparison of Figures 6.3 and Figure 6.6 illustrates that Total Accuracy is more stringent than Total Acceptability as it is based on all miscues, not just those that change meaning. Select one and be consistent when evaluating several passages for a single student.

> **Pearson eText Application Exercise 6.2:** Scoring Oral Reading Miscues for Total Acceptability

---

ANALYZING ORAL READING MISCUES: MISCUE ANALYSIS

You have established a student's reading level for word recognition. It indicates that a student is above, at, or below his/her actual grade level with respect to recognizing words. What else can a student's performance tell you? You can analyze the nature of the errors made by the student during oral reading. This is called *miscue analysis*. Section 2 offers a detailed account of the research base for miscue analysis.

A student's miscues can provide information about the student's word identification strategies.

- A student can focus on letters and sounds.
- A student can pay attention to the position of a word in the sentence, for example, assuming that a verb will follow a noun.
- A student can use the context of the preceding text to predict text content. Given the sentence "Mary jumped over the chair," a student may read "The chair fell over" as opposed to "The chair toppled over."

Miscues can suggest whether the student is primarily focusing on pronunciation or meaning.

Miscues can take different forms. If the text word and the miscue share the same letters, this may indicate that the student is paying attention to letters and sounds. An example would be pronouncing "want" as "went." If the text word and the miscue are not similar, this may imply lack of knowledge of letter/sound patterns. It can also suggest lack of attention to them.

Three questions focus on what miscues say about reader use of meaning clues.

- Did the miscue change meaning? Meaning change miscues can indicate difficulty with both word pronunciation and comprehension.
- Did the student correct the miscue? Lack of correction may suggest difficulty with word identification and comprehension.
- Did the student correct miscues that did not change meaning? This can suggest a focus on word pronunciation and lack of attention to word meaning.

Miscue analysis does not address insertions or omissions. Insertions usually occur when students are predicting what is coming next. Omissions often reflect a loss of place. They can also occur because the reader cannot pronounce a word or is not willing to try. Figure 6.8 provides an example of a scored miscue analysis worksheet.

Figure 6.8 Example: Scored Miscue Analysis Worksheet

Name: Freddie   Selection: Fox and Mouse

1. Text Word	2. Miscue	3. Miscues with Similar Letter–Sound Patterns	4. Miscues That Changed Meaning	5. Miscues That Were Corrected	6. Miscues That Did Not Change Meaning	7. Miscues That Did Not Change Meaning And Were Corrected
plant	dig				X	
watered	wanted	X	X			
dug	digged	X			X	
was	had				X	
growing	grown	X			X	
thinks	thought	X			X	
did	will		X			
few	four	X	X			
	Total 8	Total 5	Total 3	Total 0	Total 5	Total 0

Analysis of Freddie's Miscues

Freddie made 8 miscues (Column 2). Five of the eight miscues had similar letter–sound patterns to the text word (Column 3). $5 \div 8 = 63\%$. This suggests that Freddy is attempting to use letter/sound patterns.

Three of the eight miscues that changed meaning (Column 4) were not corrected. $3 \div 8 = 38\%$. This suggests that Freddie did not pay attention to word meaning.

Similarly, five of the eight miscues that did not change meaning (Column 6) were not corrected. $5 \div 8 = 63\%$. This suggests that Freddie paid attention to letter-sound relationships but not word meaning.

Usually the total of each column will tell you what you need to know about the nature of your student's miscues. While miscue analysis can indicate the strategies used by the student during oral reading, percentages should not be interpreted rigidly. Miscue analysis offers general suggestions for how students are processing text, and such observations should be made in relation to the student's comprehension score on the passage.

> **Pearson eText Application Exercise 6.3:** Oral Reading Miscue Analysis

EVALUATING AUTOMATICITY

Rate of oral and silent reading can suggest automaticity of word identification. If a reader reads relatively quickly, one can assume that the words are no longer being decoded. However, the student still uses knowledge of letter–sound relationships when reading words, even those that are read automatically. Words recognized automatically (i.e., within one second) are often termed *sight vocabulary,* despite the fact that letter–sound relationships are used to read words automatically also (Ehri, 2014; Miles, Rubin, & Gonzalez-Frey, 2018).

Both oral and silent reading rates are quite variable. Difficult or unfamiliar passages tend to be read more slowly. Reading rate also varies according to reader purpose. If the student is reading to learn or remember text content, this is typically done at a slower rate than pleasure reading. Reading rate also varies across individuals. Some readers are naturally faster than others. For these reasons, any guidelines for evaluating reading rate must be interpreted generally.

The *QRI-7* provides the examiner with a method for determining oral and silent reading rates as measured in words per minute. The number of words in the passage multiplied by 60 and divided by the number of seconds it took to read the passage will yield a word-per-minute score (WPM). Words correct per minute (WCPM) is calculated by taking the number of correctly read words, multiplied by 60 and divided by the number of seconds it took to read the passage.

Our pilot data reflect readers reading at their instructional level. We found that there was wide variation in the rates, despite a steady growth in rate as reading level increased. We offer these rates as *suggestive* of the rates of typical readers when processing text at their instructional level. We also offer ranges for words per minute (WPM) and words correct per minute (WCPM) (see Tables 6.1 and 6.2). Kame'enui and Simmons (2001) have suggested that although a WPM score measures rate or speed, a WCPM score addresses both speed and accuracy.

It is up to the examiner to choose which index of rate to compute. Much depends on the purpose of the assessment. If the purpose is to identify a student's instructional level, WPM will suffice. If, however, the assessment focuses on a student's ability to handle text at his or her grade level, WCPM might be more appropriate.

Table 6.1 Ranges of Oral Reading Rate and Correct Rate of Students Reading at Instructional Level Oral Reading

Level	Words per Minute (WPM)	Words Correct per Minute (WCPM)
Pre-primer—P	23–59	13–55
Pre-primer—NP	22–64	11–59
Primer	28–66	10–52
First	37–77	20–68
Second	43–89	19–77
Third	56–104	53–101
Fourth	57–115	54–112
Fifth	65–121	62–118

Note: P = Pictured passages; NP = Non-pictured passages.

Table 6.2 Ranges of Silent Reading Rate of Student Reading at an Instructional Level

Level	Words per Minute (WPM)
Fifth	73–175
Sixth	91–235
Middle School	
Narrative	119–233
Expository	105–189
High School	65–334

EVALUATING PROSODY

Prosody is reading with expression. Research on measures of prosody were discussed in Section 2. Valencia et al. (2010) found that fourth- and sixth-graders' levels of prosody were better predictors of comprehension than WCPM. We have included a prosody scale in *QRI-7* materials for grades 1 through 6.

Prosody Rating Scale

If the student is reading first- or second-grade material, judge their prosody after one minute. If the student reads for three minutes or more, then judge their prosody with the three-minute reading. Circle the number below that best represents the student's oral reading of this text.

4	3	2	1
Reads primarily in larger, meaningful phrase groups. Some or most of the story is read with expression.	Reads primarily in three- or four-word phrase groups. Little or no expressive interpretation is present.	Reads primarily in two-word phrases with some three- or four-word groupings. Word groupings may be awkward.	Reads primarily word-by-word with occasional two-word or three-word phrases.

Our data on instructional level reading illustrate that students become more accurate and read more quickly as their instructional level increases. In contrast, retelling and comprehension remain similar. The retelling score is affected by the length of the passages, so as students read longer and more difficult text, their memory for details is challenged. Details of these findings can be found in Section 13.

Section 7

Assessing Comprehension: Questions and Retellings

⌄	**Chapter Outline**

General Procedures
Scoring Explicit Questions
Scoring Implicit Questions

Criteria for Determining Reading Levels
Use of Explicit and Implicit Questions to Gather Information About Comprehension

Analysis of Retelling: Elementary and Middle School
General Procedures
Scoring Retelling

Retelling Examples
Narrative Text
Expository Text

Retelling: Upper Middle School and High School

Using Look-Backs

GENERAL PROCEDURES

You can assess a student's comprehension of *QRI-7* passages in three ways:

- **Ask the Comprehension Questions provided at the end of each passage (examiner's copy)**—The number of correct answers is used to assign independent, instructional, and frustration levels.

- **Ask the student to retell the selection**—Unlike the questions that follow each passage, retelling performance does not determine reading level. However, it can provide insights about the nature of the reader's comprehension. Evaluate the retelling qualitatively by using the Retelling Scoring Sheet found at the end of each passage (examiner's copy). Each scoring sheet covers the important ideas contained in the passage.

- **Read the selection to the student to assess listening comprehension**—Using the same materials and comprehension assessments (i.e., questions and retelling), you can assess whether the student can understand grade-level text if it is read to him or her.

Order of the Tasks.   The student is asked to retell what he or she has read or listened to immediately after reading the text, and then the questions are asked. There are two types of questions: *explicit* and *implicit*. The answers to *explicit* questions are present in the passage. They indicate whether the student understood and remembered information that was directly stated by the author. Answers to *implicit* questions are not present in the passage. Answering these questions requires an inference. The reader must identify clues in the passage and use them to correctly answer implicit questions.

A student's performance in answering both explicit and implicit questions following reading is the second score used to determining a reading level. In Section 6 we discussed how to evaluate oral reading. In this section we discuss how to evaluate comprehension of text that is read orally, silently, or listened to. Comprehension of silent reading is particularly important for evaluating a student's performance in grades 4 and above as silent reading of textbooks is a common expectation in upper-level classrooms.

Scoring Explicit Questions

Answers to explicit questions must come from the text. Score explicit questions as either right or wrong. Do not accept an answer that comes from prior knowledge, or an answer that is not present in the text. What if an answer does not match the words of the answer key? If the answer includes the same information in different words, mark it as correct. For example, consider the text

"The Bear and the Rabbit" on p. 164.

Once there was a very big bear.

He lived in the woods.

He was sad because he didn't have anyone to play with.

He said to his father, "How can I find a friend?"

The first question is "Why was the bear sad at the beginning of the story?" The student answered as follows: "There was this big bear, and he didn't have any friends, and he felt bad about that." This would be an acceptable answer.

Do not count an answer as correct if the response comes from prior knowledge, even if it is accurate. For example, on the third-grade passage "Cats: Lions and Tigers in Your House," (p. 214) the following explicit question is asked: "How are lions, tigers, and cats alike?" If a student says that they all have sharp teeth or they all have fur, this would be an incorrect answer. While such information is accurate, it is not stated explicitly in the passage.

Scoring Implicit Questions

In a similar way, you cannot consider an implicit question correct if the answer is not related to a clue in the passage. If the answer comes from a student's prior knowledge, do not count it as correct. For example, an implicit question following the "Amelia Earhart" passage (p. 237) is "Why do you think her plane was never found?" A student might answer, "Because it burned up." This is a reasonable answer probably drawn from the student's prior knowledge. However, the passage clearly states that her plane disappeared over the Pacific Ocean. This would imply it sank. There is no indication in the text that suggests it burned up. When the student's answer to an implicit question obviously comes from background knowledge, acknowledge that it is correct and then ask, "But what do the clues in the passage tell you?" If the student answers the prompt correctly, it should be counted as correct.

The pre-primer passages do not have implicit comprehension questions. However, students often answer an explicit question by using information from the pictures. For example, in the "Just Like Mom" passage, one question is: "Name one thing that the girl can do just like Mom." Children often answered the question by using information from the pictures instead of the text, such as "water the flowers." While such responses are incorrect answers to the explicit questions, they represent correct answers to implicit questions.

CRITERIA FOR DETERMINING READING LEVELS

Passages have 5, 6, 8, or 10 questions. The guide that follows each passage indicates the number of correct questions needed to attain an independent level (90% or above), an instructional level (67% to 89%), or a frustration level (below 67%). The following criteria are provided on the examiner's answer key for each passage, depending on its level.

Guidelines for Determining Reading Levels

Pre-Primer Level: 5 Questions	
Independent Level:	5 correct
Instructional Level:	4 correct
Frustration Level:	0–3 correct
Primer and First-Grade Levels: 6 Questions	
Independent Level:	6 correct
Instructional Level:	4–5 correct
Frustration Level:	0–3 correct
Second-Grade Through Sixth-Grade Questions	
Independent Level:	8 correct
Instructional Level:	6–7 correct
Frustration Level:	0–5 correct
Middle School and High School	
Independent Level:	9–10 correct
Instructional Level:	7–8 correct
Frustration Level:	0–6 correct

Use of Explicit and Implicit Questions to Gather Information About Comprehension

Determining percentage scores for both explicit and implicit questions allows for easy comparisons. For example, at levels 2–6, there are a total of eight questions. Four questions are explicit in nature; their answers can be found in the text. To determine a percentage for explicit questions, divide the number of explicit questions that were answered correctly by the total number of explicit questions. For example, if the student correctly answered three explicit questions, divide three by the total number of explicit questions (four) to determine that 75% of explicit questions were answered correctly.

Four questions are implicit. To answer them correctly, the reader must make use of clues in the text. If the student correctly answered one of the implicit questions, divide one by four to determine that only 25% of implicit questions were correctly answered. Analyzing and differentiating a student's ability to answer explicit and implicit questions can provide valuable information for intervention instruction. A large difference between the two scores on two or more passages may suggest that the student needs instruction either in identifying what was stated explicitly or in using text clues to draw inferences. Section 13 describes how to compare performance on explicit and implicit questions under the heading, "What is the relationship between explicit and implicit comprehension?"

ANALYSIS OF RETELLING: ELEMENTARY AND MIDDLE SCHOOL

Analysis of retellings can answer the following questions:

- Do the retellings of narrative material include setting, goal, events, and resolution?
- Do the retellings of expository material include the main ideas and supporting details?
- Are the retellings accurate?
- Are the retellings sequential?
- Do the retellings suggest that the student understood what was read?

Remember, a retelling is not used to determine independent, instructional, and frustration levels. However, it can provide valuable information with implications for instruction. For example, if the student does not retell the central parts of a narrative, s/he may not understand the basic structural elements of a story. Similarly, if the student does not organize an expository retelling around the main idea and supporting details, he or she may not understand the structure of paragraphs in informational text.

Questions to Consider When Analyzing a Student's Retelling

Were elements of narrative structure (setting, goal, events, resolution) included?

Were elements of expository structure (main idea, details) included?

Was the retelling accurate?

Was the retelling sequential?

Does the retelling suggest that the student understood the text?

General Procedures

After the student has finished reading a selection and before you ask the questions, remove the passage and ask the student to retell the passage as if it were being told to someone who had never read it. Removing the passage is unnecessary if you read the selection to the student. Each passage has a Retelling Scoring Sheet for recording what the student says. Do not offer hints or direct suggestions, such as "Can you remember why Tom Thumb lost the race?" You will find it helpful at first to record the retelling and use the audio for scoring later. As you become familiar with the individual passages, you can often score the retelling directly onto the Retelling Scoring Sheet while the student is talking.

Scoring Retelling

Compare the clauses recalled by the student with those on the Retelling Scoring Sheet. The scoring sheets for each passage were designed based on what was most frequently recalled by students in our pilot sample, as well as an analysis of important idea units. Place a check mark next to each clause on the scoring sheet that was recalled by the student. In narrative text, note the degree to which the retelling includes elements of narrative structure: setting, goal, events and resolution. In expository text, determine whether the student includes main ideas with supporting details. Obviously, a student will not recall in the exact words of the text, so synonyms and paraphrases are acceptable.

Examining a student's retelling can provide insights into the student's comprehension:

- **Characteristics of proficient readers:** When reading narratives, proficient readers direct their attention to the main character, the character's goals, events that focused on attaining the goals, and the solution. When reading expository material, they concentrate on the topic of the text, what the author says about the topic (details) and the author's main ideas. Asking a student to retell the text suggests the nature of the student's focus, i.e., what he or she paid attention to when reading the passage.

- **Characteristics of readers who struggle:** Readers who struggle often concentrate on identifying words as opposed to comprehending the text. If word identification is not automatic, comprehension will suffer. The reader who primarily focuses on identifying words has few cognitive resources to support comprehension. Struggling readers understand that words should be accurately identified using letters and sounds, but they often have little idea of what to do in addition to identifying words. Because they have read little on their own and/or have not been read to on a regular basis, they do not understand the structure of narrative and expository texts and how knowledge of structure can assist comprehension.

In Section 13, Table 13.2 presents the proportion of correct scores on conceptual knowledge, retelling, comprehension, and total comprehension (when look-backs were counted) on narrative and expository texts as a function of readability levels from the fourth through high school. Differences between the retelling of narrative and expository texts were found only at the fourth-grade and upper middle school levels.

Pearson eText
Video Example 7.1

Scoring Reading
This video includes an example of how retelling is introduced to the student and how it is scored. The student is told about the retelling before reading the oral passage, and again just before asking the student to retell the passage. Pay attention to how the examiner confirms the directions are understood.

RETELLING EXAMPLES

Narrative Text

Two retellings: Jon and Luke. The students' words on the Retelling Scoring Sheet are in italics.

Jon's Retelling. Jon, a second-grade struggling reader, was asked to read "The Surprise," a first-grade text (See p. 157 in *QRI-7*). His retelling was as follows. "It was Sam's birthday in a few days and he wanted a game, a bike, and a dog. The bike cost too much. So his father found a puppy. It was brown. It put out its paw. He paid for it. On Sam's birthday they gave him the puppy. It didn't say what he named it, but they all sang 'Happy Birthday.'"

Retelling Scoring Sheet for "The Surprise"

Setting Background

__x__   Sam's birthday was in two days. *Jon said, "It was Sam's birthday in a few days." The omission of "in two days" did not change meaning.*

_____   He was going to be seven years old.

Goal

__x__   He wanted a PlayStation game or he wanted a new bike. *Jon was given credit for "game" although he did not state the specific type of game, and for "bike."*

__x__   But most of all he wanted a dog. *Jon included this in his retelling.*

Events

_____   His father went to look for a present.

_____   First, he went into the toy store.

_____ He saw the PlayStation that Sam wanted.

_____ But his father didn't have enough money.

_____ Then he saw a red bike that Sam would love!

__x__ But that also cost too much. *Jon said, "the bike cost too much."*

_____ He drove to the animal care center.

_____ It was hard to choose just one dog.

_____ Finally, he sat down outside of a cage.

__x__ A brown fuzzy puppy came up to him. *Jon was given credit for "brown."*

__x__ The puppy put his paw on the cage. *Jon was given credit for "it put out its paw."*

_____ It seemed like he was saying take me home.

_____ "OK, little pup, I'll take you home," said Dad.

__x__ He paid for the puppy. *Jon was given credit for "he paid for it."*

_____ and they put a HOLD note on his cage.

Resolution

_____ The next day Sam and his father went for a ride.

_____ His father drove to the animal care center.

_____ Sam didn't understand why they were there.

__x__ The worker gave Sam the brown fuzzy puppy. *Jon was given credit for "they gave him the puppy."*

__x__ and everyone sang "Happy Birthday." *Jon was given credit for "they all sang 'Happy Birthday.'"*

1. Do the retellings of narrative material include setting, goal, events, and resolution?

   Yes, Jon's retelling included setting, goal, events, and resolution.

2. Are the retellings accurate? *Yes*

3. Are the retellings sequential? *Yes*

4. Do the retellings suggest that the student understood what was read? *Yes*

Summary: Jon's retelling contained comments that were related to setting, goal, events, and resolution. They focused on important parts of the narrative and were accurate. The retelling suggests that Jon's comprehension of a first-grade narrative is acceptable. Contrast his performance with that of Luke, who is a second-grader.

Luke's Retelling. "It was this kid's birthday. He was going to have a big party and get lots of presents. His father went shopping. He couldn't find anything he liked. He found a dog and he put it in a cage. He gave it to Sam and they all sang 'Happy Birthday.'"

Setting Background

__x__ Sam's birthday was in two days. *It was this kid's birthday.*

_____ He was going to be seven years old. *Luke's statement that "He would probably have a big party and get a lot of presents" was not in the text. It obviously came from prior knowledge of birthday celebrations.*

Goal

_____ He wanted a PlayStation game or he wanted a new bike.

_____ But most of all he wanted a dog. *The goal statements were not mentioned by Luke.*

Events

___x___ His father went to look for a present. *"His father went shopping" was interpreted as synonymous with "went to look for a present."*

_____ First, he went into the toy store.

_____ He saw the PlayStation that Sam wanted.

_____ But his father didn't have enough money.

_____ Then he saw a red bike that Sam would love!

_____ But that also cost too much. *Luke's statement that "He couldn't find anything" does not focus on the cost of the presents.*

_____ He drove to the animal care center.

_____ It was hard to choose just one dog.

_____ Finally, he sat down outside of a cage.

_____ A brown fuzzy puppy came up to him.

_____ The puppy put his paw on the cage.

_____ It seemed like he was saying take me home.

___x___ "OK, little pup, I'll take you home," said Dad. *Luke was given credit for the statement "He found a dog." The fact that he intended to take the dog home can be interpreted as finding a dog. Luke's statement that "he put it in a cage" is inaccurate as the father did not do this. According to the narrative, the dog remained in the cage.*

_____ He paid for the puppy.

_____ and they put a HOLD note on his cage.

Resolution

_____ The next day Sam and his father went for a ride.

_____ His father drove to the animal care center.

_____ Sam didn't understand why they were there.

_____ The worker gave Sam the brown fuzzy puppy. *Luke's retelling suggests that the father gave Sam the puppy, which is inaccurate.*

___x___ and everyone sang "Happy Birthday." *Luke was given credit for "they all sang 'Happy Birthday.'"*

1. Do the retellings of narrative material include setting, goal, events, and resolution?
   Luke included only one element of setting, two events, and one element of resolution.

2. Are the retellings accurate? *The few comments that Luke made were accurate.*

3. Are the retellings sequential? *Yes, although they were few, they were sequential.*

4. Do the retellings suggest that the student understood what was read? *Somewhat.*

Summary: Luke's retelling was very general and sparse. It did not indicate that Luke understood important details, such as cost being an important factor in finding a present.

Pearson eText Application Exercise 7.1: Analyzing a Retelling of Narrative Text

Expository Text

There are two retellings: Alicia and Kyra.

Alicia's Retelling. Alicia, a third-grader, read a second-grade passage, "Whales and Fish." (See p. 190 in *QRI-7*). Her retelling was as follows: "It's about whales and fish. They live in water but they are really different. Whales breathe air like we do but fish get air from the water. It didn't say how. Mother whales have babies but mother fish lay eggs. It didn't say if they are there when the eggs hatch. But they are also the same. They both have flippers and fins, which help them swim."

Retelling Scoring Sheet for Alicia's Retelling of "Whales and Fish"

Main Idea

___x___ Whales and fish both live in the water. *Alicia stated that "whales and fish live in water."*

___x___ But they are different in many ways. *Alicia described them as "really different."*

Details

_____ Whales are large animals.

_____ They must come to the top of the water to get air.

___x___ Whales breathe in air through a hole in the top of their heads. *Alicia stated that "whales breathe air." While she neglected to say how they did it, she recognized the most important part of the sentence.*

_____ At the same time, they blow out old air.

___x___ Fish take in air from the water. *Alicia stated that "fish get air from the water."*

___x___ Mother whales give birth to live whales. *Alicia said that "mother whales have babies."*

_____ The baby whale comes to the top of the water right away for air.

_____ The baby drinks milk from its mother for about a year.

_____ Most mother fish lay eggs. *Alicia stated that "mother fish lay eggs."*

_____ The babies are born when the eggs hatch.

_____ Right after they are born, the baby fish must find their own food.

Main Idea

___x___ Whales and fish are alike in some ways too. *Alicia said "they are also the same."*

Details

___x___ Whales and fish have flippers on their sides. *Alicia said "they have flippers."*

___x___ They have fins on their tails. *Alicia: "and fins."*

___x___ Flippers and fins help whales and fish swim. *Alicia: "which help them swim."*

_____ Fins move and push the water away.

1. Do the retellings of expository material include the main ideas and supporting details? *Yes*

2. Are the retellings accurate? *Yes*

3. Are the retellings sequential? *Yes*

4. Do the retellings suggest that the student understood what was read? *Yes*

Summary: Alicia identified all three main ideas. She offered relevant details. Her retelling of the selection was accurate.

Kyra's Retelling. Kyra, a second-grader, read the same passage. Her retelling follows: "It's about whales. They live in water and they are very big. They have a hole in their head. They blow air out of the hole. They have big babies who start eating right away. Fish have little babies and their mother feeds them. They both have flippers. And they have tails."

Retelling Scoring Sheet for Kyra's Retelling of "Whales and Fish"

Main Idea

___x___ Whales and fish both live in the water. *Kyra was given credit because she did include fish later in her retelling.*

_____ But they are different in many ways.

Details

___x___ Whales are large animals. *Kira's statement "the whales are very big" was acceptable.*

_____ They must come to the top of the water to get air.

_____ Whales breathe in air through a hole in the top of their heads. *Kira's statement that whales "have a hole in their head" is accurate but she did not describe its function, which is important to the text.*

___x___ At the same time, they blow out old air. *Kira's statement that "they blow air out of the hole" is acceptable.*

_____ Fish take in air from the water.

_____ Mother whales give birth to live whales.

_____ The baby whale comes to the top of the water right away for air.

_____ The baby drinks milk from its mother for about a year.

_____ Most mother fish lay eggs.

_____ The babies are born when the eggs hatch.

_____ Right after they are born, the baby fish must find their own food. *She makes an incorrect statement that their mothers feed the fish.*

Main Idea

_____ Whales and fish are alike in some ways too.

Details

___x___ Whales and fish have flippers on their sides. *Kyra's statement that "they both have flippers" is acceptable.*

_____ They have fins on their tails.

_____ Flippers and fins help whales and fish swim.

_____ Fins move and push the water away.

    1. Do the retellings of expository material include the main ideas and supporting details? *Kyra identified one main idea and several details.*

    2. Are the retellings accurate? *The retelling was sparse, and some of it was accurate.*

    3. Are the retellings sequential? *No*

    4. Do the retellings suggest that the student understood what was read? *No*

Summary of Kyra's Retelling: Kyra's retelling indicated that she did not remember or did not comprehend that the passage was a comparison of whales and fish, how they are alike and different. She remembered some key details but did not grasp the central idea, that whales and fish are alike and different.

Pearson eText Application Exercise 7.2: Analyzing a Retelling of Expository Text

---

RETELLING: UPPER MIDDLE SCHOOL AND HIGH SCHOOL

Evaluating the retelling of the longer selections at the upper middle school and high school levels poses a somewhat different problem. Because of the length of these selections and their concept density, do not expect a complete and lengthy retelling. Recall may take the form of a summary or gist statements. For example, one student retold the second section of "World War I" by saying, "It's about how the war ended and what the guys who won wanted to get for themselves and the part that Wilson played with his ideas for peace." Such summary statements represent few ideas that are explicitly stated in the text, but they do demonstrate the student's overall understanding. Upper-level passages are often too long for a student to remember and retell all events. Combining retelling with look-backs can address this issue.

USING LOOK-BACKS

During normal administration procedures, the examiner asks the student to answer questions without the benefit of the accompanying text. Student success in answering is heavily dependent on memory for what was read. It is impossible to know whether an incorrect answer resulted from poor comprehension during reading or inadequate memory after reading. As students read longer and more concept-dense text, memory constraints may also interfere with the ability to answer explicit or implicit questions. This is especially true with unfamiliar expository text.

Scoring comprehension without look-backs may underestimate a student's comprehension on long and/or conceptually dense texts. For example, Jonah read the "Life Cycles of Stars" passage and, when answering questions without look-backs, attained a frustration score of 40%. When he could look back, he raised his comprehension score to 90%, an independent level. Note that you would not use look-backs if you are assessing listening comprehension because you have already determined that the student did not read accurately enough for him or her to comprehend lower-level material, therefore he or she did not have the word recognition skills to effectively look back in the text.

Think about the last time you read a selection on a very unfamiliar topic. You probably comprehended what you were reading, but afterward you may have been able to recall only a small portion of it. If someone asked you a direct question, you might not have been able to provide the answer. Did this mean that you were a poor reader? On the contrary, looking back in the text allowed you to locate the answer to the question you were asked. Skilled readers employ the look-back strategy naturally and efficiently as a way of increasing and maintaining comprehension.

To initiate the look-back process the examiner should model how to find an answer to a question by looking back in the text. Then the student should be asked to look back to find an answer to a question. Our pilot data suggested that students with instructional levels at or above third grade could do this readily. For this reason, we recommend adding look-backs to the process of assessing comprehension. After scoring the questions and determining the level, give the student the text and ask whether she or he can look back to locate answers that were unknown and/or correct erroneous answers. Score the look-backs as correct or incorrect, and use this result to determine a level for comprehension with look-backs. The criteria are included at the end of each examiner copy of the text.

Many students in our pilot study who read the high school passages attained frustration levels in their initial attempts to answer questions. However, the majority raised their scores to an instructional or independent level following look-backs. For this reason, we believe that any determination of reading level on the high school passages *should be based on the use of look-backs.*

Students vary in their ability to use look-backs. Some know exactly where to find the information. Others do not seem to know how to begin and look to the examiner for guidance. In such cases, you may point to the area where the relevant material can be found. However, to receive credit for a look-back, the student should exhibit relatively independent performance. Answering implicit questions demands the identification of clues provided in the reading passage. If a student's look-back is unsuccessful, probe to see whether the student's inability to answer an implicit question is due to lack of background knowledge or to lack of attention to the clues in the text. For example, tell the student the correct answer and ask him or her to find the clue in the text. You can also point out the clue and see whether the student can use it to arrive at the correct answer. Such procedures provide valuable diagnostic information; however, do not give credit for such examiner-supported answers.

In other words, comprehension with look-backs is most representative of reading performance on the high school passages. For all passages from third grade through high school, we believe that a reading level based on a combination of questions answered without *and* with look-backs is more representative of what skilled readers do when faced with concept-dense and unfamiliar text.

There are other ways to utilize the look-back procedure to obtain information about a student's reading needs. You can choose a passage that proved difficult to the student and ask him or her to look back and indicate specific parts that were especially troublesome. You can ask the student to identify "something you found hard or something you didn't understand" and can ask a few questions to confirm that the chosen element actually was difficult and not selected at random. If the student says that everything was hard, reverse the procedure and ask her or him to find one or two things that were a bit easier than the rest.

Adding Look-Backs to Assess a Student's Comprehension

- For students at/above third-grade level
- Determine the level for questions without looking back
- Model the look-back process
- Ask students to look back in order to:
  - locate unknown answers
  - correct erroneous answers
- Determine the level for comprehension with look-backs
- Determination of reading level on high school passages should always be based on look-backs

---

Our analysis showed that students with a reading instructional level at third grade or higher were able to answer more questions when allowed to look back. In general, students were better able to increase their explicit comprehension by one question because the answers to the questions were stated directly in the text and were complex details that taxed memory. We believe that allowing students reading at the third-grade level and above the opportunity to look back in text provides the examiner with useful information to separate problems in comprehension versus memory. Details on the analyses can be found in Section 13.

Assessing Strategic Reading: Think-Alouds

 Chapter Outline

Definition of Think-Alouds

Modeling Think-Alouds

Examples of Think-Alouds
Emory's Think-Aloud Comments

Stella's Think-Aloud Comments

Carol's Think-Aloud Comments

DEFINITION OF THINK-ALOUDS

Think-alouds are a reader's verbalizations in reaction to reading a selection. The student reads a passage and stops at set points to think out loud, that is, to explain his or her reaction to the text. This allows you to observe the nature of the student's comprehension. Able readers are not passive. They engage in a variety of mental activities as they read. They are aware of what they comprehend and what they do not understand. They restate text content in their own words and connect the text to their own lives. They ask themselves questions about the text and attempt to find answers. They meet unknown words and try to determine their meaning. Think-alouds can suggest the mental activities used by the reader.

Think-aloud comments take two forms: those that suggest that the reader comprehends the text and those that show lack of understanding. Think-aloud comments can indicate that the student engages in good reader behaviors such as identifying main ideas, accurately restating text content, and asking relevant questions. Think-alouds can also reveal reader behaviors that suggest lack of comprehension, such as ignoring topics and main ideas and offering irrelevant comments. However, scoring think-alouds is not an exact science, and two individuals can interpret a student's comments differently.

In *QRI*-7, three of the level 6 passages ("The Early Life of Lois Lowry", "Building Pyramids" and "Clouds and Precipitation"), and five of the upper middle school and high school passages ("Jaimé Escalanté", "Immigration—Part 2," "Life Cycles of Stars—Part 2," "Word War I—Part 2," and "Characteristics of Viruses—Part 2") provide the opportunity to examine a student's comprehension by asking the student to think aloud while reading. The passages are formatted with **//** to indicate when the student should stop reading to think aloud, and the examiner copies provide space for you to write the student's response.

Figure 8.1 is included at the end of each think-aloud passage. Use it to complete a record of the student's think-aloud comments by placing a check mark after the appropriate comment for each think-aloud statement.

Figure 8.1 also provides a blueprint for designing an intervention curriculum. The think-aloud comments that suggest understanding represent the good reader behaviors that all struggling readers need to master. At an appropriate instructional reading level, an intervention instructor should teach struggling readers to perform the comprehension activities described as think-aloud comments that suggest understanding of the text.

Figure 8.1

Think-Aloud Comments That Suggest Understanding

Restates text content accurately

Offers relevant comment

Asks relevant question

Recognizes topic/main idea

Identifies personally

Paraphrases/summarizes appropriately

Draws a valid inference based on personal experience

Draws a valid inference based on text information

Think-Aloud Comments That Suggest Lack of Understanding

Restates text content inaccurately

Offers irrelevant comment

Asks irrelevant question

Does not recognize topic/main idea

Does not identify personally

Paraphrases/summarizes inappropriately

Draws an invalid inference based on personal experience

Draws an invalid inference based on text information

MODELING THINK-ALOUDS

Select a topic from a social studies or science text that the student would find interesting. Begin by offering a short explanation of thinking aloud. "When people read, they usually think about what they are reading. Sometimes they think to themselves, and other times they think aloud and share their thoughts with others. I'm going to show you how to think aloud by reading this text, and when I come to the two slash marks, I will tell you what I am thinking. After I have shown you how to do this, then it will be your turn."

We have chosen a sixth-grade passage on the mining boom to illustrate thinking aloud. Read aloud the first two sections while the student follows along in his or her copy of the text. Read what is written in italics, and make it sound like you are really thinking aloud. You can also include your own comments if you wish.

The Mining Boom.   The mining boom in the western United States had begun with the California Gold Rush of 1849. When the Gold Rush ended, miners looked for new opportunities. The merest rumor of gold sent them racing east in search of new strikes. // *The title tells me it's about mining (Recognizes topic/main ideas). But I am not sure about the* *word "boom." It usually means a loud noise but that doesn't fit here. (Asks relevant questions). I read a book about the Gold Rush and how lot of people died, and most of them never really found any gold, which was too bad. (Identifies personally. Offers relevant comments about the text.)*

Gold and Silver Strikes. In 1859, two young prospectors struck gold in the Sierra Nevada Mountains. Suddenly, another miner, Henry Comstock, appeared. "The land is mine," he cried and demanded to be made a partner. From then on, Comstock boasted about "his" mine. The strike became known as the Comstock Lode. A lode is a rich vein of gold or silver. *// I wonder why the two miners just let him butt in like that and take over? Did he have any proof that he owned the land? (Identifies personally. Asks relevant questions.)*

Comstock and his partners often complained about the heavy blue sand that was mixed in with the gold. It clogged the devices used for separating the gold and made the gold hard to reach. When the Mexican miners took the "danged blue stuff" to an expert in California, tests showed it was loaded with silver. Comstock had stumbled onto one of the richest silver mines in the world. *// Comstock wasn't much of a miner if he didn't check the blue stuff himself. He was certainly very lucky, but I don't think it was fair that he should make all the money when it was the Mexicans who found out what the blue sand was. (Offers relevant comments. Identifies personally.)*

[At this point, you may ask the student whether he or she would rather read silently to each // signal or have you continue to read orally. Do what the student prefers and continue to the end of the selection.]

Miners moved into many other areas of the West. Some found valuable ore in Montana and Idaho. Others struck it rich in Colorado. In the 1870s, miners discovered gold in the Black Hills of South Dakota. In the late 1890s, thousands rushed north to Alaska after major gold strikes were made there. *// Well, they found ore in different states other than California, such as Montana and Alaska. (Paraphrases/ summarizes appropriately). I wonder if they still mine gold in the U.S.? (Asks relevant questions).*

Boom Towns and Ghost Towns. Towns sprang up near all the major mining sites. First, miners built a tent city near the diggings. Then, thousands of people came to supply the miners' needs. Traders brought mule teams loaded with tools, food, and clothing. Merchants hauled in wagon loads of supplies and set up stores. *// This makes a lot of sense. You go where the business is. If I were living then, I probably wouldn't have wanted to be a miner, but I wouldn't mind being a shopkeeper. It was probably an easier job. (Identifies personally. Offers relevant comments.)*

Soon, wood-frame houses, hotels, restaurants, and stores replaced the tents. For example, it took less than a year for the mining camp at the Comstock Lode to become the boom town of Virginia City, Nevada. *// I just figured out why they were called boom towns. Business was really booming there. I never thought of it that way before. (Identifies personally.)* Many boom towns lasted for only a few years. When the gold or silver was gone, miners moved away. Without miners for customers, businesses often had to close. In this way, a boom town could quickly go bust and turn into a ghost town. Still, some boom towns survived and prospered even after the mines shut down. In these towns, miners stayed and found new ways to make a living. *// They probably became farmers or raised cattle. Maybe they made stuff like furniture, wagons, or guns. The ones who stayed had to be pretty clever to survive. (Offers relevant comments.) I don't think I would have liked to have lived then. (Identifies personally.)*

The surge of miners into the West created problems. Mines and towns polluted clear mountain streams. Miners cut down forests to get wood for buildings. Few miners got rich quickly. Much of the gold and silver lay deep underground. It could be reached only with costly machinery. Eventually, most mining in the West was taken over by large companies that could afford to buy the equipment. *// This doesn't make a lot of sense to me. How did they know it was underground if it was so deep? (Asks relevant questions). Well, I learned some new stuff, and that is always a good thing. (Identifies personally.)*

Source: From *The American Nation* by James West Davidson, Pedro Castillo, and Michael B. Stoff. © 2002 Pearson Education, Inc., or its affiliates. Adapted by permission. All Rights Reserved.

Able readers mentally engage in a variety of think-aloud activities as they read. The above example contains think-aloud comments that show understanding and involvement in the text. Unfortunately, the think-alouds of struggling readers often show an absence of good reader behaviors. Think-alouds can identify what a struggling reader pays attention to and suggest a focus for intervention instruction.

EXAMPLES OF THINK-ALOUDS

Emory

Emory, a seventh-grader, achieved at an instructional level after orally reading a sixth-grade narrative passage, "The Early Life of Lois Lowry." However, his prosody was poor as he tended to read word by word with little expression. Emory achieved at an instructional level for comprehension, correctly answering four explicit and two implicit questions. However, his retelling was sparse, and he did not retell events in sequential order. The examiner asked him to silently read the passage "Building Pyramids" and stop at designated parts to explain what was in his mind.

Emory's Think-Aloud Comments

QRI Text: Ancient Egyptian kings are best known for the huge structures they built called pyramids. These large stone buildings served as houses or tombs for the dead. The Egyptians believed that kings, or pharaohs, remained gods even after death, and that pyramids were their palaces. Kings were buried with their possessions. The Egyptians thought that kings took their possessions with them to the afterlife or the life that continued after death.

Emory's think-aloud comments: *The kings took a lot of stuff with them because they thought they would still be alive.* (Restates text content accurately.) *Did anyone check on them to see if they really were alive?* (Asks irrelevant questions.)

QRI Text: Because the afterlife was more important than life on earth, the Egyptians took great care in preparing kings for burial. They believed the bodies of the pharaohs needed to be <u>preserved</u>. They used a process called mummification.

Emory's think-aloud comments: *They made mummies.* (Restates text content accurately.) *Why were they called mummies?* (Asks relevant questions.)

QRI Text: Mummification took 70 days. First, the Egyptians removed all organs except the heart from the body. Then they rubbed oils and perfumes over the body. Next, they wrapped the body in linen bandages. Finally, the mummy, or preserved body, was placed in a coffin and put into a tomb.

Emory's think-aloud comments: *They bandaged the kings and put them in a coffin and put them in the tomb.* (Restates text content accurately.) *I know why they put perfume on them. It's so they wouldn't smell. It kind of makes sense. If they thought the king was really alive, he wouldn't smell and wouldn't need perfume to cover it up. If they thought he was dead, why waste the perfume?* (Offers relevant comments. Asks relevant questions.)

QRI Text: Archaeologists and historians estimate that some pyramids took about 20 years to build and that slave labor was not used. When the Nile River was

Pearson eText
Video Example 8.1

Modeling Think-Alouds
This video includes an example of an examiner explaining and modeling thinking-aloud to a fifth-grade student. The material that the examiner is using is titled *The Mining Boom* and it can be found on p.69–71 of this text.

flooding, farmers could not work in their fields. They were then available to work on a pyramid.

Emory's think-aloud comments: *Why did farmers work on the pyramids? Farmers have other things to do.* (Asks irrelevant questions. Offers irrelevant comments. Indicates lack of understanding of the text: "When the Nile River was flooding, farmers could not work in their fields.")

QRI Text: Perhaps as many as 20,000 workers cut more than two million blocks of heavy stone from cliffs to the south. Then they dragged the stones with rope to ramps that led to the building site.

Emory's think-aloud comments: *What is a ramp? How did they cut stones?* (Asks relevant questions.) *I'll bet they got tired fast. Stones are heavy. I helped my grandpa build a rock wall around our garden, and I was really tired, and my legs and arms were awfully sore.* (Draws a valid inference based on personal experience.)

QRI Text: Building the tombs was important but many people died because the work was difficult and dangerous. Workers labored eight hours every day for ten days in a row. Then they received one day of rest.

Emory's think-aloud comments: *Sometimes they got to rest.* (Restates text content accurately.)

QRI Text: They were paid with food. The pharaohs counted on the tomb builders to be both committed and courageous. Because no one knew how long the pharaoh would live, they had to work quickly and accurately.

Emory's think-aloud comments: *Why didn't the king live very long? I thought they already buried him.* (Offers irrelevant comments. Asks irrelevant questions.)

Emory

Think-Aloud Comments That Suggest Understanding

Restates text content accurately	√ √ √
Indicates understanding of the text	
Offers relevant comments	√
Asks relevant questions	√ √ √
Recognizes topic/main ideas	
Identifies personally	
Paraphrases/summarizes appropriately	
Draws a valid inference based on personal experience	√
Draws a valid inference based on text information	

Think-Aloud Comments That Suggest Lack of Understanding

Restates text content inaccurately	
Indicates lack of understanding of the text	
Offers irrelevant comments	√ √
Asks irrelevant questions	√ √ √
Does not recognize topic/main ideas	
Does not identify personally	
Paraphrases/summarizes inappropriately	
Draws an invalid inference based on personal experience	
Draws an invalid inference based on text information	

Analysis: Emory primarily restated the last sentence in each think-aloud paragraph. He either ignored or did not remember the preceding information. He often offered irrelevant comments or asked irrelevant questions, which suggests lack of comprehension on his part. Intervention should focus on teaching Emory how to ask relevant questions about the text: What is the topic? What is the main idea? What details support the main idea?

Stella

Stella, an eighth-grader, achieved at an instructional level after orally reading a sixth-grade narrative passage, "Abraham Lincoln." Her oral reading was accurate but her reading rate was slow and marked by numerous pauses. When asked to retell the content, she described several aspects of the setting/background, and then stated, "There was a lot more but I don't remember it." The examiner asked her to silently read the passage "Building Pyramids" and explain what was in her mind when she finished.

Stella's Think-Aloud Comments

QRI Text: Ancient Egyptian kings are best known for the huge structures they built called pyramids. These large stone buildings served as houses or tombs for the dead. The Egyptians believed that kings, or pharaohs, remained gods even after death, and that pyramids were their palaces. Kings were buried with their possessions. The Egyptians thought that kings took their possessions with them to the afterlife or the life that continued after death.

Stella's think-aloud comments: *They thought their kings lived forever.* (Restates text accurately.) *I think kings die just like anyone else. I don't think there are many kings around anymore. Maybe in the movies or on television. I don't know why they are gone.* (Offers irrelevant comments.)

QRI Text: Because the afterlife was more important than life on earth, the Egyptians took great care in preparing kings for burial. They believed the bodies of the pharaohs needed to be preserved. They used a process called mummification.

Stella's think-aloud comments: *They made them into mummies in order to keep them. I saw a mummy once when we went to the museum. It was only the head and it was all brown and wrinkly but I thought it was kind of neat. It was really very old. I kind of felt sorry for it.* (Offers relevant comments.)

QRI Text: Mummification took 70 days. First, the Egyptians removed all organs except the heart from the body. Then they rubbed oils and perfumes over the body. Next, they wrapped the body in linen bandages. Finally, the mummy, or preserved body, was placed in a coffin and put into a tomb.

Stella's think-aloud comments: *They took him all apart.* (Restates text content accurately.) *I wonder how long the perfume lasted? I like perfume, but my mother says I have to be older before I can wear it. Do you think that's fair? I don't.* (Offers irrelevant comments.)

QRI Text: Archaeologists and historians estimate that some pyramids took about 20 years to build and that slave labor was not used. When the Nile River was flooding, farmers could not work in their fields. They were then available to work on a pyramid.

Stella's think-aloud comments: *Well, it took a long time to build a pyramid. I wonder what they did if the king died before it was ready? Where would they put him? What if they forgot where they put him? I put things away and then I can't find them, and then later on I do and that makes me happy.* (Restates the text content accurately. Asks irrelevant questions.) *I guess the farmers never got a vacation.* (Draws a valid inference based on text information.)

QRI Text: Perhaps as many as 20,000 workers cut more than two million blocks of heavy stone from cliffs to the south. Then they dragged the stones with rope to ramps that led to the building site.

Stella's think-aloud comments: *It took a lot of people to build a pyramid. Why didn't they put the stones in carts instead of dragging them? People don't drag stones. They pile them up or throw them. How would you drag stones? Dragging them would be awfully hard to do. How big were the stones? Some stones can weigh a lot.* (Restates text content accurately. Asks irrelevant questions.)

QRI Text: Building the tombs was important but many people died because the work was difficult and dangerous. Workers labored eight hours every day for ten days in a row. Then they received one day of rest.

Stella's think-aloud comments: *They worked eight hours like a lot of people today. Why shouldn't they get some rest after dragging all those stones instead of putting them in carts? And if it was so dangerous, why didn't they get another job? People do that you know.* (Restates text accurately. Asks irrelevant questions.) *I guess the farmers never got any kind of vacation. They probably didn't have vacations. It was all work, work, work!* (Draws a valid inference based on text information.)

QRI Text: They were paid with food. The pharaohs counted on the tomb builders to be both committed and courageous. Because no one knew how long the pharaoh would live, they had to work quickly and accurately.

Stella's think-aloud comments: *But what if the king dies before it is ready? Where would they put him? He would probably get all smelly so they had better really wrap him up somehow. I hate bad smells.* (Asks relevant questions. Offers irrelevant comments.)

Stella

Think-Aloud Comments That Suggest Understanding

Restates text content accurately	√ √ √ √
Offers relevant comments	√
Asks relevant questions	√
Recognizes topic/main ideas	
Identifies personally	
Paraphrases/summarizes appropriately	
Draws a valid inference based on personal experience	
Draws a valid inference based on text information	√ √

Think-Aloud Comments That Suggest Lack of Understanding

Restates text content inaccurately	
Offers irrelevant comments	√ √ √
Asks irrelevant questions	√ √ √
Does not recognize topic/main ideas	
Does not identify personally	
Paraphrases/summarizes inappropriately	
Draws an invalid inference based on personal experience	
Draws an invalid inference based on text information	

Analysis: Stella is easily diverted from comprehension of explicit text content. She primarily uses text content as a bridge for recalling and commenting on her own experiences. She needs to maintain a focus on what the text says, not on what it reminds her of. Helping Stella to rephrase the text in her own words would help her comprehension.

Carol

Carol, a middle school student, was asked to think aloud in order to determine why she was experiencing difficulty in reading. Although she scored at a middle school instructional level for both word recognition and comprehension, her grades were poor. Carol described reading as "boring" and stated that she never remembered what she read. The examiner asked Carol to silently read the *QRI-7* passage on immigration and describe what she understood.

Carol's Think-Aloud Comments

QRI Text: Leaving home required great courage. The voyage across the Atlantic or Pacific was often miserable. Most immigrants could afford only the cheapest berths. Ship owners jammed up to 2,000 people in steerage, as the airless rooms below decks were called. On the return voyage, cattle and cargo filled these same spaces. In such close quarters, diseases spread rapidly.

Carol's think-aloud comments: *They came on dirty boats and got very sick.* (Restates text content accurately. Recognizes topic/main ideas.) *They must have really wanted to come here* (Draws a valid inference based on text information.)

QRI Text: For most European immigrants the voyage ended in New York City. There, after 1886, they saw the giant Statue of Liberty in the harbor. The statue was a gift from France to the United States. The Statue of Liberty became a symbol of the hope and freedom offered by the United States.

Carol's think-aloud comments: *They saw the Statue of Liberty. It came from France.* (Restates text content accurately.)

QRI Text: Many immigrants had heard stories that the streets in the United States were paved with gold. Once in the United States, the newcomers had to adjust their dreams to reality. They immediately set out to find work. European peasants living on the land had little need for money, but it took cash to survive in the United States. Through friends, relatives, labor contractors, and employment agencies, the new arrivals found jobs.

Carol's think-aloud comments: *They really had a lot to do once they got here.* (Offers relevant comments. Recognizes topic/main ideas.) *They were very determined and didn't give up.* (Draws a valid inference based on text information.)

QRI Text: Most immigrants stayed in the cities where they landed. The slums of the cities soon became packed with poor immigrants. By 1900, one such neighborhood on the lower east side of New York had become the most crowded place in the world.

Carol's think-aloud comments: *New York was very crowded because the immigrants didn't move away. It must have been really hard.* (Restates text content accurately. Offers relevant comments.)

Ethnic Neighborhoods

QRI Text: Immigrants adjusted to their new lives by settling in neighborhoods with their own ethnic group. An ethnic group is a group of people who share a common culture. Across the United States, cities were patchworks of Italian, Irish, Polish, Hungarian, German, Jewish, and Chinese neighborhoods. Within these ethnic neighborhoods, newcomers spoke their own language and celebrated special holidays with food prepared as in the old country.

Carol's think-aloud comments: *They all stayed together with people like them, which was nice for them. I would have wanted to stay with my family and friends.* (Recognizes topic/main ideas. Offers relevant comment. Identifies personally.)

Becoming Americans

QRI Text: Often newcomers were torn between the old traditions and American ways. Still, many struggled to learn the language of their new nation. Learning English was an important step toward becoming a citizen. The process of becoming part of another culture is called assimilation. Many Americans opposed the increase in immigration. They felt the newcomers would not assimilate because their languages, religions, and customs were too different. However, they were wrong.

Carol's think-aloud comments: *They learned English, but it was hard. And a lot of Americans didn't want them.* (Restates text content accurately.)

QRI Text. Children assimilated more quickly than their parents. They learned English in school and then helped their families learn to speak it. Because children wanted to be seen as American, they often gave up customs their parents honored. They played American games and dressed in American-style clothes.

Carol's think-aloud comments: *The kids got along all right.* (Offers relevant comments.)

Carol	
Think-Aloud Comments That Suggest Understanding	
Restates text content accurately	√ √ √ √
Offers relevant comments	√ √ √ √
Asks relevant questions	
Recognizes topic/main ideas	√ √ √
Identifies personally	√
Paraphrases/summarizes appropriately	
Draws a valid inference based on personal experience	
Draws a valid inference based on text information	√ √
Think-Aloud Comments That Suggest Lack of Understanding	
Restates text content inaccurately	
Offers irrelevant comments	
Asks irrelevant questions	
Does not recognize topic/main ideas	
Does not identify personally	
Paraphrases/summarizes inappropriately	
Draws an invalid inference based on personal experience	
Draws an invalid inference based on text information	

Analysis: Carol's think-aloud statements were brief and accurate, and she offered relevant comments about the text. She drew valid inferences based on the text and recognized topics and main ideas. However, she ignored supportive details. Understanding details that support a main idea is an important aspect of comprehension. Ignoring relevant details limits the nature of a reader's comprehension.

Pearson eText Application Exercise 8.1: Analyzing Job's Think-Aloud

Section 9

Recording, Analyzing, and Using Results of the *QRI-7*

 ## Chapter Outline

Reviewing the Purposes of the *QRI-7*

Completing the Student Summary Form

Using the Student Summary Form to Plan Intervention Instruction

Selecting Materials for Intervention Instruction

Selecting Instructional Strategies for Intervention Instruction

Using the *QRI-7* to Indicate Growth and Monitor Progress

Reading Performance Case Studies

REVIEWING THE PURPOSES OF THE *QRI-7*

There are two overall purposes of the *QRI-7*: Identification of an instructional reading level and identification of the strengths and weaknesses of the reader. Knowing these allows you to select materials at an appropriate level—that is, materials that can be read and understood with your support—and develop effective instruction.

Previous sections have described how to administer various aspects of the *QRI-7*. The focus of this section is to review the purpose and content of the *QRI-7* and provide a structure for organizing and recording assessment results.

Word Lists

- Assess accuracy of word identification
- Assess automaticity of word identification
- Determine starting point for reading the initial passage

Passages

- Determine a student's independent, instructional, or frustration levels
  - Word identification in context (pre-primer 1 through high school)
  - Comprehension (pre-primer through high school)
- Assess a student's ability to comprehend different types of text
  - Narrative and expository text
  - Familiar and unfamiliar text

- Text with pictures (pre-primer 1 through third grade) and without pictures (fourth grade through high school)
- Assess a student's ability to retell passage content
- Assess a student's ability to answer different forms of questions
  - Explicit (literal) questions
  - Implicit (inferential) questions
- Assess a student's ability to use look-backs to locate missing or incorrect information (third grade through high school)
- Assess the variety and quality of a student's think-alouds (sixth grade through high school)
- Assess a student's ability to answer different forms of inferential questions
- Assess a student's ability to summarize (fourth grade through high school)
- Assess a student's listening level (first grade through high school)

Pearson eText Teacher Resource: Blank Student Summary Form—Printer Friendly

Assessing a student's ability to read passages accurately and with comprehension allows you to determine reading levels: independent, instructional, and frustration.

- The independent level is the level at which a student can read successfully without assistance.
- The instructional level is the level at which an individual can read successfully with comprehension given appropriate support by a teacher.
- The frustration level is the level at which a reader is not able to read with adequate word identification and/or comprehension.

Determining a level for word identification involves recording pronunciation errors. Determining a level for comprehension involves asking explicit and implicit questions. Additional assessment activities include asking students to retell passage content and to look back in the text to correct errors.

COMPLETING THE STUDENT SUMMARY FORM

A careful analysis of data on a student's performance provides a basis for your instructional recommendations. Use the Student Summary Form in Figure 9.1 to record your results. A completed sample of this form is provided in Figure 9.2.

USING THE STUDENT SUMMARY FORM TO PLAN INTERVENTION INSTRUCTION

How can you make sense of all this information in order to design or describe an intervention that best addresses the student's needs? At this point, your role is to analyze the information you have collected to determine whether the student has a reading problem that requires intervention. Ask yourself the following questions about the student's reading and use the answers to set directions for intervention.

How accurate and automatic is the student in identifying words?   Reading fluency or automaticity in identifying words is dependent on a student's automatic word recognition. The total correct automatic score on the word lists suggests that the student is or is not automatic in identifying words at different levels of difficulty. Students reading at instructional level typically decode only two more words than they recognize automatically. Therefore, if a student recognizes many fewer words automatically than the total number he or she can read correctly, sight vocabulary instruction using methods appropriate for the student's level is warranted.

Figure 9.1 Student Summary Form

Name _____ Date: _____ Grade _____

Word Lists

Grade Level	_____ _____ _____ _____ _____
Total Correct Automatic	_____ _____ _____ _____ _____
Total Correct Identified	_____ _____ _____ _____ _____
Total Number Correct	_____ _____ _____ _____ _____

Level: Independent (Ind), Instructional (Ins), Frustration (F)

_____ _____ _____ _____ _____

What is the student's highest instructional level on the word lists? _____

Does the student use letter–sound patterns to identify words? _____

Does the student focus on the beginning of words, the middle, and/or the end? _____

Does the student identify words automatically at the instructional level? _____

o– – – – – – Five lines are provided to accommodate the results to up to five word lists administered in a session. Results for each list administered should be filled in vertically on the form. The same goes for the passages section below.

Passages

Passage Name*	_____ _____ _____ _____ _____
Type: Narrative (N), Social Studies (SS), Science (S)	_____ _____ _____ _____ _____
Readability Level (Grade)	_____ _____ _____ _____ _____

o– – – – – – Five lines are provided to accommodate the results of up to five passages administered in a session. Abbreviate the title of the passages here by using a keyword from the title (e.g., Write "Nile" if the student read "The Lifeline of the Nile"). On the last page of the summary form you will find a section where you write the full titles of the passages you administered.

Concept Questions

Do the student's answers to the concept questions suggest that the topic is familiar or unfamiliar? _____ _____ _____ _____ _____

Word Identification Oral Reading

Number of Miscues	_____ _____ _____ _____ _____
Level Total Accuracy	_____ _____ _____ _____ _____
Level Total Acceptability	_____ _____ _____ _____ _____

Are student miscues similar to original words in letter–sound patterns? _____

Do student miscues change meaning? _____

Does the student correct meaning change miscues? _____

Retelling

Does the student retell narrative text using the elements of story structure (i.e., character, goal/problem, events, resolution)? _____ _____ _____ _____ _____

Does the student retell an instructional-level expository text citing main ideas and relevant details? _____ _____ _____ _____ _____

Figure 9.1 continued

Comprehension Without Lookbacks

Total Explicit Questions Correct _____ _____ _____ _____ _____

Total Implicit Questions Correct _____ _____ _____ _____ _____

Comprehension Level (Ind, Ins, F) _____ _____ _____ _____ _____

Comprehension with Lookbacks
(Use with reading levels third grade and above)

Total Explicit Questions Correct _____ _____ _____ _____ _____

Total Implicit Questions Correct _____ _____ _____ _____ _____

Comprehension Level (Ind, Ins, F) _____ _____ _____ _____ _____

Remember: Total Passage Level is determined by taking the **lower** of the two results from Word Identification and Comprehension Question scoring. For example, if the student's miscue total on a passage indicates *instructional* level, but the number of comprehension questions correct indicates *frustration* level, then the total passage level is **frustration**. Figure 4.7 on p. 36 provides guidelines for determining total passage level.

Total Passage Level

Independent, Instructional, Frustration _____ _____ _____ _____ _____

Instructional Level

What is the student's level in narrative text? _____

What ability (e.g., word identification or comprehension) prevented the student from having a higher instructional level in narrative text? _____

What is the student's level in expository text? _____

What ability (e.g., word identification or comprehension) prevented the student from having a higher instructional level in expository text? _____

Think-Alouds

Does the student offer comments that suggest understanding, lack of understanding, or both?

_____

Mode of Reading

Does the student's comprehension differ when reading orally versus silently? _____

If so, which is better? _____

Intervention Emphasis

What are the most important skill/s to work on in intervention? _____

_____

What types of materials (narrative, social studies, science) should be used? _____

_____

What levels of materials will be used? _____

*Full Name of Passage(s) Used:

Additional Notes:

Figure 9.2 Example of Completed Student Summary Form

Student Summary Form

Name _Danika_   Date: _____   Grade _6_

Word Lists

Grade Level	4	5	6	UMS
Total Correct Automatic	10	4	3	0
Total Correct Identified	9	10	11	12
Total Number Correct	19	14	14	12

Level (Independent (Ind), Instructional (Ins), Frustration (F))

Ind   Ins   Ins   Frus

What is the student's highest instructional level on the word lists? _6_

Does the student use letter-sound patterns to identify words? _yes_

Does the student focus on the beginning of words, the middle and/or the end? _yes_

Does the student identify words automatically at the instructional level? _no_

Passages

Passage Name* _Lowry   Nile   Temp   Oxygen_

Type (Narrative (N), Social Studies (SS), Science (S))

_N   SS   S   S_

Readability Level _6   6   6   5_

Concept Questions

Concept Questions (Familiar, Unfamiliar)

_7   7   U   U_

Do the student's answers to the concept questions suggest that the topic is familiar? _yes for_
narrative and one social studies. No for science

Word Identification Oral Reading

Number of Miscues	8	24	19	25
Level Total Accuracy	Ind	Ins	Ins	Ins
Level Total Acceptability	Ind	Ins	Frus	Frus

Are student miscues similar to original words in letter-sound patterns? _yes_

Do student miscues change meaning? _yes_

Does the student correct meaning change miscues? _occasionally_

Retelling

Retains narrative structure _yes   yes_

Retains expository structure _no   no_

Does the student retell an instructional level narrative text using the elements of story structure (i.e., character, goal/problem, events, resolution)? _yes_

Does the student retell an instructional level expository text citing main ideas and relevant details?
_no_

(continued)

Figure 9.2 continued

Comprehension Without Lookbacks

Total Explicit Questions Correct	4	4	3	3	
Total Implicit Questions Correct	2	2	2	1	
Comprehension Level (Ind, Ins, F)	Ins	Ins	Frus	Frus	

Comprehension With Lookbacks (Use with reading levels Grade 3 and above)

Total Explicit Questions Correct	4	4	3	3	
Total Implicit Questions Correct	3	3	2	1	
Comprehension Level (Ind, Ins, F)	Ins	Ins	Frus	Frus	

Total Passage Level

Independent, Instructional, Frustration	Ins	Ins	Frus	Frus	

Instructional Level

What is the student's level in narrative text? _6_

What ability (i.e., word identification or comprehension) prevented the student from having a higher instructional level in narrative text? _Comprehension_

What is the student's level in expository text? _6 for social studies Below 6 science_

What ability (i.e., word identification or comprehension) prevented the student from having a higher instructional level in expository text? _comprehension_

Think Alouds

Does the student offer comments that suggests understanding, lack of understanding, or both?
Both

Mode of Reading

Does the student's comprehension differ when reading orally versus silently? _yes_

If so, which is better? _Oral reading_

Intervention Emphasis

What is the most important skill to work on in intervention? _Comprehension_

What types of materials (narrative, expository or both) will be used? _Expository_

What levels of materials will be used? _5 and 6_

*Full Name of Passage(s) _The Early Life of Lois Lowry_
The Lifeline of the Nile
Temperature and Humidity
How Does Your Body Take in Oxygen?

Additional Notes

Is there a difference between a student's ability to identify words in context and words in isolation? For many readers, the instructional levels attained on the word lists will match the instructional levels achieved for word accuracy in familiar text. However, some readers recognize far more words in context. If the oral reading of these students is fluent and expressive—that is, demonstrates prosody—a lower score on the word list does not represent a serious area of concern.

What does the instructional level suggest about a student's reading ability? *Reading disability* is defined as a serious discrepancy between a student's chronological grade level and the level at which the student can read familiar narrative material. For fourth-graders and above, a gap of two or more years between the student's highest instructional level and his/her actual grade level suggests a serious reading problem. For children in third grade and below, a gap of one year suggests the same.

How can instructional levels vary? All of us have different reading levels depending upon the topic and structure of the text. Many of us are more adept at comprehending narrative and expository passages that are based on familiar topics and genres, such as novels, world news, book reviews, and editorials. On the other hand, most people would probably struggle with a chapter on quantum physics. A student's instructional level will vary depending upon the type of passages read. A student may have different instructional levels for literature, social studies, and science texts. An instructional level for a familiar narrative is usually higher than an instructional level for unfamiliar expository material.

Assessment for struggling readers often focuses solely on narrative passages. Once a reading level for narratives is established, the assessment session ends. Neglecting to determine a student's ability in reading expository text presents an incomplete picture of the student's skills. Many readers score a year or two below their narrative level when asked to read expository text. Performance in expository text should be assessed and included in the intervention. Instruction that focuses only on narrative text will not automatically transfer to social studies and science. The differences in the content and structure of the disciplines is too great.

Which mode of reading (oral or silent) represents strengths for the student? It is natural for young readers to do better in oral reading because this is emphasized during the early elementary grades. However, as the student moves through the grades, s/he must become increasingly efficient at silent reading. A middle school student whose instructional level for oral reading is higher than for silent reading will be at a disadvantage in coping with the demands of textbook reading. For students in grade 4 and above, assessment of both oral and silent reading is strongly recommended.

How does the student perform with look-backs and without look-backs? A student can raise his or her comprehension score by engaging in look-backs to find clues that suggest correct answers to questions. Some students use look-backs more effectively with narrative or expository text. If the student is not a fluent reader, he or she often will not be able to effectively look back in the text to find clues to answering implicit questions. Typically, this type of reader will attempt to reread the entire text again. On the other hand, if a student can effectively look back in the text, it suggests both automatic word recognition and memory of the location of the text clues.

SELECTING MATERIALS FOR INTERVENTION INSTRUCTION

As described in previous sections, one role of the assessment examiner is to identify a student's instructional levels in narrative and expository text—that is, the levels of text that can be read with acceptable word recognition and comprehension. Knowing the instructional level of a reader allows you to select materials at an appropriate level—that is, materials that can be read and understood with the support of the intervention specialist.

The notion that a reader has one reading level is inaccurate. Readers generally have multiple levels: a level for familiar narratives, a lower level for social studies text and perhaps an even lower level for science material. Often, however, assessment stops when an instructional level for narrative text is identified. Assuming that a level for narrative text is the same as the level for expository material can deny a student appropriate instruction.

Narrative text focuses on a character's problem and how it is resolved. It often involves familiar concepts and situations that the reader can recognize and identify with. On the other hand, expository text frequently centers on unfamiliar topics and the main idea of a passage is seldom stated explicitly. A fourth-grade science text on plant structure will be more conceptually difficult than a fourth grade narrative on the career of Amelia Earhart. Similarly, a sixth-grade passage on building pyramids will be easier to comprehend than a sixth grade text on clouds and precipitation. One cannot assume that reading and discussing narratives will transfer to social studies and science material. Likewise, one cannot assume that reading and comprehending social studies will transfer to science text.

For many years it has been recommended that intervention text should be at a student's instructional reading level. However, because most readers have different instructional levels for narrative and nonfiction text, a single level of text for intervention may not be possible when intervention includes both fiction and nonfiction text.

Because an inability to comprehend classroom texts is probably what initiates a recommendation for literacy assessment, the best material for intervention instruction should be similar to classroom materials. If your student has an instructional level of fourth grade for science, use a fourth-grade text. Similarly, if his/her instructional level for social studies is sixth grade, use a sixth-grade social studies text for intervention instruction. If textbooks are not used in the classroom, use the materials that are.

SELECTING INSTRUCTIONAL STRATEGIES FOR INTERVENTION INSTRUCTION

In some cases, the individual who conducted the assessment is also the individual who designs and carries out intervention instruction. In other cases, student information is summarized and passed on to another individual. If you are the individual responsible for carrying out the intervention instruction, asking the following questions will help you to design appropriate instruction.

What types of text should be the focus of intervention instruction?   For students with reading levels at first through second grade, narrative text is most appropriate. For struggling readers in grade 3 and above, focus on both narrative and expository text, using regular classroom textbooks at their instructional level.

What level of text should be the focus of intervention instruction?   Begin by focusing on instructional level text. As students improve, move gradually to the next highest level. The instructional level should gradually become the independent level. You may find yourself using passages at different levels for the same student: a higher level for narrative material and a lower level for expository.

Should oral or silent reading be emphasized in intervention?   Oral reading is most appropriate for students at first- through third-grade reading levels. For struggling readers in grades 4 and above, begin with a focus on assisted oral reading where you and the students read orally together. As you read and reread narrative text, identify characters' problems and solutions. As you read and reread expository materials, determine main ideas and supporting details. Gradually transfer a focus on oral reading to silent reading.

What type of questions should be asked in intervention?   Struggling readers are not used to asking questions as they read. They are more accustomed to answering them, often with little success. Teach your students to ask questions as they read. For narrative text, focus questions on identifying characters, settings, problems, and solutions. For expository text, focus questions on identifying the topics, main ideas, and relevant details.

How can students' word identification be improved?   Model how letters represent sounds and ask students to build words by adding, deleting, and changing letters. Demonstrate how a word such as *jump* can take on different meanings such as *jumps, jumped, jumping,* and *jumper.*

How can student vocabulary be improved?   Teach word meanings based on words selected from the text, not from vocabulary word lists. Ask students to point out unknown words after oral and/or silent reading, and use these as your focus for instruction. Explain how the meaning of prefixes and suffixes affect the meaning of the root word.

How can student comprehension be improved?   One of the best ways to improve comprehension is to build background for important conceptual knowledge in the text. This knowledge building is particularly important in expository texts because they are typically about unfamiliar technical topics. In addition, teach the student/s to focus on text structure. It can provide a format for knowing what to look for during reading. When reading narratives, ask questions and form summaries based on the components of character, setting, problem, and solution. For expository text, stress the structures of description, sequence, cause and effect, problem/solution, and comparison/contrast.

How can look-backs be used effectively?   The ability to look back in the text and locate information is a characteristic of effective readers. Use look-backs as a regular part of text discussion. Model the process of rereading parts of text in order to find answers to questions.

How can think-alouds help a student's comprehension?   Thinking aloud should be a regular part of discussion between teacher and students. Instead of asking the all-too-typical literal and inferential questions, teach students to ask their own questions by engaging in the process of thinking aloud as they read.

USING THE *QRI-7* TO INDICATE GROWTH AND MONITOR PROGRESS

An individually administered QRI-7 can be used to analyze reading growth. Several studies have suggested that passages on the QRI are sensitive to a 10-week intervention and long-term change (Leslie & Allen, 1999). In addition, the QRI has also been extensively used by literacy researchers to evaluate student progress. Representative articles describing this use are found in the References and are marked with an asterisk.

Pre-and post-assessment can take two forms. You can administer a passage prior to the intervention or at the beginning of the school year, and then administer the same passage as a post-test. Select the passage that best reflects a student's reading level or a passage that best reflects your instructional focus. This is usually a narrative passage. However, if the focus of intervention is expository text, choose an expository selection.

Do not assess student growth on a monthly basis but check progress at several (three to four) points during the school year. You can re-administer the original passage that was used to determine reading level. If the student has moved to an independent level in that passage, select a passage at the next higher level for post-test administration.

Pre- and post-intervention passages must be administered in much the same way. Both should employ the same genre (i.e., both narrative, both social studies, or both science), use either oral or silent reading, and use the same comprehension components: retelling and questions with or without look-backs.

We are often asked about the validity of administering the same passage. Will students naturally perform better on the second administration just because they read the same passage previously? If the times of administration are spaced far enough apart, this may not be an issue. At one of our reading centers, the pre-test passage is routinely used as the post-test passage after the completion of an entire semester. We have noted that many children actually seem unaware that they had read the passage previously. However, if you are concerned about this and you feel that a student's performance on the post-test is suspect, administer a different passage of the same kind (narrative, social studies, or science) and level of difficulty as the post-test. This may be a more viable option if the duration of the intervention is relatively short or if you are concerned that memory for the initial passage may confound comprehension performance on the same passage. If you choose this option, the two passages should be as similar as possible. They should be at the same readability level, of the same structure (narrative or expository), and of the same level of familiarity. Table 13.6 in Section 13 provides average comprehension scores on each passage, which indicate the easier and harder passages within a level.

READING PERFORMANCE CASE STUDIES

This section includes in-depth, interactive case studies for two different students: Amy (second grade), and Jared (seventh grade). In these exercises, you will use *QRI* assessment data and artifacts to complete a multi-step analysis of each student's reading performance. The purpose is to apply what you have learned about scoring, analyzing, and using *QRI-7* results. Each exercise includes a set of short answer questions to guide your analysis.

Analyzing Amy's Reading Performance—Amy, a second-grader, was referred for assessment because of poor performance in her classroom reading group. Complete the following four exercises to apply what you know about using the *QRI-7* in order to analyze Amy's reading performance. As you complete each exercise, be sure to fill out a Student Summary Form for Amy.

Pearson eText Teacher Resource: Blank Student Summary Form—Printer Friendly

The completed summary form will be useful when answering questions in exercise 9.4.

> **Pearson eText Application Exercise 9.1:** Amy's Word List Performance

> **Pearson eText Application Exercise 9.2:** Amy's Passage Performance

> **Pearson eText Application Exercise 9.3:** Amy's Retelling and Comprehension Performance

> **Pearson eText Application Exercise 9.4:** Determining Amy's Instructional Reading Level and Intervention Emphasis

Analyzing Jared's Reading Performance—Jared, a seventh-grader, is experiencing difficulties in school, especially in social studies and science classes. Complete the following six exercises to apply what you know about using the *QRI-7* to analyze reading performance. As you complete each part of the exercise, fill out a Student Summary Form for Jared.

Pearson eText Application Exercise 9.5: Jared's Word List Performance

Pearson eText Application Exercise 9.6: Jared's Social Studies Passage Performance (Oral)

Pearson eText Application Exercise 9.7: Jared's Narrative Passage Performance (Silent)

Pearson eText Application Exercise 9.8: Jared's Think Aloud Performance

Pearson eText Application Exercise 9.9: Jared's Oral vs. Silent Reading Comprehension

Pearson eText Application Exercise 9.10: Intervention Emphasis for Jared

Pearson eText Teacher Resource: Blank Student Summary Form—Printer Friendly

The completed summary form will be useful when answering questions in exercise 9.10.

Section 10
QRI-7 Test Materials: Word Lists and Level-Diagnostic Passages

Pearson eText Teacher Resources: In the section outline below, each passage title is a clickable link that will open a printable PDF version of the passage and the accompanying examiner copies. You can also print the word list materials by clicking on the appropriate headers.

Student Word Lists

Student Reading by Analogy Lists

Examiner Word Lists

Reading by Analogy Examiner Lists

Pre-Primer 1 Passages
"I Can" (Narrative/Pictures)
"I See" (Narrative/Pictures)

Pre-Primer 2 Passages
"Just Like Mom" (Narrative/Pictures)
"People at Work" (Expository/Pictures)

Pre-Primer 3 Passages
"Lost and Found" (Narrative)
"Spring and Fall" (Narrative)
Examiner Copies

Primer Passages
"A Night in the City" (Narrative/Pictures)
"Fox and Mouse" (Narrative/Pictures)
"The Pig Who Learned to Read" (Narrative/Pictures)
"Who Lives Near Lakes?" (Expository/Pictures)
"Living and Not Living" (Expository)
Examiner Copies

Level 1 Passages
"The Surprise" (Narrative/Pictures)
"Marva Finds a Friend" (Narrative/Pictures)
"The Bear and the Rabbit" (Narrative/Pictures)
"Air" (Expository)
"The Brain and the Five Senses" (Expository/Pictures)
Examiner Copies

Level 2 Passages
"The Family's First Trip" (Narrative)
"The Lucky Cricket" (Narrative/Pictures)
"Father's New Game" (Narrative/Pictures)
"Whales and Fish" (Expository)
"Seasons" (Expository)
Examiner Copies

Level 3 Passages
"A Special Birthday for Rosa" (Narrative)
"The Friend" (Narrative)
"A New Friend from Europe" (Narrative)
"Cats: Lions and Tigers in Your House" (Expository)
"Where Do People Live?" (Expository)
"Wool: From Sheep to You" (Expository)
Examiner Copies

Level 4 Passages
"Amelia Earhart" (Narrative)
"Tomie dePaola" (Narrative)
"Early Railroads" (Expository/Pictures)
"Plant Structures for Survival" (Expository/Pictures)
Examiner Copies

Level 5 Passages
"Margaret Mead" (Narrative)
"Patricia McKissack" (Narrative)
"Farming on the Great Plains" (Expository/Pictures)
"How Does Your Body Take in Oxygen?" (Expository/Pictures)
Examiner Copies

Level 6 Passages
"Abraham Lincoln" (Biography)
"The Early Life of Lois Lowry" (Biography/Think-Aloud)

"The Lifeline of the Nile" (Social Studies/Pictures)
"Building Pyramids (Social Studies/Pictures/Think-Aloud)
"Temperature and Humidity" (Science/Pictures)
"Clouds and Precipitation" (Science/Pictures/Think-Aloud)
Examiner Copies

Middle School Passages: Literature
"Jaime Escalanté: Teacher Extraordinaire" (Biography/Think-Aloud)

Middle School Passages: Social Studies
"Immigration—Part 1" (Social Studies/Pictures)
"Immigration—Part 2" (Social Studies/Pictures/Think-Aloud)

Middle School Passages: Science
"Life Cycles of Stars—Part 1" (Science/Pictures)
"Life Cycles of Stars—Part 2" (Science Pictures/Think-Aloud)
Examiner Copies

High School Passages: Social Studies
"World War I—Part 1" (Social Studies/Pictures)
"World War I—Part 2" (Social Studies/Pictures/Think-Aloud)

High School Passages: Science
"Characteristics of Viruses—Part 1" (Science/Pictures)
"Characteristics of Viruses—Part 2" (Science/Pictures/Think-Aloud)
Examiner Copies

Student Word Lists

1. can
2. I
3. of
4. me
5. the
6. in
7. at
8. with
9. a
10. he
11. go
12. to
13. see
14. do
15. on
16. was
17. she

1. make
2. same
3. like
4. all
5. were
6. my
7. work
8. best
9. play
10. just
11. some
12. they
13. people
14. look
15. too
16. other
17. place
18. where
19. under
20. help

You can print all student and examiner copies from Section 10.

Student Word Lists

1. from	1. bear	1. stone
2. need	2. father	2. excited
3. going	3. find	3. shiny
4. what	4. sound	4. else
5. special	5. friend	5. picked
6. thing	6. song	6. promise
7. why	7. thought	7. pieces
8. again	8. keep	8. suit
9. want	9. enough	9. push
10. animals	10. brain	10. though
11. sing	11. air	11. begins
12. went	12. knew	12. food
13. jump	13. put	13. light
14. read	14. heard	14. visit
15. said	15. afraid	15. clue
16. live	16. wind	16. breathe
17. there	17. choose	17. insects
18. one	18. without	18. weather
19. great	19. move	19. noticed
20. every	20. then	20. season

Student Word Lists

1. finished	1. sunlight	1. content
2. celebrate	2. desert	2. reflected
3. believe	3. crops	3. medicine
4. confused	4. traveled	4. biography
5. motion	5. favorite	5. artery
6. rough	6. adaptation	6. capture
7. engines	7. terribly	7. vessels
8. tongue	8. predator	8. tales
9. crowded	9. illustrated	9. stampede
10. wool	10. ocean	10. obstacles
11. removed	11. pilot	11. divorced
12. curious	12. dynamite	12. registration
13. silver	13. struggled	13. scarce
14. electric	14. symbolized	14. primitive
15. introduced	15. competition	15. visualize
16. enemies	16. passenger	16. bulletin
17. glowed	17. memorize	17. solitary
18. clothing	18. environment	18. fluent
19. interested	19. adventurer	19. pioneers
20. explained	20. invented	20. advantage

Student Word Lists

1. tolerate
2. possession
3. condenses
4. memories
5. abolish
6. pyramids
7. emerge
8. boundary
9. humidity
10. insistent
11. irrigated
12. thrived
13. restricted
14. evaporate
15. gauges
16. preserved
17. proclaimed
18. courageous
19. pharaohs
20. conqueror

1. imagination
2. sacrificed
3. infrared
4. fusion
5. nebula
6. persecution
7. gravity
8. nuclear
9. helium
10. migration
11. berths
12. oppressed
13. separatist
14. antagonize
15. anarchy
16. nativist
17. accompanied
18. assimilate
19. usurped
20. asteroids

1. armaments
2. alliance
3. enzyme
4. reparations
5. replicate
6. industrialized
7. armistice
8. stalemate
9. immunodeficiency
10. mediated
11. mandates
12. infectious
13. nucleic
14. chromosome
15. diminished
16. reparations
17. interception
18. influenza
19. hereditary
20. nanometers

Student Reading by Analogy Lists

1. can		1. pan	
2. in		2. pin	
3. see		3. bee	
4. at		4. rat	
5. make		5. rake	
6. same		6. fame	
7. like		7. bike	
8. place		8. race	
9. play		9. bay	
10. look		10. book	
11. keep		11. peep	
12. thing		12. sing	
13. went		13. rent	
14. jump		14. bump	
15. need		15. seed	
16. sound		16. pound	
17. knew		17. chew	
18. brain		18. stain	

Examiner Word Lists

Pre-Primer 1

	Recognized Automatically	Identified
1. can	_____	_____
2. I	_____	_____
3. of	_____	_____
4. me	_____	_____
5. the	_____	_____
6. in	_____	_____
7. at	_____	_____
8. with	_____	_____
9. a	_____	_____
10. he	_____	_____
11. go	_____	_____
12. to	_____	_____
13. see	_____	_____
14. do	_____	_____
15. on	_____	_____
16. was	_____	_____
17. she	_____	_____

Total Correct Automatic _____ /17 = _____%
Total Correct Identified _____ /17 = _____%
Total Number Correct _____ /17 = _____%

LEVELS		
Independent	Instructional	Frustration
15–17	12–14	below 12
90–100%	70–85%	below 70%

Pre-Primer 2/3

	Recognized Automatically	Identified
1. make	_____	_____
2. same	_____	_____
3. like	_____	_____
4. all	_____	_____
5. were	_____	_____
6. my	_____	_____
7. work	_____	_____
8. best	_____	_____
9. play	_____	_____
10. just	_____	_____
11. some	_____	_____
12. they	_____	_____
13. people	_____	_____
14. look	_____	_____
15. too	_____	_____
16. other	_____	_____
17. place	_____	_____
18. where	_____	_____
19. under	_____	_____
20. help	_____	_____

Total Correct Automatic _____ /20 = _____%
Total Correct Identified _____ /20 = _____%
Total Number Correct _____ /20 = _____%

LEVELS		
Independent	Instructional	Frustration
18–20	14–17	below 14
90–100%	70–85%	below 70%

Examiner Word Lists

Primer

	Recognized Automatically	Identified
1. from	_____	_____
2. need	_____	_____
3. going	_____	_____
4. what	_____	_____
5. special	_____	_____
6. thing	_____	_____
7. why	_____	_____
8. again	_____	_____
9. want	_____	_____
10. animals	_____	_____
11. sing	_____	_____
12. went	_____	_____
13. jump	_____	_____
14. read	_____	_____
15. said	_____	_____
16. live	_____	_____
17. there	_____	_____
18. one	_____	_____
19. great	_____	_____
20. every	_____	_____

Total Correct Automatic _____ /20 = _____%
Total Correct Identified _____ /20 = _____%
Total Number Correct _____ /20 = _____%

First Grade

	Recognized Automatically	Identified
1. bear	_____	_____
2. father	_____	_____
3. find	_____	_____
4. sound	_____	_____
5. friend	_____	_____
6. song	_____	_____
7. thought	_____	_____
8. keep	_____	_____
9. enough	_____	_____
10. brain	_____	_____
11. air	_____	_____
12. knew	_____	_____
13. put	_____	_____
14. heard	_____	_____
15. afraid	_____	_____
16. wind	_____	_____
17. choose	_____	_____
18. without	_____	_____
19. move	_____	_____
20. then	_____	_____

Total Correct Automatic _____ /20 = _____%
Total Correct Identified _____ /20 = _____%
Total Number Correct _____ /20 = _____%

LEVELS		
Independent	Instructional	Frustration
18–20	14–17	below 14
90–100%	70–85%	below 70%

Examiner Word Lists

Second Grade

	Recognized Automatically	Identified
1. stone	_____	_____
2. excited	_____	_____
3. shiny	_____	_____
4. else	_____	_____
5. picked	_____	_____
6. promise	_____	_____
7. pieces	_____	_____
8. suit	_____	_____
9. push	_____	_____
10. though	_____	_____
11. begins	_____	_____
12. food	_____	_____
13. light	_____	_____
14. visit	_____	_____
15. clue	_____	_____
16. breathe	_____	_____
17. insects	_____	_____
18. weather	_____	_____
19. noticed	_____	_____
20. season	_____	_____

Total Correct Automatic ____ /20 = ____%
Total Correct Identified ____ /20 = ____%
Total Number Correct ____ /20 = ____%

Third Grade

	Recognized Automatically	Identified
1. finished	_____	_____
2. celebrate	_____	_____
3. believe	_____	_____
4. confused	_____	_____
5. motion	_____	_____
6. rough	_____	_____
7. engines	_____	_____
8. tongue	_____	_____
9. crowded	_____	_____
10. wool	_____	_____
11. removed	_____	_____
12. curious	_____	_____
13. silver	_____	_____
14. electric	_____	_____
15. introduced	_____	_____
16. enemies	_____	_____
17. glowed	_____	_____
18. clothing	_____	_____
19. interested	_____	_____
20. explained	_____	_____

Total Correct Automatic ____ /20 = ____%
Total Correct Identified ____ /20 = ____%
Total Number Correct ____ /20 = ____%

Level 2

Level 3

LEVELS		
Independent	Instructional	Frustration
18–20	14–17	below 14
90–100%	70–85%	below 70%

Examiner Word Lists

Fourth Grade

	Recognized Automatically	Identified
1. sunlight	_____	_____
2. desert	_____	_____
3. crops	_____	_____
4. traveled	_____	_____
5. favorite	_____	_____
6. adaptation	_____	_____
7. terribly	_____	_____
8. predator	_____	_____
9. illustrated	_____	_____
10. ocean	_____	_____
11. pilot	_____	_____
12. dynamite	_____	_____
13. struggled	_____	_____
14. symbolized	_____	_____
15. competition	_____	_____
16. passenger	_____	_____
17. memorize	_____	_____
18. environment	_____	_____
19. adventurer	_____	_____
20. invented	_____	_____

Total Correct Automatic _____ /20 = _____%
Total Correct Identified _____ /20 = _____%
Total Number Correct _____ /20 = _____%

Fifth Grade

	Recognized Automatically	Identified
1. content	_____	_____
2. reflected	_____	_____
3. medicine	_____	_____
4. biography	_____	_____
5. artery	_____	_____
6. capture	_____	_____
7. vessels	_____	_____
8. tales	_____	_____
9. stampede	_____	_____
10. obstacles	_____	_____
11. divorced	_____	_____
12. registration	_____	_____
13. scarce	_____	_____
14. primitive	_____	_____
15. visualize	_____	_____
16. bulletin	_____	_____
17. solitary	_____	_____
18. fluent	_____	_____
19. pioneers	_____	_____
20. advantage	_____	_____

Total Correct Automatic _____ /20 = _____%
Total Correct Identified _____ /20 = _____%
Total Number Correct _____ /20 = _____%

Level 4

Level 5

LEVELS		
Independent	Instructional	Frustration
18–20	14–17	below 14
90–100%	70–85%	below 70%

Examiner Word Lists

Sixth Grade

	Recognized Automatically	Identified
1. tolerate	_____	_____
2. possession	_____	_____
3. condenses	_____	_____
4. memories	_____	_____
5. abolish	_____	_____
6. pyramids	_____	_____
7. emerge	_____	_____
8. boundary	_____	_____
9. humidity	_____	_____
10. insistent	_____	_____
11. irrigated	_____	_____
12. thrived	_____	_____
13. restricted	_____	_____
14. evaporate	_____	_____
15. gauges	_____	_____
16. preserved	_____	_____
17. proclaimed	_____	_____
18. courageous	_____	_____
19. pharaohs	_____	_____
20. conqueror	_____	_____

Total Correct Automatic _____ /20 = _____%
Total Correct Identified _____ /20 = _____%
Total Number Correct _____ /20 = _____%

Upper Middle School

	Recognized Automatically	Identified
1. imagination	_____	_____
2. sacrificed	_____	_____
3. infrared	_____	_____
4. fusion	_____	_____
5. nebula	_____	_____
6. persecution	_____	_____
7. gravity	_____	_____
8. nuclear	_____	_____
9. helium	_____	_____
10. migration	_____	_____
11. berths	_____	_____
12. oppressed	_____	_____
13. separatist	_____	_____
14. antagonize	_____	_____
15. anarchy	_____	_____
16. nativist	_____	_____
17. accompanied	_____	_____
18. assimilate	_____	_____
19. usurped	_____	_____
20. asteroids	_____	_____

Total Correct Automatic _____ /20 = _____%
Total Correct Identified _____ /20 = _____%
Total Number Correct _____ /20 = _____%

LEVELS		
Independent	Instructional	Frustration
18–20	14–17	below 14
90–100%	70–85%	below 70%

Examiner Word Lists

	Recognized Automatically	Identified
1. armaments	_____	_____
2. alliance	_____	_____
3. enzyme	_____	_____
4. reparations	_____	_____
5. replicate	_____	_____
6. industrialized	_____	_____
7. armistice	_____	_____
8. stalemate	_____	_____
9. immunodeficiency	_____	_____
10. mediated	_____	_____
11. mandates	_____	_____
12. infectious	_____	_____
13. nucleic	_____	_____
14. chromosome	_____	_____
15. diminished	_____	_____
16. reparations	_____	_____
17. interception	_____	_____
18. influenza	_____	_____
19. hereditary	_____	_____
20. nanometers	_____	_____

Total Correct Automatic _____ /20 = _____ %
Total Correct Identified _____ /20 = _____ %
Total Number Correct _____ /20 = _____ %

LEVELS		
Independent	Instructional	Frustration
18–20	14–17	below 14
90–100%	70–85%	below 70%

Reading by Analogy Examiner Lists

Name _____ Date _____ Level _____

PP1

High-Frequency Words from the Word Lists	Correct	Low-Frequency Words	Correct
can		pan	
in		pin	
see		bee	
at		rat	

PP2

make		rake	
same		fame	
like		bike	
place		race	
play		bay	
look		book	

Primer

keep		peep	
thing		sing	
went		rent	
jump		bump	

First Grade

need		seed	
sound		pound	
knew		chew	
brain		stain	
Total		Total	

I Can

I can jump. See me jump.

I can hop. See me hop.

I can run. See me run.

I can eat lunch. See me eat.

I can sleep. See me sleep.

I can dream. See me dream.

I See

I see a frog on a log.

I see an ant on a plant.

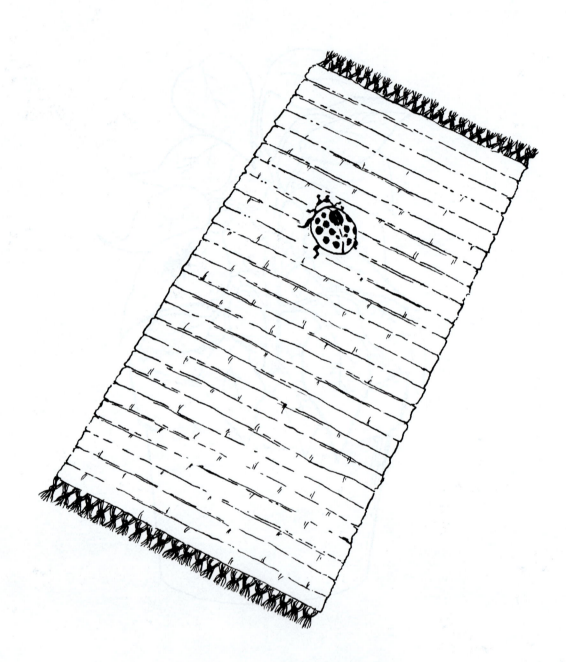

I see a bug on a rug.

I see a duck in a truck.

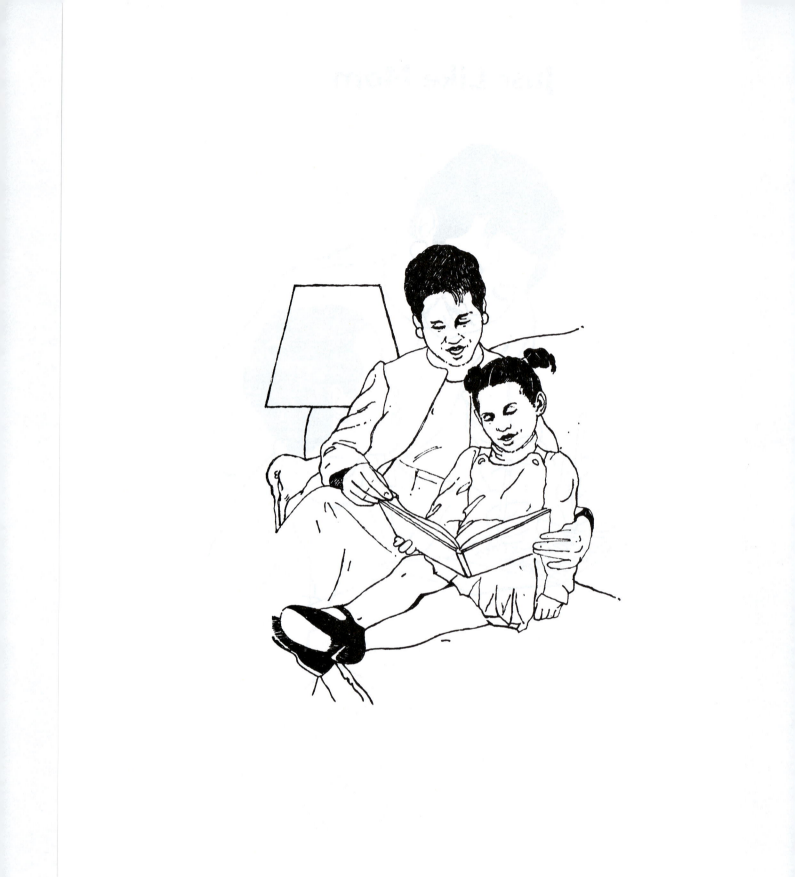

I can read.

Just like Mom.

I can go to work.

Just like Mom.

I can work at home.

Just like Mom.

I can work with numbers.

Just like Mom.

I can do lots of things.

Just like Mom.

People at Work

Some people work at home.

Other people go to work.

Why do people work?

People work to make money.

People work at many things.

Some people write at work.

Other people read at work.

Some people make things at work.

Other people sell things at work.

People work together.

Lost and Found

I lost my cat.

Where was she?

I looked inside the house.

I looked under the bed.

I looked outside too.

I lost my dog.

Where was he?

I looked inside the house.

I looked under the bed.

I looked outside too.

I found my cat.

I found my dog.

Where were they?

They were in the same place.

They were under the table.

Spring and Fall

I like the spring.

When I can do many things.

I can play with my dog.

I can play with a frog.

I can play in the rain.

I can go see a train.

I like the fall.

I can do it all.

I can read a book.

I can help Mom cook.

I can ride my bike.

I can go on a hike.

In the spring and fall, there is much to do.

But what I like best is going to the zoo.

Examiner Copies

Level: Pre-Primer 1

Narrative

Concept Questions:

What does it mean to jump? (*3: both feet go up in the air; 2: student jumps; 1: run*)

_____

_____

_____ (3-2-1-0)

What does it mean to hop? (*3: jump on one foot; 2: like a bunny; 1: run*)

_____

_____

_____ (3-2-1-0)

What does it mean to sleep? (*3: shut your eyes; 2: go to bed; 1: nighttime*)

_____

_____

_____ (3-2-1-0)

What does it mean to dream? (*3: see things while sleeping; 2: sleep; 1: close your eyes*)

Score: _____ /9 = _____%

_____ FAM (≥ 55%) _____ UNFAM

Note: Underlined words are on the word list at the PP1 level.

I Can

I can jump. See me jump.

I can hop. See me hop.

I can run. See me run.

I can eat lunch. See me eat.

I can sleep. See me sleep.

I can dream. See me dream. (37 words)

Number of Total Miscues (Total Accuracy): _____

Number of Meaning-Change Miscues (Total Acceptability): _____

Total Accuracy		**Total Acceptability**
0–1 miscues _____	Independent _____	0–1 miscues
2–4 miscues _____	Instructional _____	2 miscues
5+ miscues _____	Frustration _____	3+ miscues

Rate: 37 × 60 = 2,220/_____ seconds = _____ WPM

WCPM: (37 × _____ errors) × 60 =

_____ / _____ seconds = _____ **WCPM**

Retelling Scoring Sheet for "I Can"

_____ I can jump.

_____ I can hop.

_____ I can run.

_____ I can eat lunch.

_____ I can sleep.

_____ I can dream.

Level: Pre-Primer I

Questions for "I Can"

1. What can the girl at the beginning of the story do?
   Explicit: jump

2. What can another girl in the story do?
   Explicit: hop *Note:* If the student says "play hopscotch," count it as implicitly correct.

3. What can the group of children do?
   Explicit: run

4. What can the boy in the library do?
   Explicit: sleep

5. While the boy is sleeping, what can he do?
   Explicit: dream

Number Correct Explicit: _____

Number Correct Implicit: _____

Total: _____

_____ Independent: 5 correct

_____ Instructional: 4 correct

_____ Frustration: 0–3 correct

Level: Pre-Primer 1

Narrative

Concept Questions:

What is a frog? *(3: a reptile; 2: a green animal; 1: ribbit)*

_____

_____

_____ (3-2-1-0)

What is a bug? *(3: an insect; 2: an ant/mosquito; 1: crawly)*

_____

_____

_____ (3-2-1-0)

What is a pig? *(3: animal; 2: lives on a farm; 1: smells)*

_____

_____

_____ (3-2-1-0)

Score: _____ /9 = _____%

_____ FAM (≥ 55%) _____ UNFAM

Note: Underlined words are on the word list at the PP1 level.

I See

I <u>see</u> <u>a</u> frog <u>on</u> <u>a</u> log.

I <u>see</u> an ant <u>on</u> <u>a</u> plant.

I <u>see</u> <u>a</u> bug <u>on</u> <u>a</u> rug.

I <u>see</u> <u>a</u> duck <u>in</u> <u>a</u> truck.

I <u>see</u> <u>a</u> pig <u>doing</u> <u>a</u> jig. (35 words)

Number of Total Miscues
(Total Accuracy): _____

Number of Meaning-Change Miscues
(Total Acceptability): _____

Total Accuracy		**Total Acceptability**
0–1 miscues _____	Independent _____	0–1 miscues
2–4 miscues _____	Instructional _____	2 miscues
5+ miscues _____	Frustration _____	3+ miscues

Rate: 37 × 60 = 2,220/_____ = _____ WPM

WCPM: (37 – _____ errors) × 60 =

_____ / _____ seconds = _____ WCPM

Retelling Scoring Sheet for "I See"

_____ I see a frog/on a log.

_____ I see an ant/on a plant.

_____ I see a bug/on a rug.

_____ I see a duck/in a truck.

_____ I see a pig/doing a jig (or dancing).

Level: Pre-Primer I

Questions for "I See"

1. Where was the frog?
   Explicit or implicit from picture: on a log

2. Where was the ant?
   Explicit or implicit from picture: on a plant

3. Where was the bug?
   Explicit or implicit from picture: on a rug

4. Where was the duck?
   Explicit or implicit from picture: in a truck

5. What was the pig doing?
   Explicit: a jig *Note:* If the student says "dancing," count it as implicitly correct.

Number Correct Explicit: _____

Number Correct Implicit: _____

Total: _____

_____ Independent: 5 correct

_____ Instructional: 4 correct

_____ Frustration: 0–3 correct

Level: Pre-Primer 2

Narrative

Concept Questions:

What is a mom? (*3: the woman who had you; 2: she takes care of you; 1: a lady*)

_____

_____

_____ (3-2-1-0)

What does "working at home" mean to you? (*3: doing chores; 2: cleaning my room; 1: Saturday*)

_____

_____

_____ (3-2-1-0)

What does "going to work" mean to you? (*3: going to a job; 2: getting money; 1: leaving*)

_____

_____

_____ (3-2-1-0)

Score: _____ /9 = _____%

_____ FAM (≥ 55%) _____UNFAM

Note: Underlined words are on the word lists at the PP1 or PP2 level.

Just Like Mom

I can write.

Just like Mom.

I can read.

Just like Mom.

I can go to work.

Just like Mom.

I can work at home.

Just like Mom.

I can work with numbers.

Just like Mom.

I can do lots of things.

Just like Mom. (45 words)

Number of Total Miscues (Total Accuracy):
_____

Number of Meaning-Change Miscues
(Total Acceptability): _____

Total Accuracy		**Total Acceptability**
0–1 miscues _____	Independent _____	0–1 miscues
2–4 miscues _____	Instructional _____	2 miscues
5+ miscues _____	Frustration _____	3+ miscues

Rate: 45 × 60 = 2,700/_____ seconds = _____ WPM

WCPM: (45 – _____ errors) × 60 =
_____/ _____ seconds = _____WCPM

Retelling Scoring Sheet for "Just Like Mom"

_____ I can write/The girl can write.

_____ Just like Mom./Just like her mom.

_____ I (She) can read.

_____ Just like Mom.

_____ I (She) can go to work.

_____ Just like Mom.

_____ I (She) can work at home.

_____ Just like Mom.

_____ I can work with numbers.

_____ Just like Mom.

_____ I can do lots of things.

_____ Just like Mom.

Level: Pre-Primer 2

Questions for "Just Like Mom"

Note: If a question is answered with direct reference to pictures as opposed to text, score the answer as implicitly correct.

1. Name one thing the girl can do just like Mom.
   Explicit: write, read, go to work, work at home, or work with numbers
   Implicit: water the flowers, walk to work, or write numbers

2. Name another thing the girl can do just like Mom.
   Explicit: read, write, go to work, work at home, or work with numbers, depending on the answer above
   Implicit: same as #1

3. What can the girl work with just like Mom?
   Explicit: numbers
   Implicit: pencils, paper

4. Where can the girl work just like Mom?
   Explicit: at home, or she can go to work
   Implicit: in the garden

5. Where is another place the girl can work just like Mom?
   Explicit: at home or at her workplace, depending on the answer above
   Implicit: same as #4

Number Correct Explicit: _____

Number Correct Implicit
   (*from pictures*): _____

   Total: _____

   _____ Independent: 5 correct

   _____ Instructional: 4 correct

   _____ Frustration: 0–3 correct

Level: Pre-Primer 2

Expository

Concept Questions:

Where do people work? (*3: at their jobs; 2: example of a place; 1: out*)

_____

_____

_____ (3-2-1-0)

Why do people work? (*3: to earn money; 2: so they can eat; 1: at a job*)

_____

_____

_____ (3-2-1-0)

What are different kinds of jobs? (*3: doctor, police officer, any specific job; 2: making things, selling things, etc. 1: working*)

_____

_____

_____ (3-2-1-0)

Score: _____/9 = _____%

_____ FAM (≥ 55%) _____ UNFAM

Note: Underlined words are on the word lists at the PP1 or PP2 level.

People at Work

Some <u>people</u> <u>work</u> <u>at</u> home.

<u>Other</u> <u>people</u> <u>go</u> <u>to</u> <u>work</u>.

Why <u>do</u> <u>people</u> <u>work</u>?

<u>People</u> <u>work</u> <u>to</u> <u>make</u> money.

<u>People</u> <u>work</u> <u>at</u> many things.

Some <u>people</u> write <u>at</u> <u>work</u>.

<u>Other</u> <u>people</u> read <u>at</u> <u>work</u>.

Some <u>people</u> <u>make</u> things at <u>work</u>.

<u>Other</u> <u>people</u> sell things <u>at</u> <u>work</u>.

<u>People</u> <u>work</u> together. (49 words)

Number of Total Miscues (Total Accuracy):

_____

Number of Meaning-Change Miscues (Total Acceptability): _____

Total Accuracy		Total Acceptability
0–1 miscues _____	Independent _____	0–1 miscues
2–5 miscues _____	Instructional _____	2 miscues
6+ miscues _____	Frustration _____	3+ miscues

Rate: 49 × 60 = 2,940/_____ seconds = _____ WPM

WCPM: (49 − _____ errors) × 60 = _____/_____ seconds = _____ WCPM

Retelling Scoring Sheet for "People at Work"

Details

_____ Some people work at home.

_____ Other people go to work.

_____ Why do people work?

_____ People work to make money.

_____ People work at many things.

_____ Some people write at work.

_____ Other people read at work.

_____ Some people make things at work.

_____ Other people sell things at work.

_____ People work together.

Level: Pre-Primer 2

Questions for "People at Work"

Note: If a question is answered with direct reference to pictures as opposed to text, score the answer as implicitly correct.

1. Where do people work?
   Explicit: at home or they go to work

2. What is one thing that people do at work?
   Explicit: write, read, make things, or sell things
   Implicit: fix things

3. What is another thing that people do at work?
   Explicit: write, read, make things, or sell things, depending on answer above
   Implicit: fix things

4. What is another thing that people do at work?
   Explicit: write, read, make things, or sell things, depending on answers to previous questions
   Implicit: fix things

5. What is another thing that people do at work?
   Explicit: write, read, make things, or sell things, depending on answers to previous questions
   Implicit: fix things

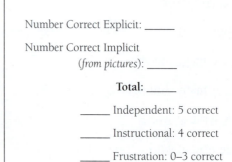

Number Correct Explicit: _____

Number Correct Implicit
(*from pictures*): _____

Total: _____

_____ Independent: 5 correct

_____ Instructional: 4 correct

_____ Frustration: 0–3 correct

Level: Pre-Primer 3

Narrative

Note: Underlined words are on the word lists at the PP1 or PP2/3 level.

Lost and Found

I lost my cat.

Where was she?

I looked inside the house.

I looked under the bed.

I looked outside too.

I lost my dog.

Where was he?

I looked inside the house.

I looked under the bed.

I looked outside too.

I found my cat.

I found my dog.

Where were they?

They were in the same place.

They were under the table. (64 words)

Retelling Scoring Sheet for "Lost and Found"

Events

_____ I lost my cat (The girl/boy lost her/his cat).

_____ I (she/he) looked inside the house.

_____ I (she/he) looked under the bed.

_____ I (she/he) looked outside too.

_____ I (she/he) lost my (her/his) dog.

_____ I (she/he) looked inside the house.

_____ I (she/he) looked under the bed.

_____ I (she/he) looked outside too.

_____ I (she/he) found my (her/his) cat.

_____ I (she/he) found my (her/his) dog.

_____ Where were they?

_____ They were in the same place.

_____ They were under the table.

Level: Pre-Primer 3

Questions for "Lost and Found"

1. What did the person in the story lose?
   Explicit: cat or dog

2. What else did the person in the story lose?
   Explicit: cat or dog, depending on the answer above

3. Where did the person in the story look?
   Explicit: inside the house, under the bed, or outside

4. Where else did the person in the story look?
   Explicit: inside the house, under the bed, or outside, depending on the answer above

5. Where did the person find the dog and cat?
   Explicit: in the same place or under the table

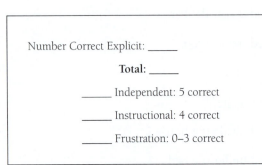

Number Correct Explicit: _____

Total: _____

_____ Independent: 5 correct

_____ Instructional: 4 correct

_____ Frustration: 0–3 correct

Level: Pre-Primer 3

Narrative

> **Concept Questions:**
>
> What does "spring" mean to you? (*3: a season with more light; it's warmer than winter; 2: rainy/flowers; 1: up*)
>
> _____
>
> _____
>
> _____ (3-2-1-0)
>
> What does "fall" mean to you? (*3: a season with less light; it's cooler than summer; 2: leaves fall; 1: down*)
>
> _____
>
> _____
>
> _____ (3-2-1-0)
>
> What does "doing something you like best" mean to you? (*3: doing your favorite thing; 2: you like it; child names an example of something they like to do; 1: fun*)
>
> _____
>
> _____
>
> _____ (3-2-1-0)
>
> **Score:** _____/9 = _____%
>
> _____ FAM (≥ 55%) _____ UNFAM

Note: Underlined words are on the word lists at the PP1 or PP2/3 level.

Spring and Fall

I like the spring.

When I can do many things.

I can play with my dog.

I can play with a frog.

I can play in the rain.

I can go see a train.

I like the fall.

I can do it all.

I can read a book.

I can help Mom cook.

I can ride my bike.

I can go on a hike.

In the spring and fall, there is much to do.

But what I like best is going to the zoo. (84 words)

> Number of Total Miscues
> (Total Accuracy): _____
>
> Number of Meaning-Change Miscues
> (Total Acceptability): _____
>
> | **Total** | **Total** |
> | **Accuracy** | **Acceptability** |
>
> 0–2 miscues _____ Independent _____ 0–2 miscues
> 3–8 miscues _____ Instructional _____ 3–4 miscues
> 9+ miscues _____ Frustration _____ 5+ miscues
>
> **Rate:** 84 × 60 = 5,040/_____seconds = _____ WPM
>
> **WCPM:** (84 – _____ errors) × 60 =
> _____/_____ seconds = _____ WCPM

Retelling Scoring Sheet for "Spring and Fall"

Details

_____ I like the spring.

_____ I can do many things.

_____ I can play with my dog.

_____ I can play with a frog.

_____ I can play in the rain.

_____ I can go see a train.

_____ I like the fall.

_____ I can do it all.

_____ I can read a book.

_____ I can help Mom cook.

_____ I can ride my bike.

_____ I can go on a hike.

_____ In spring and fall, there is much to do.

_____ But what I like best is going to the zoo.

Level: Pre-Primer 3

Questions for "Spring and Fall"

1. What can the person in the story play with in the spring?
   Explicit: a dog or a frog

2. Name another thing the person can do in the spring.
   Explicit: play with a dog or frog (depending on above), or play in the rain, or go see a train

3. What can the person in the story ride on during the fall?
   Explicit: a bike

4. What can the person in the story help Mom do?
   Explicit: cook

5. What does the person like to do best?
   Explicit: go to the zoo

Number Correct Explicit: _____

Total: _____

_____ Independent: 5 correct

_____ Instructional: 4 correct

_____ Frustration: 0–3 correct

A Night in the City

It was a Saturday night in the city.

Ben and Ruth wanted something to do.

They heard a noise from outside.

They ran to their bedroom window.

They saw people in the street.

A man had a horn.

A woman had a guitar.

They were playing together.

Soon more people came.

They all started singing.

Ben had heard the songs before.

Their father had played his iPad.

The songs were on them.

Ruth went to find their mother and father.

"Come and listen to the music," she said.

They all sat in the living room.

They listened to the music.

It went on for a long time.

Ben and Ruth fell asleep in the living room.

Mother and Father carried them to bed.

It had been a great Saturday night.

Fox and Mouse

Fox wanted to plant a garden.

Mouse helped him.

They put the seeds in the ground.

They watered the seeds.

Then they waited.

One night Mouse went to the garden.

He dug up one of the seeds.

He wanted to see if it was growing.

The seed looked good to eat.

"It is only one seed," thought Mouse.

"Fox will not know who ate the seed."

The next night Mouse went to the garden again.

He dug up one seed and ate it.

He did this every night.

After a few weeks, all the seeds were gone.

"I wonder why the seeds didn't grow," said Fox.

Mouse didn't say a word.

So Fox planted more seeds.

And Mouse helped him.

The Pig Who Learned to Read

Once there was a pig.

His name was Pete.

He lived on a farm.

He was not like other pigs.

He was special.

He wanted to learn to read.

His father said, "But pigs can't read!"

"I don't care," said Pete.

"I want to read."

Who Lives Near Lakes?

adh272010/Fotolia

Many animals live near lakes.

Turtles sit on rocks.

They like to be in the sun.

You can see ducks near a lake.

There may be baby ducks.

The babies walk behind the mother duck.

There are fish in lakes.

You can see them when they jump out of the water.

People live near lakes too.

They like to see the animals.

Living and Not Living

Some things around us live.

Others are not living.

Things that live need air.

Things that live need food.

Things that live need water.

Things that live move and grow.

Animals are living things.

Plants are living things.

Is paper living?

No, but it comes from something living.

Paper comes from trees.

Is a wagon living?

No, it moves but it is not living.

Level: Primer

Expository

> **Concept Questions:**
>
> What do plants need to grow? (3: *water, soil, and light [two of them]; 2: any one of water, soil, and light; someone to weed around them 1: someone to plant them*)
>
> _____
> _____
> _____ (3-2-1-0)
>
> What do living things do? (3: *move/eat/sleep; 2: run/walk; 1: live*)
>
> _____
> _____
> _____ (3-2-1-0)
>
> What are things that have never been alive? (3: *things that don't breathe; 2: any example such as table/chair, etc.; 1: dead*)
>
> _____
> _____
> _____ (3-2-1-0)
>
> **Score:** _____/9 = _____ %
>
> _____ FAM (≥ 55%) _____ UNFAM

Note: Underlined words are on the word lists at the PP2/3 or primer level.

Living and Not Living

Some things around us live.

Others are not living.

Things that live need air.

Things that live need food.

Things that live need water.

Things that live move and grow.

Animals are living things.

Plants are living things.

Is paper living?

No, but it comes from something living.

Paper comes from trees.

Is a wagon living?

No, it moves but it is not living. (64 words)

> Number of Total Miscues
> (Total Accuracy): _____
>
> Number of Meaning-Change Miscues
> (Total Acceptability): _____
>
> | **Total Accuracy** | | **Total Acceptability** |
> |---|---|---|
> | 0–1 miscues _____ | Independent _____ | 0–1 miscues |
> | 2–6 miscues _____ | Instructional _____ | 2–3 miscues |
> | 7+ miscues _____ | Frustration _____ | 4+ miscues |
>
> **Rate:** 64 × 60 = 3,840/_____ seconds = _____ WPM
>
> **WCPM:** (64 − _____errors) × 60 = _____/ _____ seconds = _____ WCPM

Retelling Scoring Sheet for "Living and Not Living"

Main Idea

_____ Some things live.

_____ Others are not living.

Details

_____ Things that live need air.

_____ They need food.

_____ They need water.

_____ They move and grow.

_____ Animals are living.

_____ Plants are living.

_____ Paper is not living.

_____ It comes from something living.

_____ It comes from trees.

_____ A wagon is not living.

Questions for "Living and Not Living"

1. Name two things that living things need.
Explicit: air, food, water

2. What do living things do?
Explicit: move and grow

3. What two things did your reading say were living things?
Explicit: animals and plants

4. What causes a plant to die?
Implicit: it doesn't have food or water or air

5. What living thing does paper come from?
Explicit: trees

6. Why isn't a wagon that moves a living thing?
Implicit: it does not grow

Number Correct Explicit: _____

Number Correct Implicit: _____

Total: _____

_____ Independent: 6 correct

_____ Instructional: 4–5 correct

_____ Frustration: 0–3 correct

The Surprise

Sam's birthday was in two days.

He was going to be seven years old.

He wanted a PlayStation game.

He also wanted a new bike.

But most of all he wanted a dog.

His father went to look for a present.

First, he went into the toy store.

He saw the PlayStation that Sam wanted.

But his father didn't have enough money.

Then he saw a red bike that Sam would love!

But that also cost too much.

But one day the bear was sitting by a river.

He was singing softly to himself.

A rabbit lived near the river.

He looked out of his hole when he heard the bear's song.

He thought, "Anyone who sings like that must be nice.

Maybe I don't need to be afraid of him.

It would be nice to have a friend."

The rabbit went and got his horn.

Very softly he began to play.

His music went well with the bear's song.

The bear looked around.

He couldn't see the rabbit.

Slowly, the rabbit walked up to the bear.

He kept playing and the bear kept singing.

They were both happy that they had found a friend.

And a bird joined in the song.

Air

Air is all around us.

But we can't see it.

How do we know it is there?

There are many ways.

We can see what air does.

Moving air is called wind.

Wind moves plants.

Wind moves dirt.

Strong winds can move heavy things.

Strong winds can even move a house.

We can weigh air.

We can weigh two balloons.

The one with a lot of air weighs more.

We can see what air does.

We can weigh air.

Then we know it is there.

The Brain and the Five Senses

All people have five senses.

People have eyes, ears, a nose, a mouth, and hands.

Each of the senses is part of the brain.

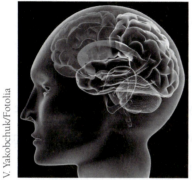

The brain makes the senses work.

People hear with their ears.

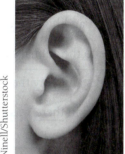

People see with their eyes.

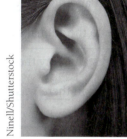

They smell with their noses.

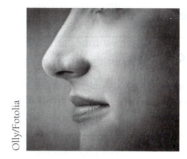

They taste with their mouths.

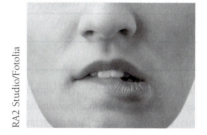

People touch things with their hands.

But, without the brain people would not see, hear, smell, taste, or touch.

The brain makes all our senses work.

Level: One

Number of Total Miscues
(Total Accuracy): _____

Number of Meaning-Change Miscues
(Total Acceptability): _____

Total Accuracy		Total Acceptability
0–6 miscues _____	Independent _____	0–6 miscues
7–27 miscues _____	Instructional _____	7–14 miscues
28+ miscues _____	Frustration _____	15+ miscues

Rate: 266 × 60 = 15, 960/_____ seconds = _____ WPM

WCPM: (266 _____ errors) × 60 = _____/ _____
_____ seconds = _____ WCPM

Oral Reading Prosody Scale—QRI-7

Directions: Please circle the number below that best represents the student's one-minute oral reading of this passage.

4	3	2	I
Reads primarily in larger, meaningful phrase groups. Some or most of the story is read with expression.	Reads primarily in three- or four-word phrase groups. Little or no expressive interpretation is present.	Reads primarily in two-word phrases with some three- or four-word groupings. Word groupings may be awkward.	Reads primarily word-by-word with occasional two-word or three-word phrases.

Retelling Scoring Sheet for "Marva Finds a Friend"

Setting/Background

____ One rainy day Marva heard a funny sound
____ She looked out and saw a little gray cat with white feet.
____ It was wet and it looked hungry.
____ Marva picked up the cat/or she brought the cat inside.
____ Mother gave the cat some food and the cat ate it all up!

Goal

____ Marva said, "I will name this cat Boots. I will take care of it."
____ "This cat may belong to somebody," her mother said.
____ Marva felt sad. "But I want you to be *my* cat."

Events

____ That night Mother looked in the newspaper.
____ She saw an ad that read, "Lost. Gray cat with white feet."
____ Marva started to cry, "But I want to keep Boots."
____ "We have to call the number," said her mother.
____ The next day a woman and a girl came to the house.
____ The girl cried, "That's my cat, Boots!"
____ The girl took Boots and she thanked Marva and her mother.

Resolution

____ The girl said, "Why don't you come over and play with Boots and me?"
____ Marva was sad to give up Boots, but she was happy that she'd made a new friend.
____ Marva's mother knew what to get Marva for her birthday.

Questions for "Marva Finds a Friend"

1. What did Marva find outside her window?
   Explicit: a cat

2. What did Marva's mother do with the cat?
   Explicit: dried it with a towel; *or* gave it some food

3. What did Marva want to do with the cat?
   Explicit: keep it

4. What did Marva's mother do after she looked in the newspaper?
   Implicit: called the phone number listed in the paper

5. What happened the next day?
   Explicit: the people that owned the cat came over and got the cat

6. How are Marva and the girl who owned the cat alike?
   Implicit: they both like cats; *or* they both named the cat Boots

Number Correct Explicit: _____

Number Correct Implicit: _____

Total: _____

_____ Independent: 6 correct

_____ Instructional: 4–5 correct

_____ Frustration: 0–3 correct

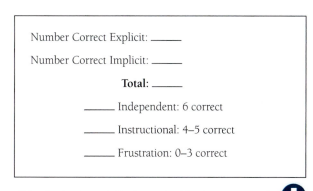

Level: One

3. What was the bear doing as he sat by the river?
   Explicit: singing

4. What did the rabbit think when he heard the bear singing?
   Explicit: that the bear must be nice; *or* he doesn't have to be afraid of him; *or* it would be nice to have a friend

5. What did the rabbit do?
   Explicit: went and got his horn; *or* played his horn

6. Why did the bear and the rabbit become friends?
   Implicit: because of their love of music

Number Correct Explicit: _____

Number Correct Implicit: _____

Total: _____

_____ Independent: 6 correct

_____ Instructional: 4–5 correct

_____ Frustration: 0–3 correct

Level: One

Expository

Note: Underlined words are on the primer or *first*-grade word lists.

Air

Air is all around us.

But we can't see it.

How do we know it is there?

There are many ways.

We can see what air does.

Moving air is called wind.

Wind moves plants.

Wind moves dirt.

Strong winds can move heavy things.

Strong winds can even move a house.

We can weigh air.

We can weigh two balloons.

The one with a lot of air weighs more.

We can see what air does.

We can weigh air.

Then we know it is there. (85 words)

Oral Reading Prosody Scale—QRI-7

Directions: Please circle the number below that best represents the student's one-minute oral reading of this passage.

4	3	2	1
Reads primarily in larger, meaningful phrase groups. Some or most of the story is read with expression.	Reads primarily in three- or four-word phrase groups. Little or no expressive interpretation is present.	Reads primarily in two-word phrases with some three- or four-word groupings. Word groupings may be awkward.	Reads primarily word-by-word with occasional two-word or three-word phrases.

Level I

Level: One

Retelling Scoring Sheet for "The Brain and the Five Senses"

____ All people have five senses.
____ People have eyes, ears, a nose,
____ a mouth, and hands.
____ Each of the senses is part of the brain.
____ The brain makes the senses work.
____ People hear with their ears.
____ People see with their eyes.
____ They smell with their noses.
____ They taste with their mouths.
____ People touch things with their hands.
____ But, without the brain people would not see, hear,
____ (people would not) taste, or smell, or touch.
____ The brain makes all our senses work.

Questions for "The Brain and the Five Senses"

1. Why is the brain important to the senses?
   Implicit: it makes the senses work

2. What do you use to taste things?
   Explicit: my mouth

3. Name one of the senses.
   Explicit: seeing, hearing, smelling, tasting, or touching

4. Name another one of the senses.
   Explicit: seeing, hearing, smelling, tasting, or touching (depending on what was said in response to #3.)

5. What would happen to the senses if the brain wasn't working right?
   Implicit: they wouldn't work right, either

6. Name another one of the senses.
   Explicit: seeing, hearing, smelling, tasting, or touching (depending on what was said in response to #3 and #4)

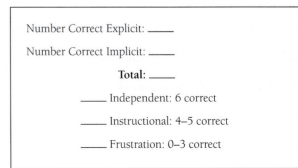

Number Correct Explicit: _____

Number Correct Implicit: _____

Total: _____

____ Independent: 6 correct

____ Instructional: 4–5 correct

____ Frustration: 0–3 correct

The Family's First Trip

Thomas lived in a small town with only 2,000 people. It was June 12th and Thomas was excited. His family was planning a trip to Atlanta to visit his aunt. Unlike his hometown, Atlanta is a big city. Thomas had never traveled to a big city before. He had to decide what to bring. It was a two day car trip. So he needed to take along things to keep him busy in the car. He was reading a book and decided to bring it. But he realized that he couldn't read all the time in the car. If he read too much he would get dizzy. He had to think of something that wouldn't use his eyes. He decided to bring his iPad.

Thomas knew that they would be going out to dinner. Another night they were going to a country music show. He brought long pants and a shirt for going out to dinner. But the music show would be outside. He brought a pair of shorts and a T-shirt for that. He had enough clothes, books, and his iPad. What else did he need? He almost forgot his toothbrush and pajamas! He would have been embarrassed if he had forgotten them!

The first day of driving went quickly for Thomas as he read his book and listened to music. His parents were looking for a hotel to stay in. Thomas and his sister begged their parents to find a place with a swimming pool. Luckily they had remembered to pack their swimming suits. Their parents found a small hotel with a heated pool. Thomas and his sister got in their suits and spent an hour in the pool before dinner. The first part of their trip was fun. They looked forward to seeing their aunt the next day.

Mary and Susan came out of their room. They didn't see anything to play with. They thought that their father had forgotten to think of a new game for them to play. Then Susan noticed a piece of paper on the floor. She picked it up and read it aloud. "I'm cold but I give off heat. I'm light when I'm open but dark when I'm closed. What am I? Open me and you'll find the next clue." The girls walked around their house thinking. They came into the kitchen and looked around. "That's it!" yelled Mary. "The refrigerator!" She opened the door and found the next clue taped to the inside of the door. The girls were off again in search of the next clue. After an hour they had found five clues. The person who had fixed the washer was just leaving as Susan found the last clue. It read, "Nice job, girls. Let's go to a movie!"

Whales and Fish

Whales and fish both live in the water, but they are different in many ways. Whales are large animals that live in the water. Even though whales live in the water, they must come to the top of the water to get air. When they come to the top of the water, whales breathe in air through a hole in the top of their heads. At the same time, they blow out old air. Whales don't get air like fish. Fish take in air from the water.

Mother whales give birth to live whales. The baby whale must come to the top of the water right away for air. The baby drinks milk from its mother for about a year. Then it finds its own food. Fish have babies in a different way. Most mother fish lay eggs. The babies are born when the eggs hatch. Right after they are born, the baby fish must find their own food.

Whales and fish are alike in some ways too. Whales and fish have flippers on their sides. They also have fins on their tails. Flippers and fins help whales and fish swim. Fins move and push the water away.

Level: Two

Resolution

___ "I did save her!" said the cricket.
___ "If I hadn't jumped on her she would have picked up the stone with the snake.
___ Maybe I am lucky after all."

Questions for "The Lucky Cricket"

1. Where did the story take place?
   Explicit: in a garden

2. At the beginning of the story, why did Ling-Ling keep the cricket she found?
   Explicit: because she thought it would bring her luck

3. Why did Ling-Ling think that the cricket was lucky after she'd seen the crane?
   Implicit: it looked at her for a long time; it nodded its head at her; it seemed to communicate with her; *or* she thought it came to her because of the cricket

4. Why did the cricket want to get away from Ling-Ling?
   Implicit: because he didn't think he was lucky

5. What did Ling-Ling see when she sat on the bridge?
   Explicit: a goldfish

6. Why did Ling-Ling want to pick up the shiny stone in the water?
   Explicit: she wanted to give it to her grandmother

7. How did the cricket surprise Ling-Ling when she reached to pick up the stone?
   Implicit: he jumped out of her pocket and landed on her neck

8. Why did the cricket decide at the end that he was lucky after all?
   Implicit: he thought that maybe he was lucky because he had saved her from picking up the snake

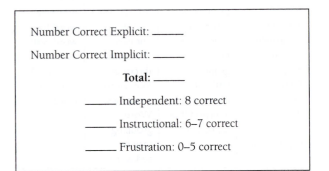

Number Correct Explicit: _____

Number Correct Implicit: _____

Total: _____

_____ Independent: 8 correct

_____ Instructional: 6–7 correct

_____ Frustration: 0–5 correct

Level: Two

Narrative

Note: Underlined words are on the first-grade or second-grade word lists.

Father's New Game

It was a cold winter day. Too cold for Mary and Susan to go outside. They wanted something interesting to do. They went to their father and asked if he would take them to a movie. He said, "I'm sorry, girls. Someone is coming to see why the washer isn't working. If you'll play by yourselves for a while, I'll think of a new game for you. But you must promise to stay in your room until I call you."

"OK," said Mary and Susan.

Father wrote notes on pieces of paper and left them around the house. Each note gave a clue as to where to find the next note. Just as the person came to look at the washer, Father called to them. "Mary, Susan, you can come out now!" Then he went into the basement. Mary and Susan came out of their room. They didn't see anything to play with. They thought that their father had forgotten to think of a new game for them to play. Then Susan noticed a piece of paper on the floor. She picked it up and read it aloud. "I'm cold but I give off heat. I'm light when I'm open but dark when I'm closed. What am I? Open me and you'll find the next clue." The girls walked around their house thinking. They came into the kitchen and looked around. "That's it!" yelled Mary. "The refrigerator!" She opened the door and found the next clue taped to the inside of the door. The girls were off again in search for the next clue. After an hour they had found five clues. The person who had fixed the washer was just leaving as Susan found the last clue. It read, "Nice job, girls. Let's go to a movie!" (298 words)

Level 2

A New Friend from Europe

Mrs. Wagner was reading a story to her fifth-grade class. While Joseph listened carefully, he also watched the new boy. Ivan looked sad and confused and Joseph could understand why. Mrs. Wagner had introduced Ivan to the class about a week ago. Ivan was from a country in Europe. It had a very long name that Joseph found hard to pronounce. Ivan's parents were both dead and he had spent most of his life in an orphanage. Then Mr. and Mrs. Mayer adopted him and brought him to America. Mrs. Wagner explained that Ivan did not speak English, but she was sure he would learn it very soon. No wonder Ivan looked sad and confused. Joseph would feel that way if he could not understand the story that Mrs. Wagner was reading.

Joseph wanted to make friends with Ivan, but he didn't know how to do this if Ivan could not understand English. That night, Joseph asked his parents what he should do. Father thought a bit and then he answered, "You know, Joseph, words are not the only way to communicate with people. You can let Ivan know you want to be friends by the look on your face and the gestures you make. You can share things with Ivan such as a special treat from your lunch or perhaps a toy."

Joseph thought about this when he went to bed. Before he fell asleep, he had a plan. Joseph loved trains. He had played with toy trains since he was a baby. He had his own model train set and he had many books about trains. The next morning, Joseph chose his favorite book. It had beautifully colored pictures of trains from the first steam engines to the sleek modern diesel engines of today. Joseph also liked to draw trains and he tucked one of his pictures between the pages of the book.

After lunch, Joseph walked toward Ivan who, as usual, was sitting alone on the playground. When Ivan looked up, Joseph smiled. He sat down next to Ivan, pointed to himself, and said, "I'm Joseph." Then he took the train book out of his backpack. He placed it on Ivan's knees and slowly began to turn the pages. Ivan seemed very interested and once, he put his hand over Joseph's to stop him from turning the page. Ivan looked for a long time at a picture of a silver streamliner crossing a bridge over a deep ravine. When he came to Joseph's drawing, he pointed at Joseph. His whole expression indicated that he was asking if Joseph drew the picture. Joseph nodded and Ivan smiled.

The next day, it was raining heavily. Joseph knew that the class would spend recess indoors. So, he added something new to his backpack. When lunch was over, Joseph walked over to Ivan who seemed glad to see him. Joseph took out his drawing tablet and his set of colored pencils. Then he opened the train book to the picture of the streamliner and began to draw the engine. Ivan watched closely. After a bit, Joseph handed the tablet to Ivan and held out the pencils.

Ivan paused for a second. Then he took a pencil and continued the drawing. The boys worked together to draw and color the silver streamliner. When they were finished, Joseph made a sharp forward motion with his arm and said "Whoosh!" to indicate that the train went fast. Ivan made the same motion. "It goes fast," said Joseph. "Fast," Ivan repeated, and both boys laughed.

Cats: Lions and Tigers in Your House

House cats, lions, and tigers are part of the same family. When animals are part of the same family, they are alike in many ways. House cats are like lions and tigers in many ways, too. When kittens are first born, they drink milk from their mothers. Lions and tigers drink milk from their mothers, too. When kittens are born, they have claws, just like big cats. Claws are used by lions, tigers, and kittens to help them keep away enemies. As kittens get bigger, they learn to hunt from their mother. House cats hunt in the same way that lions and tigers do. They hide and lie very still. When the animal they are hunting comes close, they jump on it and grab it by the back of the neck. Cats kill other animals by shaking them and breaking their necks.

Lions, tigers, and house cats show when they are afraid in the same ways, too. Their fur puffs up, making them look bigger. They hiss and spit, too. Those are their ways of saying, "I'm afraid, don't come closer."

A cat's tongue has many uses. Because it is rough with little bumps on it, it can be used as a spoon. A cat drinks milk by lapping it. Because of the bumps, the milk stays on the tongue until the cat can swallow it. If you feel the top of a cat's tongue, it is rough. This makes the tongue good for brushing the cat's hair. Lions and tigers clean themselves with their tongues just like house cats do.

Where Do People Live?

People live in different places. Some people live in a city. Others live in the country. Still other people live in between the city and the country. They live in suburbs. Why do people live in these different places?

People live in the city to be near their jobs. Cities have lots of factories, schools, and offices. People work in these buildings. If people don't want to drive a long way to their jobs, they live in the city. There are many other things to do in the city. Cities have museums and zoos. They also have many movie theaters.

People live in the country to be close to their jobs, too. Many people who live in the country are farmers. They plant crops on their land. They may sell their crops or may use them to feed the animals that live on the farm. Farmers raise cows, pigs, and chickens. The main food that these animals eat is grain. There are other things to do in the country. You can find a river to fish in or take walks in the woods. Life in the country is quiet.

Some people live in between the country and the city. They live in suburbs. Some people think that people who live in the suburbs have the best of both worlds. They live close to their jobs in the city. The suburbs are quieter than the city. They often have many movie theaters, too. It doesn't take as long to go to either the city or the country. The suburbs are more crowded than the country but less crowded than the city. Where people live depends upon what they like most.

Wool: From Sheep to You

Do you have a sweater? Do you know what it is made from? One fiber used to make sweaters is wool. Do you know where wool comes from? It comes from a sheep. However, many things must be done before the wool on a sheep can be woven or knitted to make clothing for you.

First, the wool must be removed from the sheep. People shear the wool off the sheep with electric clippers somewhat like a barber uses when he gives haircuts. Like our hair, the sheep's wool will grow back again. Most sheep are shorn only once a year. After the wool is removed, it must be washed very carefully to get out all the dirt. When the locks of wool dry, they are combed or carded to make all the fibers lie in the same direction. It is somewhat like combing or brushing your hair. Then the wool is formed into fine strands. These can be spun to make yarn. The yarn is knitted or woven into fabric. The fabric is made into clothing.

Yarn can also be used to knit sweaters by hand. Sweaters made from wool are very warm. They help keep you warm even when they are damp. Just think, the sweater you wear on a winter day may once have been on a sheep.

Level: Three

Narrative

Concept Questions:

What does "celebration" mean? *(3: to have an event because someone is joyful about something; 2: a party; Cinco de Mayo; birthday; 1: have a cake)*

_____

_____

_____ (3-2-1-0)

What does it mean for you to miss someone? *(3: that you want to be with them; you long for them; 2: I miss my grandma, or another person; 1: the ball doesn't hit them)*

_____

_____

_____ (3-2-1-0)

If you are sad, how can someone cheer you up? *(3: by being with you or doing something fun with you; by comforting you; 2: by playing _____ [student names a particular sport/ game]; by telling jokes; 1: funny)*

_____

_____

_____ (3-2-1-0)

How many candles are on a birthday cake? *(3: as many as the years you've lived/as many years you are old; 2: student gives an example like "7"; 1: light)*

_____

_____

_____ (3-2-1-0)

Score: _____/12 = _____%

_____ FAM (≥ 55%) _____ UNFAM

Note: Underlined words are on the second-grade or third-grade word lists.

A Special Birthday for Rosa

Today was the day Rosa had eagerly been waiting for, her birthday! She was very happy, but she also felt sad. This would be the first birthday that she would <u>celebrate</u> without all her family around her. The company that Rosa's father worked for had given him a wonderful promotion. But this meant that Rosa, her parents, and her little brother, Jóse, had to move to another state. Rosa liked her new home and friends. But she really wanted to <u>celebrate</u> her birthday with her grandparents, aunts, uncles, and cousins all around her.

They had sent presents, but it wouldn't be the same if she couldn't thank them in person. They wouldn't be there to watch her blow out all the candles. And what kind of a birthday would it be without listening to her grandparents' stories about growing up in Italy and Cuba? Also, four people could never sing as loudly or joyfully as her whole family could sing together!

That night, Mama made Rosa's favorite meal. Afterward, there was a beautiful cake. Mama, Papa, and Jose sang "Happy Birthday" while the eight candles <u>glowed</u>. Rosa made a wish, took a deep breath, and blew out all the candles. "I know I

Level: Three

won't get what I wished for," she said to herself, "but I'm going to wish for it anyway."

Then it was time for the presents. Rosa's father had connected his computer to their TV. He turned on his computer and typed in a Skype number. Suddenly, there on the television screen was the rest of Rosa's family smiling and waving and wishing her a happy birthday. One by one, each person asked Rosa to open the present they had sent. Then they <u>explained</u> why they had chosen that gift especially for Rosa. After all the presents were unwrapped, her family sang some favorite songs and Rosa, her mother, father, and Jóse joined in.

Then, Rosa's grandfather spoke to her. "Rosa, this is a new story, one you have never heard before. I am going to tell it to you as a special birthday gift. It is about my first birthday in this country when I was very lonely for my friends and family. It is about how I met your grandmother." When Grandfather was <u>finished</u>, he and Grandmother blew Rosa a kiss and the family said goodbye.

Rosa felt wonderful. It was almost like having her family in the room with her. Rosa hugged her

parents and her little brother. "I didn't think I would get my wish, but I did," she said. That night, when Mama and Papa came to say goodnight to Rosa, they found her in bed, already asleep. It had been the best birthday ever. (452 words)

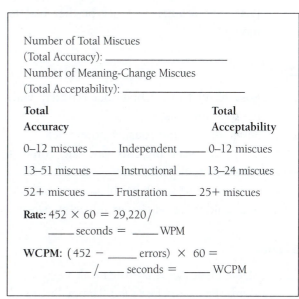

Number of Total Miscues
(Total Accuracy): _____
Number of Meaning-Change Miscues
(Total Acceptability): _____

Total Accuracy			**Total Acceptability**
0–12 miscues _____	Independent	_____	0–12 miscues
13–51 miscues _____	Instructional	_____	13–24 miscues
52+ miscues _____	Frustration	_____	25+ miscues

Rate: $452 \times 60 = 29,220/$
_____ seconds = _____ WPM

WCPM: $(452 -$ _____ errors$) \times 60 =$
_____ / _____ seconds = _____ WCPM

Oral Reading Prosody Scale—QRI-7

Directions: Please circle the number below that best represents the student's three-minute oral reading of this passage.

4	3	2	I
Reads primarily in larger, meaningful phrase groups. Some or most of the story is read with expression.	Reads primarily in three- or four-word phrase groups. Little or no expressive interpretation is present.	Reads primarily in two-word phrases with some three- or four-word groupings. Word groupings may be awkward.	Reads primarily word-by-word with occasional two-word or three-word phrases.

Level 3

Level: Three

Retelling Scoring Sheet for "A Special Birthday for Rosa"

Setting/Background

_____ Today was Rosa's birthday.

_____ She was happy, but she also felt sad.

_____ This would be the first birthday she would celebrate without all her family

_____ Rosa, her parents, and her brother had to move.

Goal

_____ Rosa wanted to celebrate her birthday with her grandparents,

_____ aunts, uncles, and cousins around her.

_____ They had sent presents but she couldn't thank them in person.

_____ They wouldn't watch her blow out candles.

_____ She couldn't listen to her grandparents' stories.

Events

_____ Mama made Rosa's favorite meal.

_____ Mama, Papa, and Jóse sang "Happy Birthday."

_____ Rosa made a wish.

_____ "I know I won't get it," she said to herself, "but I'm going to wish for it anyway."

_____ She blew out all the candles.

_____ Rosa's father turned on his computer and typed in a Skype number.

_____ On the television screen was the rest of Rosa's family smiling and waving

_____ and wishing her a happy birthday.

_____ Each person asked Rosa to open the present they sent.

_____ They explained why they chose that gift for Rosa.

_____ Her family sang favorite songs and Rosa, her mother, her father, and Jóse joined in.

_____ Grandfather spoke to Rosa.

_____ "This is a new story; one you have never heard before.

_____ I am going to tell it as a special birthday gift.

_____ It's about my first birthday in this country when I was very lonely.

_____ It is about how I met your grandmother."

_____ When Grandfather was finished, he and Grandmother blew Rosa a kiss.

Resolution

_____ Rosa felt wonderful.

_____ "I didn't think I would get my wish but I did," she said.

_____ When Mama and Papa came to say goodnight,

_____ they found Rosa already asleep.

Questions for "A Special Birthday for Rosa"

1. The story took place on what day?
   Explicit: Rosa's birthday

2. At the beginning of the story, what was Rosa's problem?
   Implicit: she would not be celebrating her birthday with her whole family

Level: Three

3. How old was Rosa on this birthday?
Implicit: eight

4. What did Rosa wish for before she blew out the candles?
Implicit: that she would be able to spend her birthday with her whole family

5. What was on the iPad?
Explicit: the rest of Rosa's family wishing her a happy birthday

6. What special birthday gift did her grandfather give her?
Explicit: he told her a story about when he came to the United States and how he met her grandmother

7. How did the Skype call help to solve Rosa's problem?
Implicit: it brought her family to her; *or* it helped her miss her family less

8. What was Rosa doing at the end of the story when her parents came to say goodnight?
Explicit: sleeping

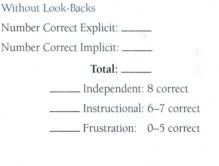

Without Look-Backs

Number Correct Explicit: _____

Number Correct Implicit: _____

Total: _____

_____ Independent: 8 correct

_____ Instructional: 6–7 correct

_____ Frustration: 0–5 correct

With Look-Backs

Number Correct Explicit: _____

Number Correct Implicit: _____

Total: _____

_____ Independent: 8 correct

_____ Instructional: 6–7 correct

_____ Frustration: 0–5 correct

Level 3

Level: Three

Narrative

Note: Underlined words are on the second-grade or third-grade word lists.

The Friend

Once upon a time there was a boy named Mark. Mark loved to go to the ocean and play his flute. One day he was playing his flute when a school of dolphins swam by. They leaped in the air every 30 seconds. Mark could almost predict when they would leap again. He watched them for a long time because he was so <u>interested</u> in their play. That day he decided that he wanted to learn more about dolphins. Mark went to the library.

The next weekend he took a boat and rowed out about as far as he had seen the dolphins before. He started playing his flute, trying to mimic the pulsed sounds he had heard on tapes of dolphin sounds. He had learned that they make two kinds of pulsed sounds. One kind is called sonar and is used to locate dolphins and objects. The other kind of sound is a burst pulse that tells the emotional state of the dolphin. Mark was trying to mimic sonar. Soon, about 400 yards away, he saw the roll of the dolphins. The boat bounced in the waves as the dolphins came closer. They seemed to be <u>curious</u> about the sounds coming from the boat. Suddenly, the boat tipped sharply, and Mark fell out. Somehow, he held on to his flute. Mark was a good swimmer, but he was too far from land to swim. The only thing to do was to try to mimic the sound of a dolphin in trouble. Maybe then the dolphins would help him to land. Kicking strongly, he kept himself up above the water. He blew high, burst pulse sounds. Just when he was about to go under water, he felt a <u>push</u> against his leg. Again,

Level: Three

and again a dolphin <u>pushed</u> him. She managed to keep his face above water as she gently <u>pushed</u> him to shore. Mark couldn't <u>believe</u> what was happening. He got safely to shore, although the boat was never seen again. As he sat on the beach, still shaking from fear, he realized that he had reached his goal. He had surely learned a lot about dolphins that day! (360 words)

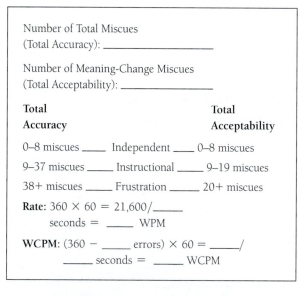

Number of Total Miscues
(Total Accuracy): _____

Number of Meaning-Change Miscues
(Total Acceptability): _____

Total Accuracy		Total Acceptability
0–8 miscues _____	Independent	_____ 0–8 miscues
9–37 miscues _____	Instructional	_____ 9–19 miscues
38+ miscues _____	Frustration	_____ 20+ miscues

Rate: $360 \times 60 = 21{,}600/$_____
seconds = _____ WPM

WCPM: $(360 -$ _____ errors$) \times 60 =$ _____$/$
_____ seconds = _____ WCPM

Oral Reading Prosody Scale—*QRI-7*

Directions: Please circle the number below that best represents the student's three-minute oral reading of this passage.

4	3	2	1
Reads primarily in larger, meaningful phrase groups. Some or most of the story is read with expression.	Reads primarily in three- or four-word phrase groups. Little or no expressive interpretation is present.	Reads primarily in two-word phrases with some three- or four-word groupings. Word groupings may be awkward.	Reads primarily word-by-word with occasional two-word or three-word phrases.

Retelling Scoring Sheet for "The Friend"

Setting/Background

_____ There was a boy named Mark.
_____ Mark loved to go to the ocean and play his flute.
_____ A school of dolphins swam by.
_____ They leaped every 30 seconds.

Goal

_____ Mark wanted to learn more about dolphins.

Events

_____ Mark went to the library.
_____ The next weekend he took a boat and rowed out where he had seen the dolphins.
_____ He played his flute to mimic the sounds of dolphins.
_____ One sound is sonar, which is used to locate things.
_____ Another kind is a burst pulse that tells how the dolphin feels.
_____ Mark saw the roll of the dolphins.
_____ The boat bounced in the waves as the dolphins came closer.
_____ The boat tipped, and Mark fell out.
_____ Mark was a good swimmer, but he was too far from land.
_____ He tried to mimic the sound of a dolphin in trouble
_____ so the dolphins would help him.
_____ Kicking strongly, he kept himself above water.
_____ A dolphin pushed him to shore.

Resolution

_____ He got safely to shore.
_____ He realized he had learned a lot about dolphins.

Level 3

Level: Three

Questions for "The Friend"

1. What instrument did Mark play?
   Explicit: the flute

2. Where did Mark go to learn more about dolphins?
   Explicit: the library

3. How did Mark learn about the dolphin sounds?
   Implicit: he read about them; *or* he listened to tapes
   If the student says, "He went to the library," ask, "How did that help him learn about dolphins?"

4. What two kinds of sounds do dolphins make?
   Explicit: sonar, or sounds to locate objects, and burst pulse, or sounds to indicate emotions

5. Why was Mark trying to mimic sonar?
   Implicit: to see if the dolphins would come to him

6. Why did the boat tip over?
   Implicit: the dolphins came close enough to cause waves

7. What did Mark do to save himself?
   Implicit: he tried to make a burst pulse sound like a dolphin in trouble, hoping a dolphin would come to help him
   If the student says, "He kicked strongly," ask, "What other thing did Mark do?"

8. How did Mark get to shore?
   Explicit: a dolphin pushed him to shore

Without Look-Backs

Number Correct Explicit: _____

Number Correct Implicit: _____

Total: _____

_____ Independent: 8 correct

_____ Instructional: 6–7 correct

_____ Frustration: 0–5 correct

With Look-Backs

Number Correct Explicit: _____

Number Correct Implicit: _____

Total: _____

_____ Independent: 8 correct

_____ Instructional: 6–7 correct

_____ Frustration: 0–5 correct

Level 3

Level: Three

Note: Underlined words are on the second-grade or third-grade word lists.

A New Friend from Europe

Mrs. Wagner was reading a story to her fifth-grade class. While Joseph listened carefully, he also watched the new boy. Ivan looked sad and confused and Joseph could understand why. Mrs. Wagner had introduced Ivan to the class about a week ago. Ivan was from a country in Europe. It had a very long name that Joseph found hard to pronounce. Ivan's parents were both dead and he had spent most of his life in an orphanage. Then Mr. and Mrs. Mayer adopted him and brought him to America. Mrs. Wagner explained that Ivan did not speak English, but she was sure he would learn it very soon. No wonder Ivan looked sad and confused. Joseph would feel that way if he could not understand the story that Mrs. Wagner was reading.

Joseph wanted to make friends with Ivan, but he didn't know how to do this if Ivan could not understand English. That night, Joseph asked his parents what he should do. Father thought a bit and then he answered, "You know, Joseph, words are not the only way to communicate with people. You can let Ivan know you want to be friends by the look on your face and the gestures you make. You can share things with Ivan such as a special treat from your lunch or perhaps a toy."

Joseph thought about this when he went to bed. Before he fell asleep, he had a plan. Joseph loved trains. He had played with toy trains since he was a baby. He had his own model train set and he

Level 3

Level: Three

_____ Joseph took out his drawing tablet and his set of colored pencils.

_____ Then he opened the train book to the picture of the streamliner

_____ and began to draw the engine.

_____ Ivan watched closely.

_____ Joseph handed the tablet to Ivan and held out the pencils.

_____ Ivan took a pencil and continued the drawing.

_____ The boys worked together to draw and color the silver streamliner.

_____ Joseph made a motion with his arm and said "Whoosh!" to show that the train went fast.

_____ "It goes fast," said Joseph.

_____ "Fast," Ivan repeated, and both boys laughed.

Questions for "A New Friend from Europe"

1. What was one of the reasons why Ivan might have looked sad?
   Implicit: he had moved to a new country; _or_ he didn't know anyone; _or_ his parents were dead; _or_ he was raised in an orphanage; _or_ he didn't understand what the teacher was saying

2. What did Joseph want?
   Explicit: to be friends with Ivan

3. Why was it difficult for Joseph to become friends with Ivan?
   Explicit: Ivan didn't speak English

4. How did Joseph's father help his son solve his problem?
   Implicit: he gave him suggestions about how to communicate with Ivan

5. What did Joseph bring to school the first time to show Ivan?
   Explicit: book of trains _or_ his drawing of a train

6. How do we know that Ivan was interested in becoming friends with Joseph?
   Implicit: his facial expressions changed; _or_ he smiled at Joseph

7. What did Joseph begin to draw at recess the second day?
   Explicit: the streamliner

8. What did Joseph do at the end of the story to help Ivan learn English?
   Implicit: he said "whoosh" and used gestures, then said the word "fast," which Ivan repeated

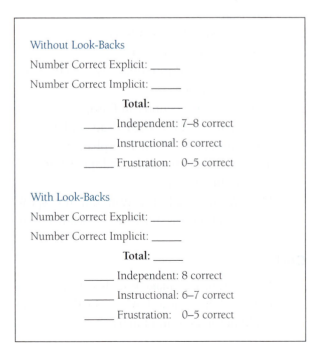

Without Look-Backs

Number Correct Explicit: _____

Number Correct Implicit: _____

      Total: _____

_____ Independent: 7–8 correct

_____ Instructional: 6 correct

_____ Frustration: 0–5 correct

With Look-Backs

Number Correct Explicit: _____

Number Correct Implicit: _____

      Total: _____

_____ Independent: 8 correct

_____ Instructional: 6–7 correct

_____ Frustration: 0–5 correct

Level 3

Level: Three

Expository

Note: Underlined words are on the second-grade or third-grade word lists.

Cats: Lions and Tigers in Your House

House cats, lions, and tigers are part of the same family. When animals are part of the same family, they are alike in many ways. House cats are like lions and tigers in many ways, too. When kittens are first born, they drink milk from their mothers. Lions and tigers drink milk from their mothers, too. When kittens are born, they have claws just like big cats. Claws are used by lions, tigers, and kittens to help them keep away <u>enemies.</u> As kittens get bigger, they learn to hunt from their mother. House cats hunt in the same way that lions and tigers do. They hide and lie very still. When the animal they are hunting comes close, they jump on it and grab it by the back of the neck. Cats kill other animals by shaking them and breaking their necks.

Lions, tigers, and house cats show when they are afraid in the same ways, too. Their fur puffs up, making them look bigger. They hiss and spit, too. Those are their ways of saying, "I'm afraid, don't come closer."

A cat's <u>tongue</u> has many uses. Because it is <u>rough</u> with little bumps on it, it can be used as a spoon. A cat drinks milk by lapping it. Because of the bumps, the milk stays on the <u>tongue</u> until the cat can swallow it. If you feel the top of a cat's <u>tongue</u>, it is <u>rough</u>. This makes the tongue good for brushing the cat's hair. Lions and tigers clean themselves with their <u>tongues</u> just like house cats do. (261 words)

Level: Three

Number of Total Miscues
(Total Accuracy): _____

Number of Meaning-Change Miscues
(Total Acceptability): _____

Total Accuracy		Total Acceptability
0–6 miscues _____	Independent _____	0–6 miscues
7–27 miscues _____	Instructional _____	7–14 miscues
28+ miscues _____	Frustration _____	15+ miscues

Rate: 261 × 60 = 15,660/_____
    seconds = _____ WPM

WCPM: (261 − ____ errors) × 60 = _____ /
    _____ seconds = _____ WCPM

Oral Reading Prosody Scale—QRI-7

Directions: Please circle the number below that best represents the student's three-minute oral reading of this passage.

4	3	2	1
Reads primarily in larger, meaningful phrase groups. Some or most of the story is read with expression.	Reads primarily in three- or four-word phrase groups. Little or no expressive interpretation is present.	Reads primarily in two-word phrases with some three- or four-word groupings. Word groupings may be awkward.	Reads primarily word-by-word with occasional two-word or three-word phrases.

Retelling Scoring Sheet for "Cats: Lions and Tigers in Your House"

Main Idea

____ Cats, lions, and tigers are part of the same family.
____ They are alike in many ways.

Details

____ When kittens are first born, they drink milk from their mothers.
____ Lions and tigers drink milk from their mothers.
____ Kittens have claws.

____ Lions, tigers, and kittens use claws to keep away enemies.
____ Cats hunt in the same way that lions and tigers do.
____ They jump on the animal
____ and grab it by the neck.
____ Cats kill animals by breaking their necks.
____ When lions, tigers, and cats are afraid, their fur puffs up.
____ They hiss and spit.
____ Because a cat's tongue is rough with bumps,
____ it can be used as a spoon.
____ A cat drinks milk by lapping it.
____ Because of the bumps,
____ the milk stays on the tongue until the cat can swallow it.
____ Lions and tigers clean themselves
____ with their tongues just like cats.

Questions for "Cats: Lions and Tigers in Your House"

1. What is this passage mostly about?
   Implicit: that cats, lions, and tigers are alike in many ways

2. How are lions, tigers, and cats alike?
   Explicit: any one of the ways presented in the story: milk from their mothers as babies; they have claws; the way they hunt; the way they show fear; *or* the uses of their tongues

Level: Three

3. What is another way that lions, tigers, and cats are alike?
   Explicit: any other of the above responses

4. What is still another way that lions, tigers, and cats are alike?
   Explicit: any other of the above responses

5. What does a cat do when it is scared or trapped in a corner?
   Implicit: it hisses, spits, or puffs up

6. Why is it important for cats to have claws when they're born?
   Implicit: for protection from their enemies

7. Why is the top of a cat's tongue rough?
   Implicit: because of the bumps on it; *or* so it can drink

8. Why doesn't milk fall off a cat's tongue?
   Explicit: because of the bumps that make cups on the tongue

Level 3

Level: Three

Expository

Note: Underlined words are on the second-grade or third-grade word lists.

Where Do People Live?

People live in different places. Some people live in a city. Others live in the country. Still other people live in between the city and the country. They live in suburbs. Why do people live in these different places?

People live in the city to be near their jobs. Cities have lots of factories, schools, and offices. People work in these buildings. If people don't want to drive a long way to their jobs, they live in the city. There are many other things to do in the city. Cities have museums and zoos. They also have many movie theaters.

People live in the country to be close to their jobs, too. Many people who live in the country are farmers. They plant crops on their land. They may sell their crops or may use them to feed the animals that live on the farm. Farmers raise cows, pigs, and chickens. The main food that these animals eat is grain. There are other things to do in the country. You can find a river to fish in or take walks in the woods. Life in the country is quiet.

Some people live in between the country and the city. They live in suburbs. Some people think that people who live in the suburbs have the best of both worlds. They live close to their jobs in the city. The suburbs are quieter than the city. They often have many movie theaters, too. It doesn't take as long to go to either the city or the country. The suburbs are more crowded than the country but less crowded than the city. Where people live depends upon what they like most. (279 words)

Level: Three

Number of Total Miscues
(Total Accuracy): _____

Number of Meaning-Change Miscues
(Total Acceptability): _____

Total Accuracy		Total Acceptability
0–6 miscues _____	Independent _____	0–6 miscues
7–28 miscues _____	Instructional _____	7–14 miscues
29+ miscues _____	Frustration _____	15+ miscues

Rate: 279 × 60 = 16,740 / _____ seconds = _____ WPM

Correct WPM: (279 − ____ errors) × 60 = _____ /
_____ seconds = _____ WCPM

Oral Reading Prosody Scale—QRI-7

Directions: Please circle the number below that best represents the student's three-minute oral reading of this passage.

4	3	2	1
Reads primarily in larger, meaningful phrase groups. Some or most of the story is read with expression.	Reads primarily in three- or four-word phrase groups. Little or no expressive interpretation is present.	Reads primarily in two-word phrases with some three- or four-word groupings. Word groupings may be awkward.	Reads primarily word-by-word with occasional two-word or three-word phrases.

Retelling Scoring Sheet for "Where Do People Live?"

Main Idea
_____ People live in different places.

Details
_____ Some people live in the city.
_____ Others live in the country.
_____ Others live in the suburbs.

Main Idea
_____ People live in the city to be near their jobs.

Details
_____ Cities have factories, schools, and offices.
_____ People work in these buildings.
_____ There are many things to do in the city.
_____ Cities have museums and zoos.
_____ They have movie theaters.

Main Idea
_____ People live in the country to be close to their jobs.

Details
_____ Many people are farmers.
_____ They plant crops.
_____ Farmers raise cows, pigs, and chickens.
_____ These animals eat grain.
_____ There are other things to do in the country.
_____ You can find a river to fish in
_____ or take walks in the woods.
_____ Life in the country is quiet.

Main Idea
_____ Some people think that people who live in the suburbs have the best of both worlds.

Details
_____ They live close to their jobs in the city.
_____ The suburbs are quieter than the city.
_____ The suburbs are more crowded than the country
_____ but less crowded than the city.

Questions for "Where Do People Live?"

1. What is this passage mostly about?
   Implicit: why people live where they do

Level 3

Level: Three

Number of Total Miscues
(Total Accuracy): _____

Number of Meaning-Change Miscues
(Total Acceptability): _____

Total Accuracy				**Total Acceptability**
0–5 miscues	_____	Independent	_____	0–5 miscues
6–23 miscues	_____	Instructional	_____	6–12 miscues
24+ miscues	_____	Frustration	_____	13+ miscues

Rate: 221 × 60 = 13,260/_____ seconds = _____ WPM

WCPM: (221 − _____ errors) × 60 = _____/
_____ seconds = _____ WCPM

Oral Reading Prosody Scale—QRI-7

Directions: Please circle the number below that best represents the student's three-minute oral reading of this passage.

4	3	2	1
Reads primarily in larger, meaningful phrase groups. Some or most of the story is read with expression.	Reads primarily in three- or four-word phrase groups. Little or no expressive interpretation is present.	Reads primarily in two-word phrases with some three- or four-word groupings. Word groupings may be awkward.	Reads primarily word-by-word with occasional two-word or three-word phrases.

Retelling Scoring Sheet for "Wool: From Sheep to You"

Main Idea

_____ Many things have to be done before wool can be woven or knitted to make clothing.

Details

_____ Wool is a fiber that comes from a sheep and is used to make sweaters.

_____ The wool must be removed from the sheep.

_____ People shear the wool off the sheep with electric clippers.

_____ The wool will grow back again.

_____ Most sheep are shorn once a year.

_____ After the wool is removed, it must be washed to get out the dirt.

_____ When the locks are dry, they are combed to make the fibers lie in the same direction.

_____ It is like combing or brushing your hair.

_____ Then the wool is formed into strands that can be spun to make yarn.

_____ The yarn is knitted or woven into fabric.

_____ The fabric is made into clothing and knitted into sweaters.

_____ Sweaters made from wool are very warm even when they are damp.

Questions for "Wool: From Sheep to You"

1. What is this passage mainly about?
   Implicit: how wool is made; *or* what you do to wool in order to use it

2. What is the first step in the making of wool?
   Explicit: cutting it off the sheep

Level: Three

3. What do people use to cut wool off sheep?
Explicit: electric clippers; electric scissors; electric shears (*electric* must be in the answer)

4. Why can sheep give wool for many years?
Implicit: because it grows back after it is cut off

5. What is done to the wool after it is washed and dried?
Explicit: it is combed

6. What happens to wool fibers after they are combed?
Explicit: the fibers lie in the same direction

7. What different things can people do with the wool yarn?
Implicit: knit; weave into fabric; make into clothing

8. Why would it be good to wear a wool sweater out in the snow?
Implicit: it will keep you warm even when it's damp.
Note: If the student omits the idea of dampness and says only, "It will keep you warm," ask, "Why would it be especially warm in the snow?"

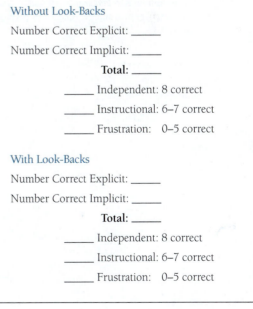

Without Look-Backs

Number Correct Explicit: _____

Number Correct Implicit: _____

      Total: _____

_____ Independent: 8 correct

_____ Instructional: 6–7 correct

_____ Frustration: 0–5 correct

With Look-Backs

Number Correct Explicit: _____

Number Correct Implicit: _____

      Total: _____

_____ Independent: 8 correct

_____ Instructional: 6–7 correct

_____ Frustration: 0–5 correct

Amelia Earhart

Amelia Earhart was an adventurer and a pioneer in the field of flying. She did things no other woman had ever done before.

During World War I, Earhart worked as a nurse. She cared for pilots who had been hurt in the war. Earhart listened to what they said about flying. She watched planes take off and land. She knew that she, too, must fly.

In 1928, Earhart became the first woman to cross the Atlantic in a plane. But someone else flew the plane. Earhart wanted to be more than just a passenger. She wanted to fly a plane across the ocean herself. For four years, Earhart trained to be a pilot. Then, in 1932, she flew alone across the Atlantic to Ireland. The trip took over fourteen hours.

Flying may seem easy today. However, Earhart faced many dangers. Airplanes had just been invented. They were much smaller than our planes today. Mechanical problems happened quite often. There were also no computers to help her. Flying across the ocean was as frightening as sailing across it had been years before. Earhart knew the dangers she faced. However, she said, "I want to do it because I want to do it. Women must try to do things as men have tried. When they fail, their failure must be a challenge to others."

Earhart planned to fly around the world. She flew more than twenty thousand miles. Then, her plane disappeared somewhere over the huge Pacific Ocean. People searched for a long time and many gave up. Earhart and her plane were never found, but people are still looking.

Adapted from *Scott Foresman Social Studies, Grade 4: Regions of Our Country and Our World,* copyright © 1983 by Scott Foresman and Co. Adapted by permission of Pearson Education, Inc.

Tomie dePaola

Tomie dePaola has illustrated over 200 books. He has also authored over 100 of the books he has illustrated. Tomie was born in 1934 in Connecticut, one of four children. When he was a young boy, Tomie's mother read to him as a young boy, and encouraged his early interest in art. His father loved to take pictures and there are many home movies of the dePaola family. Tomie knew what he wanted to do when he grew up by the time he was five years old. One day he came home from kindergarten and told his mother he was "going to draw pictures for books, sing and dance on stage, and paint all the scenery."

In elementary school he was gifted in his ability to learn songs after hearing them only once and to memorize poems. But he had a terrible time memorizing math facts. He told his second-grade teacher he was not going to be an "arithmetic-er." He was going to be an artist. He thought writing numbers on paper was a waste of good paper that could be used to draw pictures. In fourth grade Tomie sent a drawing to Walt Disney and was excited to get an answer. Mr. Disney suggested that Tomie "continue to practice."

One of his favorite childhood memories was the building of his family's new home at 26 Fairmont Avenue. As the house was being built, he found a lot of blank walls to draw on. He drew pictures of his family with chalk. Think how he felt when the walls were painted! At night he drew pictures on his sheets until his mother stopped him.

Tomie's writings show the complex feelings of children in a world of grown-ups. One of his major gifts as a writer is the way he uses his childhood memories to remind adults what they were like as children. And more importantly, his books help children see themselves grow to face the adult world. Examples of stories from his childhood include *The Art Lesson,* a book about an understanding teacher, and *The Baby Sister,* a book about the arrival of a new baby to the family.

Early Railroads

Railroads began as rails laid down in a road. The rails were made of wood topped with iron. Horses pulled carts running along the rails. The rails were smoother than the roads so the horses could pull the carts faster than they could pull wagons over roads.

Then Peter Cooper got a better idea. Why not develop a steam engine, or locomotive, to pull the carts? He believed a steam engine would be able to pull heavier loads faster than horses could.

In 1830, Cooper built a steam-powered engine. It was small and weighed barely a ton. Because of its small size, it became known as the Tom Thumb, named after a tiny hero in old English stories. Cooper wanted to let people know about his new machine, so he advertised a race between the Tom Thumb and a gray horse.

On an August day that year, the locomotive and the gray horse lined up side by side. Cooper stood at the controls of the Tom Thumb. The race began. At first the horse pulled ahead. Then the train picked up speed and soon it was neck and neck with the horse. Then Tom Thumb pulled ahead and a great cheer went up.

But suddenly a safety valve in the engine broke. The locomotive slowed and then fell behind the horse. Although Tom Thumb lost the race, steam engines would soon take over from horses.

Over the next 20 years, railroads replaced canals as the easiest and cheapest way to travel. By 1840, the United States had about 3,000 miles of railroad tracks. This was almost twice as much as Europe. A person could travel about 90 miles by railroad in just a few hours. Such a trip took a day and a half by horse-drawn wagon.

cityanimal/Fotolia

From *Scott Foresman Social Studies: The United States, Pupil Edition, Grade 5.* Copyright © 2003 Pearson Education, Inc. or its affiliates. Adapted by permission. All Rights Reserved.

Plant Structures for Survival

Plants and animals live in many different environments—hot, cold, wet, dry. But no matter where they live, all living things have basic needs that must be met. Any structure or behavior that helps a living thing meet those needs and survive in its environment is called an adaptation.

Plants need sunlight to live and grow. Many plants have special adaptations for getting sunlight. Vines climb up the sides of taller plants or objects where there is more sunlight. Water lilies have large, round leaves called pads that can take in more sunlight than small leaves. The giant water lily pads are so big that you could stand on them without sinking!

Plants also need water. In cold climates, water is frozen in ice and snow for part of the year. Plants that live in these areas have adaptations to help them conserve water. Because trees and other plants lose water through their leaves, some trees lose their leaves before the weather gets cold. Pine trees, such as Christmas trees, do not lose their leaves. However, their leaves are very thin and have a waxy covering that helps keep the trees from losing water. This adaptation helps pine trees survive during the cold winter months.

Plants that grow in very dry places have special adaptations for getting and storing water. The cactus plant lives in the desert where it doesn't rain very often. A cactus has long, shallow roots that cover a large area. When it rains, the roots can absorb a great deal of water very quickly. The cactus stores the extra water. Its thick, waxy covering is an adaptation that helps keep moisture inside the plant.

Level: Four

Biography: Narrative

Concept Questions:

Who was Amelia Earhart? (*3: a famous woman who tried to fly around the world, or the first woman who flew across the Atlantic alone; 2: a famous woman, or an adventurer, or a pilot. 1: a girl/woman*)

_____

_____

_____ (3-2-1-0)

What were the dangers of flying a small plane 100 years ago? (*3: no definition is possible; 2: there was no computer to guide them, or mechanical problems, or planes were new to the world; 1: they'd crash*)

_____

_____

_____ (2-1-0)

What is an adventurer? (*3: someone who does something unusual or exciting; 2: examples: an animal trainer, a scuba diver, etc.; 1: a place to go*)

_____

_____

_____ (3-2-1-0)

What are women's rights? (*3: legal rights given to women, or the same legal rights as men; 2: to work, to drive, to fly, or to choose to work at home; 1: cleaning, cooking*)

_____

_____

_____ (3-2-1-0)

Score: _____/11 = _____%

_____ FAM (≥ 55%) _____UNFAM

Note: Underlined words are on the third-grade or fourth-grade word lists.

Amelia Earhart

Amelia Earhart was an <u>adventurer</u> and a pioneer in the field of flying. She did things no other woman had ever done before.

During World War I, Earhart worked as a nurse. She cared for <u>pilots</u> who had been hurt in the war. Earhart listened to what they said about flying. She watched planes take off and land. She knew that she, too, must fly.

In 1928, Earhart became the first woman to cross the Atlantic in a plane. But someone else flew the plane. Earhart wanted to be more than just a <u>passenger</u>. She wanted to fly a plane across the <u>ocean</u> herself. For four years, Earhart trained to be a <u>pilot</u>. Then, in 1932, she flew alone across the Atlantic to Ireland. The trip took over fourteen hours.

Flying may seem easy today. However, Earhart faced many dangers. Airplanes had just been <u>invented</u>. They were much smaller than our planes today. Mechanical problems happened quite often. There were also no computers to help her. Flying across the <u>ocean</u> was as frightening as sailing across it had been years before. Earhart knew the dangers she faced. However, she said, "I want to

Level: Four

do it because I want to do it. Women must try to do things as men have tried. When they fail, their failure must be a challenge to others."

Earhart planned to fly around the world. She flew more than twenty thousand miles. Then, her plane disappeared somewhere over the huge Pacific Ocean. People searched for a long time and many gave up. Earhart and her plane were never found, but people are still looking. (268 words)

Adapted from *Scott Foresman Social Studies, Grade 4: Regions of Our Country and Our World,* copyright © 1983 by Scott Foresman and Co. Adapted by permission of Pearson Education, Inc.

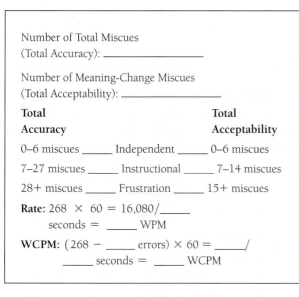

Number of Total Miscues
(Total Accuracy): _____

Number of Meaning-Change Miscues
(Total Acceptability): _____

Total Accuracy | **Total Acceptability**

0–6 miscues _____ Independent _____ 0–6 miscues

7–27 miscues _____ Instructional _____ 7–14 miscues

28+ miscues _____ Frustration _____ 15+ miscues

Rate: 268 × 60 = 16,080/_____
seconds = _____ WPM

WCPM: (268 − _____ errors) × 60 = _____/
_____ seconds = _____ WCPM

Oral Reading Prosody Scale—QRI-7

Directions: Please circle the number below that best represents the student's three-minute oral reading of this passage.

4	3	2	1
Reads primarily in larger, meaningful phrase groups. Some or most of the story is read with expression.	Reads primarily in three- or four-word phrase groups. Little or no expressive interpretation is present.	Reads primarily in two-word phrases with some three- or four-word groupings. Word groupings may be awkward.	Reads primarily word-by-word with occasional two-word or three-word phrases.

Retelling Scoring Sheet for "Amelia Earhart"

Setting/Background

_____ Amelia Earhart was an adventurer.

_____ During World War I she was a nurse who cared for pilots who had been hurt.

_____ Earhart watched planes take off and land.

Goal

_____ She knew that she must fly.

_____ Earhart was the first woman to cross the Atlantic in a plane.

_____ Someone else flew the plane.

_____ She wanted to fly a plane across the ocean.

Events

_____ Earhart trained to be a pilot.

_____ In 1932 she flew alone across the Atlantic to Ireland.

_____ Earhart faced dangers.

_____ Airplanes were smaller.

_____ There were no computers.

_____ Earhart said women must try to do things as men have tried.

_____ Earhart planned to fly around the world.

Level 4

Level: Four

Resolution

_____ Her plane disappeared over the Pacific Ocean.
_____ People searched for a long time, and many gave up.
_____ Earhart and her plane were never found.
_____ People are still looking.

Questions for "Amelia Earhart"

1. What was Amelia Earhart's main goal?
   Implicit: to fly; *or* to do things that were challenging

2. What was Amelia Earhart doing in a plane when she first crossed the Atlantic?
   Explicit: she was a passenger

3. How long did it take Amelia Earhart when she flew alone across the Atlantic?
   Explicit: over fourteen hours

4. Why would flying *alone* across the Atlantic be an especially dangerous thing to do?
   Implicit: it was a long trip; there was no one to help with problems; *or* there was no one to help her stay awake or give her a break

5. What was one of the dangers of flying in those early days?
   Explicit: small planes; mechanical problems; *or* no computers

6. How do we know Amelia Earhart believed in equal rights for women?
   Implicit: she said women should try to do things just as men have tried

7. What was Amelia Earhart trying to do when her plane disappeared?
   Explicit: fly around the world

8. Why do you think her plane was never found?
   Implicit: probably sank in the ocean; ocean was so big; *or* plane was very small

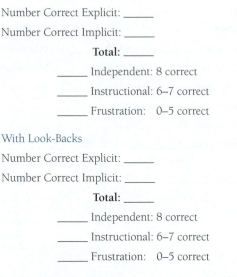

Without Look-Backs
Number Correct Explicit: _____
Number Correct Implicit: _____
            Total: _____
            _____ Independent: 8 correct
            _____ Instructional: 6–7 correct
            _____ Frustration: 0–5 correct

With Look-Backs
Number Correct Explicit: _____
Number Correct Implicit: _____
            Total: _____
            _____ Independent: 8 correct
            _____ Instructional: 6–7 correct
            _____ Frustration: 0–5 correct

Level 4

Level: Four

Biography: Narrative

Note: Underlined words are on the third-grade or fourth-grade word lists.

Tomie dePaola

Tomie dePaola has illustrated over 200 books. He has also authored over 100 of the books he has illustrated. Tomie was born in 1934 in Connecticut, one of four children. When he was a young boy, Tomie's mother read to him and encouraged his early interest in art. His father loved to take pictures and there are many home movies of the dePaola family. Tomie knew what he wanted to do when he grew up by the time he was five years old. One day he came home from kindergarten and told his mother he was "going to draw pictures for books, sing and dance on stage, and paint all the scenery."

In elementary school he was gifted in his ability to learn songs after hearing them only once and to memorize poems. But he had a terrible time memorizing math facts. He told his second-grade teacher he was not going to be an "arithmetic-er." He was going to be an artist. He thought writing numbers on paper was a waste of good paper that could be used to draw pictures. In fourth grade Tomie sent a drawing to Walt Disney and was excited to get an answer. Mr. Disney suggested that Tomie "continue to practice."

One of his favorite childhood memories was the building of his family's new home at 26 Fairmont Avenue. As the house was being built, he found a lot of blank walls to draw on. He drew pictures of his family with chalk. Think how he

Level: Four

felt when the walls were painted! At night he drew pictures on his sheets until his mother stopped him.

Tomie's writings show the complex feelings of children in a world of grown-ups. One of his major gifts as a writer is the way he uses his childhood memories to remind adults what they were like as children. And more importantly, his books help children see themselves grow to face the adult world. Examples of stories from his childhood include *The Art Lesson,* a book about an understanding teacher, and *The Baby Sister,* a book about the arrival of a new baby to the family. (355 words)

Number of Total Miscues
(Total Accuracy): _____

Number of Meaning-Change Miscues
(Total Acceptability): _____

Total Accuracy		**Total Acceptability**
0–8 miscue _____ Independent	_____	0–8 miscue
9–36 miscues _____ Instructional	_____	9–19 miscues
37+ miscues _____ Frustration	_____	20+ miscues

Rate: 355 × 60 = 21,300/_____
    seconds = _____ WPM

WCPM: (355 − _____ errors) × 60 = _____/
    _____ seconds = _____ WCPM

Level 4

Oral Reading Prosody Scale—QRI-7

Directions: Please circle the number below that best represents the student's three-minute oral reading of this passage.

4	3	2	1
Reads primarily in larger, meaningful phrase groups. Some or most of the story is read with expression.	Reads primarily in three- or four-word phrase groups. Little or no expressive interpretation is present.	Reads primarily in two-word phrases with some three- or four-word groupings. Word groupings may be awkward.	Reads primarily word-by-word with occasional two-word or three-word phrases.

Retelling Scoring Sheet for "Tomie dePaola"

Setting/Background

_____ Tomie dePaola has illustrated over 200 books.
_____ He has authored over 100 books.
_____ When he was a young boy, dePaola's mother read to him and encouraged his interest in art.
_____ His father loved to take pictures, and there are many movies of the family.

Goal

_____ Tomie knew what he wanted to do when he grew up by the time he was five years old.
_____ One day he came home from kindergarten and told his mother
_____ he was going to draw pictures for books, sing and dance on stage, and paint the scenery.

Events

_____ He was gifted in his ability to learn songs after hearing them once and to memorize poems.
_____ But he had a terrible time memorizing math facts.
_____ He told his teacher he was not going to be an "arithmetic-er."
_____ He was going to be an artist.
_____ He thought writing numbers on paper was a waste of paper that could be used to draw pictures.

Level: Four

_____ In fourth grade, Tomie sent a drawing to Walt Disney and was excited to get an answer.

_____ Mr. Disney suggested that Tomie continue to practice.

_____ One of his favorite memories was the building of his family's new home.

_____ As the house was being built he found a lot of blank walls to draw on.

_____ He drew pictures of his family with chalk.

_____ At night he drew pictures on his sheets until his mother stopped him.

Resolution

_____ Tomie's writings show the feelings of children in a world of grown-ups.

_____ One of his major gifts is the way he uses his childhood memories to remind adults what they were like as children.

_____ His books help children see themselves grow to face the adult world.

_____ Examples include _The Art Lesson,_ about an understanding teacher,

_____ and _The Baby Sister,_ about the arrival of a new baby.

Questions for "Tomie dePaola"

1. Who is Tomie dePaola?
Explicit: an author and illustrator of children's books (either is acceptable)

2. What did Tomie tell his mother one day after kindergarten?
Explicit: that he wanted to draw pictures for books; _or_ sing and dance on stage; _or_ paint all the scenery (The student must provide two of the three answers above. If the student says, "He wanted to be an artist," ask, "What specific things did he tell his mother he wanted to do?")

3. In second grade, what could Tomie memorize well?
Explicit: songs; or poems

4. What did Walt Disney tell Tomie to do?
Explicit: practice

5. What examples in the story tell us that Tomie would draw on anything?
Implicit: he drew on the walls of his new home when it was being built; _or_ he drew on his sheets

6. How did Tomie's artistic abilities get him into trouble?
Implicit: he got in trouble with his mother for drawing on his sheets

7. Why might adults like Tomie's books?
Implicit: they remind adults what they were like as children

8. What ideas in the story tell us why Tomie wrote the book _The Art Lesson?_
Implicit: Tomie was an artist; _or_ he loved drawing; _or_ he had an understanding teacher

Without Look-Backs

Number Correct Explicit: _____
Number Correct Implicit: _____

Total: _____

Independent: 8 correct
Instructional: 6–7 correct
Frustration: 0–5 correct

With Look-Backs

Number Correct Explicit: _____
Number Correct Implicit: _____

Total: _____

Independent: 8 correct
Instructional: 6–7 correct
Frustration: 0–5 correct

Level 4

Level: Four

Social Studies: Expository

Note: Underlined words are on the third-grade or fourth-grade word lists.

Early Railroads

Railroads began as rails laid down in a road. The rails were made of wood topped with iron. Horses pulled carts running along the rails. The rails were smoother than the roads so the horses could pull the carts faster than they could pull wagons over roads.

Then Peter Cooper got a better idea. Why not develop a steam <u>engine</u>, or locomotive, to pull the carts? He <u>believed</u> a steam <u>engine</u> would be able to pull heavier loads faster than horses could.

In 1830, Cooper built a steam-powered <u>engine</u>. It was small and weighed barely a ton. Because of its small size, it became known as the Tom Thumb, named after a tiny hero in old English stories. Cooper wanted to let people know about his new machine, so he advertised a race between the Tom Thumb and a gray horse.

On an August day that year, the locomotive and the gray horse lined up side by side. Cooper stood at the controls of the Tom Thumb. The race began. At first the horse pulled ahead. Then the train picked up speed and soon it was neck and neck with the horse. Then Tom Thumb pulled ahead and a great cheer went up.

Level 4

Level: Four

But suddenly a safety valve in the <u>engine</u> broke. The locomotive slowed and then fell behind the horse. Although Tom Thumb lost the race, steam <u>engines</u> would soon take over from horses.

Over the next 20 years, railroads replaced canals as the easiest and cheapest way to travel. By 1840, the United States had about 3,000 miles of railroad tracks. This was almost twice as much as Europe. A person could travel about 90 miles by railroad in just a few hours. Such a trip took a day and a half by horse-drawn wagon. (297 words)

From *Scott Foresman Social Studies: The United States, Pupil Edition, Grade 5.* Copyright © 2003 Pearson Education, Inc. or its affiliates. Adapted by permission. All Rights Reserved.

Number of Total Miscues
(Total Accuracy): _____

Number of Meaning-Change Miscues
(Total Acceptability): _____

Total Accuracy		**Total Acceptability**
0–7 miscues _____	Independent _____	0–7 miscues
8–31 miscues _____	Instructional _____	8–16 miscues
32+ miscues _____	Frustration _____	17+ miscues

Rate: 297 × 60 = 17,820/_____ seconds = _____ WPM

WCPM: (297 − _____ errors) × 60 = _____/
_____ seconds = _____ WCPM

Oral Reading Prosody Scale—*QRI-7*

Directions: Please circle the number below that best represents the student's three-minute oral reading of this passage.

4	3	2	1
Reads primarily in larger, meaningful phrase groups. Some or most of the story is read with expression.	Reads primarily in three- or four-word phrase groups. Little or no expressive interpretation is present.	Reads primarily in two-word phrases with some three- or four-word groupings. Word groupings may be awkward.	Reads primarily word-by-word with occasional two-word or three-word phrases.

Retelling Scoring Sheet for "Early Railroads"

Main Idea

_____ Railroads began as rails on a road.

Details

_____ Horses pulled carts on the rails.
_____ The rails were smoother than the roads.
_____ Horses could pull the carts faster.

Main Idea

_____ Peter Cooper got an idea.

Details

_____ Why not develop a steam engine?
_____ An engine would be able to pull heavier loads faster.

Main Idea

_____ Cooper built a steam engine.

Details

_____ It was small
_____ and became known as the Tom Thumb.

Main Idea

_____ Cooper wanted people to know about his engine.

Level 4

Level: Four

Details

_____ He advertised a race between the Tom Thumb and a horse.

_____ At first the horse pulled ahead.

_____ It was neck and neck.

_____ Then Tom Thumb pulled ahead.

_____ But a valve broke.

_____ The locomotive fell behind the horse.

Main Idea

_____ Engines would take over from horses.

Details

_____ Railroads replaced canals as ways to travel.

_____ A person could travel 90 miles by railroad in a few hours.

Questions for "Early Railroads"

1. What is this passage mainly about?
   Implicit: a race between the first steam engine and a horse; *or* how the steam engine replaced the horse in hauling things and people

2. Why did Peter Cooper build a steam engine?
   Implicit: it could pull heavier loads and go faster than horses
   (If the students says, "to make money," ask, "Why would it make money?")

3. Why was the first steam engine called Tom Thumb?
   Explicit: it was small and Tom Thumb was small

4. Why did Cooper set up the race between Tom Thumb and the horse?
   Explicit: to let people know about the engine

5. How do you know that people who watched the race wanted Tom Thumb to win?
   Implicit: they cheered when Tom Thumb pulled ahead

6. Even though the horse won the race, why could you say that Tom Thumb really won?
   Implicit: because steam engines later replaced horses

7. Why did the horse win the race?
   Explicit: a part of the locomotive's engine broke

8. By 1840, what country had more miles of railroad track?
   Explicit: United States

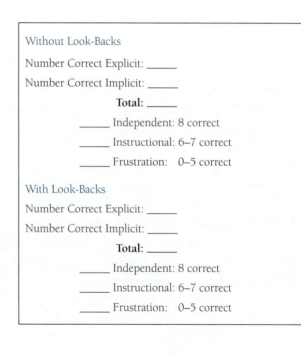

Without Look-Backs

Number Correct Explicit: _____

Number Correct Implicit: _____

   Total: _____

   _____ Independent: 8 correct

   _____ Instructional: 6–7 correct

   _____ Frustration: 0–5 correct

With Look-Backs

Number Correct Explicit: _____

Number Correct Implicit: _____

   Total: _____

   _____ Independent: 8 correct

   _____ Instructional: 6–7 correct

   _____ Frustration: 0–5 correct

Level 4

Level: Four

Science: Expository

Note: Underlined words are on the third-grade or fourth-grade word lists.

Plant Structures for Survival

Plants and animals live in many different environments—hot, cold, wet, dry. But no matter where they live, all living things have basic needs that must be met. Any structure or behavior that helps a living thing meet those needs and survive in its environment is called an adaptation.

Plants need sunlight to live and grow. Many plants have special adaptations for getting sunlight. Vines climb up the sides of taller plants or objects where there is more sunlight. Water lilies have large, round leaves called pads that can take in more sunlight than small leaves. The giant water lily pads are so big that you could stand on them without sinking!

Plants also need water. In cold climates, water is frozen in ice and snow for part of the year. Plants that live in these areas have adaptations to help them conserve water. Because trees and other plants lose water through their leaves, some trees lose their leaves before the weather gets cold. Pine trees, such as Christmas trees, do not lose their leaves. However, their leaves are very thin and have a waxy covering that helps keep the trees from losing water. This adaptation helps pine trees survive during the cold winter months.

Plants that grow in very dry places have special adaptations for getting and storing water. The cactus plant lives in the desert where it doesn't rain very often. A cactus has long, shallow roots

Level 4

Level: Four

that cover a large area. When it rains, the roots can absorb a great deal of water very quickly. The cactus stores the extra water. Its thick, waxy covering is an <u>adaptation</u> that helps keep moisture inside the plant. (278 words)

From *Scott Foresman Science, Teacher Edition, Grade 4.* Copyright © 2000 by Pearson Education, Inc. or its affiliates. Used by permission. All Rights Reserved.

Number of Total Miscues
(Total Accuracy): _____

Number of Meaning-Change Miscues
(Total Acceptability): _____

Total Accuracy		**Total Acceptability**
0–6 miscue _____	Independent _____	0–16 miscue
7–29 miscues _____	Instructional _____	7–15 miscues
30+ miscues _____	Frustration _____	16+ miscues

Rate: 278 × 60 = 16,680/_____ seconds = _____ WPM

WCPM: (278 − _____ errors) × 60 = _____/
_____ seconds = _____ WCPM

Oral Reading Prosody Scale—QRI-7

Directions: Please circle the number below that best represents the student's three-minute oral reading of this passage.

4	3	2	1
Reads primarily in larger, meaningful phrase groups. Some or most of the story is read with expression.	Reads primarily in three- or four-word phrase groups. Little or no expressive interpretation is present.	Reads primarily in two-word phrases with some three- or four-word groupings. Word groupings may be awkward.	Reads primarily word-by-word with occasional two-word or three-word phrases.

Retelling Scoring Sheet for "Plant Structures for Survival"

Main Idea

_____ Plants and animals live in different environments.

Details

_____ All plants have needs.
_____ An adaptation is a structure or behavior
_____ that helps a plant meet needs and/or survive.

Main Idea

_____ Plants need sunlight to live and/or grow.

Details

_____ Plants have adaptations for getting sunlight.
_____ Vines climb up
_____ where there is more sunlight.
_____ Water lilies have leaves
_____ that can take in more sunlight.

Main Idea

_____ Plants also need water.

Details

_____ In cold climates, water is frozen.
_____ Plants have adaptations to conserve water.
_____ Because plants lose water through their leaves,
_____ they lose leaves
_____ before the weather gets cold.
_____ Pine trees do not lose their leaves.
_____ Their leaves are thin
_____ and have a waxy covering
_____ that keep the trees from losing water.

Main Idea

_____ Plants in very dry areas have adaptations for getting and/or storing water.

Level: Four

Details

_____ A cactus has roots
_____ that cover a large area.
_____ The roots can absorb a great deal of water.
_____ The cactus stores extra water.
_____ Its thick and/or waxy covering is an adaptation
_____ that keeps moisture inside the plant.

Questions for "Plant Structures for Survival"

1. What was the most important idea in what you read?
   Implicit: that plants develop structures to help them live (survive) in certain climates

2. What is an adaptation?
   Explicit: any structures; *or* a behavior that helps a living thing to survive in its environment

3. What is one example of how a plant adapts to get more sunlight?
   Explicit: a vine grows up a tall plant to get more sunlight; *or* lily pads grow very large to capture sunlight

4. Why do some trees lose their leaves before the weather gets cold?
   Explicit: to prevent the tree from losing water through its leaves

5. Why don't pine trees lose water through their leaves?
   Implicit: their leaves are very thin *and* are protected by a waxy substance

6. Describe the root system of a cactus.
   Explicit: long; *or* shallow

7. How is the root system of a cactus an example of adaptation to the desert?
   Implicit: the roots can absorb the small amounts of rain that fall in the desert

8. How are a cactus and a pine tree alike?
   Implicit: both are covered by a waxy substance that prevents loss of water

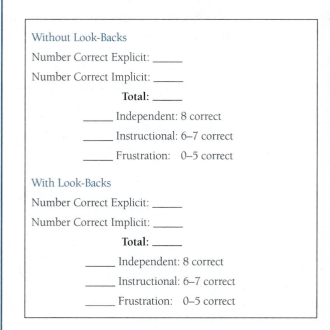

Without Look-Backs

Number Correct Explicit: _____

Number Correct Implicit: _____

Total: _____

_____ Independent: 8 correct

_____ Instructional: 6–7 correct

_____ Frustration: 0–5 correct

With Look-Backs

Number Correct Explicit: _____

Number Correct Implicit: _____

Total: _____

_____ Independent: 8 correct

_____ Instructional: 6–7 correct

_____ Frustration: 0–5 correct

Level 4

Margaret Mead

Margaret Mead had always been interested in the ways of life of people from other lands. When Mead went to college, she took a class in anthropology. This is the study of how different people live. Mead decided to make this her career. She wanted to study primitive people before modern ways of living destroyed their culture.

Mead realized that living with a people is the only effective way to learn about them. She chose a village in Samoa to investigate. Several islands make up Samoa, which is in the Pacific Ocean. Mead worked hard to prepare for Samoa. She studied languages like the Samoan language. She read everything she could about the Samoan people. She read about their food and how they built their homes. She read about their ceremonies, their past history, and their taboos. But she wanted to learn much more.

Finally, Mead arrived in Samoa. At first life was difficult for her. She was alone. She was not fluent in the Samoan language. She lived in a house with no walls and no electricity or gas. It had no running water and no bathroom. One day she said to herself, "I can't go on" in Samoan. Then she thought that maybe she could continue after all. Mead became fluent in the Samoan language, and the people soon regarded her as one of the villagers. She listened to their talk, their jokes, and their gossip. They told her their problems. Mead felt that being a woman assisted her in learning more about the lives of these people. Instead of having to go on hunts with the men, Mead stayed with the women. She observed the children playing and learned how food was prepared. She made efforts to get the older people to recount tales of the past.

Mead learned many things from the Samoan people. She always took notes and kept careful records. These notes were used to write her first book, which was called *Coming of Age in Samoa*. It made her famous. Mead spent the rest of her life studying and writing about primitive ways of life that no longer exist today.

From *Our People* by Nelle Dederick et al. Copyright © 1979 by Ginn and Company. Adapted by permission of Pearson Education, Inc. All Rights Reserved.

Patricia McKissack

Patricia McKissack is the author of biographies of famous African Americans and of several picture books. Two of her most widely known picture books are *Mirandy and Brother Wind* and *Flossie & the Fox*. Patricia was the oldest of three children whose family moved to St. Louis, Missouri, when she was very young. Her parents divorced when she was ten, and her mother moved to -Nashville, Tennessee, to be close to her parents. Her grandparents in Nashville were very important in Patricia's life. They gave her a lot of love and attention, particularly her grandfather, who, she says, "spoiled her rotten." Her grandfather was a great storyteller, and he would always include Patricia's or her siblings' names in his stories. He told a story of a girl named Pat who could outsmart foxes, and we all know that foxes are smart. This story forms the foundation of Patricia's famous book, *Flossie & the Fox*. His stories are the inspiration for many of her picture books.

Patricia began to see herself as an author in third grade. She wrote a poem, and her teacher put it on the bulletin board and said she liked it. It was thrilling to have other people read and respond to something she had written. She was forever scribbling ideas and thoughts down for future reference, and she realized early that she wanted to be a writer. But she was told black people couldn't do that. "Girl, you better take something you can do. You'd better be a teacher." Despite this advice, reading and writing remained an important part of her life. She kept a journal, and always kept a diary. She spent a lot of time in the -Nashville Public Library because it was one public place that was open to blacks. Every week she checked out three books, the maximum allowed. The minute she was done, she went back for more. Fairy tales and myths were her favorite, but she was troubled because she never saw people who looked like her in the stories. She searched the libraries for books with African American characters and found them in books of nonfiction. She began reading biographies of people like Mary McLeod Bethune, and her search led her to the poetry of Langston Hughes. She even searched the encyclopedia for pictures of African Americans.

In college Patricia majored in English and Education. Again, she was steered toward getting a teaching certificate "so you can have something to do when you graduate." She became a teacher, and when she taught eighth grade, she was bothered by the lack of material for African American children. She loved the poetry of Paul Laurence Dunbar that her mother had read to her, so she wrote her first biography of Dunbar. She continued to write biographies of important African Americans such as Frederick Douglass, W. E. B. Du Bois, Martin Luther King Jr., and Jesse Jackson. She remained committed to writing strong, accurate, and appealing stories about African Americans to improve the self-esteem of African American children and to encourage all children to have an open mind toward cultures different from their own.

Farming on the Great Plains

In the 1800s, the Great Plains was a vast region of dry grasslands. People did not think it would ever make good farmland. As a result, the Great Plains attracted very few pioneers.

The United States government decided to try to encourage people to move to the Great Plains. In 1862, Congress passed the Homestead Act. This act offered free land to pioneers willing to start new farms. If you were a man over the age of 21, a woman whose husband had died, or the head of a family, you could claim 160 acres of land. You had to pay a small registration fee, usually about $10. You also had to farm your land and live on it for five years. Then the land was yours. Settlers who claimed land through this law were called homesteaders.

It was not easy to establish a farm on the Great Plains. The grasses, or sod, had thick tangled roots. The roots reached several inches down into the soil. Before planting crops, farmers had to dig through this sod. Great Plains farmers soon became known as sodbusters.

After ripping up the sod, most homesteaders used it to build houses. There were few trees or rocks so sod was a useful building material. Houses built from blocks of sod stayed cool in the summer. They were warm in the winter and were fireproof. Unfortunately for the homesteaders, the sod walls were often home to bugs, mice, and snakes.

The homesteaders faced many obstacles such as harsh weather conditions and deadly natural disasters. Spring often brought tornadoes, hailstorms, and flooding. Summers could mean scorching heat and frequent droughts. In fall, the prairie grass dried and settlers had to watch for prairie fires. Winter brought bitter cold along with ice storms and blizzards.

Farmers also faced the dreaded grasshopper. In the mid-1870s, millions of grasshoppers swarmed across the Great Plains. They darkened the sky and covered the ground in layers up to six inches high. The insects ate everything in their path, crops, grass, even fences and axe handles.

Barbulat/Fotolia

From *Scott Foresman Social Studies: The United States: Pupil Edition, Grade 5*. Copyright © 2003 by Pearson Education, Inc. or its affiliates. Adapted by permission. All Rights Reserved.

How Does Your Body Take in Oxygen?

Preparing Air for Your Lungs

About one-fifth of the air that you breathe in is a gas called oxygen. Your cells must have oxygen to do their work. Without oxygen, cells will die—some within 3–5 minutes. When you breathe in, your respiratory system brings air containing oxygen into your body. The cells in your body use the oxygen, and as they work, the cells produce carbon dioxide. This gas leaves your body as waste when you breathe out.

The respiratory system includes your nose, your lungs, and the tubes that connect them. Air enters the body through the nose, which has the job of getting the air ready for the lungs. If air is very cold, dry, or dirty it could damage your lungs. Your nose warms, moistens, and cleans the air that you breathe in. The blood supply and mucus in your nose keeps it warm and moist. The hairs in your nose capture the dust from the air.

After the air is warmed, moistened, and cleaned it goes to the throat and down the trachea, or windpipe. The trachea divides into two bronchial tubes, each of which goes into a lung.

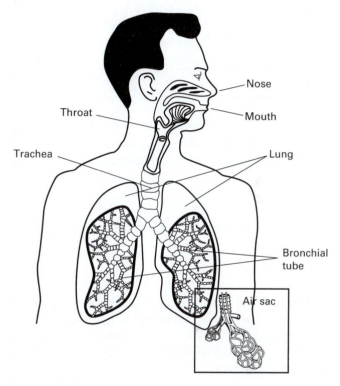

Inside the Lungs

Inside the lungs, the bronchial tubes divide into smaller and smaller tubes. The smallest tubes lead to clusters of tiny pouches called air sacs. A net of tiny blood vessels surrounds each air sac. Inhaled air, which is rich in oxygen enters the air sacs. At this moment, the blood in the vessels around the air sacs contains a lot of carbon dioxide, which the blood has picked up from body cells. That blood contains little oxygen. An air exchange quickly takes place. Oxygen passes from the air sacs into the blood vessels. The blood now has oxygen to deliver to body cells. Look at the picture above to help you visualize this description. At the same time that oxygen passes out of the air sacs, carbon dioxide passes from the blood vessels into the air sacs. The carbon dioxide leaves your body when you exhale.

From *Scott Foresman Science, Teacher Edition, Grade 5*. Copyright © 2000 by Pearson Education, Inc. or its affiliates. Reprinted by permission. All Rights Reserved.

Level: Five

Biography: Narrative

Concept Questions:

Who was Margaret Mead? *(3: an anthropologist; 2: a scientist; 1: a famous woman)*

_____

_____

_____ (3-2-1-0)

How do we learn about different people? *(Note: no 3-point responses are possible; 2: by spending time with them; 1: by reading about them, seeing a movie about them, watching them)*

_____

_____

_____ (2-1-0)

What are primitive people? *(3: people who have basic life skills, but no technology, written language, or industry; 2: people without electricity, or people without inside plumbing; 1: people who live in rural parts of Africa or Asia or South America)*

_____

_____

_____ (3-2-1-0)

What are problems in learning a new language? *(Note: no 3-point responses; 2: hard to hear the sounds or learn the vocabulary; 1: embarrassed by pronunciation)*

_____

_____

_____ (2-1-0)

Score: _____/10 = _____%

_____FAM (≥ 55%) _____UNFAM

Note: Underlined words are on the fourth-grade or fifth-grade word lists.

Margaret Mead

Margaret Mead had always been interested in the ways of life of people from other lands. When Mead went to college, she took a class in anthropology. This is the study of how different people live. Mead decided to make this her career. She wanted to study <u>primitive</u> people before modern ways of living destroyed their culture.

Mead realized that living with a people is the only effective way to learn about them. She chose a village in Samoa to investigate. Several islands make up Samoa, which is in the Pacific <u>Ocean</u>. Mead worked hard to prepare for Samoa. She studied languages like the Samoan language. She read everything she could about the Samoan people. She read about their food and how they built their homes. She read about their ceremonies, their past history, and their taboos. But she wanted to learn much more.

Finally, Mead arrived in Samoa. At first life was difficult for her. She was alone. She was not <u>fluent</u> in the Samoan language. She lived in a house with no walls and no electricity or gas. It had no running water and no bathroom. One day she said to herself, "I can't go on" in Samoan. Then she thought that maybe she could continue after all. Mead became <u>fluent</u> in the Samoan language, and the people soon regarded her

Level: Five

as one of the villagers. She listened to their talk, their jokes, and their gossip. They told her their problems. Mead felt that being a woman assisted her in learning more about the lives of these people. Instead of having to go on hunts with the men, Mead stayed with the women. She observed the children playing and learned how food was prepared. She made efforts to get the older people to recount <u>tales</u> of the past.

Mead learned many things from the Samoan people. She always took notes and kept careful records. These notes were used to write her first book, which was called *Coming of Age in Samoa*. It made her famous. Mead spent the rest of her life studying and writing about <u>primitive</u> ways of life that no longer exist today. (357 words)

From *Our People* by Nelle Dederick et al. Copyright © 1979 by Ginn and Company. Adapted by permission of Pearson Education, Inc. All Rights Reserved.

Number of Total Miscues
(Total Accuracy): _____

Number of Meaning-Change Miscues
(Total Acceptability): _____

Total Accuracy	Total Acceptability
0–8 miscues _____Independent _____	0–8 miscues
9–37 miscues _____Instructional _____	9–19 miscues
38+ miscues _____Frustration _____	20+ miscues

Rate: 357 × 60 = 21,420/_____seconds = _____ WPM

WCPM: (357 − _____ errors) × 60 = _____/ _____seconds = _____WCPM

Oral Reading Prosody Scale—QRI-7

Directions: Please circle the number below that best represents the student's 3-minute oral reading of this passage.

4	3	2	1
Reads primarily in larger, meaningful phrase groups. Some or most of the story is read with expression.	Reads primarily in three- or four-word phrase groups. Little or no expressive interpretation is present.	Reads primarily in two-word phrases with some three- or four-word groupings. Word groupings may be awkward.	Reads primarily word-by-word with occasional two-word or three-word phrases.

Retelling Scoring Sheet for "Margaret Mead"

Background/Setting

_____ When Margaret Mead went to college, she took a class in anthropology.
_____ She decided to make this her career.

Goal

_____ She wanted to study primitive people.
_____ She chose a village in Samoa to investigate.

Events

_____ Margaret Mead studied languages like the Samoan language.
_____ She read about Samoan food and how they built their homes.
_____ When she arrived in Samoa her house had no walls.
_____ Life was difficult because she lived in a house with no electricity.
_____ She said, "I can't go on" in Samoan.
_____ Then she thought that she could continue.
_____ The people regarded/thought of her as one of the villagers because
_____ she listened to their jokes, and their gossip.
_____ Instead of having to go on hunts with the men,

Level 5

Level: Five

_____ Margaret Mead stayed with the women.
_____ She observed the children playing
_____ and learned how food was prepared.

Resolutions

_____ She wrote a book called *Coming of Age in Samoa.*
_____ It made her famous.

Questions for "Margaret Mead"

1. What was Margaret Mead's main goal?
   Implicit: to study primitive people

2. What people did Margaret Mead choose to investigate?
   Explicit: people in Samoa

3. Name one thing Margaret Mead read about to prepare her for Samoa.
   Explicit: homes; food; ceremonies; Samoa's history; taboos; *or* the Samoan language

4. Give one reason why life in Samoa was difficult at first.
   Explicit: she was alone; there were no walls, electricity, running water, or bathroom; *or* she was not fluent in the language

5. What made Margaret Mead decide she would be able to stay in Samoa?
   Implicit: when she talked to herself in Samoan and realized she knew the language

6. Why was Margaret Mead able to learn a lot about the family life of the Samoans?
   Implicit: she stayed with the women and children; *or* the women and children talked to her

7. Why did Margaret Mead want to hear the stories of the Samoans' past?
   Implicit: she wanted to learn as much about them as she could

8. What did Margaret Mead do with the notes and records she kept?
   Explicit: she wrote a book

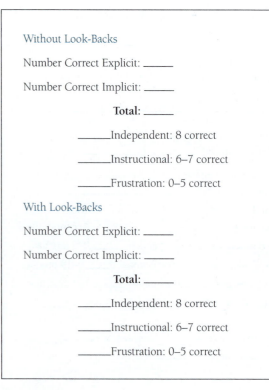

Without Look-Backs

Number Correct Explicit: _____

Number Correct Implicit: _____

        Total: _____

_____Independent: 8 correct

_____Instructional: 6–7 correct

_____Frustration: 0–5 correct

With Look-Backs

Number Correct Explicit: _____

Number Correct Implicit: _____

        Total: _____

_____Independent: 8 correct

_____Instructional: 6–7 correct

_____Frustration: 0–5 correct

Level 5

Level: Five

Biography: Narrative

Note: Underlined words are on the fourth-grade or fifth-grade word lists.

Patricia McKissack

Patricia McKissack is the author of biographies of famous African Americans and of several picture books. Two of her most widely known picture books are *Mirandy and Brother Wind* and *Flossie & the Fox*. Patricia was the oldest of three children whose family moved to St. Louis, Missouri, when she was very young. Her parents divorced when she was ten, and her mother moved to Nashville, Tennessee, to be close to her parents. Her grandparents in Nashville were very important in Patricia's life. They gave her a lot of love and attention, particularly her grandfather, who, she says, "spoiled her rotten." Her grandfather was a great storyteller, and he would always include Patricia's or her siblings' names in his stories. He told a story of a girl named Pat who could outsmart foxes, and we all know that foxes are smart. This story forms the foundation of Patricia's famous book, *Flossie & the Fox*. His stories are the inspiration for many of her picture books.

Level 5

Level: Five

Level 5

Patricia began to see herself as an author in third grade. She wrote a poem, and her teacher put it on the <u>bulletin</u> board and said she liked it. It was thrilling to have other people read and respond to something she had written. She was forever scribbling ideas and thoughts down for future reference, and she realized early that she wanted to be a writer. But she was told black people couldn't do that. "Girl, you better take something you can do. You'd better be a teacher." Despite this advice, reading and writing remained an important part of her life. She kept a journal, and always kept a diary. She spent a lot of time in the Nashville Public Library because it was one public place that was open to blacks. Every week she checked out three books, the maximum allowed. The minute she was done, she went back for more. Fairy <u>tales</u> and myths were her <u>favorite</u>, but she was troubled because she never saw people who looked like her in the stories. She searched the libraries for books with African American characters and found them in books of nonfiction. She began reading biographies of people like Mary McLeod Bethune, and her search led her to the poetry of Langston Hughes. She even searched the encyclopedia for pictures of African Americans.

In college Patricia majored in English and Education. Again, she was steered toward getting a teaching certificate "so you can have something to do when you graduate." She became a teacher, and when she taught eighth grade, she was bothered by the lack of material for African American children. She loved the poetry of Paul Laurence Dunbar that her mother had read to her, so she wrote her first <u>biography</u> of Dunbar. She continued to write biographies of important African Americans such as Frederick Douglass, W. E. B. DuBois, Martin Luther King Jr., and Jesse Jackson. She remained committed to writing strong, accurate, and appealing stories about African Americans to improve the self-esteem of African American children and to encourage all children to have an open mind toward cultures different from their own. (521 words)

Number of Total Miscues
(Total Accuracy): _____

Number of Meaning-Change Miscues
(Total Acceptability): _____

Total Accuracy		**Total Acceptability**
0–12 miscues _____ Independent		_____ 0–12 miscues
13–54 miscues _____ Instructional		_____ 13–28 miscues
55+ miscues _____ Frustration		_____ 29+ miscues

Rate: $521 \times 60 = 31{,}260/$ seconds _____ = _____ WPM

WCPM: ($521 -$ _____ errors) $\times 60 =$ _____ /
_____ seconds = _____ WCPM

Level: Five

Retelling Scoring Sheet for "Patricia McKissack"

Setting/Background

_____ Patricia McKissack is the author of biographies of famous African Americans and of picture books.

_____ Two of her most widely known books are *Mirandy and Brother Wind* and *Flossie & the Fox.*

_____ Patricia was the oldest of three children whose family moved to St. Louis, Missouri, when she was very young.

_____ Her parents divorced when she was ten and

_____ her mother moved to Nashville, Tennessee, to be close to her parents.

_____ Her grandparents were very important in Patricia's life,

_____ particularly her grandfather who "spoiled her rotten."

_____ Her grandfather was a storyteller,

_____ and he would always include Patricia's name or her siblings' names in his stories.

_____ His stories are the inspiration for many of Patricia's books.

Goal

_____ Patricia began to see herself as an author in third grade.

Events

_____ She wrote a poem and her teacher put it on the bulletin board and said she liked it.

_____ It was thrilling to have people read something she had written.

Goal

_____ She wanted to be a writer.

Events

_____ But she was told black people couldn't do that and that she'd better be a teacher.

_____ Reading and writing remained an important part of her life.

_____ She kept a journal and always kept a diary.

_____ She spent a lot of time in the public library because it was one place that was open to blacks.

_____ Every week she checked out three books, the maximum allowed.

_____ The minute she was done, she went back for more.

_____ She was troubled because she never saw people who looked like her in the stories.

Goal

_____ She searched the libraries for books with African American characters.

Events

_____ She found them in biographies in nonfiction.

_____ She even searched the encyclopedia for pictures of African Americans.

_____ In college Patricia majored in English and Education.

_____ When she taught eighth grade, she was bothered by the lack of material for African American children.

Level 5

Level: Five

Resolution

_____ She loved the poetry of Paul Laurence Dunbar so she wrote her first biography of Dunbar.

_____ She continued to write biographies of important African Americans,

_____ such as Frederick Douglass/or W. E. B. Du Bois/or Martin Luther King Jr./or Jesse Jackson.

Goal

_____ Throughout her life, she remained committed to writing strong and accurate stories

_____ about African Americans to improve the self-esteem of African American children

_____ and to encourage all children to have an open mind toward different cultures.

Questions for "Patricia McKissack"

1. Who was Patricia McKissack?
   Explicit: an author of biographies and picture books. If the student says, "an author," ask, "What kinds of books did she write?" Either type of book is acceptable.

2. Who was the most influential in developing Patricia's love of story?
   Implicit: her grandfather

3. How did Patricia's third-grade teacher encourage her writing?
   Explicit: she liked a poem Patricia had written and put it on the bulletin board. (Both ideas must be included.)

4. Why did some people tell Patricia to be a teacher rather than an author?
   Implicit: they told her blacks couldn't become authors; *or* they told her she should "do something she could do"

5. How do we know that Patricia was determined to be an author?
   Implicit: reading and writing remained important to her (despite the advice to become a teacher); she went to the library a lot and kept reading; *or* she kept a journal and a diary

6. Why did Patricia decide to write biographies of African American people?
   Explicit: she found few books in the library on African Americans; *or* when she taught eighth grade there were few books written about African Americans

Level 5

Level: Five

7. Name two persons that Patricia McKissack has written biographies about.
Explicit: Paul Laurence Dunbar, Martin Luther King Jr., W. E. B. Du Bois, Frederick Douglass, or Jesse Jackson

8. How do we know that Patricia McKissack would want children who are *not* African American to read her books?
Implicit: by reading her books children would learn about other cultures; *or* she wants all children to have an open mind toward cultures different from their own

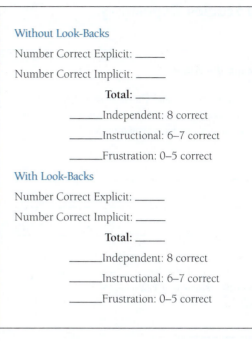

Without Look-Backs

Number Correct Explicit: _____

Number Correct Implicit: _____

        Total: _____

_____Independent: 8 correct

_____Instructional: 6–7 correct

_____Frustration: 0–5 correct

With Look-Backs

Number Correct Explicit: _____

Number Correct Implicit: _____

        Total: _____

_____Independent: 8 correct

_____Instructional: 6–7 correct

_____Frustration: 0–5 correct

Level 5

Level: Five

Social Studies: Expository

Concept Questions:

What are the Great Plains? (*3: central part of the United States, area with few trees, area with a lot of farms; 2: made up of a group of states, has a lot of tornadoes; 1: is big, not fancy*)

_____

_____

_____ (3-2-1-0)

What is a homesteader? (*3: a settler, a pioneer, someone who got land through the Homestead Act; 2: a farmer, a hard worker, someone who lived a long time ago; 1: lives in a home*)

_____

_____

_____ (3-2-1-0)

What is sod? (*3: grass, turf; 2: it's green, has to be cut, on your lawn; 1: a good thing; a lot of people have it*)

_____

_____

_____ (3-2-1-0)

What is a natural disaster? (*3: it's something bad that is caused by nature, when people are hurt or killed by a tornado, a bad thing but people don't cause it; 2: when volcanoes erupt; a tsunami, a hurricane, a big storm; 1: I saw one on television, they happen all the time*)

_____

_____

_____ (3-2-1-0)

Score: _____/12 = _____%

_____FAM (≥ 55%) _____UNFAM

Note: Underlined words are on the fourth-grade or fifth-grade word lists.

Farming on the Great Plains

In the 1800s, the Great Plains was a vast region of dry grasslands. People did not think it would ever make good farmland. As a result, the Great Plains attracted very few <u>pioneers</u>.

The United States government decided to try to encourage people to move to the Great Plains. In 1862, Congress passed the Homestead Act. This act offered free land to <u>pioneers</u> willing to start new farms. If you were a man over the age of 21, a woman whose husband had died, or the head of a family, you could claim 160 acres of land. You had to pay a small <u>registration</u> fee, usually about $10. You also had to farm your land and live on it for five years. Then the land was yours. Settlers who claimed land through this law were called homesteaders.

It was not easy to establish a farm on the Great Plains. The grasses, or sod, had thick tangled roots. The roots reached several inches down into the soil. Before planting <u>crops</u>, farmers had to dig through this sod. Great Plains farmers soon became known as sodbusters.

After ripping up the sod, most homesteaders used it to build houses. There were few trees or rocks so sod was a useful building material. Houses

Level: Five

built from blocks of sod stayed cool in the summer. They were warm in the winter and were fireproof. Unfortunately for the homesteaders, the sod walls were often home to bugs, mice, and snakes.

The homesteaders faced many obstacles such as harsh weather conditions and deadly natural disasters. Spring often brought tornadoes, hailstorms, and flooding. Summers could mean scorching heat and frequent droughts. In fall, the prairie grass dried and settlers had to watch for prairie fires. Winter brought bitter cold along with ice storms and blizzards.

Farmers also faced the dreaded grasshopper. In the mid-1870s, millions of grasshoppers swarmed across the Great Plains. They darkened the sky and covered the ground in layers up to six inches high. The insects ate everything in their path, crops, grass, even fences and axe handles. (343 words)

From Scott Foresman Social Studies: The United States, Pupil Edition, Grade 5. Copyright © 2003 by Pearson Education, Inc. or its affiliates. Adapted by permission. All Rights Reserved.

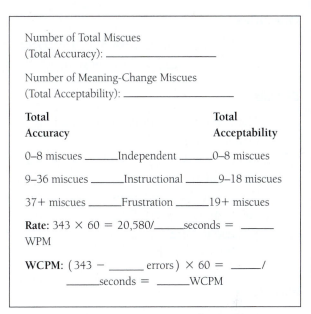

Number of Total Miscues
(Total Accuracy): _____

Number of Meaning-Change Miscues
(Total Acceptability): _____

Total Accuracy	**Total Acceptability**
0–8 miscues _____Independent _____0–8 miscues	
9–36 miscues _____Instructional _____9–18 miscues	
37+ miscues _____Frustration _____19+ miscues	

Rate: $343 \times 60 = 20{,}580/$_____seconds = _____ WPM

WCPM: $(343 -$ _____ errors$) \times 60 =$ _____/ _____seconds = _____WCPM

Oral Reading Prosody Scale—QRI-7

Directions: Please circle the number below that best represents the student's 3-minute oral reading of this passage.

4	3	2	I
Reads primarily in larger, meaningful phrase groups. Some or most of the story is read with expression.	Reads primarily in three- or four-word phrase groups. Little or no expressive interpretation is present.	Reads primarily in two-word phrases with some three- or four-word groupings. Word groupings may be awkward.	Reads primarily word-by-word with occasional two-word or three-word phrases.

Retelling Scoring Sheet for "Farming on the Great Plains"

Main Idea

_____ The Great Plains were dry grasslands.

Details

_____ People did not think it would make good farmland.

_____ It attracted very few pioneers.

Level 5

Level: Five

Main Idea

_____ The U.S. government passed the Homestead Act to encourage people to move there.

Details

_____ The Homestead Act offered free land
_____ to a man over 21,
_____ to a woman whose husband had died,
_____ and to the head of a family.
_____ You could claim 160 acres.
_____ You had to pay a $10 fee.
_____ You had to farm your land
_____ and live on it for five years.

Main Idea

_____ It was not easy to farm.

Details

_____ The grasses had tangled roots
_____ several inches down in the soil.
_____ Farmers had to dig through the sod.
_____ They became known as sodbusters.

Main Idea

_____ Homesteaders used sod to build houses.

Details

_____ Houses stayed cool in summer.
_____ They were warm in winter.
_____ They were fireproof.
_____ The walls contained bugs, mice, and/or snakes.

Main Idea

_____ The homesteaders faced harsh weather and natural disasters.

Details

_____ Spring brought tornadoes, hailstorms, and/or flooding.
_____ Summers could mean heat and/or drought.
_____ In fall, settlers had to watch for fires.
_____ Winter brought cold, ice storms, and/or blizzards.

Main Idea

_____ Farmers also faced grasshoppers.

Details

_____ Millions of grasshoppers swarmed across the Great Plains.
_____ They darkened the sky.
_____ They covered the ground six inches high.
_____ They ate everything in their path,
_____ crops, grass, fences, and/or axe handles.

Comments/Observations

Questions for "Farming on the Great Plains"

1. What is this passage mainly about?
   Implicit: the difficulties of farming on the Great Plains

2. Why did the Homestead Act attract pioneers to the Great Plains?
   Implicit: it offered free land

3. How long did farmers have to live on the land before it became theirs?
   Explicit: five years

Level: Five

4. Why did Great Plains farmers become known as sodbusters?
Implicit: they had to dig up or bust the sod before they could plant crops

5. Give one reason why sod was a good material for building houses.
Explicit: warmth in winter; coolness in summer; fireproof; *or* few rocks or trees available

6. Name one obstacle that homesteaders faced in the spring.
Explicit: tornadoes; *or* hailstorms; *or* floods

7. What obstacle did homesteaders face in the fall?
Explicit: prairie fires

8. Why would the grasshoppers cause a lot of hardship to the farmers?
Implicit: they ate crops and tools

Without Look-Backs

Number Correct Explicit: _____

Number Correct Implicit: _____

Total: _____

_____ Independent: 8 correct

_____ Instructional: 6–7 correct

_____ Frustration: 0–5 correct

With Look-Backs

Number Correct Explicit: _____

Number Correct Implicit: _____

Total: _____

_____ Independent: 8 correct

_____ Instructional: 6–7 correct

_____ Frustration: 0–5 correct

Level 5

Level: Five

Science: Expository

Concept Questions:

What does the word "moist" mean? (*3: damp, wet;
2: rain, tears, a towel; 1: my forehead when I run*)

_____

_____

_____ (3-2-1-0)

Why does your body need oxygen? (*3: in order to
breathe, to stay alive; 2: you don't know it's there, it's in the
air; 1: it's a good thing*)

_____

_____

_____ (3-2-1-0)

Why is it important to breathe through your nose?
(*3: the nose cleans the air you breathe in, it warms what you
breathe in; 2: it is easier than breathing through your mouth;
1: you would die if you couldn't breathe*)

_____

_____

_____ (3-2-1-0)

How does the air that you breathe get into your bloodstream? (*3: it goes to the lungs where there are blood vessels;
2: the lungs are involved, or if it didn't, we would die; 1: it's
how the body works*)

_____

_____

_____ (3-2-1-0)

Score: _____/12 = _____%

_____FAM (≥ 55%) _____UNFAM

Note: Underlined words are on the fourth-grade or fifth-grade
word lists.

About one-fifth of the air that you breathe in is a gas
called oxygen. Your cells must have oxygen to do their
work. Without oxygen, cells will die—some within
3–5 minutes. When you breathe in, your respiratory
system brings air containing oxygen into your body.
The cells in your body use the oxygen, and as they
work, the cells produce carbon dioxide. This gas
leaves your body as waste when you breathe out.

The respiratory system includes your nose, your
lungs, and the tubes that connect them. Air enters the
body through the nose, which has the job of getting the
air ready for the lungs. If air is very cold, dry, or dirty it
could damage your lungs. Your nose warms, moistens,
and cleans the air that you breathe in. The blood supply
and mucus in your nose keeps it warm and moist. The
hairs in your nose <u>capture</u> the dust from the air.

After the air is warmed, moistened, and
cleaned it goes to the throat and down the
trachea, or windpipe. The trachea divides into two
bronchial tubes, each of which goes into a lung.

Inside the Lungs

Inside the lungs, the bronchial tubes divide into
smaller and smaller tubes. The smallest tubes lead

Level 5

Level: Five

to clusters of tiny pouches called air sacs. A net of tiny blood <u>vessels</u> surrounds each air sac. Inhaled air, which is rich in oxygen enters the air sacs. At this moment, the blood in the vessels around the air sacs contains a lot of carbon dioxide, which the blood has picked up from body cells. That blood contains little oxygen. An air exchange quickly takes place. Oxygen passes from the air sacs into the blood <u>vessels</u>. The blood now has oxygen to deliver to body cells. Look at the picture above to help you <u>visualize</u> this description. At the same time that oxygen passes out of the air sacs, carbon dioxide passes from the blood <u>vessels</u> into the air sacs. The carbon dioxide leaves your body when you exhale. (344 words)

From Scott Foresman Science, Teacher Edition, Grade 5. Copyright © 2000 by Pearson Education, Inc. or its affiliates. Reprinted by permission. All Rights Reserved.

Number of Total Miscues
(Total Accuracy): _____

Number of Meaning-Change Miscues
(Total Acceptability): _____

Total Accuracy		Total Acceptability	
0–8 miscues _____	Independent	_____	0–8 miscues
9–36 miscues _____	Instructional	_____	9–18 miscues
37+ miscues _____	Frustration	_____	19+ miscues

Rate: 344 × 60 = 20,640/_____ seconds = _____ WPM

WPM: (344 − _____ errors) × 60 = _____/_____ seconds = _____ WCPM

Oral Reading Prosody Scale—QRI-7

Directions: Please circle the number below that best represents the student's 3minute oral reading of this passage.

4	3	2	1
Reads primarily in larger, meaningful phrase groups. Some or most of the story is read with expression.	Reads primarily in three- or four-word phrase groups. Little or no expressive interpretation is present.	Reads primarily in two-word phrases with some three- or four-word groupings. Word groupings may be awkward.	Reads primarily word-by-word with occasional two-word or three-word phrases.

Retelling Scoring Sheet for "How Does Your Body Take in Oxygen?"

Main Idea

_____ Your cells must have oxygen to do their work.

Details

_____ About one-fifth of the air you breathe is oxygen.
_____ Without oxygen, cells will die.
_____ When you breathe in, air brings oxygen into your body.
_____ The cells use the oxygen,
_____ and produce carbon dioxide.
_____ Carbon dioxide leaves your body when you breathe out.

Main Idea

_____ Your respiratory system includes your nose, lungs, and the tubes that connect them.

Details

_____ Air enters the body through the nose.
_____ The nose gets the air ready for your lungs.

Level 5

Level: Five

_____ Cold, dry, and/or dirty air could damage your lungs.

_____ Your nose warms, moistens, and/or cleans the air.

_____ The blood supply and mucus keep the air warm and/or moist.

_____ The hairs capture the dust from the air.

Main Idea

_____ After the air is warmed, moistened, and/or cleaned, it leaves the nose.

Details

_____ It goes to the throat

_____ and down the trachea/windpipe

_____ into the lungs.

_____ The trachea divides into two bronchial tubes,

_____ and each goes into a lung.

_____ The tubes divide into smaller tubes.

_____ The tubes lead to pouches/air sacs.

_____ A net of blood vessels surrounds each air sac.

Main Idea

_____ An air exchange takes place.

Details

_____ Blood vessels contain carbon dioxide.

_____ The blood contains little oxygen.

_____ Oxygen passes from the air sacs into the blood vessels.

_____ The blood has oxygen to deliver to cells.

_____ Carbon dioxide passes from the blood vessels into the air sacs.

_____ Carbon dioxide leaves your body when you exhale.

Questions for "How Does Your Body Take in Oxygen?"

1. What is _one_ of the main ideas of what you have read thus far?
   Implicit: that oxygen is needed by cells; _or_ that the air is cleaned and moistened by your nose before it enters the lungs; _or_ how air is exchanged inside your lungs

2. Why do your cells need oxygen?
   Explicit: to do their work; they need it to live

3. When the cells use the oxygen, what other gas do they make?
   Explicit: carbon dioxide

Level: Five

4. How is the air that you breathe cleaned *and* moistened?
   Explicit: nose hairs clean it, and blood supply *and/or* mucous warms and moistens it.

5. Why can't you hold your breath for 20 minutes?
   Implicit: your body would force you to breathe to keep your cells alive

6. Explain how air goes from your nose to your lungs.
   Explicit: it goes to your throat and down the windpipe or trachea through the bronchial tubes to the lungs (If the student omits "throat," the answer is still correct, but the student must describe the air going down the windpipe or trachea and through the bronchial tubes.)

7. Why are there two bronchial tubes?
   Implicit: because there are two lungs, and so a tube is connected to each one

8. Why is it important that tiny blood vessels surround each air sac?
   Implicit: so that the oxygen can enter the bloodstream and carbon dioxide can be released from the blood into the lungs to exhale; *or* so the air exchange (carbon dioxide for oxygen) can take place

---

Without Look-Backs

Number Correct Explicit: _____

Number Correct Implicit: _____

   Total: _____

   _____Independent: 8 correct

   _____Instructional: 6–7 correct

   _____Frustration: 0–5 correct

With Look-Backs

Number Correct Explicit: _____

Number Correct Implicit: _____

   Total: _____

   _____Independent: 8 correct

   _____Instructional: 6–7 correct

   _____Frustration: 0–5 correct

Level 5

Abraham Lincoln

When Abraham Lincoln was nineteen years old, he visited the city of New Orleans, Louisiana. He saw things he would never forget. He saw black people being sold in slave markets. They were chained together and treated like animals. Lincoln watched little children being sold to strangers and taken away from their parents. Lincoln was heartbroken and these memories stayed with him for the rest of his life. Although slavery was allowed in many states of the Union, Lincoln believed that it was wrong and he was not afraid to say so.

In 1858, Lincoln ran for the United States Senate against Stephen Douglas. There was much talk about slavery. Should the owning of slaves be allowed in new states that were just coming into the Union? Douglas said that the decision to own slaves was up to each individual person. Lincoln said that slavery must not be allowed to spread because it was wrong. But he knew that it would not be easy to end slavery in those states that had allowed it for so many years. Lincoln believed it was important to keep the United States strong. He felt that slavery weakened the country. In one speech, he said the country could not last half slave and half free. He said, "A house divided against itself cannot stand." Lincoln lost the election to the Senate, but he became well known for his views. In 1860 he ran for president of the United States.

The slave states opposed Lincoln as president. They did not want to abolish slavery. They threatened to leave the Union if Lincoln was elected. When he became president, the slave states carried out their threat. A terrible war broke out between the northern and southern states. At times, members of the same family were fighting against one another.

In 1863, Lincoln gave an order called the Emancipation Proclamation, which ended slavery. The war finally ended two years later. The southern states once more became part of the Union, but slavery was no longer allowed. No more would little children be torn from their parents and sold to strangers. Abraham Lincoln had achieved his goal.

The Early Life of Lois Lowry

Lois Lowry, author of two Newbery Award–winning books, *Number the Stars* (1990) and *The Giver* (1994), was born in Hawaii in 1937. Like many authors she uses childhood events and her feelings about them as ideas for her books. Because her father was an army dentist, the family moved often, rarely settling in one place for more than a few years. Perhaps because of the many moves and Lois's shy personality, making friends was difficult, and Lois became very close with her older sister, Helen.//

By the time she was three years old Lois could read, and books became a central part of her life. Already a keen observer of the world around her, she found that books fed her active imagination. Lois's mother fostered her love of books by reading to the children frequently. When Lois was 9 and her sister, Helen, was 12, their mother read *The Yearling* to them. The life of one of the characters, Jody, made Lois want to be a boy. She wanted to have a life like Jody's, to be poor, living in a swamp, having animals as friends. Jody was only one of the characters who filled Lois's life with adventure.//

Her love of books drew her to the public library. When she was 10 years old, she found a book called *A Tree Grows in Brooklyn*. The title piqued her curiosity and she decided to check it out. The librarian told her it was not a book for children, but Lois was insistent. Before Lois arrived home the librarian had called to warn her mother that Lois had checked out a book that was not suitable for children. Her mother was polite but not concerned. She had read the book herself and recalled nothing that would harm her 10-year-old daughter. Lois loved the book and wanted to be like Francie, making a better life for herself through grit and determination. Lois was drawn to characters with lives of adventure, and given the right opportunity Lois would explore the world herself.//

After World War II Lois's father was stationed in Japan. Lois, her mother, sister, and younger brother, Jon, joined him there in 1948. The family lived in an American enclave where all the houses were American style, all the neighbors were American, and the little community had its own movie theater, church, library, and elementary school. Lois didn't understand why they lived in this enclave with the excitement of Tokyo all around them. At 11 years of age, Lois often sneaked out of the American area to explore the city of Tokyo. She still remembers the smells: fish and charcoal; and the sounds: music, shouting, and the clatter of wooden wheels. But most of all she remembers children her own age dressed in dark blue school uniforms.//

Although she saw the children frequently, she never spoke to them. They must have found her curious, a light-haired girl riding her bicycle alone in the city. Through her journeys she came face to face with the tragedy of war. She found families whose homes had been destroyed living in packing boxes. The images of Tokyo, like all the other experiences of her early life, remain with her and emerge in her stories.//

Lois began writing for young people in the mid-1970s at the suggestion of an editor of a publishing company. She has been writing for young people ever since. Her goal as a writer for young people is to help her readers cope with the difficulties of being young in a world that doesn't always respect youth.//

The Lifeline of the Nile

The Nile River is the longest river in the world. It begins in East Africa and flows northward into Egypt. Surrounded by hot, sandy deserts, the Nile brought life to the people who lived by it. In ancient Egypt, the Nile irrigated land that stretched about five miles on both sides of the river. This is where Egyptian civilization began and agriculture thrived.

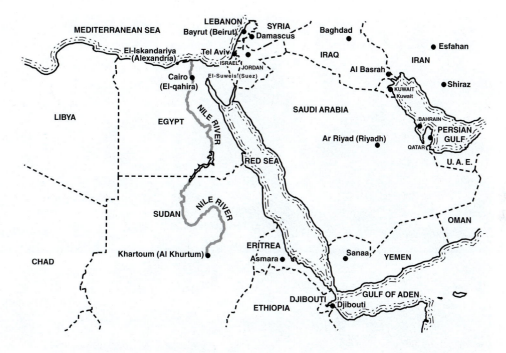

The Nile overflowed because of heavy rains in East Africa. People living near the Nile planted seeds after the floods and harvested in late summer. They called this area "black land" because the land was very fertile. Wheat and barley were the most important crops in ancient Egypt. Papyrus was another valuable crop. The Egyptians used its stems to make paper. The papermaking process involved cutting thin strips from the plant's stem and pressing them together. When the pressed strips dried, they produced a smooth surface. Papyrus became widely used for record keeping.

The Nile was also a means of transporting goods; however, the geography of the Nile caused some roadblocks for travelers. Six cataracts or waterfalls break up the flow of the Nile. The cataracts made it impossible to sail south to East Africa without taking a boat out of the water and carrying it. Because the river moves from south to north, a boat also needed sails to move it.

The Nile gave the Egyptians many gifts but it also caused problems. Although the Nile did flood regularly, it did not always do so in the same way. Sometimes heavy rains caused too much water to overflow. Crops were destroyed and people lost their lives. Other times, the Nile did not flood enough and crops could not grow. When this happened, Egyptians used the food they stored from surplus harvests.

From *Scott Foresman Social Studies: The World, Grade 6*. Copyright © 2003 Pearson Education, Inc. or its affiliates. Adapted by permission. All Rights Reserved.

Building Pyramids

Ancient Egyptian kings are best known for the huge structures they built called pyramids. These large stone buildings served as houses or tombs for the dead. The Egyptians believed that kings, or pharaohs, remained gods even after death, and that pyramids were their palaces. Kings were buried with their possessions. The Egyptians thought that kings took their possessions with them to the afterlife or the life that continued after death.//

Richard Nowitz/Digital Vision/Getty Images

Because the afterlife was more important than life on earth, the Egyptians took great care in preparing kings for burial. They believed the bodies of the pharaohs needed to be preserved. They used a process called mummification.//

Mummification took 70 days. First, the Egyptians removed all organs except the heart from the body. Then they rubbed oils and perfumes over the body. Next, they wrapped the body in linen bandages. Finally, the mummy, or preserved body, was placed in a coffin and put into a tomb.//

Archaeologists and historians estimate that some pyramids took about 20 years to build and that slave labor was not used. When the Nile River was flooding, farmers could not work in their fields. They were then available to work on a pyramid.//

Perhaps as many as 20,000 workers cut more than two million blocks of heavy stone from cliffs to the south. Then they dragged the stones with rope to ramps that led to the building site.

Building the tombs was important but many people died because the work was difficult and dangerous. Workers labored eight hours every day for ten days in a row. Then they received one day of rest.//

They were paid with food. The pharaohs counted on the tomb builders to be both committed and courageous. Because no one knew how long the pharaoh would live, they had to work quickly and accurately.//

From Scott Foresman Social Studies: The World, Grade 6. Copyright © 2003 Pearson Education, Inc. or its affiliates. Adapted by permission. All Rights Reserved.

Temperature and Humidity

When you go outside the air temperature is often the first weather condition that you notice. In the summer, if the sun has been out the air usually feels warm. On hot days the air temperature can be above 90°. If there are clouds the air often feels cooler because the clouds have blocked some of the heat from the sun's rays. The air is cooler at very high altitudes because the air is less dense and the warm ground is too far away to affect air temperature. Also, there are fewer molecules to absorb the sun's energy.

Humidity is moisture in the air in the form of a gas called water vapor. This water vapor comes from oceans, lakes, rainfall, and other sources from which water evaporates into the air.

Sometimes the air has more water vapor than at other times. The amount of water vapor that the air can hold depends largely on the air temperature. The warmer the air temperature the more water vapor it can hold.

Meteorologists refer to relative humidity when reporting how much water vapor is in the air. Relative humidity is a ratio that compares the amount of water vapor in the air to the largest amount of moisture the air can hold at that temperature. A 65% relative humidity means the air is holding 65% of the water vapor it can hold at that temperature.

Once the air has reached 100 percent relative humidity, it can't hold any more water vapor. When this happens water vapor condenses, or changes from a gas to a liquid. The temperature at which water vapor condenses is called a dew point. Water droplets form on a plant when the night air cools and reaches its dew point.

Serkucher/Fotolia

From *Scott Foresman Science, Teacher Edition, Grade 6*. Copyright © 2000 Pearson Education, Inc. or its affiliates. Reprinted by permission. All Rights Reserved.

Clouds and Precipitation

Clouds are mostly water. To understand how clouds form, remember how changes in temperature affect humidity.//

Think of a clear spring day when the sun warms the ground, which in turn warms the air. Warm air holds a certain amount of water, and warm air rises. Eventually, the warm air cools when it joins the cooler air away from the ground. At the cooler temperature the air cannot hold as much water vapor. As the water vapor separates from the air, it connects with dust and microscopic particles of salt to form tiny drops of water. They are so small and light that they float in the air. Collections of millions of these droplets form clouds.//

As clouds move in the wind and evaporate, they may take on different shapes. Clouds may be classified into a few basic kinds with a few different shapes.//

The types of clouds are classified according to their height above the ground. And the names of clouds give a clue to their appearance. For example, low clouds that are close to the ground are usually thick, even sheets. The term *strato* means "sheetlike," so the low sheetlike clouds are called stratus clouds. You can see these clouds in the first photo.

Hasky2/Shutterstock

Middle-level clouds may appear in groups in an otherwise blue sky. *Cumulo* means "pile or heap," so these middle-level groups of clouds are a type of cumulus cloud. These are pictured in the second photo below.

robodread/Fotolia

High clouds that are wispy with curled edges across a background of blue sky are called cirrus clouds because *cirro* means "curl." The third photo is a good example of cirrus clouds.// Finally, there are clouds that build upon each other into very high vertical clouds. Because they occur in heaps, they are a type of cumulus cloud, but because they often result in thunderstorms they are called cumulonimbus, because *nimbo* means "rain."

Clouds are associated with rain and snow. Most rain that occurs in the United States begins as snow. Ice crystals that are high in the cirrus clouds grow when more and more water vapor condenses on them.//

Eventually, they become so heavy that the crystals start to fall. When ice crystals fall through clouds, they may collide and combine with other ice crystals or water droplets. When the crystals become too heavy to float in the air, they drop as precipitation.//

If all the bands of air that the crystals fall through are cold, then the precipitation reaches the ground as snow. If the ice crystals fall far enough through warm air, they reach the ground as rain.

Sometimes if a band of cold air is near the ground, the rain becomes colder and freezes when it hits the ground. This is freezing rain that becomes ice on the ground, making walking and driving dangerous.//

Hail is formed when ice crystals are thrown up and down within a cumulonimbus cloud. Water collects on the crystal as it falls through the cloud and freezes on the crystal as it rises higher in the cloud. The hailstone grows larger in this way until it becomes too heavy to float and then falls to the ground.//

From *Scott Foresman Science, Teacher Edition, Grade 6*. Copyright © 2000 Pearson Education, Inc. or its affiliates. Reprinted by permission. All Rights Reserved.

Level: Six

Biography: Narrative

Concept Questions:

Who was Abraham Lincoln? (*3: the 16th president of the United States; 2: the man who stopped slavery; a famous man during the Civil War; a president; 1: a famous man*)

_____

_____

_____
(3-2-1-0)

What are the evils of slavery? (*3: it is immoral to own people, or slaves have to work but don't earn money, or their bosses make them do hard work with few breaks; 2: it's against religious teachings, or it's not right to own anyone; 1: it's the devil*)

_____

_____

_____
(3-2-1-0)

Why was the Civil War fought? (*3: the South wanted to secede from the country, or the North wanted to free slaves and the South didn't; 2: because the North and South couldn't agree on something; 1: people liked to fight*)

_____

_____

_____
(3-2-1-0)

What were the results of the Civil War? (*3: the Union was preserved, or slavery was not allowed, or the federal government showed to be superior to states; 2: many men were killed, or family members fought against each other; 1: peace happened, or there was no more fighting*)

_____

_____

_____
(3-2-1-0)

Score: _____/12 = _____%

_____FAM (≥ 55%)_____UNFAM

Note: Underlined words are on the sixth-grade word list.

Abraham Lincoln

When Abraham Lincoln was nineteen years old, he visited the city of New Orleans, Louisiana. He saw things he would never forget. He saw black people being sold in slave markets. They were chained together and treated like animals. Lincoln watched little children being sold to strangers and taken away from their parents. Lincoln was heartbroken and these <u>memories</u> stayed with him for the rest of his life. Although slavery was allowed in many states of the Union, Lincoln believed that it was wrong and he was not afraid to say so.

In 1858, Lincoln ran for the United States Senate against Stephen Douglas. There was much talk about slavery. Should the owning of slaves be allowed in new states that were just coming into the Union? Douglas said that the decision to own slaves was up to each individual person. Lincoln said that slavery must not be allowed to spread because it was wrong. But he knew that it would not be easy to end slavery in those states that had allowed it for so many years. Lincoln believed that it was important to keep the United States strong. He felt that slavery weakened the country. In one speech, he said the country could not last half slave and half free. He said, "A house divided against itself cannot stand." Lincoln lost the election to

Level 6

Level: Six

the Senate, but he became well known for his views. In 1860 he ran for president of the United States.

The slave states opposed Lincoln as president. They did not want to abolish slavery. They threatened to leave the Union if Lincoln was elected. When he became president, the slave states carried out their threat. A terrible war broke out between the northern and southern states. At times, members of the same family were fighting against one another.

In 1863, Lincoln gave an order called the Emancipation Proclamation, which ended slavery. The war finally ended two years later. The southern states once more became part of the Union, but slavery was no longer allowed. No more would little children be torn from their parents and sold to strangers. Abraham Lincoln had achieved his goal. (360 words)

Number of Total Miscues
(Total Accuracy): _____

Number of Meaning-Change Miscues
(Total Acceptability): _____

Total Accuracy		Total Acceptability
0–8 miscues _____Independent	_____	0–8 miscues
9–37 miscues _____Instructional	_____	9–19 miscues
38+ miscues _____Frustration	_____	20+ miscues

Rate: $360 \times 60 = 21{,}600/$_____ seconds = _____ WPM

WCPM: $(360 -$ _____ errors$) \times 60 =$ _____/
_____ seconds = _____WCPM

Oral Reading Prosody Scale—QRI-7

Directions: Please circle the number below that best represents the student's three-minute oral reading of this passage.

4	3	2	1
Reads primarily in larger, meaningful phrase groups. Some or most of the story is read with expression.	Reads primarily in three- or four-word phrase groups. Little or no expressive interpretation is present.	Reads primarily in two-word phrases with some three- or four-word groupings. Word groupings may be awkward.	Reads primarily word-by-word with occasional two-word or three-word phrases.

Retelling Scoring Sheet for "Abraham Lincoln"

Setting/Background

_____ When Abraham Lincoln was nineteen, he visited New Orleans, Louisiana.
_____ He saw things he would never forget.
_____ He saw black people being sold in slave markets.
_____ They were chained together and treated like animals.
_____ Lincoln watched children being sold to strangers
_____ and taken away from their parents.

Goal

_____ Lincoln believed that slavery was wrong.
_____ He was not afraid to say so.

Events

_____ Lincoln ran for the Senate against Stephen Douglas.
_____ Lincoln said that slavery must not spread.
_____ He felt that slavery weakened the country.
_____ Lincoln lost the election to the Senate.
_____ He ran for president.
_____ The slave states opposed Lincoln.
_____ They did not want to abolish slavery.

Level: Six

_____ They threatened to leave the Union if Lincoln was elected.

_____ When Lincoln became president, a war broke out between the states.

Resolution

_____ Lincoln gave an order, the Emancipation Proclamation, which ended slavery.

_____ The war ended.

_____ The southern states once more became part of the Union, but slavery was not allowed.

_____ Abraham Lincoln had achieved his goal.

Questions for "Abraham Lincoln"

1. What was Abraham Lincoln's main goal?
   Implicit: to end slavery in the United States

2. Name one thing that Abraham Lincoln saw in the slave markets of New Orleans.
   Explicit: blacks chained together; blacks treated like animals; blacks being sold; children being separated from parents; or children being sold to strangers

3. How did the sights of the slave market influence Abraham Lincoln's later life?
   Implicit: he was against slavery and fought to end it; or it made him sick, and he wanted to stop it

4. What office did Abraham Lincoln run for against Stephen Douglas?
   Explicit: he ran for the U.S. Senate

5. What did the southern states threaten to do if Abraham Lincoln was elected president?
   Explicit: leave the Union

6. Why did the southern states oppose Abraham Lincoln as president?
   Implicit: he was against slavery, and he would fight to end it in their states

7. How did Abraham Lincoln's prediction, "A house divided against itself cannot stand," come true?
   Implicit: the war between the states broke out

8. What did the Emancipation Proclamation do?
   Explicit: it ended slavery

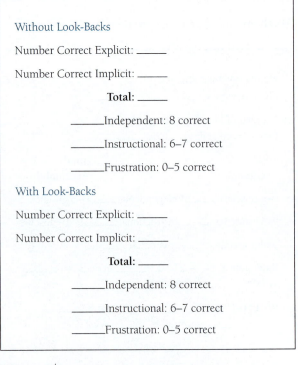

Without Look-Backs

Number Correct Explicit: _____

Number Correct Implicit: _____

      Total: _____

_____ Independent: 8 correct

_____ Instructional: 6–7 correct

_____ Frustration: 0–5 correct

With Look-Backs

Number Correct Explicit: _____

Number Correct Implicit: _____

      Total: _____

_____ Independent: 8 correct

_____ Instructional: 6–7 correct

_____ Frustration: 0–5 correct

Level 6

Level: Six

Biography: Narrative

Concept Questions:

Who is Lois Lowry? (*3: a writer of adult and children's books; 2: she wrote The Giver and Number the Stars; a writer; 1: a woman*)

_____

_____

_____ (3-2-1-0)

What does "imagination" mean? (*3: to think of something that isn't real; to make something in your mind that hasn't happened; 2: to have a friend that isn't real; 1: to think*)

_____

_____

_____ (3-2-1-0)

What does it mean to have a shy personality? (*3: to be uncomfortable around groups of people, or talking to people; 2: person likes to be alone, or student names a classmate who is shy; 1: a type of person*)

_____

_____

_____ (3-2-1-0)

What does "emerge" mean? (*3: to come out of something, or to become known; 2: like a butterfly emerges from a cocoon; 1: to hide*)

_____

_____

_____ (3-2-1-0)

Score: _____/12 = _____%

_____FAM (≥ 55%) _____UNFAM

"Now I want you to read this section, and when you come to the slash (//) marks, I want you to tell me what you are thinking. Then read to the next slash mark and do the same thing. When you have finished reading, I will ask you to tell me what you remember and then I will ask you questions."

Note: Underlined words are on the sixth-grade word list.

The Early Life of Lois Lowry

Lois Lowry, author of two Newbery Award–winning books, *Number the Stars* (1990) and *The Giver* (1994), was born in Hawaii in 1937. Like many authors she uses childhood events and her feelings about them as ideas for her books. Because her father was an army dentist, the family moved often, rarely settling in one place for more than a few years. Perhaps because of the many moves and Lois's shy personality, making friends was difficult, and Lois became very close with her older sister, Helen.//

_____

_____

_____

_____

_____

By the time she was three years old Lois could read, and books became a central part of her life. Already a keen observer of the world around her, she found that books fed her active imagination. Lois's mother fostered her love of books by reading

Level 6

to the children frequently. When Lois was 9 and her sister, Helen, was 12, their mother read *The Yearling* to them. The life of one of the characters, Jody, made Lois want to be a boy. She wanted to have a life like Jody's, to be poor, living in a swamp, having animals as friends. Jody was only one of the characters who filled Lois's life with adventure.//

_____

_____

_____

_____

Her love of books drew her to the public library. When she was 10 years old, she found a book called *A Tree Grows in Brooklyn*. The title piqued her curiosity and she decided to check it out. The librarian told her it was not a book for children, but Lois was <u>insistent</u>. Before Lois arrived home the librarian had called to warn her mother that Lois had checked out a book that was not suitable for children. Her mother was polite but not concerned. She had read the book herself and recalled nothing that would harm her 10-year-old daughter. Lois loved the book and wanted to be like

Francie, making a better life for herself through grit and determination. Lois was drawn to characters with lives of adventure, and given the right opportunity Lois would explore the world herself.//

_____

_____

_____

_____

After World War II Lois's father was stationed in Japan. Lois, her mother, sister, and younger brother, Jon, joined him there in 1948. The family lived in an American enclave where all the houses were American style, all the neighbors were American, and the little community had its own movie theater, church, library, and elementary school. Lois didn't understand why they lived in this enclave with the excitement of Tokyo all around them. At 11 years of age, Lois often sneaked out of the American area to explore the city of Tokyo. She still remembers the smells: fish and charcoal; and the sounds: music, shouting, and the clatter of wooden wheels. But most of all she remembers children her own age dressed in dark blue school uniforms.//

 Copyright © 2021 Pearson Education, Inc. Reproduction is permitted for classroom use only.

Level: Six

_____

_____

_____

_____

_____

Although she saw the children frequently, she never spoke to them. They must have found her curious, a light-haired girl riding her bicycle alone in the city. Through her journeys she came face to face with the tragedy of war. She found families whose homes had been destroyed living in packing boxes. The images of Tokyo, like all the other experiences of her early life, remain with her and emerge in her stories.//

_____

_____

_____

_____

_____

Lois began writing for young people in the mid-1970s at the suggestion of an editor of a publishing company. She has been writing for young people ever since. Her goal as a writer for young people is to help her readers cope with the difficulties of being young in a world that doesn't always respect youth. //

_____

_____

_____

_____

(597 words)

Number of Total Miscues
(Total Accuracy):_____

Number of Meaning-Change Miscues
(Total Acceptability):_____

Total Accuracy		**Total Acceptability**
0–14 miscues _____Independent	_____	0–14 miscues
15–62 miscues _____Instructional	_____	15–32 miscues
63+ miscues _____Frustration	_____	33+ miscues

Rate: $597 \times 60 = 35{,}820/$_____seconds = _____ WPM

WCPM: $(597 -$ _____ errors$) \times 60 =$ _____/ _____seconds = _____WCPM

Level 6

Level: Six

Oral Reading Prosody Scale—QRI-7

Directions: Please circle the number below that best represents the student's three-minute oral reading of this passage.

4	3	2	1
Reads primarily in larger, meaningful phrase groups. Some or most of the story is read with expression.	Reads primarily in three- or four-word phrase groups. Little or no expressive interpretation is present.	Reads primarily in two-word phrases with some three- or four-word groupings. Word groupings may be awkward.	Reads primarily word-by-word with occasional two-word or three-word phrases.

Retelling Scoring Sheet for "The Early Life of Lois Lowry"

Setting/Background/Characters

_____ Lois Lowry is the author of two award-winning books,

_____ *Number the Stars* and *The Giver*.

Goal

_____ She uses childhood events and her feelings about them as ideas for her books.

Events

_____ Because her father was an army dentist, the family moved often.

_____ Because of the moves and Lois's shy personality,

_____ Lois became close with older sister, Helen.

_____ By the time she was three years old, Lois could read.

Goal

_____ Books became a central part of her life and fed her imagination.

Events

_____ Lois's mother fostered her love of books by reading to the children frequently.

_____ Their mother read *The Yearling* to them.

Goal

_____ The book made Lois want to be a boy.

_____ She wanted to have a life like Jody's, to be poor, living in a swamp, and having animals as friends.

Events

_____ Her love of books drew her to the public library.

_____ When she was 10 years old, she found a book called *A Tree Grows in Brooklyn*.

Goal

_____ The title piqued her curiosity and she decided to check it out.

Events

_____ The librarian told her it was not a book for children, but Lois was insistent.

_____ Before Lois arrived home, the librarian had called to warn her mother.

_____ Her mother was polite but not concerned.

_____ She had read the book herself and recalled nothing that would harm her daughter.

_____ Lois loved the book.

Goals

_____ Lois wanted to be like Francie, making a better life

_____ through grit and determination.

_____ Lois was drawn to characters with lives of adventure.

_____ And given the opportunity, Lois would explore the world.

Events

_____ After World War II, Lois's father was stationed in Japan.

_____ Lois and her mother, sister, and brother joined him there.

_____ The family lived in an American enclave

Level: Six

_____ where the houses were in an American style and all the neighbors were American.

_____ The community had a movie theater, church, library, and school.

_____ Lois didn't understand why they lived there with the excitement of Tokyo around them.

Goal

_____ Lois often sneaked out to explore Tokyo.

Events

_____ She still remembers the smells of fish and charcoal

_____ and the sounds of music, shouting, and the clatter of wheels.

_____ She remembers the children dressed in dark blue school uniforms.

_____ She never spoke to them.

_____ They must have found her curious, riding her bicycle alone.

_____ She came face to face with the tragedy of war.

_____ She found families whose homes had been destroyed

_____ living in packing boxes.

_____ The images of Tokyo remain,

_____ like all other early experiences, and emerge in her stories.

Resolution

_____ Lois began writing for young people

_____ at the suggestion of an editor of a publishing company.

_____ She has been writing for young people ever since.

Goal

_____ Her goal is to help readers cope with the difficulties

_____ of being young in a world that doesn't always respect youth.

Questions for "The Early Life of Lois Lowry"

1. Who is Lois Lowry?
   Explicit: author of books for young people. If the student says only, "An author," ask, "Who does she write for?" or "What kind of author?"

2. According to the story, where does Lois Lowry get the ideas for her books?
   Explicit: from things that happened to her as a child and how she felt about them

3. How did the fact that Lois learned to read very young affect her childhood?
   Implicit: books fed her imagination; or they became a central part of her life

4. Why didn't Lois's mother get upset when Lois checked out _A Tree Grows in Brooklyn_ from the library?
   Explicit: her mother had read it and didn't see anything in it that would harm Lois

Level: Six

5. How might Lois's understanding of the main characters in *The Yearling* and *A Tree Grows in Brooklyn* have affected her behavior in Japan?
Implicit: she wanted to have adventures like the characters, so she sneaked out of the American enclave to explore Tokyo

6. What does Lois remember about Tokyo?
Explicit: its smells—fish and charcoal; its sounds—music, shouting, and the clatter of wooden wheels; *or* children her age dressed in dark blue school uniforms.One example of each sound or smell must be provided. If the student says, "Its sounds and smells," ask, "Can you name one smell and one sound?"

7. Why didn't Lois speak to the Japanese school children her age?
Implicit: she was shy; *or* she didn't speak their language

8. Why does Lois write about the difficulties of being young?
Implicit: to help them cope with similar problems; *or* because she had problems when she was young. If the student just names a problem, such as being shy or having to move a lot, ask, "Why would this influence Lois to write about the difficulties of young people?"

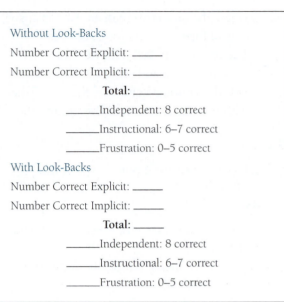

Without Look-Backs

Number Correct Explicit: _____

Number Correct Implicit: _____

         Total: _____

_____Independent: 8 correct

_____Instructional: 6–7 correct

_____Frustration: 0–5 correct

With Look-Backs

Number Correct Explicit: _____

Number Correct Implicit: _____

         Total: _____

_____Independent: 8 correct

_____Instructional: 6–7 correct

_____Frustration: 0–5 correct

Think-Aloud Summary

Think-Aloud Comments That Suggest Understanding

Restates text content accurately   _____

Offers relevant comment   _____

Asks relevant question   _____

Recognizes topic/main idea   _____

Identifies personally   _____

Paraphrases/summarizes appropriately   _____

Draws a valid inference based on personal experience   _____

Draws a valid inference based on text information   _____

Think-Aloud Comments That Suggest Lack of Understanding

Restates text content inaccurately   _____

Offers irrelevant comment   _____

Asks irrelevant question   _____

Does not recognize topic/main idea   _____

Does not identify personally   _____

Paraphrases/summarizes inappropriately   _____

Draws an invalid inference based on personal experience   _____

Draws an invalid inference based on text information   _____

Level 6

Level: Six

Social Studies: Expository

> **Concept Questions:**
>
> What happens when there is a flood? (*3: a lot of water covers areas that are usually dry; 2: homes are ruined, people sometimes die; 1: it's a bad thing, or I saw pictures on television*)
>
> _____
>
> _____
>
> _____ (3-2-1-0)
>
> What does it mean if something thrives? (*3: it flourishes/prospers/grows well; 2: plants have a lot of flowers or vegetables, a person succeeds; 1: my grandfather's garden, something that is working*)
>
> _____
>
> _____
>
> _____ (3-2-1-0)
>
> What is meant by fertile land? (*3: land that produces a lot of crops, land that has a lot of things necessary for growing plants; 2: big corn fields, where there are a lot of farms, not the desert; 1: what I saw when we went to Iowa*)
>
> _____
>
> _____
>
> _____ (3-2-1-0)
>
> What is a harvest? (*3: crops that are picked or cut down; 2: corn, wheat, tomatoes, etc.; 1: my uncle had one*)
>
> _____
>
> _____
>
> _____ (3-2-1-0)
>
> **Score:** _____/12 = _____%
>
> _____FAM (≥ 55%) _____UNFAM

Note: Underlined words are on the sixth-grade word list.

The Lifeline of the Nile

The Nile River is the longest river in the world. It begins in East Africa and flows northward into Egypt. Surrounded by hot, sandy deserts, the Nile brought life to the people who lived by it. In ancient Egypt, the Nile irrigated land that stretched about five miles on both sides of the river. This is where Egyptian civilization began and agriculture thrived.

The Nile overflowed because of heavy rains in East Africa. People living near the Nile planted seeds after the floods and harvested in late summer. They called this area "black land" because the land was very fertile. Wheat and barley were the most important crops in ancient Egypt. Papyrus was another valuable crop. The Egyptians used its stems to make paper. The papermaking process involved cutting thin strips from the plant's stem and pressing them together. When the pressed strips dried, they produced a smooth surface. Papyrus became widely used for record keeping.

The Nile was also a means of transporting goods; however, the geography of the Nile caused some roadblocks for travelers. Six cataracts or waterfalls break up the flow of the Nile. The cataracts made it impossible to sail south to East

Level: Six

Africa without taking a boat out of the water and carrying it. Because the river moves from south to north, a boat also needed sails to move it.

The Nile gave the Egyptians many gifts but it also caused problems. Although the Nile did flood regularly, it did not always do so in the same way. Sometimes heavy rains caused too much water to overflow. Crops were destroyed and people lost their lives. Other times, the Nile did not flood enough and crops could not grow. When this happened, Egyptians used the food they stored from surplus harvests. (295 words)

From *Scott Foresman Social Studies: The World*, Grade 6. Copyright © 2003 Pearson Education, Inc. or its affiliates. Adapted by permission. All Rights Reserved.

Number of Total Miscues
(Total Accuracy): _____

Number of Meaning-Change Miscues
(Total Acceptability): _____

Total Accuracy		**Total Acceptability**
0–7 miscues _____ Independent _____		0–7 miscues
8–30 miscues _____ Instructional _____		8–16 miscues
31+ miscues _____ Frustration _____		17+ miscues

Rate: 295 × 60 = 17,700/_____ seconds = _____ WPM

WCPM: (295 − _____ errors) × 60 = _____/ _____ seconds = _____ WCPM

Oral Reading Prosody Scale—QRI-7

Directions: Please circle the number below that best represents the student's three-minute oral reading of this text.

4	3	2	I
Reads primarily in larger, meaningful phrase groups. Some or most of the story is read with expression.	Reads primarily in three- or four-word phrase groups. Little or no expressive interpretation is present.	Reads primarily in two-word phrases with some three- or four-word groupings. Word groupings may be awkward.	Reads primarily word-by-word with occasional two-word or three-word phrases.

Retelling Scoring Sheet for "The Lifeline of the Nile"

Main Idea

_____ The Nile River brought life to Egyptians.

Details

_____ The Nile is the longest river in the world.
_____ The Nile irrigated land
_____ for five miles on both sides of the river.
_____ Egyptian civilization began.
_____ Agriculture thrived.

Main Idea

_____ The land was very fertile.

Details

_____ The Nile overflowed
_____ because of heavy rains.
_____ People planted seeds after the floods
_____ and harvested in summer.
_____ Wheat, barley, and/or papyrus were important crops.
_____ The Egyptians used papyrus to make paper/ keep records.

Main Idea

_____ The Nile was a means of transportation but there were problems.

Level 6

Level: Six

Details

_____ Cataracts/waterfalls made it impossible to sail south

_____ without taking a boat out of the water.

_____ Because the river moves from south to north,

_____ a boat needed sails to move it.

Main Idea

_____ The Nile gave gifts to the Egyptians but also caused problems.

Details

_____ Sometimes rains caused too much water to overflow.

_____ Crops were destroyed,

_____ and people lost their lives.

_____ Other times, the Nile did not flood enough,

_____ and crops could not grow.

_____ Egyptians used the food they stored from surplus harvests.

Questions for "The Lifeline of the Nile"

1. What is this passage mainly about?
   Implicit: the importance of the Nile River to ancient Egypt; or how the Nile helped Egypt

2. Why did the Nile River overflow?
   Explicit: because of heavy rains in East Africa

3. Name one important crop that the Egyptians grew.
   Explicit: wheat; barley; *or* papyrus

4. How do we know the ancient Egyptians were a literate people—that is, they could read and write?
   Implicit: papyrus was an important crop that they used to make paper

5. Why did the Egyptians store surplus food?
   Implicit: in case the Nile did not flood enough and crops were poor

6. What is another word for waterfall?
   Explicit: cataract

7. In what direction did the Nile flow?
   Explicit: from south to north

8. Why would a boat need a sail to travel to the south?
   Implicit: you would be going against the current

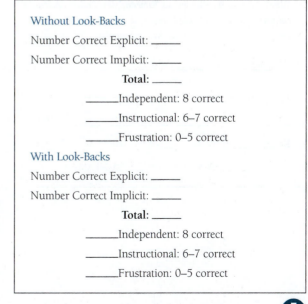

Without Look-Backs

Number Correct Explicit: _____

Number Correct Implicit: _____

Total: _____

_____ Independent: 8 correct

_____ Instructional: 6–7 correct

_____ Frustration: 0–5 correct

With Look-Backs

Number Correct Explicit: _____

Number Correct Implicit: _____

Total: _____

_____ Independent: 8 correct

_____ Instructional: 6–7 correct

_____ Frustration: 0–5 correct

Level 6

Level: Six

Social Studies: Expository

Concept Questions:

What are pyramids? (3: *ancient Egyptian tombs, structures in the shape of a triangle; 2: they were made of heavy blocks of stone, or tourists visit them, or there are mummies inside; 1: they were in a movie about mummies*)

_____

_____

_____ (3-2-1-0)

What is a pharaoh? (3: *an ancient Egyptian ruler or king, or a ruler they thought was a god; 2: a powerful person, people had to obey him; 1: they may be in a museum*)

_____

_____

_____ (3-2-1-0)

What is a mummy? (3: *a body that is preserved, or an ancient dead Egyptian; 2: it's wrapped in strips of cloth; it died a long time ago; 1: they're scary*)

_____

_____

_____ (3-2-1-0)

What is an archaeologist? (3: *someone who studies ancient cultures; 2: a very educated person, or someone who digs to find bodies; 1: "ist" means he does something*)

_____

_____

_____ (3-2-1-0)

Score: _____/12 = _____%

_____FAM (≥ 55%) _____UNFAM

"Now I want you to read this section, and when you come to the slash (//) marks, I want you to tell me what you are thinking. Then read to the next slash mark and do the same thing. When you have finished reading, I will ask you to tell me what you remember and then I will ask you questions."

Note: Underlined words are on the sixth-grade word list.

Building Pyramids

Ancient Egyptian kings are best known for the huge structures they built called <u>pyramids</u>. These large stone buildings served as houses or tombs for the dead. The Egyptians believed that kings, or <u>pharaohs</u>, remained gods even after death, and that <u>pyramids</u> were their palaces. Kings were buried with their <u>possessions</u>. The Egyptians thought that kings took their <u>possessions</u> with them to the afterlife or the life that continued after death.//

_____

_____

_____

_____

_____

Because the afterlife was more important than life on earth, the Egyptians took great care in preparing kings for burial. They believed the

Level: Six

bodies of the pharaohs needed to be <u>preserved</u>.

They used a process called mummification.//

_____

_____

_____

_____

Mummification took 70 days. First, the

Egyptians removed all organs except the heart from

the body. Then they rubbed oils and perfumes over

the body. Next, they wrapped the body in linen

bandages. Finally, the mummy, or <u>preserved</u> body,

was placed in a coffin and put into a tomb.//

_____

_____

_____

Archaeologists and historians estimate that

some <u>pyramids</u> took about 20 years to build and

that slave labor was not used. When the Nile River

was flooding, farmers could not work in their fields.

They were then available to work on a <u>pyramid</u>.//

_____

_____

_____

Perhaps as many as 20,000 workers cut more

than two million blocks of heavy stone from cliffs

to the south. Then they dragged the stones with

rope to ramps that led to the building site.

Building the tombs was important but many

people died because the work was difficult and

dangerous. Workers labored eight hours every day for

ten days in a row. Then they received one day of rest.//

_____

_____

_____

They were paid with food. The pharaohs

counted on the tomb builders to be both

committed and <u>courageous</u>. Because no one knew

how long the pharaoh would live, they had to work

quickly and accurately.//

Level 6

Level: Six

_____

_____

_____

_____

_____

(303 words)

_____

Number of Total Miscues
(Total Accuracy): _____

Number of Meaning-Change Miscues
(Total Acceptability): _____

Total Accuracy	Total Acceptability
0–7 miscues _____Independent	_____0–7 miscues
8–32 miscues _____Instructional	_____8–16 miscues
33+ miscues _____Frustration	_____17+ miscues

Rate: (If you used this passage as a think-aloud passage, rate cannot be calculated, and prosody cannot be rated)
303 × 60 = 18,180/_____seconds = _____WPM

WCPM: (303 − errors) × 60 = _____/
_____seconds = _____WCPM

Oral Reading Prosody Scale—QRI-7

Directions: Circle the number below that best represents the student's 3-minute oral reading of this text.

4	3	2	1
Reads primarily in larger, meaningful phrase groups. Some or most of the story is read with expression.	Reads primarily in three- or four-word phrase groups. Little or no expressive interpretation is present.	Reads primarily in two-word phrases with some three- or four-word groupings. Word groupings may be awkward.	Reads primarily word-by-word with occasional two-word or three-word phrases.

Retelling Scoring Sheet for "Building Pyramids"

Main Idea

_____ Egyptian kings built pyramids.

Details

_____ These buildings served as tombs.
_____ The Egyptians believed that kings remained gods after death.
_____ Pyramids were their palaces.
_____ Kings were buried with their possessions.
_____ The Egyptians thought that kings took their possessions to the afterlife.

Main Idea

_____ The Egyptians took care in preparing kings for burial.

Details

_____ They preserved the bodies.
_____ They used mummification.
_____ Mummification took 70 days.
_____ The Egyptians removed all organs except the heart.
_____ They rubbed oil and perfumes over the body.
_____ They wrapped the body in bandages.
_____ The mummy was placed in a coffin and put into a tomb.

Level 6

Level: Six

Main Idea

_____ Archaeologists estimate that pyramids took 20 years to build.

Details

_____ Slave labor was not used.
_____ When the Nile River was flooding, farmers could not work in their fields.
_____ They worked on pyramids instead.
_____ As many as 20,000 workers cut blocks of heavy stone and dragged them to the site.

Main Idea

_____ The work was difficult and/or dangerous.

Details

_____ People died.
_____ Workers labored eight hours a day for ten days.
_____ Then they received one day of rest.
_____ They were paid with food.
_____ Because no one knew how long the pharaoh would live, they had to work quickly.

Questions for "Building Pyramids"

1. What is this passage mainly about?
   Implicit: why and how pyramids were built; *or* ancient Egyptian burial practices

2. What was the purpose of pyramids?
   Explicit: they served as houses or tombs for the dead; *or* they were the dead pharaoh's palace

3. Why were pharaohs buried with their possessions?
   Explicit: the Egyptians thought the pharaoh took his possessions with him to the afterlife

4. Why did the ancient Egyptians believe the body of the pharaoh should be preserved?
   Implicit: the pharaoh would need the body in the afterlife

5. What organ did the ancient Egyptians leave in the dead pharaoh's body?
   Explicit: the heart

Level 6

Level: Six

6. Name one step in the process of mummification.
   Explicit: remove the organs; *or* rub the body with oils and perfumes; *or* wrap the body in linen

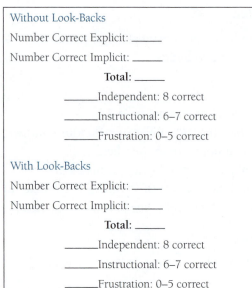

Without Look-Backs

Number Correct Explicit: _____

Number Correct Implicit: _____

   Total: _____

   _____Independent: 8 correct

   _____Instructional: 6–7 correct

   _____Frustration: 0–5 correct

With Look-Backs

Number Correct Explicit: _____

Number Correct Implicit: _____

   Total: _____

   _____Independent: 8 correct

   _____Instructional: 6–7 correct

   _____Frustration: 0–5 correct

7. Why did it take so long to build a pyramid?
   Implicit: pyramids were very large, and workers did not have modern tools; *or* workers could only work when they were not farming

Think-Aloud Summary

Think-Aloud Comments That Suggest Understanding

Restates text content accurately	_____
Offers relevant comment	_____
Asks relevant question	_____
Recognizes topic/main idea	_____
Identifies personally	_____
Paraphrases/summarizes appropriately	_____
Draws a valid inference based on personal experience	_____
Draws a valid inference based on text information	_____

8. Why was building a pyramid considered to be important work?
   Implicit: they were preparing for the pharaoh's afterlife; *or* they were working for a god

Think-Aloud Comments That Suggest Lack of Understanding

Restates text content inaccurately	_____
Offers irrelevant comment	_____
Asks irrelevant question	_____
Does not recognize topic/main idea	_____
Does not identify personally	_____
Paraphrases/summarizes inappropriately	_____
Draws an invalid inference based on personal experience	_____
Draws an invalid inference based on text information	_____

Level 6

Level: Six

Science: Expository

Note: Underlined words are on the sixth-grade word list.

Temperature and Humidity

When you go outside the air temperature is often the first weather condition that you notice. In the summer, if the sun has been out the air usually feels warm. On hot days the air temperature can be above 90°. If there are clouds the air often feels cooler because the clouds have blocked some of the heat from the sun's rays. The air is cooler at very high altitudes because the air is less dense and the warm ground is too far away to affect air temperature. Also, there are fewer molecules to absorb the sun's energy.

Humidity is moisture in the air in the form of a gas called water vapor. This water vapor comes from oceans, lakes, rainfall, and other sources from which water evaporates into the air.

Sometimes the air has more water vapor than at other times. The amount of water vapor that the air can hold depends largely on the air temperature. The warmer the air temperature the more water vapor it can hold.

Meteorologists refer to relative humidity when reporting how much water vapor is in the air. Relative humidity is a ratio that compares the amount of water vapor in the air to the largest amount of moisture the air can hold at that

Level 6

Level: Six

temperature. A 65% relative <u>humidity</u> means the air is holding 65% of the water vapor it can hold at that temperature.

Once the air has reached 100 percent relative <u>humidity</u>, it can't hold any more water vapor. When this happens water vapor <u>condenses</u>, or changes from a gas to a liquid. The temperature at which water vapor <u>condenses</u> is called a dew point. Water droplets form on a plant when the night air cools and reaches its dew point. (291 words)

From *Scott Foresman Science, Teacher Edition, Grade 6.* Copyright © 2000 Pearson Education, Inc. or its affiliates. Reprinted by permission. All Rights Reserved.

Number of Total Miscues
(Total Accuracy): _____

Number of Meaning-Change Miscues
(Total Acceptability): _____

Total Accuracy		**Total Acceptability**
0–7 miscues _____Independent	_____	0–7 miscues
8–30 miscues _____Instructional	_____	8–16 miscues
31+ miscues _____Frustration	_____	17+ miscues

Rate: 291 × 60 = 17,460/_____seconds = _____WPM

WCPM: (291 − _____ errors) × 60 = _____/
_____seconds = _____WCPM

Directions: Please circle the number below that best represents the student's three-minute oral reading of this text.

4	3	2	1
Reads primarily in larger, meaningful phrase groups. Some or most of the story is read with expression.	Reads primarily in three- or four-word phrase groups. Little or no expressive interpretation is present.	Reads primarily in two-word phrases with some three- or four-word groupings. Word groupings may be awkward.	Reads primarily word-by-word with occasional two-word or three-word phrases.

Retelling Scoring Sheet for "Temperature and Humidity"

Main Idea

_____ When you go outside you notice air temperature.

Details

_____ In the summer, if the sun has been out the air feels warm.
_____ On hot days the temperature can be above 90°.
_____ If there are clouds the air feels cooler
_____ because clouds have blocked the heat from the sun.
_____ The air is cooler at high altitudes
_____ because the air is less dense
_____ and the warm ground is too far away
_____ to affect the temperature.
_____ There are fewer molecules to absorb the sun's energy.

Main Idea

_____ Humidity is moisture in the air.

Details

_____ It is in the form of a gas/water vapor.
_____ This comes from oceans/lakes/rainfall,
_____ from which water evaporates into the air.

Level: Six

Main Idea

_____ Sometimes the air has more water vapor than at other times.

Details

_____ The amount depends on the air temperature.
_____ The warmer the air temperature,
_____ the more water vapor it can hold.

Main Idea

_____ Meteorologists refer to relative humidity when reporting humidity.

Details

_____ Relative humidity is a ratio
_____ that compares the amount of water vapor in the air
_____ to the largest amount of moisture
_____ the air can hold at that temperature.
_____ A 65% relative humidity means
_____ the air is holding 65% of the water vapor it can hold.

Main Idea

_____ Relative humidity of 100% means the air can't hold any more water vapor.

Details

_____ Water vapor changes from a gas to a liquid.
_____ The temperature at which water vapor changes is called the dew point.
_____ Water droplets form on a plant
_____ when the night air is cooled
_____ and reaches its dew point.

Questions for "Temperature and Humidity"

1. What is this section mostly about?
   Implicit: how temperature and humidity are related

2. What is humidity?
   Explicit: moisture in the air or water vapor in the air

3. Why does it feel more humid when the humidity is high in warm weather rather than in cold weather?
   Implicit: warmer air can hold more water vapor than cooler air

Level 6

Level: Six

4. What is relative humidity?

   Explicit: the ratio of the amount of water vapor in the air relative to the maximum amount the air could hold at that temperature

5. If the temperature increases and the amount of water vapor in the air stays the same, what would happen to the relative humidity, and why?

   Implicit: it would decrease because warm air can hold more humidity, so the amount of water vapor stays the same but it is a lower percentage of the maximum the warm air can hold

6. What happens when the air can't hold any more water vapor?

   Explicit: the vapor changes to a liquid

7. What is the dew point?

   Explicit: the temperature at which water vapor turns to liquid

8. Why do we find the grass wet in the morning even when it hasn't rained?

   Implicit: the temperature of the air decreased overnight. Either of the following answers are correct: the water vapor reached 100% (or its maximum) and turned to a liquid; *or* dew formed when the water vapor hit 100%.

Without Look-Backs

Number Correct Explicit: _____

Number Correct Implicit: _____

   Total: _____

_____Independent: 8 correct

_____Instructional: 6–7 correct

_____Frustration: 0–5 correct

With Look-Backs

Number Correct Explicit: _____

Number Correct Implicit: _____

   Total: _____

_____Independent: 8 correct

_____Instructional: 6–7 correct

_____Frustration: 0–5 correct

Level: Six

Science: Expository

"Now I want you to read this section, and when you come to the slash (//) marks, I want you to tell me what you are thinking. Then read to the next slash mark and do the same thing. When you have finished reading, I will ask you to tell me what you remember, and then I will ask you questions."

Note: Underlined words are on the sixth-grade word list.

Clouds and Precipitation

Clouds are mostly water. To understand how clouds form, remember how changes in temperature affect humidity.//

_____

_____

_____

_____

_____

Think of a clear spring day when the sun warms the ground, which in turn warms the air. Warm air holds a certain amount of water, and warm air rises. Eventually, the warm air cools when it joins the cooler air away from the ground. At the cooler temperature the air cannot hold as much water vapor. As the water vapor separates from the air, it connects with dust and microscopic particles of salt to form tiny drops of water. They are so small and light that they float in the air. Collections of millions of these droplets form clouds.//

_____

_____

_____

_____

_____

Level 6

Level: Six

As clouds move in the wind and <u>evaporate</u>, they may take on different shapes. Clouds may be classified into a few basic kinds with a few different shapes. //

_____

_____

_____

_____

The types of clouds are classified according to their height above the ground. And the names of clouds give a clue to their appearance. For example, low clouds that are close to the ground are usually thick, even sheets. The term *strato* means "sheet-like," so the low sheetlike clouds are called stratus clouds. You can see these clouds in the first photo.

Middle-level clouds may appear in groups in an otherwise blue sky. *Cumulo* means "pile or heap," so these middle-level groups of clouds are a type of cumulus cloud. These are pictured in the second photo below.

High clouds that are wispy with curled edges across a background of blue sky are called cirrus clouds because *cirro* means "curl." The third photo is a good example of cirrus clouds.//

_____

_____

_____

_____

Finally, there are clouds that build upon each other into very high vertical clouds. Because they occur in heaps, they are a type of cumulus cloud, but because they often result in thunderstorms they are called cumulonimbus, because *nimbo* means "rain."//

_____

_____

_____

_____

Clouds are associated with rain and snow. Most rain that occurs in the United States begins as snow. Ice crystals that are high in the cirrus clouds grow when more and more water vapor <u>condenses</u> on them.//

_____

_____

_____

_____

Level: Six

Eventually, they become so heavy that the crystals start to fall. When ice crystals fall through clouds, they may collide and combine with other ice crystals or water droplets. When the crystals become too heavy to float in the air, they drop as precipitation.//

_____

_____

_____

_____

If all the bands of air that the crystals fall through are cold, then the precipitation reaches the ground as snow. If the ice crystals fall far enough through warm air, they reach the ground as rain.

Sometimes if a band of cold air is near the ground, the rain becomes colder and freezes when it hits the ground. This is freezing rain that becomes ice on the ground, making walking and driving dangerous.//

_____

_____

_____

_____

Hail is formed when ice crystals are thrown up and down within a cumulonimbus cloud. Water collects on the crystal as it falls through the cloud and freezes on the crystal as it rises higher in the cloud. The hailstone grows larger in this way until it becomes too heavy to float and then falls to the ground.//

_____

_____

_____

_____

(528 words)

_____

From _Scott Foresman Science, Teacher Edition, Grade 6_. Copyright © 2000 Pearson Education, Inc. or its affiliates. Reprinted by permission. All Rights Reserved.

Number of Total Miscues
(Total Accuracy): _____

Number of Meaning-Change Miscues
(Total Acceptability): _____

Total Accuracy	**Total Acceptability**
0–1 miscues _____Independent	_____0–11 miscues
12–4 miscues _____Instructional	_____12–29 miscues
5+ miscues _____Frustration	_____30+ miscues

Rate (If you used this passage as a think-aloud passage, you cannot compute rate):

$528 \times 60 = 31{,}680/$_____ seconds = _____WPM

WCPM: $(528 -$ _____ errors$) \times 60 =$ _____/ _____seconds = _____WCPM

Level: Six

Oral Reading Prosody Scale—QRI-7

Directions: Circle the number below that best represents the student's 3-minute oral reading of this text.

4	3	2	1
Reads primarily in larger, meaningful phrase groups. Some or most of the story is read with expression.	Reads primarily in three- or four-word phrase groups. Little or no expressive interpretation is present.	Reads primarily in two-word phrases with some three- or four-word groupings. Word groupings may be awkward.	Reads primarily word-by-word with occasional two-word or three-word phrases.

Retelling Scoring Sheet for "Clouds and Precipitation"

Main Idea

_____ Clouds are mostly water.

Details

_____ Warm air holds water.
_____ The air rises.
_____ The air cools.
_____ The cool air cannot hold water vapor.
_____ The water vapor separates
_____ and connects with dust and salt
_____ to form drops of water.
_____ They are so small and light
_____ that they float.
_____ Millions of these droplets form clouds.

Main Idea

_____ Clouds are classified according to their height above the ground.

Details

_____ Low clouds close to the ground form sheets.
_____ *Strato* means "sheetlike,"
_____ so they are called stratus clouds.

_____ Middle-level clouds appear in groups.
_____ *Cumulo* means "pile or heap,"
_____ so these clouds are cumulus clouds.
_____ Clouds that are wispy/high/with curled edges
_____ are called cirrus clouds
_____ because *cirro* means "curl."
_____ Clouds that build into very high clouds/vertical clouds
_____ often result in thunderstorms.
_____ They are called cumulonimbus
_____ because *nimbo* means "rain."

Main Idea

_____ Clouds are associated with rain and snow.

Details

_____ Most rain begins as snow.
_____ Ice crystals grow in cirrus clouds.
_____ They become so heavy that they fall.
_____ They may combine with other crystals/water droplets.
_____ When the crystals become too heavy,
_____ they drop as precipitation.
_____ If the air is cold, the precipitation is snow.
_____ If the air is warm, the precipitation is rain.
_____ If cold air is near the ground,
_____ the rain freezes and becomes ice.
_____ Hail is formed
_____ when ice crystals are thrown up and down.
_____ Water collects and freezes on the crystal.
_____ The hailstones grow larger
_____ until they become too heavy
_____ and fall to the ground.

Questions for "Clouds and Precipitation"

1. What is this section mostly about?
   Implicit: how clouds and precipitation are related

Level: Six

2. Name one thing needed for clouds to form.
   Explicit: water vapor; *or* dust

3. How are clouds classified?
   Explicit: according to their height from the ground

4. Why are clouds named as they are?
   Implicit: because part of their name describes how they look (in Latin)

5. What does a stratus cloud look like?
   Explicit: a sheet

6. What can you predict about the weather if the clouds are cumulonimbus?
   Explicit: a thunderstorm is likely

7. What can you conclude about the atmosphere above the ground when it snows?
   Implicit: that all of [the bands of] the air above the ground is/are cold

8. What happened to an ice crystal that resulted in a golf-ball-sized hailstone?
   Implicit: it was thrown up and down a lot in a cloud that contained a lot of water

---

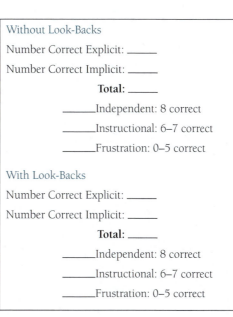

Without Look-Backs

Number Correct Explicit: _____

Number Correct Implicit: _____

      Total: _____

      _____Independent: 8 correct

      _____Instructional: 6–7 correct

      _____Frustration: 0–5 correct

With Look-Backs

Number Correct Explicit: _____

Number Correct Implicit: _____

      Total: _____

      _____Independent: 8 correct

      _____Instructional: 6–7 correct

      _____Frustration: 0–5 correct

Think-Aloud Summary

Think-Aloud Comments That Suggest Understanding

Restates text content accurately	_____
Offers relevant comment	_____
Asks relevant question	_____
Recognizes topic/main idea	_____
Identifies personally	_____
Paraphrases/summarizes appropriately	_____
Draws a valid inference based on personal experience	_____
Draws a valid inference based on text information	_____

Think-Aloud Comments That Suggest Lack of Understanding

Restates text content inaccurately	_____
Offers irrelevant comment	_____
Asks irrelevant question	_____
Does not recognize topic/main idea	_____
Does not identify personally	_____
Paraphrases/summarizes inappropriately	_____
Draws an invalid inference based on personal experience	_____
Draws an invalid inference based on text information	_____

Barbulat/Fotolia Richard Nowitz/Digital Vision/Getty Images Serkucher/Fotolia Brian Cosgrove/Dorling Kindersley, Ltd. robodread/Fotolia rck/Fotolia

Jaime Escalanté: Teacher Extraordinaire

Few teachers have movies made out of their lives, but Jaime (pronounced Hy-me) Escalanté is one of them. The movie was *Stand and Deliver*. What was it about Jaime Escalanté that made him worthy of a movie? To understand we have to go back to his family. His parents were teachers, as was his mother's father. His family lived in a rural area in the mountains that allowed him freedom to develop his imagination. And his grandfather taught him to read and count.//

When he was nine, he moved with his mother and siblings to La Paz, the capital of Bolivia. The city was big, noisy, and crowded. School was a greater shock where he faced the challenges of paying attention, following rules, and fitting in with his peers. Although he was creative, his report cards weren't good. If he didn't think that an assignment was worthwhile, he'd create his own project and many teachers didn't approve. However, one teacher discovered a key to motivate Jaime—mathematics. The interest of one teacher can make a huge difference in a student's life.//

His mother sacrificed to send him to a private high school where he fell in love with chemistry, physics, and higher mathematics. When he took an entrance exam for college, he scored the highest of all of the applicants in physics and math. In college, he met his first mentor, the elementary teacher who had shown him the wonders of math. Mr. Bilbao was now a college teacher and he mentored Jaime once again. When a physics teacher died unexpectedly, he recommended that Jaime teach the course despite Jaime having completed only one year of college.//

At age 21, Jaime was hired as a teacher and he learned how to motivate teenagers. He attracted them by sports, and then hooked them on math. He promised them A's, but made them work for them. His lifelong creed was, determination + discipline + hard work = success. He lived that creed by going to school and working at least three other jobs to support his family. Because of political unrest in Bolivia, Jaime went to the United States.//

In the United States, Jaime learned that he would have to complete college all over again to earn a teaching certificate. To enroll in a city college, an applicant must pass a test in a major subject. A test in math was the best choice for someone who knew little English. Jaime turned in his paper after 25 minutes of an anticipated two-hour exam. The glowering test administer snatched the test from Jaime's hand and began to score it. His glower faded slowly and at the end, he looked up apologetically and said, "OK. You did fine. You got every one right."//

Jaime kept going to night school while he worked at other jobs, but after eight years he still was over a year away from teacher certification. Hearing about a scholarship that would pay tuition, books, and a living allowance for one year, Jaime applied. He won the scholarship, and a year later he chose to teach in a neighborhood school. The students were Mexican American and Jaime felt that he understood the lives of these students because he too was an immigrant whose first language was Spanish. He was asked to teach "high school math" but found that it was only basic mathematical functions. Jaime was appalled that the most difficult concepts were percentages and fractions. He thought that any fifth-grader should have mastered those concepts.//

His students learned but not fast enough to satisfy Escalanté. The Advanced Placement calculus exam was just what he needed to convince people that these students could excel in higher mathematics. Garfield High did not offer the courses needed to prepare for the AP exam. How could Jaime teach prerequisite knowledge and advanced calculus in one year? He asked his students to come in before school started, stay after school, and come in on Saturdays. The first year he had 14 students, but nine dropped out. At the end of the year, four of the five students passed the AP exam, an amazing percentage! The next year eight of ten students passed showing that the first year's results were not a fluke. In 1982, his entire class passed the exam. However, to the students' surprise, each received a letter from the Educational Testing Service accusing them of cheating! The evidence was that they all missed the same question and answered in similar ways. After several months of trying to convince ETS that their scores were valid, 12 of the initial 18 students decided to retake the exam; they all passed!//

After that, Escalanté received requests for TV interviews and lectures. Any teacher who could take poor, immigrant students, and teach them the mathematics necessary to pass the AP calculus exam was exceptional and his continued success with rising numbers of students was a testament to his teaching. In 1988, the film *Stand and Deliver* was made to celebrate this amazing teacher. He died in 2010 of cancer, at the age of 79.//

Immigration—Part 1

Reasons for Immigration

Between 1866 and 1915, more than a million immigrants poured into the United States. Both push and pull factors played a part in this vast migration. Push factors are conditions that drive people from their homes. Pull factors are conditions that attract immigrants to a new area.

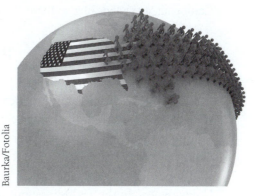

Baurka/Fotolia

Push Factors

Many immigrants were small farmers or landless farm workers. As European populations grew, land for farming became scarce. Small farms could barely support the families who worked them. In some areas, new farm machines replaced farm workers.

Another factor was political and religious persecution that pushed many people to leave their homes. In the late 1800s, the Russian government supported pogroms or organized attacks on Jewish villages. "Every night," recalled a Jewish girl who fled Russia, "they were chasing after us, to kill everyone." Millions of Jews fled Russia and eastern Europe to settle in American cities.

Persecution was also a push factor for Armenian immigrants. The Armenians lived in the Ottoman Empire (present-day Turkey). Between the 1890s and the 1920s, the Ottoman government killed a million or more Armenians. Many fled, eventually settling in California and elsewhere in the United States.

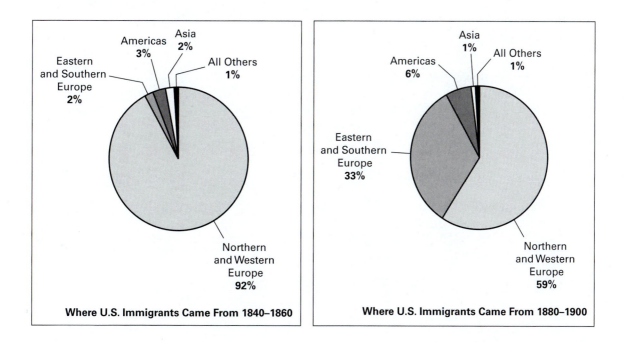

Where U.S. Immigrants Came From 1840–1860
- Americas 3%
- Asia 2%
- All Others 1%
- Eastern and Southern Europe 2%
- Northern and Western Europe 92%

Where U.S. Immigrants Came From 1880–1900
- Asia 1%
- All Others 1%
- Americas 6%
- Eastern and Southern Europe 33%
- Northern and Western Europe 59%

War and hardship were other push factors. In 1913, a civil war raged in Mexico and this caused thousands of Mexicans to cross the border into the American Southwest. Poverty and hardship in China drove many Chinese to make new homes across the Pacific. After gold was discovered in California, thousands of Chinese poured into California, attracted, like so many others, by tales of "mountains of gold."

Pull Factors

The promise of freedom and hopes for a better life attracted poor and oppressed people from Europe, Asia, and Latin America. Often one bold family member—usually a young single male—set off for the United States. Before long, he would write home with news of the rich land across the ocean or across the border. Once settled, he would send for family members to join him.

Once settled, the newcomers helped pull neighbors from the old country to the United States. In the 1800s, one out of every ten Greeks left their homes for the United States. Thousands of Italians, Poles, and eastern European Jews also sailed to America. Jobs were another pull factor. American factories needed workers and factory owners sent agents to Europe and Asia to hire workers at low wages. Steamship companies competed to offer low fares for the ocean crossing and railroads posted notices in Europe advertising cheap land in the American West.

From *The American Nation* by James West Davidson, Pedro Castillo, and Michael B. Stoff. Copyright © 2002 Pearson Education, Inc., or its affiliates. Adapted by permission. All Rights Reserved.

Immigration—Part 2

The Long Voyage

Leaving home required great courage. The voyage across the Atlantic or Pacific was often miserable. Most immigrants could afford only the cheapest berths.

Ship owners jammed up to 2,000 people in steerage, as the airless rooms below decks were called. On the return voyage, cattle and cargo filled these same spaces. In such close quarters, diseases spread rapidly.//

For most European immigrants the voyage ended in New York City. There, after 1886, they saw the giant Statue of Liberty in the harbor. The statue was a gift from France to the United States. The Statue of Liberty became a symbol of the hope and freedom offered by the United States.//

Javarman/Fotolia

Adjusting to the New Land

Many immigrants had heard stories that the streets in the United States were paved with gold. Once in the United States, the newcomers had to adjust their dreams to reality. They immediately set out to find work. European peasants living on the land had little need for money, but it took cash to survive in the United States. Through friends, relatives, labor contractors, and employment agencies, the new arrivals found jobs.//

Most immigrants stayed in the cities where they landed. The slums of the cities soon became packed with poor immigrants. By 1900, one such neighborhood on the lower east side of New York had become the most crowded place in the world.//

Ethnic Neighborhoods

Immigrants adjusted to their new lives by settling in neighborhoods with their own ethnic group. An ethnic group is a group of people who share a common culture. Across the United States, cities were patchworks of Italian, Irish, Polish, Hungarian, German, Jewish, and Chinese neighborhoods. Within these ethnic neighborhoods, newcomers spoke their own language and celebrated special holidays with food prepared as in the old country.//

Becoming Americans

Often newcomers were torn between the old traditions and American ways. Still, many struggled to learn the language of their new nation. Learning English was an important step toward becoming a citizen. The process of becoming part of another culture is called assimilation. Many Americans opposed the increase in immigration. They felt the newcomers would not assimilate because their languages, religions, and customs were too different. However, they were wrong.//

Children assimilated more quickly than their parents. They learned English in school and then helped their families learn to speak it. Because children wanted to be seen as American, they often gave up customs their parents honored. They played American games and dressed in American-style clothes.//

From *The American Nation* by James West Davidson, Pedro Castillo, and Michael B. Stoff. Copyright © 2002 Pearson Education, Inc., or its affiliates. Adapted by permission. All Rights Reserved.

Life Cycles of Stars—Part 1

Stars have life cycles, just like humans. In fact, a star is born, changes, and then dies. In contrast to the human life cycle that lasts about 75 years, the life cycle of a typical star is measured in billions of years.

Every star in the sky is at a different stage in its life cycle. Some stars are relatively young, while others are near the end of their existence. The sun is about halfway through its 10-billion-year-long life cycle.

Birth of a Star

The space between stars is not entirely empty. In some places, there are great clouds of gas and dust. Each of these clouds is a nebula. A nebula is where stars are born.

Stocktrek/Photodisc/Getty Images

The element hydrogen makes up most of a nebula. Helium and a sprinkling of dust are also present. The particles in a nebula are spread very thin. In fact, the particles are a million times less dense than the particles in the air you breathe. However, since nebulae are very large, they contain enormous amounts of matter.

Gravity causes matter to be attracted to other matter. Therefore, as a nebula travels through space, it collects more dust and gas. The clouds become packed tighter and tighter, as gravity pulls it all together. Whenever matter is packed in this way, it heats up. An especially dense part of the nebula may form a hot, spinning ball of matter. Such a ball of hot matter is called a protostar.

A protostar doesn't yet shine by ordinary light, but it does give off infrared energy. Scientists identify protostars within nebulae using infrared telescopes. A protostar eventually becomes hot enough for nuclear fusion to take place in its core. When nuclear fusion produces great amounts of energy, a star comes to life.

Low-Mass Star

Stars begin their life cycle with different masses. A star's mass determines how long its life cycle will last and how it will die. Stars with a mass less than five times that of the sun are called low-mass stars. Most stars are in this group.

A low-mass star begins its life cycle as a main-sequence star. Over a period of billions of years, its supply of hydrogen is slowly changed by nuclear fusion into helium. During this time, the star changes very little. (382 words)

From *Science Insights: Exploring Earth and Space* by M. DiSpezio, M. Linner-Luebe, M. Lisowski, B. Sparks, and G. Skoog. Copyright © 2002 by Addison Wesley Longman. Adapted by permission of Pearson Education, Inc. All Rights Reserved.

Life Cycles of Stars—Part 2

Red Giant Stage

As the hydrogen in the core of a low-mass star is used up, the core starts to collapse. The core of the star becomes denser and hotter. The increased temperature causes another kind of nuclear reaction. Helium is converted to carbon. This nuclear reaction gives off great amounts of energy, causing the star to expand. It becomes a red giant.//

The red giant stage in a star's life is relatively short. The sun will be a main-sequence star for a total of 10 billion years. But the sun will be a red giant for only about 500 million years.//

Dwarf Stage

Eventually, most of the helium in a red giant's core is changed into carbon. Nuclear fusion slows. The star cools, and gravity makes it collapse inward. The matter making up the star is squeezed together very tightly, and the star becomes a white dwarf.//

A typical white dwarf is about the size of Earth. But its matter is far denser than any matter on Earth. Eventually, the star becomes a burned-out black chunk of very dense matter that gives off no visible light. Then it is called a black dwarf.//

Life of a High-Mass Star

Stars more than six times as massive as the sun have a very different life cycle than low-mass stars. A high-mass star uses up its hydrogen at a much faster rate. After only about 50 to 100 million years, a high-mass star has no hydrogen left. At this time, the core collapses and the outer layers expand greatly. The star becomes a super giant.//

Stellar Evolution

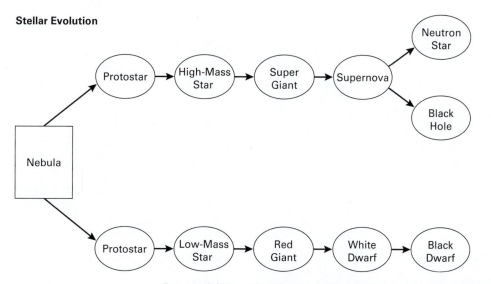

Eventually, the core of the super giant can no longer stand the pressure of the outside layers of the star. The outside layers crash in very suddenly, causing a tremendous explosion that gives off an extraordinary amount of light. Great shells of gases fly off the star. The star becomes a supernova. A supernova explosion is the most violent event known to happen in the universe.//

After a supernova explodes, only the tiny core of the star remains. This core, made up of neutrons, is called a neutron star. Neutron stars are extremely dense. Astronomers hypothesize that after a massive star undergoes a supernova explosion, it may also become a black hole. A black hole is so dense and its gravity is so strong that nothing can escape from it, not even light. Do black holes really exist? So far, scientists have no real proof. Black holes do not release light so they can't be observed directly.//

From *Science Insights: Exploring Earth and Space* by M. DiSpezio, M. Linner-Luebe, M. Lisowski, B. Sparks, and G. Skoog. Copyright © 2002 by Addison Wesley Longman. Adapted by permission of Pearson Education, Inc. All Rights Reserved.

Examiner Copies

Level: Upper Middle School

Biography: Literature

Concept Questions

What is a mentor? (*3: a supporter, a guide, a counselor, someone who takes an interest in you over time; 2: someone who likes you, someone who knows more than you do; 1: someone you like*)

_____

_____

_____ (3-2-1-0)

What is determination? (*3: willpower, having a strong purpose, working hard to accomplish goals; 2: being stubborn, wanting your own way; 1: able to determine something*)

_____

_____

_____ (3-2-1-0)

What is a creed? (*3: a belief, your principles, what you use to direct your actions; 2: it is hard to follow, people don't always agree; 1: people have it*)

_____

_____

_____ (3-2-1-0)

What does it mean to motivate someone? (*3: make people want to do something, support people so they can succeed, give people reasons for doing something; 2: be friends, be willing to listen to people's troubles; 1: talk with people*)

_____

_____

_____ (3-2-1-0)

Score: _____ /12 = _____

_____ FAM (≥ 55%) _____ UNFAM

" *Now I want you to read this section, and when you come to the slash (//) marks, I want you to tell me what you are thinking. Then read to the next slash mark and do the same thing. When you have finished reading, I will ask you to tell me what you remember, and then I will ask you questions.*"

Note: Underlined words are on the upper middle school word list.

Jaime Escalanté: Teacher Extraordinaire

Few teachers have movies made out of their lives, but Jaime (pronounced Hy-me) Escalanté is one of them. The movie was *Stand and Deliver*. What was it about Jaime Escalanté that made him worthy of a movie? To understand we have to go back to his family. His parents were teachers, as was his mother's father. His family lived in a rural area in the mountains that allowed him freedom to develop his imagination. And his grandfather taught him to read and count.//

_____

_____

_____

_____

_____

When he was nine, he moved with his mother and siblings to La Paz, the capital of Bolivia. The city was big, noisy, and crowded. School was a greater shock where he faced the challenges of paying attention, following rules, and fitting in with his peers. Although he was creative, his report cards weren't good. If he didn't think that an assignment was worthwhile, he'd create his own project and many teachers didn't approve. However, one teacher discovered a key to motivate Jaime—mathematics. The interest of one teacher can make a huge difference in a student's life.//

_____

_____

_____

_____

His mother <u>sacrificed</u> to send him to a private high school where he fell in love with chemistry, physics, and higher mathematics. When he took an entrance exam for college, he scored the highest of all of the applicants in physics and math. In college, he met his first mentor, the elementary teacher who had shown him the wonders of math. Mr. Bilbao was now a college teacher and he mentored Jaime once again. When a physics teacher died unexpectedly, he recommended that Jaime teach the course despite Jaime having completed only one year of college.//

_____

_____

_____

_____

At age 21, Jaime was hired as a teacher and he learned how to motivate teenagers. He attracted them by sports, and then hooked them on math.

He promised them A's, but made them work for them. His lifelong creed was, determination + discipline + hard work = success. He lived that creed by going to school and working at least three other jobs to support his family. Because of political unrest in Bolivia, Jaime went to the United States.//

_____

_____

_____

_____

_____

In the United States, Jaime learned that he would have to complete college all over again to earn a teaching certificate. To enroll in a city college, an applicant must pass a test in a major subject. A test in math was the best choice for someone who knew little English. Jaime turned in his paper after 25 minutes of an anticipated two-hour exam. The glowering test administer snatched the test from Jaime's hand and began to score it. His glower faded slowly and at the end, he looked up apologetically and said, "OK. You did fine. You got every one right."//

_____

_____

_____

_____

_____

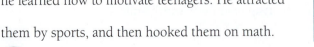

Level: Upper Middle School

Jaime kept going to night school while he worked at other jobs, but after eight years he still was over a year away from teacher certification. Hearing about a scholarship that would pay tuition, books, and a living allowance for one year, Jaime applied. He won the scholarship, and a year later he chose to teach in a neighborhood school. The students were Mexican American and Jaime felt that he understood the lives of these students because he too was an immigrant whose first language was Spanish. He was asked to teach "high school math" but found that it was only basic mathematical functions. Jaime was appalled that the most difficult concepts were percentages and fractions. He thought that any fifth-grader should have mastered those concepts.//

_____

_____

_____

_____

_____

His students learned but not fast enough to satisfy Escalanté. The Advanced Placement calculus exam was just what he needed to convince people that these students could excel in higher mathematics. Garfield High did not offer the courses needed to prepare for the AP exam. How could Jaime teach prerequisite knowledge and advanced calculus in one year? He asked his students to come in before school started, stay after school, and come in on Saturdays. The first year he had 14 students, but nine dropped out. At the end of the year, four of the five students passed the AP exam, an amazing percentage! The next year eight of ten students passed showing that the first year's results were not a fluke. In 1982, his entire class passed the exam. However, to the students' surprise, each received a letter from the Educational Testing Service accusing them of cheating! The evidence was that they all missed the same question and answered in similar ways. After several months of trying to convince ETS that their scores were valid, 12 of the initial 18 students decided to retake the exam; they all passed!//

_____

_____

_____

_____

_____

After that, Escalanté received requests for TV interviews and lectures. Any teacher who could take poor, immigrant students, and teach them the mathematics necessary to pass the AP calculus exam was exceptional and his continued success with rising numbers of students was a testament to his

Level: Upper Middle School

teaching. In 1988, the film *Stand and Deliver* was made to celebrate this amazing teacher. He died in 2010 of cancer, at the age of 79.// (847 words)//

Number of Total Miscues
(Total Accuracy): _____

Number of Meaning-Change Miscues
(Total Acceptability): _____

Total Accuracy		Total Acceptability
0–17 miscues _____	Independent _____	0–17 miscues
18–84 miscues _____	Instructional _____	18–42 miscues
85 + miscues _____	Frustration _____	43 + miscues

Rate: 847 × 60 = 50,820/_____ seconds = _____ WPM

WCPM: (847 − _____ errors) × 60 = _____/_____ seconds = _____ WCPM

Retelling Scoring Sheet for "Jaime Escalanté: Teacher Extraordinaire"

Setting/Background

_____ Few teachers have movies made out of their lives.
_____ Jaime Escalanté is one of them.
_____ His parents were teachers.
_____ His family lived in a rural area in the mountains.
_____ His grandfather taught him to read and count.

Events

_____ When he was nine, he moved to the capital of Bolivia.
_____ Although he was creative,
_____ his report cards weren't good.
_____ If he didn't think that an assignment was worthwhile,
_____ he'd create his own project
_____ and many teachers didn't approve.
_____ one teacher discovered a key to motivate Jaime—mathematics.

Goal

_____ His mother wanted him to get a good high school education.

Events

_____ He fell in love with chemistry, physics, and higher mathematics in high school.
_____ When he took an entrance exam for college
_____ he scored the highest of all of the applicants in physics and math.
_____ In college, he met his first mentor, the elementary teacher;
_____ he mentored Jaime once again.
_____ Jaime was hired as a teacher.

Goal

_____ He wanted to motivate teenagers.
_____ He promised them A's
_____ but made them work for them.
_____ His lifelong creed was, determination + discipline + hard work = success.
_____ He lived that creed.

Events

_____ Jaime moved to the United States and found he would have to complete college all over again.
_____ An applicant must pass a test in a major subject.
_____ Jaime turned in his math test after 25 minutes and got every one right.

Goal

_____ Jaime kept going to night school
_____ while he worked at other jobs.
_____ He was determined to be a teacher

Events

_____ He chose to teach in a neighborhood school.
_____ The students were Mexican American.
_____ He taught high school math
_____ but found that it was only basic mathematical functions.

Level: Upper Middle School

Goal

_____ He wanted his students to learn advanced math.

_____ His students did not learn fast enough to satisfy Escalanté.

_____ The Advanced Placement calculus exam would convince people

_____ that these students could excel in higher mathematics.

Events

_____ He asked his students to come in before and after school and on Saturdays.

_____ The first year four of the five students passed the AP exam.

_____ The next year eight of ten students passed.

_____ In 1982, his entire class passed the exam.

_____ The Educational Testing Service accusing them of cheating.

_____ Twelve of the initial 18 students retook the exam;

_____ they all passed.

Resolution

_____ Escalanté received requests for TV interviews and lectures.

_____ Any teacher who could take poor, immigrant students

_____ and teach them the mathematics

_____ necessary to pass the AP calculus exam was exceptional.

_____ The film *Stand and Deliver* was made to celebrate this amazing teacher.

Questions for "Jaime Escalanté: Teacher Extraordinaire"

1. What was the selection mostly about?
   Implicit: how Jaime Escalanté became famous and the subject of a movie

2. What members of Jaime's family were teachers?
   Explicit: mother, father, and grandfather

3. How do you know that Jaime was an independent student?
   Implicit: if he didn't think that an assignment was worthwhile, he'd create his own project, instead of doing assignments because a teacher required them

4. Why might Jaime have felt discouraged after he moved to California?
   Implicit: he had to start college over again and/or he had to learn English well enough to be able to understand instruction in English

5. Why did the test administrator glower at Jaime when he turned in his math test?
   Implicit: Jaime completed it in 25 minutes so the administrator probably thought he hadn't worked at it long enough

6. What was Jaime's opinion of the high school math curriculum?
   Explicit: he was appalled or he thought it was at a fifth-grade level

7. What did Jaime require of the students so that they would learn advanced calculus?
   Explicit: he asked them to come in before and after school and on Saturdays

8. Why did the ETS think Jaime's students cheated?
   Explicit: they all missed the same question and answered in similar ways

9. Why did people ask Jaime for lecture and TV interviews?
   Explicit: because he took poor, immigrant students and taught them math necessary to pass AP calculus

10. How did Jaime live his creed (determination + discipline + hard work = success) throughout his life?
    Implicit: he went to school full time and worked at least three jobs or he completed college a second time when he went to the United States

Without Look-Backs

Number Correct Explicit: _____

Number Correct Implicit: _____

    Total: _____

    _____ Independent: 9–10 correct

    _____ Instructional: 7–8 correct

    _____ Frustration: 0–6 correct

With Look-Backs

Number Correct Explicit: _____

Number Correct Implicit: _____

    Total: _____

    _____ Independent: 9–10 correct

    _____ Instructional: 7–8 correct

    _____ Frustration: 0–6 correct

Think-Aloud Summary

Think-Aloud Comments That Suggest Understanding

Restates text content accurately _____

Offers relevant comment _____

Asks relevant question _____

Recognizes topic/main idea _____

Identifies personally _____

Paraphrases/summarizes appropriately _____

Draws a valid inference based on personal experience _____

Draws a valid inference based on text information _____

Think-Aloud Comments That Suggest Lack of Understanding

Restates text content inaccurately _____

Offers irrelevant comment _____

Asks irrelevant question _____

Does not recognize topic/main idea _____

Does not identify personally _____

Paraphrases/summarizes inappropriately _____

Draws an invalid inference based on personal experience _____

Draws an invalid inference based on text information _____

Level: Upper Middle School

Social Studies: Expository

Immigration—Part 1

Reasons for Immigration

Between 1866 and 1915, more than a million immigrants poured into the United States. Both push and pull factors played a part in this vast migration. Push factors are conditions that drive people from their homes. Pull factors are conditions that attract immigrants to a new area.

Push Factors

Many immigrants were small farmers or landless farm workers. As European populations grew, land for farming became scarce. Small farms could barely support the families who worked them. In some areas, new farm machines replaced farm workers.

Another factor was political and religious persecution that pushed many people to leave their homes. In the late 1800s, the Russian government supported pogroms or organized attacks on Jewish villages. "Every night," recalled a Jewish girl who fled Russia, "they were chasing after us, to kill everyone." Millions of Jews fled Russia and eastern Europe to settle in American cities.

Concept Questions

What is an immigrant? (*3: someone who settles in another country; a future citizen; 2: someone who is different from citizens, someone who was not born in the United States; 1: my grandfather*)

_____

_____

_____ (3-2-1-0)

What is persecution? (*3: treating someone badly/cruelly, unfair treatment/oppression because of race or religion; 2: people can die from it, a form of abuse, bullies do it; 1: like execution*)

_____

_____

_____ (3-2-1-0)

What is hardship? (*3: suffering, difficulties, trouble; 2: sometimes due to poverty, people do not like it, you work to overcome it; not having enough to eat; 1: not good*)

_____

_____

_____ (3-2-1-0)

What does it mean to attract? (*3: appeal to people, get people's interest, entice; 2: TV ads attract, it makes you want to buy something; 1: can help or hurt someone*)

_____

_____

_____ (3-2-1-0)

Score: _____ /12 = _____ %

_____ FAM (≥ 55%) _____ UNFAM

Note: Underlined words are on the upper middle school word list.

Persecution was also a push factor for Armenian immigrants. The Armenians lived in the Ottoman Empire (present-day Turkey). Between the 1890s and the 1920s, the Ottoman government killed a million or more Armenians. Many fled, eventually settling in California and elsewhere in the United States.

War and hardship were other push factors. In 1913, a civil war raged in Mexico and this caused thousands of Mexicans to cross the border into the American Southwest. Poverty and hardship in China drove many Chinese to make new homes across the Pacific. After gold was discovered in California, thousands of Chinese poured into California, attracted, like so many others, by tales of "mountains of gold."

Pull Factors

The promise of freedom and hopes for a better life attracted poor and oppressed people from Europe, Asia, and Latin America. Often one bold family member—usually a young single male—set off for the United States. Before long, he would write home with news of the rich land across the ocean or across the border. Once settled, he would send for family members to join him.

Once settled, the newcomers helped pull neighbors from the old country to the United States. In the 1800s, one out of every ten Greeks left their homes for the United States. Thousands of Italians, Poles, and eastern European Jews also sailed to America. Jobs were another pull factor. American factories needed workers and factory owners sent agents to Europe and Asia to hire workers at low wages. Steamship companies competed to offer low fares for the ocean crossing and railroads posted notices in Europe advertising cheap land in the American West. (421 words)

From *The American Nation* by James West Davidson, Pedro Castillo, and Michael B. Stoff. Copyright © 2002 Pearson Education, Inc., or its affiliates. Adapted by permission. All Rights Reserved.

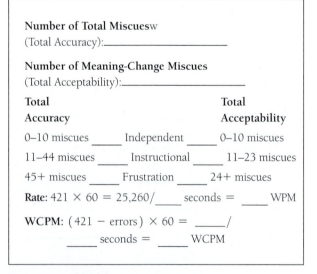

Number of Total Miscuesw
(Total Accuracy):_____

Number of Meaning-Change Miscues
(Total Acceptability):_____

Total Accuracy		Total Acceptability
0–10 miscues _____	Independent _____	0–10 miscues
11–44 miscues _____	Instructional _____	11–23 miscues
45+ miscues _____	Frustration _____	24+ miscues

Rate: 421 × 60 = 25,260/_____ seconds = _____ WPM

WCPM: (421 − errors) × 60 = _____/
_____ seconds = _____ WCPM

Retelling Scoring Sheet for "Immigration—Part 1"

Main Idea

_____ More than a million immigrants poured into the United States.

Level: Upper Middle School

Details

_____ Push factors and pull factors played a part.
_____ Push factors drive people from their homes.
_____ Pull factors are conditions that attract immigrants.

Main Idea

_____ A push factor was scarce land.

Details

_____ Many immigrants were farmers.
_____ Small farms could not support them.
_____ Machines replaced farm workers.

Main Idea

_____ Religious and political persecution were push factors.

Details

_____ The Russian government supported pogroms or attacks on Jews.
_____ Millions of Jews fled Russia and Europe.
_____ The Ottoman government killed Armenians.
_____ A million or more Armenians fled.

Main Idea

_____ War and hardship were push factors.

Details

_____ War raged in Mexico.
_____ Thousands of Mexicans crossed the border.
_____ Hardship drove Chinese across the Pacific.
_____ After gold was discovered,
_____ thousands poured into California.

Main Idea

_____ The promise of freedom/hope for a better life attracted people.

Details

_____ From Europe/Asia/Latin America,
_____ a bold young male set off for the United States.
_____ Once settled, he would send for family members.
_____ One out of every ten Greeks left their homes.
_____ Thousands of Italians, Poles, and Jews sailed to America.

Main Idea

_____ Jobs were another pull factor.

Details

_____ American factories needed workers.
_____ Owners sent agents
_____ to hire workers at low wages.
_____ Steamship companies offered low fares
_____ and railroads advertised cheap land.

Questions for "Immigration—Part 1"

1. What is this passage mostly about?
   Implicit: reasons why immigrants came to America

2. Why did farmers leave Europe and come to America?
   Explicit: land became scarce or farms could not support families

3. Why would growing populations result in scarce farming land?
   Implicit: more land would be needed for cities and places for people to live

Level: Upper Middle School

4. Name two push factors affecting immigration.
Explicit: scarce land; persecution; war; *or* hardship

5. What push factor caused Mexicans to cross the border into America?
Explicit: civil war in their country

6. Why was a young single male usually the first family member to immigrate?
Implicit: he was not burdened by a family; *or* he could get a job easier than a woman or an older man; *or* he might be more adventurous or courageous

7. Give two examples of pull factors that affected immigration.
Explicit: promise of freedom; promise of a better life; a family member who immigrated; a neighbor who immigrated; *or* jobs

8. Why would having a neighbor in America be a pull factor?
Implicit: the immigrant would know someone in America; the neighbor could help the immigrant get settled; *or* the neighbor might convince the immigrant that it was a good idea to come to America

9. Why did factory owners send agents to Europe to hire workers?
Explicit: they needed workers; *or* they could hire immigrants for low wages

10. Why would railroads advertise cheap land in the American West?
Implicit: the immigrants would have to travel on the railroads to get to the West

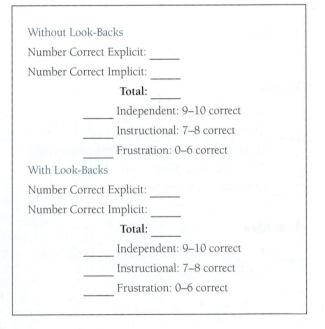

Without Look-Backs

Number Correct Explicit: _____

Number Correct Implicit: _____

        Total: _____

_____ Independent: 9–10 correct

_____ Instructional: 7–8 correct

_____ Frustration: 0–6 correct

With Look-Backs

Number Correct Explicit: _____

Number Correct Implicit: _____

        Total: _____

_____ Independent: 9–10 correct

_____ Instructional: 7–8 correct

_____ Frustration: 0–6 correct

Level: Upper Middle School

Social Studies: Expository

Concept Questions

What is a symbol? (*3: something that represents something else, a sign with a special meaning; 2: the peace symbol, the flag of our country, logos on sports uniforms 1: some are funny*)

_____

_____

_____ (3-2-1-0)

What is the difference between a dream and reality? (*3: a dream is not real, a dream may seem real but it isn't; 2: you can put things in a daydream, reality is when you are awake, dreams are for sleeping; 1: I had a bad dream a few days ago*)

_____

_____

_____ (3-2-1-0)

What do we mean by culture? (*3: shared beliefs and values; 2: kinds of food, special clothes, religious ceremonies; 1: different people have them*)

_____

_____

_____ (3-2-1-0)

Why might it be difficult to move to another country? (*3: it would be different from what you are used to; 2: you might not know the language, you might not know how they do things, you would miss your friends; 1: I have a friend from another country*)

_____

_____

_____ (3-2-1-0)

Score: _____ /12 = _____ %

_____ FAM (≥ 55%) _____ UNFAM

" *Now I want you to read this section, and when you come to the slash (//) marks, I want you to tell me what you are thinking. Then read to the next slash mark and do the same thing. When you have finished reading, I will ask you to tell me what you remember, and then I will ask you questions.*"

Note: Underlined words are on the upper middle school word list.

Immigration—Part 2

The Long Voyage

Leaving home required great courage. The voyage across the Atlantic or Pacific was often miserable. Most immigrants could afford only the cheapest berths. Ship owners jammed up to 2,000 people in steerage, as the airless rooms below decks were called. On the return voyage, cattle and cargo filled these same spaces. In such close quarters, diseases spread rapidly.**//**

_____

_____

_____

_____

_____

For most European immigrants the voyage ended in New York City. There, after 1886, they saw the giant Statue of Liberty in the harbor. The statue was a gift from France to the United States. The Statue of Liberty became a symbol of the hope and freedom offered by the United States.**//**

Level: Upper Middle School

_____

_____

_____

_____

_____

Adjusting to the New Land

Many immigrants had heard stories that the streets in the United States were paved with gold. Once in the United States, the newcomers had to adjust their dreams to reality. They immediately set out to find work. European peasants living on the land had little need for money, but it took cash to survive in the United States. Through friends, relatives, labor contractors, and employment agencies, the new arrivals found jobs.//

_____

_____

_____

_____

Most immigrants stayed in the cities where they landed. The slums of the cities soon became packed with poor immigrants. By 1900, one such neighborhood on the lower east side of New York had become the most crowded place in the world.//

_____

_____

_____

Ethnic Neighborhoods

Immigrants adjusted to their new lives by settling in neighborhoods with their own ethnic group. An ethnic group is a group of people who share a common culture. Across the United States, cities were patchworks of Italian, Irish, Polish, Hungarian, German, Jewish, and Chinese neighborhoods. Within these ethnic neighborhoods, newcomers spoke their own language and celebrated special holidays with food prepared as in the old country.//

_____

_____

_____

_____

Becoming Americans

Often newcomers were torn between the old traditions and American ways. Still, many struggled to learn the language of their new nation. Learning English was an important step toward becoming a citizen. The process of becoming part of another culture is called assimilation. Many Americans opposed the increase in immigration. They felt the newcomers would not <u>assimilate</u> because their languages, religions, and customs were too different. However, they were wrong.**//**

_____

_____

_____

_____

_____

Children assimilated more quickly than their parents. They learned English in school and then helped their families learn to speak it. Because children wanted to be seen as American, they often gave up customs their parents honored. They played American games and dressed in American-style clothes.**//**

_____

_____

_____

_____

(417 words)

_____

From *The American Nation* by James West Davidson, Pedro Castillo, and Michael B. Stoff. Copyright © 2002 Pearson Education, Inc., or its affiliates. Adapted by permission. All Rights Reserved.

Number of Total Miscues
(Total Accuracy): _____

Number of Meaning-Change Miscues
(Total Acceptability): _____

Total Accuracy		Total Acceptability	
0–10 miscues _____	Independent _____	0–10 miscues	
11–43 miscues _____	Instructional _____	11–22 miscues	
44+ miscues _____	Frustration _____	23+ miscues	

Rate (If you used this passage as a think-aloud passage, you cannot compute rate):

$417 \times 60 = 25{,}020\,/\,$ _____ seconds = _____ WPM

WCPM: (417 − _____ errors) × 60 = _____ /

_____ seconds = _____ WCPM

Retelling Scoring Sheet for "Immigration—Part 2"

Main Idea

_____ Leaving home required great courage.

Details

_____ The voyage was miserable.

_____ Ship owners jammed up to 2,000 people

_____ in airless rooms below decks.

_____ On the return voyage, cattle and cargo filled these spaces.

_____ Diseases spread rapidly.

Main Idea

_____ For most immigrants the voyage ended in New York City.

Details

_____ They saw the Statue of Liberty.

_____ The statue was a gift from France.

_____ The Statue of Liberty became a symbol of hope.

Level: Upper Middle School

Main Idea

_____ Newcomers had to adjust to their new land.

Details

_____ Through friends and relatives they found jobs.

_____ Most immigrants stayed in the cities where they landed.

_____ They settled in neighborhoods with their own ethnic group.

_____ Newcomers spoke their own language and/or celebrated holidays.

Main Idea

_____ Becoming part of another culture is called assimilation.

Details

_____ Learning English was an important step.

_____ Many Americans opposed immigration.

_____ They felt the newcomers would not assimilate.

_____ They were wrong.

Main Idea

_____ Children assimilated more quickly.

Details

_____ They learned English.

_____ They helped their families learn it.

_____ They wanted to be seen as American.

_____ They often gave up their parents' customs.

_____ They played American games

_____ and dressed in American clothes.

Questions for "Immigration—Part 2"

1. What is this passage mainly about?
   Implicit: how immigrants came to America and how they settled and adjusted

2. Give one reason why ocean voyages were so difficult.
   Explicit: immigrants could only afford the cheapest berths; they were too crowded; there was not much air; *or* disease spread rapidly

3. Why did disease spread so fast on the ocean voyages?
   Implicit: immigrants were too crowded; there was no good air; *or* cattle filled the spaces on the return voyage

4. What was one way in which the immigrants found jobs?
   Explicit: Through friends, relatives, labor contractors, *or* employment agencies

5. Why was cash so important to an immigrant?
   Implicit: they needed it for food, clothing, and rent

6. Why did immigrants stay in the crowded slums?
   Implicit: they were too poor to move; *or* they were with their own ethnic group

7. What is assimilation?
   Explicit: the process of becoming part of another culture

8. Name one element of a common culture that is mentioned in the passage.
   Explicit: language; holidays; *or* food

9. Why did some Americans oppose immigration?
   Explicit: they did not feel that the immigrants would be able to assimilate; *or* they thought the immigrants were too different

10. What might cause disagreements between immigrant children and their parents?
    Implicit: children giving up honored customs; children wanting to act like Americans; *or* children acting different from their parents

---

Without Look-Backs

Number Correct Explicit: _____

Number Correct Implicit: _____

Total: _____

_____ Independent: 9–10 correct

_____ Instructional: 7–8 correct

_____ Frustration: 0–6 correct

With Look-Backs

Number Correct Explicit: _____

Number Correct Implicit: _____

Total: _____

_____ Independent: 9–10 correct

_____ Instructional: 7–8 correct

_____ Frustration: 0–6 correct

Think-Aloud Summary

Think-Aloud Comments That Suggest Understanding

Restates text content accurately _____

Offers relevant comment _____

Asks relevant question _____

Recognizes topic/main idea _____

Identifies personally _____

Paraphrases/summarizes appropriately _____

Draws a valid inference based on personal experience _____

Draws a valid inference based on text information _____

Think-Aloud Comments That Suggest Lack of Understanding

Restates text content inaccurately _____

Offers irrelevant comment _____

Asks irrelevant question _____

Does not recognize topic/main idea _____

Does not identify personally _____

Paraphrases/summarizes inappropriately _____

Draws an invalid inference based on personal experience _____

Draws an invalid inference based on text information _____

Level: Upper Middle School

Science: Expository

Concept Questions

What are stars made of? (*3: gas, hydrogen, and/or helium, dust; 2: materials present in space; 1: things that shine*)

_____

_____

_____ (3-2-1-0)

What is gravity? (*3: force, weight, keeps us down on the ground; 2: keeps you from jumping up real high, you jump off a roof and it pulls you down; 1: it's a movie I saw*)

_____

_____

_____ (3-2-1-0)

What is mass? (*3: an amount of something, an accumulation, a lump, a heap; 2: can be of different sizes, is usually solid; 1: I read about it in science class*)

_____

_____

_____ (3-2-1-0)

What do nuclear reactions produce? (*3: energy; 2: an explosion, a change of some type; 1: people don't like them*)

_____

_____

_____ (3-2-1-0)

Score: _____ /12 = _____ %

_____ FAM (≥ 55%) _____ UNFAM

Note: Underlined words are on the upper middle school word list.

Life Cycles of Stars—Part I

Stars have life cycles, just like humans. In fact, a star is born, changes, and then dies. In contrast to the human life cycle that lasts about 75 years, the life cycle of a typical star is measured in billions of years.

Every star in the sky is at a different stage in its life cycle. Some stars are relatively young, while others are near the end of their existence. The sun is about halfway through its 10-billion-year-long life cycle.

Birth of a Star

The space between stars is not entirely empty. In some places, there are great clouds of gas and dust. Each of these clouds is a nebula. A nebula is where stars are born.

The element hydrogen makes up most of a nebula. Helium and a sprinkling of dust are also present. The particles in a nebula are spread very thin. In fact, the particles are a million times less dense than the particles in the air you breathe. However, since nebulae are very large, they contain enormous amounts of matter.

Gravity causes matter to be attracted to other matter. Therefore, as a nebula travels through space, it collects more dust and gas. The clouds become packed tighter and tighter, as gravity pulls it all together. Whenever matter is packed in this way, it heats up. An especially dense part of the nebula may form a hot, spinning ball of matter. Such a ball of hot matter is called a protostar.

Level: Upper Middle School

A protostar doesn't yet shine by ordinary light, but it does give off infrared energy. Scientists identify protostars within nebulae using infrared telescopes. A protostar eventually becomes hot enough for nuclear fusion to take place in its core. When nuclear fusion produces great amounts of energy, a star comes to life.

Low-Mass Star

Stars begin their life cycle with different masses. A star's mass determines how long its life cycle will last and how it will die. Stars with a mass less than five times that of the sun are called low-mass stars. Most stars are in this group.

A low-mass star begins its life cycle as a main-sequence star. Over a period of billions of years, its supply of hydrogen is slowly changed by nuclear fusion into helium. During this time, the star changes very little. (382 words)

From *Science Insights: Exploring Earth and Space* by M. DiSpezio, M. Linner-Luebe, M. Lisowski, B. Sparks, and G. Skoog. Copyright © 2002 by Addison Wesley Longman. Adapted by permission of Pearson Education, Inc. All Rights Reserved.

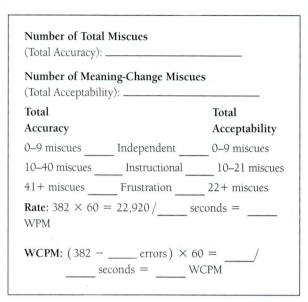

Number of Total Miscues
(Total Accuracy): _____

Number of Meaning-Change Miscues
(Total Acceptability): _____

Total Accuracy		Total Acceptability
0–9 miscues _____	Independent _____	0–9 miscues
10–40 miscues _____	Instructional _____	10–21 miscues
41+ miscues _____	Frustration _____	22+ miscues

Rate: $382 \times 60 = 22{,}920 /$ _____ seconds = _____ WPM

WCPM: $(382 - $ _____ errors$) \times 60 = $ _____ $/$ _____ seconds = _____ WCPM

Retelling Scoring Sheet for "Life Cycles of Stars—Part I"

Main Idea

_____ Stars have life cycles.

Details

_____ A star is born, changes, and dies.
_____ The life cycle is measured in billions of years.
_____ Every star is at a different stage.
_____ Some stars are young,
_____ while others are near the end of their existence.
_____ The sun is halfway through its cycle.

Main Idea

_____ A nebula is where stars are born.

Details

_____ A nebula is a cloud of gas and/or dust.
_____ Hydrogen makes up most of a nebula.
_____ Helium is also present.
_____ The particles are spread very thin.
_____ Since nebulae are very large.
_____ They contain enormous amount of matter.

Main Idea

_____ Gravity causes matter to be attracted to matter.

Level: Upper Middle School

Details

_____ A nebula travels through space.
_____ It collects more dust and gas.
_____ Gravity pulls them together.
_____ They become packed tighter and tighter.
_____ Packed matter heats up.
_____ Part of a nebula may form a dense/hot/ spinning ball of matter
_____ called a protostar.

Main Idea

_____ A protostar doesn't shine but gives off infra-red energy.

Details

_____ Scientists identify protostars with infrared telescopes.
_____ A protostar becomes hot enough for nuclear fusion to take place.
_____ When nuclear fusion produces great energy,
_____ a star comes to life.

Main Idea

_____ Stars begin their cycle with different masses.

Details

_____ A star's mass determines how long its cycle will last
_____ and how it will die.
_____ Most stars are low-mass stars.
_____ Over billions of years, the supply of hydrogen
_____ is changed into helium.

Questions for "Life Cycles of Stars— Part 1"

1. What is this passage mainly about?
   Implicit: how stars are born

2. How long is the life cycle of the sun?
   Explicit: 10 billion years

3. What is a nebula?
   Explicit: a cloud of gas and dust.

4. Why do nebulae collect more dust and gas as they move through space?
   Implicit: gravity causes dust to be attracted to other dust

5. What is a protostar?
   Explicit: a dense hot part of the nebula

6. If a protostar doesn't give off light, how do scientists know it exists?
   Implicit: it gives off infrared energy, which can be detected using infrared telescopes

7. What is the final action that causes a protostar to become a star?
   Implicit: the core becomes so hot that nuclear fusion occurs and produces great amounts of energy

8. What determines how long a star will live?
   Explicit: its mass

9. Why is gravity crucial to the birth of a star?
   Implicit: gravity packs matter, which causes it to heat up and become a protostar

10. In a low-mass star, what does hydrogen change into?
    Explicit: helium

Without Look-Backs

Number Correct Explicit: _____

Number Correct Implicit: _____

Total: _____

_____ Independent: 9–10 correct

_____ Instructional: 7–8 correct

_____ Frustration: 0–6 correct

With Look-Backs

Number Correct Explicit: _____

Number Correct Implicit: _____

Total: _____

_____ Independent: 9–10 correct

_____ Instructional: 7–8 correct

_____ Frustration: 0–6 correct

Level: Upper Middle School

Expository: Science

Concept Questions

How do stars change over time? (*3: they go through different stages, they eventually explode; 2: they get brighter or dimmer, it gets difficult for astronomers to see them; 1: I could tell you if I had a telescope*)

_____

_____

_____ (3-2-1-0)

What is a supernova? (*3: the explosion of a high-mass star; 2: a violent explosion, it gives off a lot of light; 1: something very big*)

_____

_____

_____ (3-2-1-0)

What is density? (*3: thickness, mass, bulk, compactness; 2: the amount can vary, different things can contribute to density; 1: it's a thing*)

_____

_____

_____ (3-2-1-0)

What is a black hole? (*3: after a star explodes, it might become a black hole; 2: it is very dense, it has strong gravity, nothing can escape from it, scientists are not sure it exists; 1: something in the sky*)

_____

_____

_____ (3-2-1-0)

Score: _____ /12 = _____ %

_____ FAM (≥ 55%) _____ UNFAM

"Now I want you to read this section, and when you come to the slash (//) marks, I want you to tell me what you are thinking. Then read to the next slash mark and do the same thing. When you have finished reading, I will ask you to tell me what you remember, and then I will ask you questions."

Note: Underlined words are on the upper middle school word list.

Life Cycles of Stars—Part 2

Red Giant Stage

As the hydrogen in the core of a low-mass star is used up, the core starts to collapse. The core of the star becomes denser and hotter. The increased temperature causes another kind of <u>nuclear</u> reaction. <u>Helium</u> is converted to carbon. This <u>nuclear</u> reaction gives off great amounts of energy, causing the star to expand. It becomes a red giant.**//**

_____

_____

_____

_____

_____

The red giant stage in a star's life is relatively short. The sun will be a main-sequence star for a total of 10 billion years. But the sun will be a red giant for only about 500 million years.**//**

_____

_____

_____

_____

_____

Level: Upper Middle School

Dwarf Stage

Eventually, most of the helium in a red giant's core is changed into carbon. Nuclear fusion slows. The star cools, and gravity makes it collapse inward. The matter making up the star is squeezed together very tightly, and the star becomes a white dwarf.**//**

_____

_____

_____

_____

A typical white dwarf is about the size of Earth. But its matter is far denser than any matter on Earth. Eventually, the star becomes a burned-out black chunk of very dense matter that gives off no visible light. Then it is called a black dwarf.**//**

_____

_____

_____

_____

Life of a High-Mass Star

Stars more than six times as massive as the sun have a very different life cycle than low-mass stars. A high-mass star uses up its hydrogen at a much faster rate. After only about 50 to 100 million years, a high-mass star has no hydrogen left. At this time,

the core collapses and the outer layers expand greatly. The star becomes a super giant.**//**

_____

_____

_____

_____

Eventually, the core of the super giant can no longer stand the pressure of the outside layers of the star. The outside layers crash in very suddenly, causing a tremendous explosion that gives off an extraordinary amount of light. Great shells of gases fly off the star. The star becomes a supernova. A supernova explosion is the most violent event known to happen in the universe.**//**

_____

_____

_____

_____

After a supernova explodes, only the tiny core of the star remains. This core, made up of neutrons, is called a neutron star. Neutron stars are extremely dense. Astronomers hypothesize that after a massive star undergoes a supernova explosion, it may also become a black hole. A black hole is so

Level: Upper Middle School

dense and its <u>gravity</u> is so strong that nothing can escape from it, not even light. Do black holes really exist? So far, scientists have no real proof. Black holes do not release light so they can't be observed directly.//

_____

_____

_____

_____

(420 words)

_____

From _Science Insights: Exploring Earth and Space_ by M. DiSpezio, M. Linner-Luebe, M. Lisowski, B. Sparks, and G. Skoog. Copyright © 2002 by Addison Wesley Longman. Adapted by permission of Pearson Education, Inc. All Rights Reserved.

Number of Total Miscues
(Total Accuracy): _____

Number of Meaning-Change Miscues
(Total Acceptability): _____

Total Accuracy		Total Acceptability
0–10 miscues _____ Independent _____		0–10 miscues
11–44 miscues _____ Instructional _____		11–23 miscues
45+ miscues _____ Frustration _____		24+ miscues

Rate (If you used this passage as a think-aloud passage, you cannot compute rate):

420 × 60 = 25,200/_____ seconds = _____ WPM

WCPM: (420 − _____ errors) × 60 = _____/
_____ seconds = _____ WCPM

Retelling Scoring Sheet for "Life Cycles of Stars—Part 2"

Main Idea

_____ A low-mass star becomes a red giant.

Details

_____ As the hydrogen is used up the core starts to collapse.
_____ The core becomes denser and hotter.
_____ The temperature causes a nuclear reaction.
_____ The reaction gives off great amounts of energy.
_____ The star expands.
_____ The red giant stage is short.

Main Idea

_____ The star enters the black dwarf stage.

Details

_____ The star cools,
_____ and gravity makes it collapse.
_____ The matter is squeezed together.
_____ A dwarf star is about the size of Earth,
_____ but its matter is denser.
_____ The star becomes a burned-out chunk
_____ that gives off no light.

Main Idea

_____ High-mass stars have a different life cycle.

Details

_____ When it has no hydrogen left,
_____ the core collapses,
_____ and the outer layers expand.
_____ The star becomes a super giant.
_____ The outer layers crash in,
_____ causing a tremendous explosion
_____ and an extraordinary amount of light.
_____ The star becomes a supernova,
_____ the most violent event in the universe.

Level: Upper Middle School

Main Idea

_____ After a supernova only the core/neutron star remains.

Details

_____ Neutron stars are extremely dense.
_____ It may become a black hole.
_____ A black hole is so dense
_____ and its gravity is so strong
_____ that nothing can escape from it
_____ Scientists have no proof of black holes.
_____ Black holes do not release light
_____ so they can't be observed directly.

Questions for "Life Cycles of Stars—Part 2"

1. What is this passage mainly about?
   Implicit: stages in a star's life

2. What causes all life-cycle changes in stars?
   Implicit: nuclear reactions

3. What series of events causes a star to go into the red giant stage?
   Explicit: the core collapses when hydrogen is used up, it becomes denser and hotter, another kind of nuclear reaction occurs, and the star expands

4. How long will the sun remain as a red giant?
   Explicit: 500 million years

5. How big is a typical white dwarf?
   Explicit: the size of Earth

6. What is the stage when the star becomes a chunk of dense matter that gives off no visible light?
   Explicit: black dwarf stage

Level: Upper Middle School

7. What causes the core of a high-mass star to collapse?
Implicit: lack of hydrogen

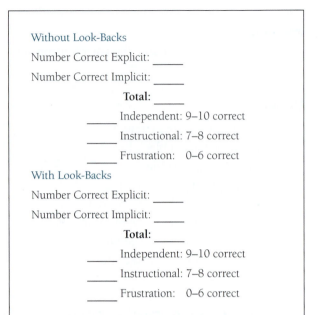

Without Look-Backs

Number Correct Explicit: _____

Number Correct Implicit: _____

Total: _____

_____ Independent: 9–10 correct

_____ Instructional: 7–8 correct

_____ Frustration: 0–6 correct

With Look-Backs

Number Correct Explicit: _____

Number Correct Implicit: _____

Total: _____

_____ Independent: 9–10 correct

_____ Instructional: 7–8 correct

_____ Frustration: 0–6 correct

8. What is one thing a star can become after a supernova explosion?
Explicit: a neutron star or a black hole

9. Why doesn't a neutron star give out light?
Implicit: it is too dense

Think-Aloud Summary

Think-Aloud Comments That Suggest Understanding

Restates text content accurately _____

Offers relevant comment _____

Asks relevant question _____

Recognizes topic/main idea _____

Identifies personally _____

Paraphrases/summarizes appropriately _____

Draws a valid inference based on personal experience _____

Draws a valid inference based on text information _____

Think-Aloud Comments That Suggest Lack of Understanding

Restates text content inaccurately _____

Offers irrelevant comment _____

Asks irrelevant question _____

Does not recognize topic/main idea _____

Does not identify personally _____

Paraphrases/summarizes inappropriately _____

Draws an invalid inference based on personal experience _____

Draws an invalid inference based on text information _____

10. Why have scientists been unable to prove the existence of a black hole?
Implicit: they can't be observed directly because they do not give off light

World War I—Part I

World War I, also known as the Great War, drew in not only the major powers of Europe, but those of America and Asia as well. Many economic and political factors caused the war. Newly industrialized nations competed with one another for trade and markets for their goods. Also, the urge for national power and independence from other nations came from old and new powers. When a new nation tried to increase its power by building a strong military, an older nation perceived the new nation as a threat to its power. Such tensions led to the division of Europe into two groups for security: one composed of Britain, France, and Russia, the other of Austria, Hungary, and Germany.

Although the factors discussed above caused the war, the final breaking point was a local conflict between Austria and Serbia, a tiny kingdom in southeastern Europe. Serbia, supported by Russia, wanted to unite with the Serbs living in the Austro-Hungarian Empire and create a Greater Serbia. Austria, supported by Germany, did not want Serbia cutting into its empire. The war officially started in August of 1914, after the assassination of the Austrian heir to the throne, who was visiting Sarajevo, near Serbia's border. The assassin was a young man with connections to the military intelligence branch of the Serbian government. Austria's attempt to punish Serbia drew Russia and its allies Britain and France into a war against Austria-Hungary and Germany. The map below illustrates the geographical location of the countries in Europe and surrounding regions in 1914.

The War Raged on Two Fronts

Germany hoped to defeat France by striking quickly through Belgium and, therefore, to minimize the danger of a two-front war. The highly trained German troops nearly reached Paris before the French stopped them. However, the Russians aided France by suddenly attacking Germany on its eastern front, and Germany sent troops from western Europe to face the attack. With the German forces diminished, the French were able to force the weakened Germans back. The war in the west became a stalemate with neither side able to achieve a victory. As a result, both sides sought new allies to help them gain victory, and the war became a world war as Japan, Italy, Portugal, Romania, and other countries joined Britain, France, and Russia. Germany and Austria-Hungary drew in Bulgaria and the Ottoman Empire, which included Turkey.

On the eastern front Russia kept part of the German army busy. Although Russia fought valiantly, it had not been prepared for war and thus was unable to defeat the Germans. Russian defeats led to a revolution that toppled the tsar of Russia. In late 1917 the new leader of Russia, Lenin, offered to make peace with Germany. As part of the treaty agreement, Germany gained coal mines and oil fields from Russia, which gave Germany power to fuel its army. More important, it allowed the war to be fought on only one front—the western front.

The United States entered the war when Germany began attacking American ships that were taking supplies to Britain and France. U.S. President Woodrow Wilson warned the Germans to stop the attacks, and for a while they did. But they announced an unrestricted submarine warfare after the British blockade shut off supplies to Germany. The final event that caused the United States to join the Allies was the interception of a telegram from the German foreign secretary to Mexico asking Mexico to ally itself with Germany and help fight the United States. Germany promised Mexico financial aid and the recovery of Texas, New Mexico, and Arizona when the Allies were defeated.

In the fall of 1918, German military leaders realized they could not win. One by one Germany's allies quit. On November 3, German sailors mutinied at Kiel, a city and port in northwest Germany. Four days later a revolution broke out in Germany. A republic was founded, and the kaiser fled to Holland.

Leaders of the new German government agreed to an armistice, which is an agreement to stop fighting. They asked that the peace settlement be based on President Wilson's Fourteen Points, which he had described in a speech to Congress in 1918. The Fourteen Points outlined the president's ideas for solving the problems that led to the war. Wilson wanted an end to secret agreements, freedom of the seas in peace and war, the reduction of armaments, the right of nationality groups to form their own nations, and an association of nations to keep the peace. In other speeches Wilson called for a negotiated peace with reasonable demands made on the losers. The Allies agreed to model the peace settlement on the Fourteen Points.

Early in the morning of November 11, 1918, the war ended. In a railroad car in the Compiègne Forest in northern France, two German delegates met Allied officials to sign the armistice. The guns were silent.

No previous war had caused such widespread horror. More than 10 million troops were killed in battle, and 20 million more were wounded. Thirteen million civilians died from war-related famine, disease, and injuries. The cost of the war was estimated at more than $350 billion. Destruction was everywhere.

World War I—Part 2

Three Leaders Dominated the Paris Peace Conference

After the armistice had been signed, the Allied nations met in Paris to discuss peace terms. Contrary to Wilson's wishes, the defeated countries were not allowed to send representatives to the peace conference. Thus, the so-called Big Three dominated the meeting: President Wilson; David Lloyd George, prime minister of Great Britain; and Georges Clemenceau, premier of France. At the conference Wilson pushed his Fourteen Points. Above all, he wanted to see a League of Nations, an international association established to keep the peace. To get the others to agree, however, he had to make compromises.//

Georges Clemenceau, known as the "Old Tiger," had led France during the darkest hours of the war. He wanted Germany to pay war damages because almost all of the fighting on the western front had been on French soil. Most of all he insisted that France be made safe from attack by Germany in the future. He wanted German power destroyed even at the cost of permanently taking much of Germany's western territories from her. Clemenceau placed little faith in Wilson's proposed "League of Nations."//

Lloyd George in turn wanted Germany's colonies for Britain. He also wanted the German navy destroyed. During the peace talks, he mediated between the idealism of Wilson and the severe terms of Clemenceau. In the resulting compromise, Wilson gave in on many details and agreed to form an alliance with Britain and France against future German attacks. Clemenceau and Lloyd George agreed to make the creation of the League of Nations part of the peace agreement, which was called the Versailles Treaty.//

Germany Lost Territory and Wealth in Its Defeat

When the German delegation arrived to sign the Versailles Treaty, they found its terms harsher than they had expected. The Germans were outraged at the war-guilt clause, which placed the entire blame for the war on Germany and its allies. They were also dismayed that many of Wilson's Fourteen Points were missing or had been weakened by changes. The first delegates from Germany refused to sign the treaty. To avoid further attacks by Allied soldiers, however, a second German delegation signed it on June 28, 1919. Even though Germany signed the treaty, there was strong resentment over its harsh terms.//

In the treaty, France won back the provinces of Alsace and Lorraine, lost to Germany in the late 1800s. The German territory west of the Rhine River, called the Rhineland, was to become a buffer zone between the two enemies. It was to be occupied by Allied troops for at least 15 years. France was also given the rich coal mines of the Saar, located on the French-German border. But after 15 years, the Saarlanders could vote to have their region go back to the German government or remain under the French. In 1935 they voted to become part of Germany again.//

In the treaty the Allies required that Germany repay much of the cost of the war, or make reparations. They wanted an immediate payment of $5 billion in cash. Two years later they billed Germany for $32 billion, plus interest. The

treaty reduced German military power and permitted Germany an army of no more than 100,000 men. The navy was allowed only six warships, some other vessels, and no submarines or military airplanes. The Germans were not alone in thinking such peace terms were unjust. Even David Lloyd George doubted the justice of the Versailles Treaty. President Wilson hoped that his dream, the League of Nations, could correct the unjust treaty later.//

New Independent Nations Were Formed

Four empires had fallen apart in the course of World War I: the German, the Austro-Hungarian, the Ottoman, and the Russian. Based partly on secret agreements made during the war, the Allies drew up treaties to divide the territory. The map shows how the empires were divided up. The western portion of the old Russian Empire lost to Germany during the war was reorganized. Finland, Latvia, Lithuania, and Estonia emerged from this territory, and part of this area was used to create Poland.//

Europe After World War I

The defeated Austro-Hungarian Empire was also divided into several new countries: Austria, Hungary, Czechoslovakia, and Yugoslavia. The creation of the new countries helped fulfill one of Wilson's Fourteen Points, the right of self-determination, or the right of people to form their own nations.//

The Ottoman Empire too was divided up. Syria, Iraq, Trans-Jordan, and Palestine were created from the Ottoman Empire. They became mandates, lands given to certain nations to develop. Syria was ruled by France, the other three by Britain. These mandates were promised independence at a future time.//

Redrawing the map of Europe, however, brought some new groups under foreign control. There were social, cultural, and language implications of this foreign control. For example, Austrians living in the southwestern part of the old Austro-Hungarian Empire came under the rule of Italy. Other German-speaking Austrians were placed under Czechoslovakian rule.//

One of the biggest problems was the newly independent Poland, created from the Polish-language provinces of prewar Austria-Hungary, Germany, and Russia. The treaty's authors gave Poland some territory in eastern Germany known as the Polish Corridor. The Polish Corridor and other areas would prove to be problems in the future because they contained many ethnic minorities. Some Germans lived in the new Polish Corridor, and to complicate matters, many Hungarians also came under Romanian control. Few of these peoples were happy about the changes, and their discontent was a dangerous sign for the future.//

From *History and Life* by T. W. Wallbank, A. Schrier, D. Maier, and P. Gutierrez-Smith. Copyright © 1993 by Scott Foresman and Company. Used by permission of Pearson Education, Inc. All Rights Reserved.

Characteristics of Viruses—Part 1

Similarities and Differences between Viruses and Cells

If you ever had a cold or the flu, you probably hosted viruses. A virus is an infectious agent made up of a core of nucleic acid and a protein coat. Viruses are not cells. Unlike plant and animal cells, a virus package does not have a nucleus, a membrane, or cellular organelles such as ribosomes, mitochondria, or chloroplasts. Although viruses are not cells, they do have organized structural parts.

Compared to even the smallest cell, a virus is tiny. The virus that causes polio, for example, measures only 20 nanometers in diameter. One nanometer is one billionth of a meter. At that size, 3000 polioviruses could line up across the period at the end of this sentence.

All viruses have at least two parts: a protective protein coat and a core of nucleic acid. The protein coat around the core of the nucleic acid is called a capsid. Depending on the virus, the capsid may consist of one or several kinds of protein. The capsid protects the viral nucleic acid core from its environment.

In cells, DNA is the hereditary material. Some viruses also contain DNA, while other viruses contain only RNA. In viruses containing RNA, the RNA functions as the hereditary material.

Compared to a cell, a virus has a relatively simple existence. Viruses do not eat, respire, or respond to environmental changes as cells do. It should not surprise you, therefore, to learn that viruses have fewer genes than cells have. While a human cell may contain about 100,000 genes and a bacterial cell about 1000, a virus may contain only 5 genes.

An Influenza Virus

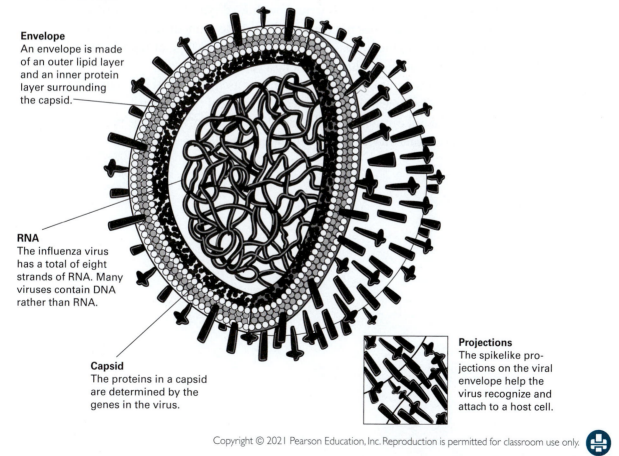

Envelope
An envelope is made of an outer lipid layer and an inner protein layer surrounding the capsid.

RNA
The influenza virus has a total of eight strands of RNA. Many viruses contain DNA rather than RNA.

Capsid
The proteins in a capsid are determined by the genes in the virus.

Projections
The spikelike projections on the viral envelope help the virus recognize and attach to a host cell.

In the figure you can see the parts of an influenza virus: a core of RNA, a surrounding capsid, and an outer covering called an envelope. An envelope is an additional protective coating usually made up of lipids, proteins, and carbohydrates. Envelopes are found only in viruses that infect animal cells. An envelope has spike-like projections that recognize and bind to complementary sites on the membrane of the cell being infected. Think about how a prickly burr sticks to objects.

Viral Replication: Ticking Time Bombs

Viruses do not reproduce, they replicate. Reproduction, which is characteristic of living things, involves cell division. Replication does not involve cell division. Viruses cannot replicate on their own. In order to replicate, viruses require a host. A host is an organism that shelters and nourishes something. Living cells host viruses. These host cells provide all the materials that viruses need to copy themselves.

When it enters a host cell, a virus may immediately begin to replicate, or it may remain relatively inactive. The viral replication process that rapidly kills a host cell is called the lytic cycle. You can follow the lytic cycle in the figure below. The lytic cycle begins when a virus invades a host cell and begins to replicate immediately, producing many new viruses. Eventually, the host cell lyses, or breaks apart, releasing the newly made viruses. The new viruses may then enter other cells and repeat the cycle.

As a child you may have had chicken pox, which is caused by a virus. While you were ill, most of the viruses were in the lytic cycle. Because your cells were being destroyed by the chicken pox virus, you showed symptoms of the disease.

Sometimes a virus does not start the lytic cycle immediately. Instead the virus enters the lysogenic cycle. The lysogenic cycle is a type of replication in which a virus does not immediately kill a host cell.

During the lysogenic cycle, viral DNA inserts itself into a host cell's chromosome. A viral DNA segment that is inserted in a bacterial chromosome is called a prophage. A host cell carrying a prophage may divide many times. The prophage is replicated every time the host cell's chromosome replicates.

Lytic Cycle

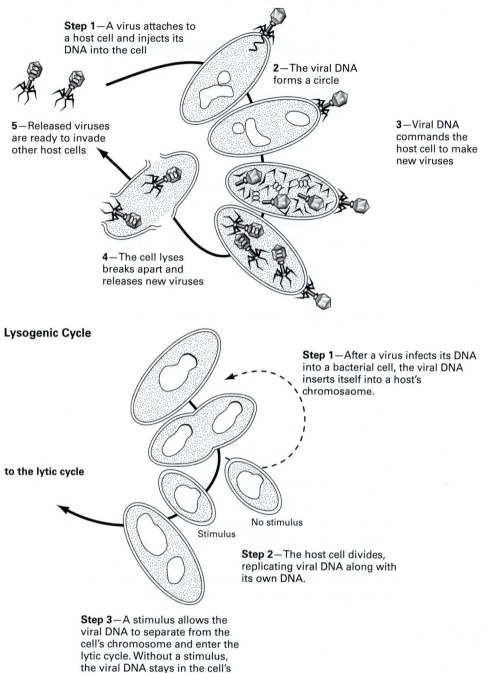

Step 1—A virus attaches to a host cell and injects its DNA into the cell

2—The viral DNA forms a circle

3—Viral DNA commands the host cell to make new viruses

5—Released viruses are ready to invade other host cells

4—The cell lyses breaks apart and releases new viruses

Lysogenic Cycle

Step 1—After a virus infects its DNA into a bacterial cell, the viral DNA inserts itself into a host's chromosaome.

to the lytic cycle

No stimulus

Stimulus

Step 2—The host cell divides, replicating viral DNA along with its own DNA.

Step 3—A stimulus allows the viral DNA to separate from the cell's chromosome and enter the lytic cycle. Without a stimulus, the viral DNA stays in the cell's chromosome.

Some prophages remain in the lysogenic cycle indefinitely. Usually, however, some type of environmental stimulus eventually results in the separation of a prophage from the chromosome of its host cell. The viral DNA then enters the lytic cycle. The virus that causes cold sores in humans can go through the lysogenic cycle, for example. Cold sores erupt when these viruses enter the lytic cycle.

From *Similarities and Differences between Viruses and Cells*, from *Biology: The Web of Life* by Eric Strauss and Marylin Lisowski. Copyright © 1998 by Addison Wesley Longman. Used by permission of Pearson Education, Inc. All Rights Reserved.

Characteristics of Viruses—Part 2

Diversity of Viruses: An Unending Supply

Classifying viruses is difficult because they are so diverse. As a result, biologists have developed several different ways of organizing viruses. Sometimes they are organized by shape, sometimes by the host they infect. Viruses may also be classified according to the way they function inside a cell.//

Shape. The arrangement of proteins in capsids determines the shape of the viruses.

Host. Viruses can be organized according to the type of host they infect. There are animal viruses, plant viruses, and bacterial viruses. Viruses that infect only bacterial cells are referred to as bacteriophages.

Many but not all viruses invade only a specific type of organism. For example, the virus that causes polio replicates only inside human host cells. The virus that causes rabies infects only the cells of a particular animal species, such as dogs and humans.//

You may wonder how viruses can be so specific. Earlier you learned that capsids and envelopes contain specific proteins. Receptor sites on host cells also contain specific proteins. If the outer proteins in a virus do not fit with the outer proteins of a cell, the virus will not attach to the cell. Without attachment, the viral nucleic acid cannot enter the host cell to replicate.//

Function. Some viruses, such as retroviruses, can also be classified based on how they function in a host. A retrovirus is a virus that contains an RNA code that replicates by first transcribing its RNA into DNA. The prefix "retro-" means "reverse." What do you think might work in reverse in this group of viruses?//

Most viruses and all organisms make RNA from DNA in the process of transcription. Retroviruses are able to make nucleic acids in reverse order from the usual process. In retroviruses DNA is made from RNA. As you can see in the figure, retroviruses have an enzyme called reverse transcriptase, which transcribes viral RNA into viral DNA inside the host cell. You can study the figure to better understand the replication of a human immunodeficiency virus (HIV). The retrovirus causes acquired immunodeficiency syndrome (AIDS).//

The Retrovirus

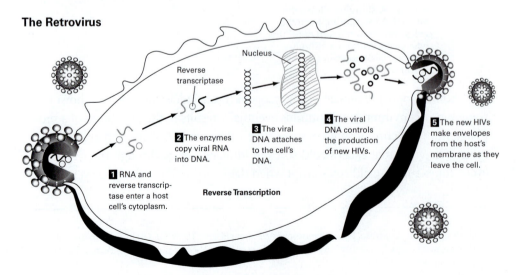

Reverse transcriptase

Nucleus

1 RNA and reverse transcriptase enter a host cell's cytoplasm.

2 The enzymes copy viral RNA into DNA.

3 The viral DNA attaches to the cell's DNA.

4 The viral DNA controls the production of new HIVs.

5 The new HIVs make envelopes from the host's membrane as they leave the cell.

Reverse Transcription

Retroviruses include tumor-producing viruses as well as HIV. Tumor-producing retroviruses and HIV follow a similar invasion pattern. Many tumor-producing viruses, however, enter the lysogenic cycle after Step 3 in the figure. Tumors do not immediately appear, but the viral DNA replicates along with the host cell DNA. Eventually many host cells will contain tumor-producing viral DNA. Using what you have learned about the lysogenic cycle, you can probably predict what will happen eventually.//

Nonviral particles. Scientists have discovered two infectious agents that have simpler structures than viruses: viroids and prions. A viroid is a single strand of pure RNA. Viroids cause plant diseases. For example, viroids have killed many coconut palm trees in the Philippines. Other viroids affect the health of crops such as potatoes and tomatoes. Unlike viruses, viroids do not have capsids protecting their nucleic acids.//

A prion is a protein molecule that can cause disease in animals. Prions are the only known infectious agents that do not contain DNA or RNA but can, nonetheless, spread throughout an organism. A prion causes a fatal disease called scrapie in sheep. Prions have also been found in the brains of cows that died from the so-called mad cow disease. Other prions are found in humans who suffer from kuru or Creutzfeldt-Jakob disease. Both of these diseases affect the central nervous system. A cure has not yet been found for diseases caused by viroids or prions.//

From *Diversity of Viruses: An Unending Supply*, from *Biology: The Web of Life* by Eric Strauss and Marylin Lisowski. Copyright © 1998 by Addison Wesley Longman. Used by permission of Pearson Education, Inc. All Rights Reserved.

Level: High School

Social Studies: Expository

Concept Questions:

What caused World War I? (*3: nations wanted control over other nations and/or independence from other nations, an heir to a throne was assassinated; 2: nations did not like or trust each other, the assassination was an excuse; 1: causes of wars are all the same*)

_____

_____

_____ (3-2-1-0)

What is a <u>stalemate</u>? (*3: an impasse, a deadlock, a standoff, no winner; 2: can go on for a long time, prevents getting anything done; 1: you don't want one in sports*)

_____

_____

_____ (3-2-1-0)

What does "unrestricted" mean? (*3: free, no limits, no rules; unhindered, no obstacles; 2: like if there were no penalties in football; like you can go where you want because there are no signs or barricades; 1: not restricted, I can do it if I want*)

_____

_____

_____ (3-2-1-0)

What is an armistice? (*3: a truce, a ceasefire, an agreement to stop fighting; 2: saves lives, gives people a chance to think about things, is often broken; 1: a holiday*)

_____

_____

_____ (3-2-1-0)

Score: _____/12 = _____ %

_____ FAM (≥ 55%) _____ UNFAM

Note: Underlined words are on the high school word list.

World War I—Part I

World War I, also known as the Great War, drew in not only the major powers of Europe, but those of America and Asia as well. Many economic and political factors caused the war. Newly <u>industrialized</u> nations competed with one another for trade and markets for their goods. Also, the urge for national power and independence from other nations came from old and new powers. When a new nation tried to increase its power by building a strong military, an older nation perceived the new nation as a threat to its power. Such tensions led to the division of Europe into two groups for security: one composed of Britain, France, and Russia, the other of Austria, Hungary, and Germany.

Although the factors discussed above caused the war, the final breaking point was a local conflict between Austria and Serbia, a tiny kingdom in southeastern Europe. Serbia, supported by Russia, wanted to unite with the Serbs living in the Austro-Hungarian Empire and create a Greater Serbia. Austria, supported by Germany, did not want Serbia cutting into its empire. The war officially started in August of 1914, after the assassination of the Austrian heir to the throne, who was visiting Sarajevo, near Serbia's border. The assassin was

Level: High School

a young man with connections to the military intelligence branch of the Serbian government. Austria's attempt to punish Serbia drew Russia and its allies Britain and France into a war against Austria-Hungary and Germany. The map illustrates the geographical location of the countries in Europe and surrounding regions in 1914.

The War Raged on Two Fronts

Germany hoped to defeat France by striking quickly through Belgium and, therefore, to minimize the danger of a two-front war. The highly trained German troops nearly reached Paris before the French stopped them. However, the Russians aided France by suddenly attacking Germany on its eastern front, and Germany sent troops from western Europe to face the attack. With the German forces diminished, the French were able to force the weakened Germans back. The war in the west became a stalemate with neither side able to achieve a victory. As a result, both sides sought new allies to help them gain victory, and the war became a world war as Japan, Italy, Portugal, Romania, and other countries joined Britain, France, and Russia. Germany and Austria-Hungary drew in Bulgaria and the Ottoman Empire, which included Turkey.

On the eastern front Russia kept part of the German army busy. Although Russia fought valiantly, it had not been prepared for war and thus was unable to defeat the Germans. Russian defeats led to a revolution that toppled the tsar of Russia. In late 1917 the new leader of Russia, Lenin, offered to make peace with Germany. As part of the treaty agreement, Germany gained coal mines and oil fields from Russia, which gave Germany power to fuel its army. More important, it allowed the war to be fought on only one front—the western front.

The United States entered the war when Germany began attacking American ships that were taking supplies to Britain and France. U.S. President Woodrow Wilson warned the Germans to stop the attacks, and for a while they did. But they announced an unrestricted submarine warfare after the British blockade shut off supplies to Germany. The final event that caused the United States to join the Allies was the interception of a telegram from the German foreign secretary to Mexico asking Mexico to ally itself with Germany and help fight the United States. Germany promised Mexico financial aid and the recovery of Texas, New Mexico, and Arizona when the Allies were defeated.

In the fall of 1918, German military leaders realized they could not win. One by one Germany's allies quit. On November 3, German sailors mutinied at Kiel, a city and port in northwest Germany. Four days later a revolution broke out in Germany. A republic was founded, and the kaiser fled to Holland.

Leaders of the new German government agreed to an armistice, which is an agreement to stop fighting. They asked that the peace settlement be based on President Wilson's Fourteen Points, which he had described in a speech to Congress in 1918. The Fourteen Points outlined the president's ideas for solving the problems that led to the war. Wilson wanted an end to secret agreements, freedom of the seas in peace and war, the reduction of armaments, the right of nationality groups to form their own nations, and an association of nations to keep the peace. In other speeches Wilson called for a negotiated peace with reasonable demands made on the losers. The Allies agreed to model the peace settlement on the Fourteen Points.

Early in the morning of November 11, 1918, the war ended. In a railroad car in the Compiègne Forest in northern France, two German delegates met Allied officials to sign the armistice. The guns were silent.

No previous war had caused such widespread horror. More than 10 million troops were killed in battle, and 20 million more were wounded. Thirteen million civilians died from war-related famine, disease, and injuries. The cost of the war was estimated at more than $350 billion. Destruction was everywhere. (865 words)

From *History and Life* by T. W. Wallbank, A. Schrier, D. Maier, and P. Gutierrez-Smith. Copyright © 1993 by Scott Foresman and Company. Used by permission of Pearson Education, Inc. All Rights Reserved.

Rate: 865 × 60 = 51,900/_____ no secs = _____ WPM

Retelling Scoring Sheet for "World War I—Part I"

Main Idea

_____ Economic and political factors caused World War I.

Details

_____ Nations competed for trade and/or markets for goods.

_____ Nations wanted power and/or independence.

_____ Old nations were threatened by new nations.

_____ Such tensions led to two groups:

_____ one composed of Britain, France, and Russia,

_____ the other of Austria, Hungary, and Germany.

Level: High School

Main Idea

_____ The breaking point was a conflict between Austria and Serbia.

Details

_____ The heir to the Austrian throne was assassinated.

_____ Austria attempted to punish Serbia

_____ and drew Russia, Britain, and France into war against Austria-Hungary and Germany.

Main Idea

_____ The war became a stalemate.

Details

_____ Neither side achieved victory.

_____ Russia attacked Germany.

_____ Germany pulled troops from France.

_____ Russian defeats led to a revolution.

_____ Russia made peace with Germany.

_____ It allowed the war to be fought on one front.

_____ The British blockade shut off supplies to Germany.

Main Idea

_____ The United States entered the war.

Details

_____ The United States sent supplies to Britain and France.

_____ Germany began attacking American supply ships.

_____ A British blockade shut off supplies to Germany.

_____ The final event was the interception of a German telegram

_____ asking Mexico to fight the United States.

_____ Germany promised Mexico financial aid and the recovery of Texas, New Mexico, and/or Arizona.

Main Idea

_____ German leaders realized they could not win.

Details

_____ Their allies quit.

_____ A revolution broke out.

_____ A republic was founded.

_____ Germany agreed to an armistice.

_____ Germany asked for a peace settlement

_____ based on President Wilson's Fourteen Points.

Main Idea

_____ The Fourteen Points outlined ideas for solving the problems that led to the war.

Details

_____ End secret agreements,

_____ have freedom of the seas,

_____ reduce armaments,

_____ grant the right of nationality groups to form their own nations,

_____ form an association of nations to keep the peace.

Main Idea

_____ The war ended on November 11, 1918.

Questions for "World War I—Part I"

1. What is this passage mostly about?
   Implicit: how World War I started and ended

2. What two types of factors caused the war?
   Explicit: economic and political

Level: High School

3. How did the old powers regard the rise of new powers?
Implicit: as competition for trade and as a military threat

4. What event finally triggered the war?
Explicit: the assassination of the Austrian heir to the throne by a Serbian; *or* by a man with ties to the military intelligence branch of the Serbian government

5. How did the Russian attack on Germany result in a stalemate?
Implicit: Germany pulled troops from France to meet the Russian attack, and France was able to force the Germans back but could not defeat them

6. How do you know that the United States favored Britain and France?
Implicit: U.S. ships were taking supplies to Britain and France

7. How do you know that Britain had a powerful navy?
Implicit: the British blockade shut off supplies to Germany

8. What final event caused the United States to join the Allies?
Explicit: the interception of a telegram from Germany to Mexico asking Mexico to ally itself with Germany and help fight the United States

9. How did the defeat of Russia on the eastern front help Germany?
Explicit: Germany gained oil fields and coal mines that gave fuel to its army; *or* it allowed the war to be fought on only one front so all their armies could be unified there

10. What events caused Germany to agree to an armistice?
Explicit: their allies quit; or sailors mutinied; or a revolution broke out

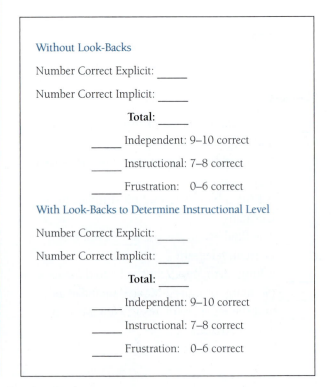

Without Look-Backs

Number Correct Explicit: _____

Number Correct Implicit: _____

       Total: _____

_____ Independent: 9–10 correct

_____ Instructional: 7–8 correct

_____ Frustration: 0–6 correct

With Look-Backs to Determine Instructional Level

Number Correct Explicit: _____

Number Correct Implicit: _____

       Total: _____

_____ Independent: 9–10 correct

_____ Instructional: 7–8 correct

_____ Frustration: 0–6 correct

Level: High School

Concept Questions:

What does "compromise" mean? (*3: where both parties agree but don't get all they want, concession, settlement, cooperation; 2: you might accept it but not like all of it, without compromise little would get done; 1: like I will take out the garbage if my sister will unload the dishwasher*)

_____

_____

_____ (3-2-1-0)

What was the League of Nations? (*3: an international organization created after World War I, a world alliance, an organization to keep the peace; 2: it didn't last very long, Wilson wanted it, it was part of the treaty that ended World War I; 1: a group of countries*)

_____

_____

_____ (3-2-1-0)

What does "mediated" mean? (*3: arbitrated, interceded, refereed, acted as a go-between; 2: you have to be patient to do it, you have to see both sides of an issue; 1: can be a good thing*)

_____

_____

_____ (3-2-1-0)

What are reparations? (*3: compensations, damages, restitutions, a way of making amends for an injury; 2: they can sometimes be unjust, you have to compromise to make them, not everyone agrees with them; 1: some people want them and some don't*)

_____

_____

_____ (3-2-1-0)

Score: _____ /12 = _____ %

_____ FAM (≥ 55%) _____ UNFAM

Now I want you to read the next section and when you come to the slash marks in the text, I want you to tell me what you are thinking. When you are done reading, I will ask you to tell me what you remember, and then I will ask you questions.

Note: Underlined words are on the high school word list.

World War I—Part 2

Three Leaders Dominated the Paris Peace Conference

After the armistice had been signed, the Allied nations met in Paris to discuss peace terms. Contrary to Wilson's wishes, the defeated countries were not allowed to send representatives to the peace conference. Thus, the so-called Big Three dominated the meeting: President Wilson; David Lloyd George, prime minister of Great Britain; and Georges Clemenceau, premier of France. At the conference Wilson pushed his Fourteen Points. Above all, he wanted to see a League of Nations, an international association established to keep the peace. To get the others to agree, however, he had to make compromises.//

_____

_____

_____

_____

_____

Level: High School

Concept Questions:

What does it mean to classify something? (*3: put into categories, organize on the basis of likenesses or differences; 2: put things in order, sort things; 1: give it a name*)

_____

_____

_____ (3-2-1-0)

What does it mean to invade something? (*3: attack, enter, grow, take over; 2: can be a good or bad thing, usually one attacker wins out; 1: my brother invaded my room*)

_____

_____

_____ (3-2-1-0)

What does it mean to be specific? (*3: exact, precise, explicit, matching; 2: an action can be specific to a situation, if you are going on a camping trip you would take specific kinds of clothes; 1: like special*)

_____

_____

_____ (3-2-1-0)

What does the prefix "retro" mean? (*3: back, backward, behind, reverse; 2: it's a movement, it signals time; 1: like a retrorocket*)

_____

_____

_____ (3-2-1-0)

Score: _____ /12 = _____ %

_____ FAM (≥ 55%) _____ UNFAM

Now I want you to read the next section, and when you come to the slash marks in the text, I want you to tell me what you are thinking. When you have finished reading, I will ask you to tell me what you remember, and then I will ask you questions.

Note: Underlined words are on the high school word list.

Characteristics of Viruses—Part 2
Diversity of Viruses: An Unending Supply

Classifying viruses is difficult because they are so diverse. As a result, biologists have developed several different ways of organizing viruses. Sometimes they are organized by shape, sometimes by the host they infect. Viruses may also be classified according to the way they function inside a cell.**//**

_____

_____

_____

_____

_____

_____

Shape. The arrangement of proteins in capsids determines the shape of the viruses.

Host. Viruses can be organized according to the type of host they infect. There are animal viruses, plant viruses, and bacterial viruses. Viruses that infect only bacterial cells are referred to as bacteriophages.

Many but not all viruses invade only a specific type of organism. For example, the virus that causes polio replicates only inside human host cells. The virus that causes rabies infects only the cells of a particular animal species, such as dogs and humans.**//**

Level: High School

Level: High School

_____

_____

_____

_____

_____

You may wonder how viruses can be so specific. Earlier you learned that capsids and envelopes contain specific proteins. Receptor sites on host cells also contain specific proteins. If the outer proteins in a virus do not fit with the outer proteins of a cell, the virus will not attach to the cell. Without attachment, the viral nucleic acid cannot enter the host cell to replicate.//

_____

_____

_____

_____

Function. Some viruses, such as retroviruses, can also be classified based on how they function in a host. A retrovirus is a virus that contains an RNA code that replicates by first transcribing its RNA into DNA. The prefix "retro-" means "reverse." What do you think might work in reverse in this group of viruses?//

_____

_____

_____

_____

Most viruses and all organisms make RNA from DNA in the process of transcription. Retroviruses are able to make nucleic acids in reverse order from the usual process. In retroviruses DNA is made from RNA. As you can see in the figure, retroviruses have an enzyme called reverse transcriptase, which transcribes viral RNA into viral DNA inside the host cell. You can study the figure to better understand the replication of a human immunodeficiency virus (HIV). The retrovirus causes acquired immunodeficiency syndrome (AIDS).//

_____

_____

_____

_____

Retroviruses include tumor-producing viruses as well as HIV. Tumor-producing retroviruses and HIV follow a similar invasion pattern. Many tumor-producing viruses, however, enter the lysogenic cycle after Step 3 in the figure. Tumors do not immediately appear, but the viral DNA replicates along with the host cell DNA. Eventually many host cells will contain tumor-producing viral DNA. Using what you have learned about the lysogenic cycle, you can probably predict what will happen eventually.//

_____

_____

_____

_____

Nonviral particles. Scientists have discovered two infectious agents that have simpler structures than viruses: viroids and prions. A viroid is a single strand of pure RNA. Viroids cause plant diseases. For example, viroids have killed many coconut palm trees in the Philippines. Other viroids affect the health of crops such as potatoes and tomatoes. Unlike viruses, viroids do not have capsids protecting their nucleic acids.//

_____

_____

_____

_____

_____

A prion is a protein molecule that can cause disease in animals. Prions are the only known infectious agents that do not contain DNA or RNA but can, nonetheless, spread throughout an organism. A prion causes a fatal disease called scrapie in sheep. Prions have also been found in the brains of cows that died from the so-called mad cow disease. Other prions are found in humans who suffer from kuru or Creutzfeldt-Jakob disease. Both of these diseases affect the central nervous system. A cure has not yet been found for diseases caused by viroids or prions.// (582 words)

_____

_____

_____

_____

(914 words)

From *Biology: The Web of Life* by Eric Strauss and Marylin Lisowski. Copyright © 1998 by Addison Wesley Longman. Used by permission of Pearson Education, Inc. All Rights Reserved.

Level: High School

Retelling Scoring Sheet for "Characteristics of Viruses—Part 2"

Main Idea

_____ Classifying viruses is difficult because they are so diverse.

Details

_____ They are organized by shape,
_____ by the host they infect,
_____ and by the way they function in a cell.
_____ There are animal viruses,
_____ plant viruses,
_____ and bacterial viruses.
_____ Many viruses invade only a specific type of organism.

Main Idea

_____ Some viruses are classified as retroviruses.

Details

_____ Retroviruses include HIV
_____ and tumor-producing viruses.
_____ A retrovirus replicates by transcribing the RNA into DNA
_____ inside the host cell.
_____ Host cells then contain tumor-producing DNA.

Main Idea

_____ Two agents with simpler structures are viroids and prions.

Details

_____ A viroid is a strand of RNA.
_____ Viroids cause plant diseases.
_____ A prion causes disease in animals.
_____ Prions have been found in cows with mad cow disease.
_____ Prions have been found in humans with nervous system diseases.
_____ A cure has not been found for such diseases.

Questions for "Characteristics of Viruses—Part 2"

1. What are the major topics included in this section?
   Implicit: any two of the following: how viruses are classified, retroviruses, and nonviral particles

2. Name three ways in which viruses are classified.
   Explicit: by shape, host, and the way they function

3. What is necessary for the virus to attach to a host?
   Explicit: the outer proteins must match

4. What is a retrovirus?
   Explicit: a virus that replicates by first transcribing its RNA into DNA

5. How do retroviruses differ from other viruses?
   Implicit: retroviruses make RNA into DNA, or viruses make RNA from DNA

6. What is the role of reverse transcriptase in a retrovirus?
   Explicit: it transcribes viral RNA into viral DNA

7. What are the two types of illnesses caused by a retrovirus?
   Explicit: AIDS and tumors (Cancer is acceptable.)

8. What happens when tumor-producing viral DNA goes into the lytic cycle?
   Implicit: tumors are produced in the host cell

9. If a person is found to be HIV positive but shows no symptoms of AIDS, what cycle is the HIV virus in?
   Implicit: the lysogenic cycle

10. How are viroids and prions alike, and how are they different?
    Implicit: they are both <u>infectious</u> agents, and/or no cure has been found for the diseases they produce but viroids cause plant diseases and prions cause animal diseases (Answer should include one likeness and one difference.)

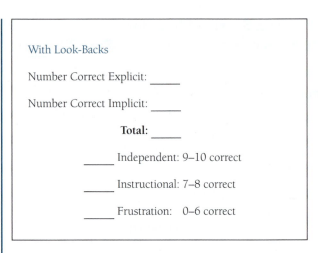

With Look-Backs

Number Correct Explicit: _____

Number Correct Implicit: _____

Total: _____

_____ Independent: 9–10 correct

_____ Instructional: 7–8 correct

_____ Frustration: 0–6 correct

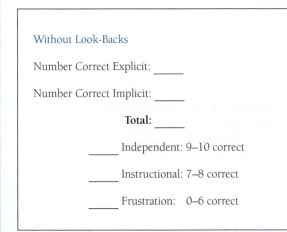

Without Look-Backs

Number Correct Explicit: _____

Number Correct Implicit: _____

Total: _____

_____ Independent: 9–10 correct

_____ Instructional: 7–8 correct

_____ Frustration: 0–6 correct

Think-Aloud Summary

Think-Aloud Comments That Suggest Understanding

Restates text content accurately   _____

Offers relevant comment   _____

Asks relevant question   _____

Recognizes topic/main idea   _____

Identifies personally   _____

Paraphrases/summarizes appropriately   _____

Draws a valid inference based on personal experience   _____

Draws a valid inference based on text information   _____

Think-Aloud Comments That Suggest Lack of Understanding

Restates text content inaccurately   _____

Offers irrelevant comment   _____

Asks irrelevant question   _____

Does not recognize topic/main idea   _____

Does not identify personally   _____

Paraphrases/summarizes inappropriately   _____

Draws an invalid inference based on personal experience   _____

Draws an invalid inference based on text information   _____

Section 11

Administering and Scoring the Inference-Diagnostic Passages

 Chapter Outline

Purpose of the Inference-Diagnostic Passages

Differences Between Level-Diagnostic and Inference-Diagnostic Passages

Choosing an Inference-Diagnostic Passage

Mode of Reading: Oral or Silent

Mode of Answering Questions

    Questions for Inference-Diagnostic Passages

    Guidelines for Determining Acceptability of Answers

    Recording Results and Identifying a Focus for Instruction

Evaluating Summaries

    Scoring and Analysis of Narrative/Biographies Summaries

    Scoring and Analysis of Expository Summaries

    Guidelines for Scoring Summaries

Summary

PURPOSE OF THE INFERENCE-DIAGNOSTIC PASSAGES

The Level-Diagnostic passages, which we have discussed in the preceding sections, are used to estimate a student's independent, instructional, and frustration reading levels. These levels are based on word identification and comprehension. The instructional reading level is the level at which a student can identify words within an accuracy level of 90–97%, and answer explicit (literal) and implicit (inferential) questions with 70–88% comprehension.

    What else can we learn in order to design effective intervention instruction? The Inference-Diagnostic passages move beyond determining a student's general reading level, and allow examiners to identify the kinds of inference questions that the student can answer successfully, which in turn identifies the type of information and questions that should be the focus of intervention instruction. The Inference-Diagnostic passages allow you to assess a student's ability to answer different forms of inference questions in three different disciplines: literature (i.e., biographies), social studies, and science. These questions parallel the type of reading that occurs in classrooms where students are expected to independently read text, ask and answer questions, and monitor their own comprehension. In other words, the inference questions focus on specific types of questions that are asked by classroom teachers, are present in classroom textbooks, and are found in state and national standards. You can find a list of such questions (prompts) in Figure 11.1.

Figure 11.1 Types of Questions Found in Inference-Diagnostic Passages

Narrative Passages	Expository Passages
Determine the theme	Determine the central idea
Explain why or how	Explain/analyze why/how
Understand meaning of words and phrases	Determine word meaning
Determine point of view	Determine point of view (social studies)
Provide text evidence	Provide text evidence
	Identify text structure
Summarize the text	Summarize the text

DIFFERENCES BETWEEN LEVEL-DIAGNOSTIC AND INFERENCE-DIAGNOSTIC PASSAGES

How are the Level-Diagnostic and Inference-Diagnostic passages different?

- **Grade level range of passages:** The range of Level-Diagnostic passages is pre-primer through high school. The range of Inferential-Diagnostic passages is fourth grade through high school.
- **When comprehension is assessed:** Level-Diagnostic passages assess comprehension at the end of the passage, whereas questions are inserted throughout Inference-Diagnostic passages. Text content necessary to answer a question precedes each question, making it immediately available to the reader. In other words, the reader does not have to search throughout an entire text in order to find an answer to a question. If the reader does not answer a question correctly, it may be due to the reader's inability to comprehend or recognize relevant information. It may also be due to a reader's difficulty in interpreting the questions.
- **Individual vs. group administered sessions:** Level-Diagnostic passages must be administered to one student at a time. Inference-Diagnostic passages can be administered to a single student, a small group, or an entire class. Administration to a single student can be oral or written. Group administration requires written answers.
- **Retelling vs. summarization:** Retelling is a Level-Diagnostic activity that indicates the amount, accuracy, and order of what the student remembers. A summary is an Inferential-Diagnostic activity that indicates whether the student recognizes the most important elements of the text. Figure 11.2 provides a full comparison of Level-Diagnostic passages and Inferential-Diagnostic passages.

Figure 11.2 Comparison of Level-Diagnostic and Inference-Diagnostic Passages

Level-Diagnostic Passages	Inference-Diagnostic Passages
For levels pre-primer through high school	For levels 4 through high school
Must be administered to individual student	Can be administered to individual student, small group, or whole class
Text preceded by concept questions	Text preceded by concept questions
Questions are literal and inferential	Questions are inferential only
Questions are asked after reading	Questions are asked during and/or after reading
Questions are placed at the end of the text	Questions are placed within the text
Students are asked to *retell* passages	Students are asked to summarize only the most important elements
Passages include narratives, social studies, and science	Passages include biographies, social studies, and science

CHOOSING AN INFERENCE-DIAGNOSTIC PASSAGE

Use the following guidelines to select an Inference-Diagnostic Passage:

- **For individual students:** Select an expository passage that is at a student's instructional level as determined by results from the Level-Diagnostic passages. We suggest an expository text because this type of text often poses more problems for students than narrative material. If time permits, the student can read both a narrative and an expository selection. You may find a distinct difference in the student's comprehension of the two different text types.

- **For a small group or the whole class:** If you are administering the passage to a group or class, select a passage level that best represents the whole group. For example, administer a fifth-grade passage to a fifth-grade class even though some students would probably score higher or lower. Your purpose is to determine the type of questions they can answer correctly, and you may find that your best readers experience difficulty with some question types.

MODE OF READING: ORAL OR SILENT?

An individual student can read the passage orally or silently. If you let the student make the decision, it may ensure that the chosen mode is one with which the reader is most comfortable. Group administration requires that participants read silently.

MODE OF ANSWERING QUESTIONS

The student(s) should have full access to the passage when answering questions. This is not an assessment of memory; it is an assessment of comprehension. A single reader can answer the questions orally, with the examiner writing down what the student says. The reader can also answer the questions in writing. Older students often prefer written answers perhaps because this format is what they are used to in their regular classrooms. Group administration requires that the students write their answers.

Questions for Inference-Diagnostic Passages

Each passage is preceded by four concept questions that allow you to determine whether the content of the section is familiar or unfamiliar. For more information, see Section 4, Factors affecting reading levels.

Questions that follow the Inference-Diagnostic passages focus on different forms of inferential comprehension. They vary according to the nature of the text: narrative or expository. See Figures 11.3 and 11.4 for a list of question stems for narrative and expository passages.

Figure 11.3 Question Stems for Narrative Text

What evidence in the text indicates	Two questions
What is the theme or central idea	Two questions
Explain/analyze why or how	Two questions
Point of view	Two questions
What does a word/phrase mean	Two questions

Figure 11.4 Question Stems for Expository Text

What is the central idea	Two questions
What is the meaning of	Two questions
Analyze why or how	Two questions
What evidence in the text indicates	Two questions
What is the structure of the text	One question
What is the point of view of	One question (social studies)

Guidelines for Determining the Acceptability of Answers

Use the following guidelines to determine whether or not an answer is acceptable:

- Some answers may contain unrelated information. If the information given does not contradict the correct answer, accept it as correct. If it does contradict the correct answer, mark the entire answer as wrong.

- If you are unsure about the acceptability of an answer, ask the student to clarify what was said. If the student is not able to do this or if you administered the passage to a group, score the answer as incorrect. It is better to focus instruction on an inference type and find it is not needed than to assume instruction is not necessary when it is.

- Some answers, both written and oral, may be relatively unintelligible even though they seem to address the question. Score them as wrong.

- Some answers may be based on a student's prior knowledge. For example, many of the vocabulary questions center on words with multiple meanings. If a student offers an accurate definition of a word but not one that fits the context of the passage, score this as incorrect. Only accept answers that are based on the text content. The vocabulary questions ask, "What is the meaning of _____ in the context of the passage?"

- If the student writes his or her answer, do not score on the basis of writing mechanics such as spelling, sentence structure, punctuation, etc. Only score on the basis of accuracy in relation to the answer key.

Recording Results and Identifying a Focus for Instruction

Once you have scored all answers, examine the student's performance in terms of the type of inference questions that were correctly answered. As described above, each passage has a chart that helps you to summarize a student's performance. There may be a pattern to a student's performance—that is, a student may correctly answer both forms of one kind of question and offer incorrect answers for another kind. The table will make this visible. Each chart is aligned with the specific order of questions as presented in the text as demonstrated in Figure 11.5.

Figure 11.5 Evaluating Performance by Inference Type
Passage: The Rise of Cattle Drives
Level 4

Determine central idea	_____	Q1	_____	Q6
Determine word meaning	_____	Q4	_____	Q8
Explain why/how	_____	Q2	_____	Q10
Provide text evidence	_____	Q5	_____	Q9
Identify text structure	_____	Q3		
Determine point of view	_____	Q7		

You have three options for filling in the performance chart:

- Record only the correct answers that offer a picture of a student's strengths (use C or ∏ to indicate correct answers).
- Record only the incorrect answers that indicate the student's need for instruction (use I or X to indicate incorrect answers).
- Record both correct and incorrect answers. If you choose this option, pay close attention to which answers are correct and incorrect as this suggests a pattern for intervention instruction.

For example, when reading Level-Diagnostic passages, Jamie, an eighth-grader, scored at a fifth-grade instructional level for social studies text. He was asked to silently read an Inference-Diagnostic passage at the fifth-grade level and answer the questions in writing. Figure 11.6 records his performance by inserting a "C" for each correct question.

Figure 11.6 Evaluating Performance by Inference Type
Passage: The Rise of Cattle Drives
Level 5

Determine central idea	__C__	Q1	_____		Q6
Determine word meaning	__C__	Q4	__C__		Q8
Explain why/how	_____	Q2	__C__		Q10
Provide text evidence	_____	Q5	_____		Q9
Identify text structure	_____	Q3			
Determine point of view	__C__	Q7			

Jamie's strengths were in understanding word meaning and recognizing an author's point of view. He demonstrated difficulty in identifying text structure and providing text evidence to support his answers. His answers also suggested that determining central idea and explaining why or how may also need an instructional focus.

EVALUATING SUMMARIES

You can also ask the student to summarize the passage. A summary is more concise than a retelling. Summaries "tap the ability to generalize text content," (Caccamise et al., 2015 p. 92). The student has access to the text while crafting the summary.

Memory for what was read should not be part of summary writing. While the summary can be oral or written, a written summary more easily lends itself to revision. It allows the student to reread and review what was written. A written summary also removes the need for you to record what the student says, and you can evaluate it at a later date. For the literature passages, the student summarizes the entire biography. For the social studies and science passages, the student summarizes a specific segment of the text. Your purpose is to determine whether a student understands how to write a narrative and/or expository summary.

What are the components of a well-crafted summary? A summary includes only the most relevant content about a specific topic (Ferretti & De La Paz, 2011). A summary of a biography focuses on the important events in a character's life. It includes why the person is famous and what difficulties challenged him or her. An expository summary includes the main idea, along with the most significant details related to this idea.

Evaluating a summary can involve two components: 1) the content of the summary, and 2) the mechanics of writing, such as spelling, punctuation, and sentence structure. We suggest that the content of the summary is most important—that is, the extent to which it includes elements that match the answer key and address the topic. You may, if you wish, evaluate writing mechanics, but they are not part of our scoring system.

Scoring and Analysis of Narrative/Biographies Summaries

The answer key for biographical summaries is organized around the elements of a narrative: setting, character(s), initiating event, further events, and ending. The summary is scored by counting the number of story elements (setting, characterizations, initiating event, episodes, and ending) included. Elements may be missing depending on the nature of the passage. For example, a setting may or may not be important to a story. To receive credit, the student only needs to include one statement within the story element category. Figure 11.7 provides an example of a narrative student summary with sample scoring.

Figure 11.7 Example of Narrative Student Summary and Scoring

The following summary was written by a seventh-grader after reading the sixth-grade text "The Legacy of Jim Thorpe." The scoring of the student's summary is presented below.

The story is about a boy who lives on an Indian reservation and his parents made him go to school when he was 6 years old. Instead of going he just ran away. Later though he joins the track and football team and becomes a star. He later did the pentathlon and became known as America's sport star of all time.

Summary of "The Legacy of Jim Thorpe"?

1. Setting

   On an Indian reservation and in Indian schools ✔

2. Characterizations

   Jim Thorpe was a talented athlete and a hard worker. _____

   He hated school. _____

   Hiram Thorpe, Jim's dad, wanted him to get an education. _____

3. Initiating Event

   Jim kept running away from Indian schools because he didn't likethe strict schedules. ✔

   Jim's father kept sending him back. _____

   Finally, his father realized that he couldn't keep Jim at school. _____

4. Event #1

   Jim was accepted into Carlisle Indian School. _____

(Continued)

(*Continued*)

It had a great sports tradition. _____

Jim showed talent at the high jump. _____

Pops Warner, the track coach, made him a member of the team. ✔ _____

5. Event #2

Jim wanted to play football, but the coach didn't want him to. _____

The coach relented and asked Jim to run downfield against defensive players. _____

No one could tackle Jim, so he became part of the football team. ✔ _____

The first year he sat on the bench. _____

Later he became a star. _____

6. Event #3

Pops Warner promised he would help Jim train for the Olympics. _____

Jim went to the Olympics in 1912 and entered the pentathlon and the decathlon. ✔ _____

He won two gold medals. _____

7. Ending

Jim was named the Male Athlete of the Half Century in 1950. ✔ _____

Total elements included in summary = 6

Total possible elements = 7

Acceptable = 5

---

*Acceptable elements:

1. On an Indian reservation and in Indian schools (*"on an Indian reservation"*)

2. Jim kept running away from Indian schools because he didn't like the strict schedules (*Instead of going he just ran away*)

3. Pops Warner, the track coach, made him a member of the team. (*he joins the track and football team*)

4. No one could tackle Jim, so he became part of the football team. (*he joins the track and football team*)

5. Jim went to the Olympics in 1912 and entered the pentathlon and the decathlon (*He later did the pentathlon*)

6. He was named the Male Athlete of the Half Century in 1950. (*became known as America's sport star of all time*)

The evaluation of this summary is made based on the number of story elements it contains and how it was organized. The student included six of the seven story elements and organized the elements in the order in which they occurred. This is an acceptable summary.

Pearson eText Application Exercise 11.1: Julio's Inference-Diagnostic Passage Performance (Narrative)

Scoring and Analysis of Expository Summaries

Like analysis of biographical summaries, scoring for expository summaries is determined by comparing the student's summary elements with those on the Summary Scoring Sheet that is part of the Answer Key. Each passage has its own list of acceptable elements. Each element is worth 1 point. Following are two students' summaries based on the same fourth-grade level text, "Linking East and West."

An acceptable text-based summary contains the following elements:

1. An introductory statement of purpose.

2. People traveled by wagons.

3. People traveled by ship.

4. People traveled by stagecoach.

5. The Pony Express carried mail.

6. The telegraph sent messages by wire.

7. A transcontinental railroad linked the East and West.

Student 1: Jenny

Jenny summarized the passage as follows: *People rode across the U.S. in the olden days in wagons. Then they made the telegraph. And then they made the railroad. When that was done, they put in a golden spike and telegraphed all over the world that it was done.*

1. An introductory statement of purpose.
   People traveled by wagons.
   People rode in wagons,
2. People traveled by ship.
3. People traveled by stagecoach.
4. The journey took months.
5. The Pony Express carried mail.

   The telegraph sent messages by wire
   Then they made the telegraph
   A transcontinental railroad linked the East and West.
   Then they made the railroad

   <u>Evaluating Summary Performance</u>
   Total elements included in student's summary = 3
   Total possible elements included in summary = 8
   Acceptable = 6
   Jennie's summary was unacceptable. She identified only 3 elements.

Student 2: Peter

Peter summarized the same passage as follows: *Well traveling wasn't very easy. The first way was by wagon which were pulled by big horses. They could sail there. And the Pony Express came. A railroad went from east to west. It took a lot of time to build. People were happy.*

1. An introductory statement of purpose
   Well traveling wasn't very easy.
2. People traveled by wagons.
   The first way was by wagon.
3. People traveled by ship.
   They could sail there.
4. People traveled by stagecoach.
5. The journey took months.
6. The Pony Express carried mail.
   And the Pony Express came next.
7. The telegraph sent messages by wire.
8. A transcontinental railroad linked the East and West.
   A railroad went from east to west.

   <u>Evaluating Summary Performance</u>
   Total elements included in student's summary = 5
   Total possible elements included in summary = 8
   Acceptable = 6
   Peter's summary was unacceptable. He identified 5 elements.

Guidelines for Scoring Summaries

Evaluation of a written summary carries some uncertainty due to the following factors:

- Students seldom use the words from the text when crafting their summary.
- Summaries of inference passages represent a first effort; that is, they have not been fine-tuned or received input from a teacher or peer.
- Summaries may be somewhat disorganized, and may display questionable sentence structure and include lack of clarity.
- Summaries may include opinion and may represent a combination of accurate, inaccurate, and unrelated information.
- Summaries may contain elements based solely on prior knowledge.

Unacceptable information can take several forms, which we illustrate with examples from summaries of the fourth-grade selection, "Linking East and West."

- Statements related to the topic of the summary but not present in the answer key because they lack importance. Ex: *Pony Express riders were teenagers.*
- Repetitions of previously stated information. Ex: *People traveled by stagecoach. The stagecoach took them west.*
- Information that is not relevant to the intent of the summary. Ex: *The Pony Express was like a relay.*
- Information that is inaccurate. Ex: *The Pony Express started in 1861.*
- Information that is not text-based. Ex: *The Pony Express probably needed a lot of horses.*
- A personal statement on the part of the student. Ex: *The Pony Express was a good idea.*

Accept a student's paraphrase as long as it matches the meaning of the answer key unit. For example, *"big ships took people to the west"* is a match for *"people traveled by ship."* *"Ships were fun to ride in"* is not a match. Personal comments and observations are not text-based. *"Ships move funny and can make you sick, so a lot of travelers felt bad"* is not an acceptable match.

Pearson eText Application Exercise 11.2: Arthur's Inference-Diagnostic Passage Performance (Social Studies)

Pearson eText Application Exercise 11.3: Paula's Inference-Diagnostic Passage Performance (Science)

Summary

The Inference-Diagnostic materials are included to provide an analysis of a student's ability to answer different types of inferential questions. The questions are phrased the same in narrative and expository materials and ask the student to:

- Find evidence to support an answer
- Identify a theme or central idea in a text
- Explain why or how ideas in the text relate
- Determine the meaning of a word in the context of a sentence

- Determine point of view (in literature and social studies)
- Identify text structure (social studies and science)

The Inference-Diagnostic materials are designed to be used at a student's instructional level, so it is necessary to administer the Level-Diagnostic materials first to find the instructional level. We compared students' performance on the Inference-Diagnostic materials to the instructional levels reported by teachers using the Level-Diagnostic *QRI-5* materials. In all cases students scored lower on the Inference-Diagnostic materials than on the *QRI-5* materials. This finding was not surprising because the inference questions recommended by state and national standards were anticipated to be much more difficult than the questions on previous editions of the *QRI*. Our previous research with the *CARA* found that even students who met state proficiency standards answered only about 50% of the inference questions correctly.

Section 12
Inference-Diagnostic Materials

Pearson eText Teacher Resource: In the chapter outline below, each passage title is a clickable link that will open a printable PDF version of the passage and the accompanying examiner copies.

 ## Chapter Outline

Grade 4
Cynthia Rylant: The Development of an Author (Biography)
Linking East and West (Social Studies/Picture)
How Do Organisms Compete for Resources? (Science/Picture)
Examiner Copies

Grade 5
Jane Goodall, Goddess of the Apes (Biography)
The Rise of Cattle Drives (Social Studies/Picture)
The Body's Transportation System (Science/Picture)
Examiner Copies

Grade 6
The Legacy of Jim Thorpe (Biography)
From Dynasty to Dynasty (Social Studies/Picture)
What Causes Weather? (Science/Picture)
Examiner Copies

Middle School
Malcolm X: The Development of a Separatist (Biography)
A Wave of Nativism (Social Studies/Picture)
What Is a Comet? (Science/Picture)
Examiner Copies

High School
The Life of Georgia O'Keeffe: The Artist and the Woman (Biography)
America Adjusts to Peace (Social Studies/Picture)
The Kingdoms of Life (Science/Picture)
Examiner Copies

Biography

Cynthia Rylant: The Development of an Author

"Cynthia Rylant, I know that name." If the name is familiar, you may have read her books. Her well-known series, "Henry and Mudge," is about a family and their dog. Other series are "Poppleton" and "Mr. Putter & Tabby," about a man and his cat. These books describe being lonely and the need to be loved. Rylant writes about deep emotions that her characters feel, and the reader feels them, too. A book reviewer once wrote that her books have "**undeniable punch**."

1. **What do the topics of Ms. Rylant's books tell us about how she felt about animals?**

2. **What does "undeniable punch" mean in the sentence, "A book reviewer once wrote that her books have 'undeniable punch'"?**

Cynthia's childhood was not happy. Her father was in the army and he struggled with the army's rules. He began drinking too much and fought with her mother. Rylant describes her parents' fighting as an "**ongoing cyclone**." When she was four years old, her mother left her dad and they moved to Beaver, West Virginia. Her mother had to earn money to support them, so she went to nursing school. But the school was in another state, so Cynthia lived with her grandparents. She missed her parents terribly, but she felt loved by her grandparents and cousins. Her life was full of hearing adults tell stories and exploring the mountains. The mountains are the setting for many of her books.

3. **What do the words "ongoing cyclone" mean in the sentence, "Rylant describes her parents' fighting as an *ongoing cyclone*"?**

When Cynthia first moved to West Virginia her father wrote to her often. He told her how much he loved her and hoped to see her soon. But after a while his letters stopped coming. When she was twelve, he began to write to her again. He invited her to visit him, but it never happened. He became very ill and died on her thirteenth birthday. His death hurt her deeply. She wrote in her autobiography, "It is hard to lose someone, even harder to lose him twice, and beyond description to lose him without a goodbye either time."

4. **Explain how events in Cynthia's childhood led her to write about being lonely and needing to be loved.**

5. **What is a theme so far, and what details in the text support the theme?**

Cynthia had many boyfriends in high school, but in her senior year her boyfriend broke up with her. At the time her heart was broken, but it turned out well. She was forced to look beyond getting married and living in a mobile home. She went to college and her first English course opened a new world. She read the works of great writers. But being from a tiny town in West Virginia, she thought her writing would never measure up. After college she went to graduate school to earn a master's degree and become a high school teacher. There, she met a young man who shared her love of literature. They married and, unable to find a teaching job, she got a job in a public library. Although she had used libraries in college, she'd never been to a public library! Beaver, West Virginia, had no library, so she read only comic books and later romance novels. In the public library she discovered children's literature and found that many picture books were written for children! Although she loved her job, she left it after five months when her son was born.

6. Describe how Cynthia's goals change from her junior year in high school to her final year of college.

7. From whose point of view is this biography written, and how do you know?

8. How did Cynthia's point of view of writers affect her view of herself as a writer?

Most writers have times of day when they choose to write. Some get up early and write during the day. Others write at night, but Cynthia had no choice. She wrote whenever she could, which was usually between Nate's feedings and naps. One night when Nate was six months old Cynthia began to write stories about her childhood. She began, "When I was young in the mountains..." An hour later she was finished. She wrote a simple cover letter, "Dear Editor, I hope you like this book." Two months later she received a letter from an editor saying that he'd like to publish her book.

9. Provide details from the text that show how dedicated to writing Cynthia was.

It took two years for the book to be published and she was not happy with the illustrations in the book. The book said that her grandfather came home covered with the black dust of a coal mine and only his lips were clean. But in the picture only his hat was black. She complained to the publisher and succeeded in getting the drawing changed. The book was honored as a Notable Book by the American Library Association. This was the beginning of a great writing career. She wrote nine books in the next nine years! Her writing has been described as brave, perceptive, and having an honest voice.

Ms. Rylant continues to write books in the "Henry and Mudge" series that she began over 25 years ago. She also continues to write the "Mr. Putter & Tabby" and "Poppleton" series. In the past ten years she has begun two new series, "Annie and Snowball" and "Brownie & Pearl." This child from West Virginia has become an award-winning writer.

10. What is a theme of this biography, and what details support the theme?

Summarize this text.

Social Studies

Linking East and West

It was not easy to get across the United States in the 1850s. There were thousands of miles of railroad tracks, but they were mostly in the eastern part of the country. To reach the West, people traveled in wagons pulled by oxen or horses. The only other way was by ship. Either way, the journey could take months. People began looking for faster ways to move people and mail across the United States.

1. **The topic of the above paragraph is "linking the East and West." What is the central idea?**

In 1858, travelers were offered a new way to cross the country, the stagecoach. Stagecoaches were horse-drawn wagons that traveled in stages, or short sections. If the weather was good, stagecoaches could bring people and bags of mail from Missouri to California in only 25 days.

In 1860, a new business called the Pony Express began delivering mail from Missouri to California in just 10 days. The Pony Express was like a 2,000-mile relay race. Each express rider rode about 75 miles. Then he handed his bags of mail on to a new rider. The riders were mostly teenagers, some as young as 13.

The Pony Express was soon put out of business by an invention called the telegraph. The telegraph sent messages along wires using electricity. An American inventor named Samuel Morse developed a way to send telegraph messages using a code called Morse Code. The first telegraph line across the country was completed in October 1861. Morse Code messages could now be sent from coast to coast in just a few minutes!

2. **The topic of the above paragraph is "the telegraph." What is the central idea?**

3. **Analyze why the telegraph put the Pony Express out of business.**

The telegraph allowed news to travel quickly, but it did not help people or goods cross the country. Many people believed that the best way to link East and West would be to build a transcontinental railroad, a railroad across the continent. President Abraham Lincoln agreed. In 1862, the United States government gave two companies the **right** to start building the railroad. The Union Pacific began building track west from Omaha, Nebraska. The Central Pacific began building east from Sacramento, California.

4. **What is the meaning of "right" in the context of the above passage?**

5. **What evidence in the text indicates that the Pony Express and Morse Code did not completely link the East and the West?**

Building the Railroad

Both railroad companies faced serious difficulties. One problem was finding enough workers for this huge project. The Union Pacific hired former Civil War soldiers, former slaves, and Irish and German immigrants. The Central Pacific's workforce was also **diverse**. It included thousands of Chinese immigrants. The two railroad companies raced against each other. Each company was paid in land and money for every mile of track it completed. Central Pacific workers built tracks over steep mountain slopes. Chinese workers had the difficult work of blasting tunnels through solid rock. Many Chinese workers were killed in dynamite accidents.

6. **What is the meaning of "diverse" in the context of the above passage?**

On the Great Plains, Union Pacific workers came into conflict with Native Americans. As the railroad moved west, the tracks began to cross their traditional hunting grounds. Many Native American leaders did not want the railroad to cross this land. "We do not want you here," a Lakota chief named Red Cloud told Union Pacific workers. "You are scaring away the buffalo." However, the Union Pacific continued building. U.S. soldiers began guarding the railroad workers. The track moved west.

7. **Which text structure best explains how the author organized the above two paragraphs?**

    _____ *description of important features* _____ *explanation of steps in a sequence*

    _____ *account of cause and effect* _____ *explanation of problem and solution*

    _____ *comparison/contrast of two or more things*

    Give a reason from the text for your answer. For example, if you choose description, tell what is being described. If you choose sequence, list one or two steps. For cause and effect, state a cause or effect mentioned in the text. For problem and solution, tell what the problem is or describe the solution. For comparison, tell what is being compared or contrasted.

8. **Analyze why the Central Pacific had a more difficult time building the railroad than the Union Pacific.**

9. **What was the point of view of the U.S. government regarding the views of the Native Americans?**

The Golden Spike

On May 10, 1869, the tracks of the Union Pacific and Central Pacific finally met at Promontory Point, Utah Territory. A golden spike was hammered into the track. This symbolized the success of the project. The message "Done" was telegraphed around the nation. There were celebrations from New York to San Francisco.

Steven Miller/Fotolia

10. What evidence in the text indicates that the entire nation supported the building of the transcontinental railroad?

Summarize what the text says about different ways to link the East and West.

Taken from: *The United States* (2011). Glenview, IL: Scott Foresman Pearson. ISBN-13: 978-0-328-52028-2, pp. 539–543.

Science

How Do Organisms Compete for Resources?

Organisms compete for resources in an ecosystem. Predators survive by eating prey.

Competition

A watering hole is a good place to see the animals on the African savannah. You might see zebras, giraffes, gazelles, wildebeests, and other animals. How can an ecosystem have enough resources for so many organisms?

Competition is the struggle among organisms to survive in a habitat with limited resources. Like all organisms, the animals on the savannah need food, water, and a place to live. The animals that survive compete successfully for these resources.

Different species live in different places. Those that do live together have different needs. Organisms with different needs can live together with little competition. Zebras and wildebeests can graze together on the savannah because they have different diets. Zebras prefer the tall, coarse grasses. When zebras eat those grasses, they expose the shorter grasses, which wildebeests then eat.

1. **The topic of the above paragraph is "different species." What is the central idea?**

Competition happens when organisms in an ecosystem have similar needs. An ecosystem can't always meet its organisms' needs. Resources, including water, food, and shelter, are limited. Organisms with helpful adaptations will survive. Others will die.

When Resources Are Scarce

Sometimes members of the same species compete. This might happen if **resources** become scarce, for example by drought. If water in the savannah is scarce, zebras that can **survive** with less water might survive. Those that need more water might not.

Competition also occurs between different species. Like wildebeests, gazelles eat short, tender grass. If drought reduces the number of grass plants, wildebeests and gazelles will compete for the limited resource.

2. **Analyze why competition occurs between species.**

3. **What is the meaning of "resources" in the context of the above passage?**

4. **What is the meaning of "survive" in the context of the above passage?**

Predators and Prey

Animals use different methods to get the food they need. Some animals eat plants. But they can be food for other animals. An animal that feeds on other animals is called a predator. The animal that a predator eats is called a prey.

The number of predators that an ecosystem can support depends on the number of prey. And the number of prey depends on how many predators there are. It's a balancing act. As the number of predators increases, more prey are eaten. The number of prey gets smaller. When that happens, the predators do not have enough food, and some will die. As a result, fewer prey are eaten, and more prey survive to become food for more predators. The number of predators increases again.

5. The topic of the above paragraph is "predators and prey." What is the central idea?

6. Which text structure best explains how the author organized the above paragraph?

_____ *description of important features* _____ *explanation of steps in a sequence*
_____ *account of cause and effect* _____ *explanation of problem and solution*
_____ *comparison/contrast of two or more things*

Give a reason from the text for your answer. For example, if you choose description, tell what is being described. If you choose sequence, list one or two steps. For cause and effect, state a cause or effect mentioned in the text. For problem and solution, tell what the problem is or describe the solution. For comparison, tell what is being compared or contrasted.

Adaptations

Both predators and prey have adaptations that help them survive. Many predators are adapted to hunt and kill. They may be fast or have a keen sense of smell, hearing, or sight to help them locate prey. Some predators have behaviors that help them catch prey. Pack animals, such as wolves, work as a group to attack individuals from a herd. Alligators and crocodiles float with only their eyes and nostrils out of water. Strong jaw muscles and sharp teeth help them grab their meal.

Not all predators chase after their prey. A jellyfish has hundreds of stinging cells on its tentacles. Chemicals in these cells can paralyze the prey, which then can be eaten.

dlrz4114/Fotolia

7. What evidence in the text indicates that predators do not always hunt alone?

Prey are adapted to avoid predators. Some prey animals secrete a poison and are brightly colored to warn away predators. Others mimic, or look like, a dangerous animal. Some prey depend on camouflage to make them look like something else, such as a plant, stick, or rock.

8. What evidence in the text indicates that prey can kill predators?

9. Analyze how predators and prey are alike.

10. Analyze how the adaptations of predator and prey are different.

Summarize what the text says about why species compete.

Taken from: *Life Science* (2008). Glenview, Il: Pearson Scott Foresman. ISBN-13: 978-0-328-30450-9, pp. 176–178.

Level 4

Biography

Level 4

```
┌─────────────────────────────────────────────────┐
│ Concept Questions                                 │
│                                                   │
│ What does the word emotions mean? (3: feelings; 2: likes │
│ and dislikes, to cry/be happy; 1: it means to move) │
│                                                   │
│ _____ │
│                                                   │
│ _____ │
│                                    (3-2-1-0)      │
│ _____ │
│                                                   │
│ What does the word undeniable mean? (3: true, cannot be │
│ denied; can't be questioned; 2: to say you didn't do something; │
│ 1: to try to get out of trouble)                  │
│                                                   │
│ _____ │
│                                                   │
│ _____ │
│                                    (3-2-1-0)      │
│ _____ │
│                                                   │
│ What does the phrase measure up mean? (3: to compare │
│ positively to something else; to be equal to; 2: say if you and │
│ your brother are compared; 1: height, to see how tall you are) │
│                                                   │
│ _____ │
│                                                   │
│ _____ │
│                                    (3-2-1-0)      │
│ _____ │
│                                                   │
│ What does it mean for someone to be perceptive? (3: sensi- │
│ tive [see, hear, smell, feel] to things, aware; 2: to understand; │
│ 1: good at something)                             │
│                                                   │
│ _____ │
│                                                   │
│ _____ │
│                                    (3-2-1-0)      │
│ _____ │
│                                                   │
│ Score: _____ /12 = _____ %                        │
│        _____ FAM (≥ 55%) _____ UNFAM              │
└─────────────────────────────────────────────────┘
```

Cynthia Rylant: The Development of an Author

"Cynthia Rylant, I know that name." If the name is familiar, you may have read her books. Her well-known series, "Henry and Mudge," is about a family and their dog. Other series are "Poppleton" and "Mr. Putter & Tabby," about a man and his cat. These books describe being lonely and the need to be loved. Rylant writes about deep emotions that her characters feel, and the reader feels them too. A book reviewer once wrote that her books have "undeniable punch."

1. **What do the topics of Ms. Rylant's books tell us about how she felt about animals?**
   Answer: She loves animals because they are main characters in her series books.
   Inference Type: Support statements about a text

2. **What does "undeniable punch" mean in the sentence, "A book reviewer once wrote that her books have 'undeniable punch'"?**
   Answer: The reader of her stories feels the character's feelings/emotions.
   Inference Type: Understand the meaning of words/phrases

Cynthia's childhood was not happy. Her father was in the army and he struggled with the army's rules. He began drinking too much and fought with her mother. Rylant describes her parents' fighting as an "ongoing cyclone." When she was four years old, her mother left her dad and they moved to Beaver, West Virginia. Her mother had to earn money to support them, so she went to nursing school. But the school was in another state, so Cynthia lived

Level 4

with her grandparents. She missed her parents terribly, but she felt loved by her grandparents and cousins. Her life was full of hearing adults tell stories and exploring the mountains. The mountains are the setting for many of her books.

3. **What do the words "ongoing cyclone" mean in the sentence, "Rylant describes her parents' fighting as an *ongoing cyclone*"?**
Answer: Their fighting was noisy and wild like a cyclone (storm).
Inference Type: Understand the meaning of words/phrases

When Cynthia first moved to West Virginia her father wrote to her often. He told her how much he loved her and hoped to see her soon. But after a while his letters stopped coming. When she was twelve, he began to write to her again. He invited her to visit him, but it never happened. He became very ill and died on her thirteenth birthday. His death hurt her deeply. She wrote in her autobiography, "It is hard to lose someone, even harder to lose him twice, and beyond description to lose him without a goodbye either time."

4. **Explain how events in Cynthia's childhood led her to write about being lonely and needing to be loved.**
Answer: Her parents separated, and her mother couldn't care for her, so she was sent to live with her grandparents; OR She missed her parents a lot OR her father died when she was 13 and she hadn't seen him since she was four. She wrote about experiences of being lonely and wanting to be loved.
Inference Type: Explain why/how

5. **What is a theme so far, and what details support the theme?**
Answer: Cynthia's childhood was difficult OR that the actions of parents affect their children. Details included her parents' separation, that she had to live apart from them; she missed them terribly. The theme must be stated as well as text details that support it.
Inference Type: Determine the theme

Cynthia had many boyfriends in high school, but in her senior year her boyfriend broke up with her. At the time her heart was broken, but it turned out well. She was forced to look beyond getting married and living in a mobile home. She went to college and her first English course opened a new world. She read the works of great writers. But being from a tiny town in West Virginia, she thought her writing would never measure up. After college she went to graduate school to earn a master's degree and become a high school teacher. There, she met a young man who shared her love of literature. They married and, unable to find a teaching job, she got a job in a public library. Although she had used libraries in college, she'd never been to a public library! Beaver, West Virginia, had

Level 4

no library, so she read only comic books and later romance novels. In the public library she discovered children's literature and found that many picture books were written for children! Although she loved her job, she left it after five months when her son was born.

6. **Describe how Cynthia's goals change from her junior year in high school to her final year of college.**
   Answer: In high school she wanted only to get married and live in a mobile home, but in college she decided to become a teacher.
   Inference Type: Explain why/how

7. **From whose point of view is this biography written, and how do you know?**
   Answer: Third person because the writer uses the words "she" and "Ms. Rylant."
   Inference Type: Determine point of view

8. **How did Cynthia's point of view of writers affect her view of herself as a writer?**
   Answer: She was inspired by writers but believed that they lived in a world far different from her own OR she felt that being from a small town meant that she didn't have the experiences of successful writers, so she couldn't be one.
   Inference Type: Determine point of view

Most writers have times of day when they choose to write. Some get up early and write during the day. Others write at night, but Cynthia had no choice. She wrote whenever she could, which was usually between Nate's feedings and naps. One night when Nate was six months old, Cynthia began to write stories about her childhood. She began, "When I was young in the mountains..." An hour later she was <u>finished</u>. She wrote a simple cover letter, "Dear Editor, I hope you like this book." Two months later she received a letter from an editor saying that he'd like to publish her book.

9. **Provide details from the text that show how dedicated to writing Cynthia was.**
   Answer: She wrote in between her child's naps and feedings.
   Inference Type: Support statements about a text

It took two years for the book to be published, and she was not happy with the illustrations in the book. The book said that her grandfather came home covered with the black dust of a coal miner and only his lips were clean. But in the picture only his hat was black. She complained to the publisher and succeeded in getting the drawing changed. The book was honored as a Notable Book by the American Library Association. This was the beginning of a great writing career. She wrote nine books in the next nine years! Her writing has been described as brave, perceptive, and having an honest voice.

Ms. Rylant continues to write books in the "Henry and Mudge" series that she began over 25 years ago. She also continues to write the "Mr. Putter & Tabby" and "Poppleton" series. In

Level 4

the past ten years she has begun two new series, "Annie and Snowball" and "Brownie & Pearl." This child from West Virginia has become an award-winning writer.

10. **What is a theme of this biography, and what details support your theme?**
   Answer: Theme 1: People with difficult childhoods often become writers. Details: Her parents separated, and her mother couldn't take care of her for four years. Theme 2: If you have a passion for something you do it despite all odds. Details: She did so at any time that she could, in between her baby's naps and feedings. The theme must be supported by details from the text.
   <u>Inference Type: Determine the theme</u>

Words = 768. Lexile = 810.

Evaluating Performance by Inference Type

Support statements about a text	_____ Q1	_____ Q9
Understand the meaning of words/phrases	_____ Q2	_____ Q3
Explain why/how	_____ Q4	_____ Q6
Determine point of view	_____ Q7	_____ Q8
Determine the theme	_____ Q5	_____ Q10

Summarize the text. The summary is scored by counting the number of story elements (setting, characterizations, initiating event, episodes, and ending) included. To receive credit the student only needs to include one statement within the story element category. The elements that are bolded were included in most summaries.

1. **Character: one point** _____
   It is a story about a little girl who loved to write

It's about Cynthia Rylant, an author of children's books

Her books are about being lonely and/or wanting to be loved

2. **Initiating Event: one point** _____
   Her parents fought, or they separated (when she was four)
   She lived with her grandparents when her mother went to school

3. **Event: one point** _____
   Her father died when she was young/she missed her father greatly

4. **Event: one point** _____
   She went to college
   She became a teacher
   She wanted to be a writer

5. **Event: one point** _____
   She got married and had a son
   She wrote whenever she could/or whenever her baby slept

6. **Event: one point** _____
   She wrote her first book about her childhood
   She got the book published

7. **Ending: one point** _____
   She has written several different book series
   She has won a writing award

Evaluating Summary Performance

Total elements included in student's summary = _____

Total possible elements included in summary = 7

Acceptable = 5

Level 4

Social Studies

Concept Questions

What is a telegraph? (*3: A way of communicating through wires, a way of sending messages; 2: it's faster than a letter, it tells you something; you could read it; 1: television, like a graph*)

_____

_____

_____ (3-2-1-0)

What does *transcontinental* mean? (*3: Across a continent, coast to coast; 2: it goes a long way, trains do it; 1: we live on a continent*)

_____

_____

_____ (3-2-1-0)

What does it mean to link something? (*3: connect, join, put together; 2: a chain has links, links have to be strong; 1: dad linked my iPad*)

_____

_____

_____ (3-2-1-0)

What is a conflict? (*3: argument; disagreement, fight; 2: it could be between two nations, some are good, and some are bad; 1: it happens sometime, I had one with my brother*)

_____

_____

_____ (3-2-1-0)

Score: _____ /12 = _____ %

_____ FAM (≥ 55%) _____ UNFAM

Linking East and West

It was not easy to get across the United States in the 1850s. There were thousands of miles of railroad tracks, but they were mostly in the eastern part of the country. To reach the West, people <u>traveled</u> in wagons pulled by oxen or horses. The only other way was by ship. Either way, the journey could take months. People began looking for faster ways to move people and mail across the United States.

1. **The topic of the above paragraph is "linking the East and West." What is the central idea?**
   Answer: It was difficult to get across the United States; OR people traveled to the west in wagons or by ship.
   <u>Inference Type: Determine the central idea</u>

   In 1858, travelers were offered a new way to cross the country, the stagecoach. Stagecoaches were horse-drawn wagons that <u>traveled</u> in stages, or short sections. If the weather was good, stagecoaches could bring people and bags of mail from Missouri to California in only 25 days.

   In 1860, a new business called the Pony Express began delivering mail from Missouri to California in just 10 days. The Pony Express was like a 2,000-mile relay race. Each express rider rode about 75 miles. Then he handed his bags of mail on to a new rider. The riders were mostly teenagers, some as young as 13.

   The Pony Express was soon put out of business by an invention called the telegraph.

Level 4

The telegraph sent messages along wires using electricity. An American inventor named Samuel Morse developed a way to send telegraph messages using a code called Morse Code.

The first telegraph line across the country was completed in October 1861. Morse Code messages could now be sent from coast to coast in just a few minutes!

2. **The topic of the above paragraph is "the telegraph." What is the central idea?**
   Answer: The telegraph sent messages across wires; OR the telegraph replaced the Pony Express; OR the telegraph was faster than the Pony Express.
   Inference Type: Determine the central idea

3. **Why did the telegraph put the Pony Express out of business?**
   Answer: It sent messages across wires, not land; OR it did not need horses or riders; OR it was faster.
   Inference Type: Explain why or how

   The telegraph allowed news to travel quickly, but it did not help people or goods cross the country. Many people believed that the best way to link East and West would be to build a transcontinental railroad, a railroad across the continent. President Abraham Lincoln agreed. In 1862, the United States government gave two companies the **right** to start building the railroad. The Union Pacific began building track west from Omaha, Nebraska. The Central Pacific began building east from Sacramento, California.

4. **What is the meaning of "right" in the context of the above passage?**
   Answer: Allowed to do something.
   Inference Type: Determine word meaning

5. **What evidence in the text indicates that the Pony Express and Morse Code did not completely link the East and the West?**
   Answer: They did not help people or goods to cross the country.
   Inference Type: Providing text evidence

Building the Railroad

Both railroad companies faced serious difficulties. One problem was finding enough workers for this huge project. The Union Pacific hired former Civil War soldiers, former slaves, and Irish and German immigrants. The Central Pacific's workforce was also **diverse**. It included thousands of Chinese immigrants. The two railroad companies raced against each other. Each company was paid in land and money for every mile of track it completed. Central Pacific workers built tracks over steep mountain slopes. Chinese workers had the difficult work of blasting tunnels through solid rock. Many Chinese workers were killed in <u>dynamite</u> accidents.

Level 4

6. **What is the meaning of "diverse" in the context of the above passage?**
   Answer: Different; not all alike; not the same.
   <u>Inference Type: Determine word meaning</u>

On the Great Plains, Union Pacific workers came into conflict with Native Americans. As the railroad moved west, the tracks began to cross their traditional hunting grounds. Many Native American leaders did not want the railroad to cross this land. "We do not want you here," a Lakota chief named Red Cloud told Union Pacific workers. "You are scaring away the buffalo." However, the Union Pacific continued building. U.S. soldiers began guarding the railroad workers. The track moved west.

7. **Which text structure best explains how the author organized the above two paragraphs?**
   _____ *description of important features*
   _____ *explanation of steps in a sequence*
   _____ *account of cause and effect*
   _____ *explanation of problem and solution*
   _____ *comparison/contrast of two or more things*

   Give a reason from the text for your answer. For example, if you choose description, tell what is being described. If you choose sequence, list one or two steps. For cause and effect, state a cause or effect mentioned in the text. For problem and solution, tell what the problem is or describe the solution. For comparison, tell what is being compared or contrasted.
   Answer: Compare/contrast: The author compares the Union Pacific and the Central Pacific. OR

Description: The author describes difficulties faced by the Central Pacific and the Union Pacific.
<u>Inference Type: Identify text structure</u>

Note: This question has two separate answers: identification of structure and explanation of reason.

8. **Explain why the Central Pacific had a more difficult time building the railroad than the Union Pacific.**
   Answer: The Central Pacific had to build across mountains; OR the Central Pacific had to use dynamite and/or blast through rock; OR many workers died building the Central Pacific.
   <u>Inference Type: Explain why or how</u>

9. **What was the point of view of the U.S. government regarding the views of the Native Americans?**
   Answer: They did not agree with the Native Americans; OR they wanted building the railroads to continue; OR they were ready to use force because they sent soldiers to protect the workers.
   <u>Inference Type: Determine point of view</u>

The Golden Spike

On May 10, 1869, the tracks of the Union Pacific and Central Pacific finally met at Promontory Point, Utah Territory. A golden spike was hammered into the track. This <u>symbolized</u> the success of the project. The message "Done" was telegraphed around the nation. There were celebrations from New York to San Francisco.

Level 4

Level 4

10. **What evidence in the text indicates that the entire nation supported the building of the transcontinental railroad?**

    Answer: When it was finished, there were celebrations from New York to San Francisco.

    Inference Type: Providing text evidence

Taken from: *The United States* (2011). Glenview, IL: Scott Foresman Pearson. ISBN-13: 978-0-328-52028-2, pp. 539–543. Words = 563. Lexile = 860L.

Evaluating Performance by Inference Type

Determine central idea	____ Q1	____ Q2
Determine word meaning	____ Q4	____ Q6
Explain why/how	____ Q3	____ Q8
Provide text evidence	____ Q5	____ Q10
Identify text structure	____ Q7	
Determine point of view	____ Q9	

Summarize what the text says about different ways to link the East and West.

An acceptable text-based summary contains the following elements:

1. *An introductory statement of purpose.*
2. *People traveled by wagons.*
3. *People traveled by ship.*
4. *People traveled by stagecoach.*
5. *The journey took months.*
6. *The Pony Express carried mail.*
7. *The telegraph sent messages by wire.*
8. *A transcontinental railroad linked the East and West.*

Evaluating Summary Performance

Total elements included in student's summary = ____

Total possible elements included in summary = 8

Acceptable = 6

Level 4

Science

Concept Questions

What does it mean to compete? (*3: go against, oppose, fight someone, take different sides; 2: someone wins, and someone loses, teams in a football game, countries compete; 1: my brother and I do it, people can die*)

_____

_____

_____ (3-2-1-0)

What is a species? (*3: type, kind, class, group, category; 2: it can be a plant or an animal, maple trees and fir trees; 1: you find them everywhere*)

_____

_____ (3-2-1-0)

What is a prey? (*3: a target, an animal hunted by others, what you're trying to kill, what a predator hunts; 2: a lion hunts a gazelle, animals eat them, it's a crocodile's lunch; 1: it's not a good thing*)

_____

_____

_____ (3-2-1-0)

What does it mean to adapt? Answer: (*3: get used to things, change; adjust; 2: don't stand out; be like others; 1: what I did when we moved here*)

_____

_____ (3-2-1-0)

Score: _____ 12= _____ %

_____ FAM (≥55%) _____ UNFAM

How Do Organisms Compete for Resources?

Organisms compete for resources in an ecosystem. Predators survive by eating prey.

Competition

A watering hole is a good place to see the animals on the African savannah. You might see zebras, giraffes, gazelles, wildebeests, and other animals. How can an ecosystem have enough resources for so many organisms?

Competition is the struggle among organisms to survive in a habitat with limited resources. Like all organisms, the animals on the savannah need food, water, and a place to live. The animals that survive compete successfully for these resources.

Different species live in different places. Those that do live together have different needs. Organisms with different needs can live together with little competition. Zebras and wildebeests can graze together on the savannah because they have different diets. Zebras prefer the tall, coarse grasses. When zebras eat those grasses, they expose the shorter grasses, which wildebeests then eat.

Level 4

1. **The topic of the above paragraph is "different species." What is the central idea?**
   Answer: Species that live together have different needs; OR species with different needs can live together.
   <u>Inference Type: Determine the central idea</u>

<u>Competition</u> happens when organisms in an ecosystem have similar needs. An ecosystem can't always meet its organisms' needs. Resources, including water, food, and shelter, are limited. Organisms with helpful adaptations will survive. Others will die.

When Resources Are Scarce

Sometimes members of the same species compete. This might happen if **resources** become scarce, for example by drought. If water in the savannah is scarce, zebras that can **survive** with less water might survive. Those that need more water might not.

<u>Competition</u> also occurs between different species. Like wildebeests, gazelles eat short, tender grass. If drought reduces the number of grass plants, wildebeests and gazelles will compete for the limited resource.

2. **Analyze why competition occurs between species.**
   Answer: Competition occurs if species have the same needs; OR competition occurs if resources are limited.

<u>Inference Type: Explain why or how</u>

3. **What is the meaning of "resources" in the context of the above passage?**
   Answer: Supplies; things that are necessary for life; food and/or water.
   <u>Inference Type: Determine word meaning</u>

4. **What is the meaning of "survive" in the context of the above passage?**
   Answer: Live; not die.
   <u>Inference Type: Determine word meaning</u>

Predators and Prey

Animals use different methods to get the food they need. Some animals eat plants. But they can be food for other animals. An animal that feeds on other animals is called a <u>predator</u>. The animal that a <u>predator</u> eats is called a prey.

The number of predators that an ecosystem can support depends on the number of prey. And the number of prey depends on how many <u>predators</u> there are. It's a balancing act. As the number of <u>predators</u> increases, more prey are eaten. The number of prey gets smaller. When that happens, the <u>predators</u> do not have enough food, and some will die. As a result, fewer prey are eaten, and more prey survive to become food for more <u>predators</u>. The number of predators increases again.

Level 4

5. The topic of the above paragraph is "predators and prey." What is the central idea?
Answer: The number of predators depends on the number of prey and/or the number of prey depends on the number of predators.
Inference Type: Determine the central idea

6. Which text structure best explains how the author organized the above paragraph?
_____*description of important features*
_____*explanation of steps in a sequence*
_____*account of cause and effect*
_____*explanation of problem and solution*
_____*comparison/contrast of two or more things*

Give a reason from the text for your answer. For example, if you choose description, tell what is being described. If you choose sequence, list one or two steps. For cause and effect, state a cause or effect mentioned in the text. For problem and solution, tell what the problem is or describe the solution. For comparison, tell what is being compared or contrasted.
Answer: Cause and Effect: The author describes causes for change in the number of predators and prey. OR Description: The author describes how numbers of predators and prey change.
Inference Type: Identify text structure

Note: This question has two separate answers: identification of structure and explanation of reason.

Adaptations

Both predators and prey have adaptations that help them survive. Many predators are adapted to hunt and kill. They may be fast or have a keen sense of smell, hearing, or sight to help them locate prey. Some predators have behaviors that help them catch prey. Pack animals, such as wolves, work as a group to attack individuals from a herd. Alligators and crocodiles float with only their eyes and nostrils out of water. Strong jaw muscles and sharp teeth help them grab their meal.

Not all predators chase after their prey. A jellyfish has hundreds of stinging cells on its tentacles. Chemicals in these cells can paralyze the prey, which then can be eaten.

7. What evidence in the text indicates that predators do not always hunt alone?
Answer: Pack animals/wolves work as a group.
Inference Type: Provide text evidence

Prey are adapted to avoid predators. Some prey animals secrete a poison and are brightly colored to warn away predators. Others mimic, or look like, a dangerous animal. Some prey depend on camouflage to make them look like something else, such as a plant, stick, or rock.

Taken from: *Life Science* (2008). Glenview, IL: Pearson Scott Foresman. ISBN-13: 978-0-328-30450-9, pp. 176–178. 549 words 790L.

8. What evidence in the text indicates that prey can kill predators?
Answer: Some prey secrete a poison.
Inference Type: Provide text evidence

Level 4

9. **Analyze how predators and prey are alike.**
   Answer: Both have adaptations or ways that help them stay alive.
   <u>Inference Type: Explain why or how</u>

10. **Analyze how the adaptations of predator and prey are different.**
    Answer: Predators are adapted to hunt and kill, and prey are adapted to avoid predators.
    <u>Inference Type: Explain why or how</u>

Evaluating Performance by Inference Type

Determine central idea	_____Q1_____Q5
Determine word meaning	_____Q3_____Q4
Explain why/how	_____Q2_____Q9_____Q10
Provide text evidence	_____Q7_____Q8
Identify text structure	_____Q6

Summarize what the text says about competition between species.

An acceptable text-based summary contains the following elements:

1. *An introductory statement of purpose.*
2. *Competition is the struggle of species to survive.*
3. *Competition occurs when resources are limited.*
4. *Resources include food,*
5. *water,*
6. *and shelter.*
7. *Competition occurs between organisms with similar needs.*
8. *Competition also occurs between different species.*

Evaluating Summary Performance

Total elements included in student's summary = _____

Total possible elements included in summary = 8

Acceptable = 6

Biography

Jane Goodall, Goddess of the Apes

Jane Goodall is the most recognizable living scientist in the Western world. Her work with chimpanzees in Tanzania has been reported in books and movies. Her study of chimps happened despite her being a slight young woman without a formal education. This biography will explain how it happened.

Jane's mother, Vanne, introduced her to nature through walks in their back yard. She drew Jane's attention to the smallest of creatures, from insects to birds. A story from when Jane was eighteen months old suggests the scientist she would become. She discovered a bed of earthworms and hid them in her bedroom with some under her pillow. Her nanny ran to Vanne, reporting that Jane would not give them up. Vanne explained to Jane that the worms would die if she kept them in her room overnight because they needed soil. Amazingly, Jane understood and returned the worms to the garden. Her interest in nature continued to grow. Her first field study occurred when she was five years old. Her grandmother asked her to gather some eggs from the henhouse. Jane wanted to see how the hens laid the eggs. Four hours later a hen stood up and an egg came out. Jane returned to the house tired but pleased. As usual, her mother patiently listened to Jane's story. A few years later a neighbor's dog **turned a light bulb on in her head** when he taught Jane that animals have personalities and feelings of their own. Years later, she reflected that Rusty's lessons made her study of animals more insightful.

1. **Explain how events in Jane's childhood suggest the kind of work she would do as an adult.**

2. **What does the phrase "turned a light bulb on in her head" mean in the sentence toward the end of the last paragraph?**

After high school she did not know what to do. Her family could not afford to send her to college, and her grades were only good in the subjects she liked. So, she did what many young women of the time did; she took secretarial courses. After working as a secretary for a few years she took a job at a company that made documentary films. She was charged with selecting the music for the films. The work was more interesting, and she took advantage of life in London by going to lectures, concerts, and having a social life. She was relatively content until she received a letter from an old school friend inviting her to visit her in Kenya, Africa. She quit her job and went to live with her family to save money. She worked long hours as a waitress and after 15 months had enough money for a ticket to Kenya. The sailing to Africa took two weeks and she loved every minute. On her way to her friend's farm she spied a giraffe by the roadside. At that moment she realized that she was really in Africa. After spending five months with her friend's family, she realized that she wanted to stay in Africa and work with animals. At a party she was told if she wanted to work with animals, she had to talk with Louis Leakey. So typical to Jane, she called the famous scientist and they arranged to meet.

They met at his office in the National Museum in Nairobi. He was impressed with her knowledge of Africa and animals, especially since she had no formal education. When she explained that she wanted to work with animals, he offered her a position as his assistant! He wanted to study the animal most closely related to humans. They agreed that the study of chimps, which share over 95% of their genetic material with humans, would be the key.

3. **What is a theme so far?**

4. **What is the author's point of view of Jane, and how does that affect how the biography is told?**

5. **Using details from the text, explain why it was unusual that Louis Leakey hired Jane to be his assistant.**

There were permissions to get and funds to be raised. Jane was not allowed to go into Gombe alone. So, ever the adventurer, Vanne went along. After two years, they left for Kenya. Her work at Gombe always began early in the morning. Imagine going into a jungle and sitting for hours waiting to see or hear a chimp. It took her three months before the chimps came anywhere close to her. She noticed that chimps traveled in a group of six or fewer with a mother with children and two to three adult males. Soon she realized that the total group included about 50 chimps.

After about five months, Vanne wanted to return to England. Although she didn't participate directly in Jane's research, she worked with the Africans in many ways. For example, she ministered medicines to them and learned their customs. Jane benefited from her mother's kindness to the Africans for many years.

In the next few months, Jane made two important discoveries. First, she learned that chimps ate meat, not just plants. Second, she watched a chimp put a small blade of grass into a termite hill. When he pulled out the grass, it was covered with termites! Jane had discovered that chimps use tools, something that was thought to be uniquely human. Those were only two of the many discoveries made by Jane Goodall. She published a book titled *The Chimpanzees of Gombe,* in 1986, which remains the most comprehensive work on chimpanzee behavior ever published. You can learn more about her by watching Animal Planet and HBO.

6. **Explain how chimps and humans are the same and different.**

7. **How does the narrator continue to reflect a point of view of Jane from the events in the story?**

8. **What does the title of this biography, "Jane Goodall, Goddess of the Apes," mean?**

9. **Explain how Jane and her mother are the same and different, citing details from the text.**

10. **What is the theme of this biography, and how did Jane respond to challenges?**

Summarize the text.

Social Studies

The Rise of Cattle Drives

While farmers were struggling to survive on the Great Plains, the cattle ranching industry was developing farther south. The first cows were brought to North America by the Spanish in the early 1600s. By the end of the Civil War, there were about 5 million cattle in Texas. They were a tough breed known as Texas longhorns.

In the 1860s, longhorns sold for about $4 each in Texas. But they were worth about $40 each in the growing cities of the East, where beef was scarce. Cattle ranchers realized they could make huge profits, but only if they could figure out a way to get their cattle across the country.

The solution was the cattle drive. On cattle drives, cowboys drove, or moved, huge herds of cattle north to the new railroad lines **extending** across the Great Plains. The cattle drives began in Texas and ended in towns along the railroad. From these towns, cattle were shipped by train to eastern cities.

Some of these towns, like Abilene, Kansas, became known as cow towns. In 1871 alone, about 700,000 longhorns trampled through the dirt streets of Abilene.

Jeff Schultes/Fotolia

1. The topic of the above paragraph is cattle drives. What is the central idea?

2. Analyze why cattle ranchers wanted to get their cattle to eastern cities.

3. Which text structure best explains how the author organized the above two paragraphs?

_____*description of important features*_____*explanation of steps in a sequence*
_____*account of cause and effect*_____*explanation of problem and solution*
_____*comparison/contrast of two or more things*

Give a reason from the text for your answer. For example, if you choose description, tell what is being described. If you choose sequence, list one or two steps. For cause and effect, state a cause or effect mentioned in the text. For problem and solution, tell what the problem is or describe the solution. For comparison, tell what is being compared or contrasted.

4. What is the meaning of "extending" in the context of the above passage?

5. What evidence in the text indicates that a cattle drive was only one part of getting the cattle to eastern markets?

Cowboy Life

In 1866, Charles Goodnight and his partner Oliver Loving drove their herd of 2,000 longhorns north from Texas to Colorado. This route soon became known as the Goodnight Loving Trail. "There were many hardships and dangers," wrote Charles Goodnight. But overall, he remembered his days on the trail as the happiest time of his life. "Most of the time we were solitary adventurers in a great land as fresh and new as a spring morning."

Cowboys were a diverse group. About a third of all cowboys were Mexican Americans or African Americans. Many were very young. An African American cowboy named Nat Love began working on cattle drives when he was just 15. Love later became famous for his cowboy skills. He wrote a book about his adventures on the cattle trail. Cowboys like Nat Love lived a **hard**, dangerous, and lonely life on the long cattle drives. They worked 16-hour days on horseback, seven days a week. At night, they took turns watching the herd.

6. The topic of the above two paragraphs is "cowboy life." What is the central idea?

7. What was the point of view of Charles Goodnight regarding the cattle drives?

8. What is the meaning of "hard" in the context of the above passage?

9. What evidence in the text indicates that people were interested in the life of a cowboy?

Cattle drives usually covered about 10 miles a day. The large herds moved along slowly, grazing as they walked. But longhorns were nervous animals, and there was the constant danger of a stampede. In a stampede, entire herds of longhorns took off running wildly. They could trample horses and people, or charge into rivers and drown. To try to keep the animals calm, cowboys would sing to them.

By the late 1880s, the cattle drives came to an end. One cause was the growing conflict between cattle ranchers and farmers on the Great Plains. To keep cattle off their farmland, homesteaders began fencing in their land. They used a new type of fence made of barbed wire, or twisted wire with sharp points. Barbed wire fences, which were cheap and easy to build, began enclosing the vast open plains. Expanding railroad lines also helped end the cattle drives. As new railroad lines reached into Texas, it was no longer necessary for ranchers to drive their cattle north.

Throughout the late 1800s, new railroad lines brought thousands of people to the West. Towns at the western end of railroad lines, such as Los Angeles, California, and Seattle, Washington, soon grew into important cities.

10. Analyze why cattle drives came to an end.

Summarize what the text says about a cowboy's job on cattle drives.

_____

Taken from: *The United States* (2011) Glenview, IL: Scott Foresman Pearson. ISBN-13: 978-0-328-52028-2, pp. 550–552.

Science

The Body's Transportation System

The circulatory system is the body's transportation system. It moves food and oxygen to each cell and then takes away cells' wastes. The system includes the heart, blood, and blood vessels.

Blood

Red Blood Cells   Platelets   White Blood Cells

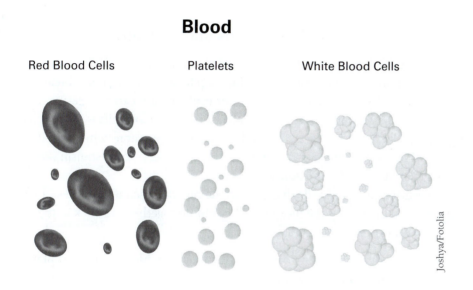

Joshya/Fotolia

Blood

Your blood has several different parts. Each part has a different job. The biggest part of your blood is a straw-colored liquid called plasma. The cells in your body depend on the blood's plasma to carry food to them from the digestive system. Plasma also carries away the cells' wastes. Cells get their water from the plasma as well. Finally, plasma moves some chemicals from one part of the body to another. For example, adrenaline is a chemical made by glands in your lower back. Your blood carries adrenaline from these glands to your heart and muscle cells as a signal to be more active.

1. **Which text structure best explains how the author organized the above two paragraphs?**

   _____*description of important features* _____*explanation of steps in a sequence*
   _____*account of cause and effect*_____*explanation of problem and solution*
   _____*comparison/contrast of two or more things*

   Give a reason from the text for your answer. For example, if you choose description, tell what is being described. If you choose sequence, list one or two steps. For cause and effect, state a cause or effect mentioned in the text. For problem and solution, tell what the problem is or

describe the solution. For comparison, tell what is being compared or contrasted.

2. Analyze why blood plasma is necessary to cells.

Red Blood Cells

Your cells need oxygen to get energy from food. The red blood cells carry oxygen to your body's cells. These cells are bright red when they are carrying oxygen. After they give the oxygen to the cells, their color turns a darker red.

White Blood Cells and Platelets

Different kinds of white blood cells work hard to protect your body against germs and other harmful things. Some white blood cells wrap around and break down germs, pieces of waste matter, dead cells, or cells that are carrying germs. Others make chemicals that kill germs. The number of white blood cells is always changing. When the body needs to fight infection, it makes more white blood cells. Not all white blood cells are actually in the blood vessels. Some squirm their way between your body cells and attack germs there.

Platelets are pieces of cells that float in the blood. When a blood vessel is cut, platelets are there to stop the bleeding. They **clump** together and stick to the edges of the cut. They help form a clot.

3. The topic of the above two paragraphs is "white blood cells and platelets." What is the central idea?

4. What is the meaning of "clump" in the context of the above passage?

5. Analyze how red blood cells and white blood cells have different jobs.

6. What evidence in the text indicates that we would probably die without white blood cells?

Blood Vessels

The blood vessels can be thought of as highways your blood uses to move through your body. The three kinds of blood vessels are arteries, capillaries, and veins. Arteries are blood vessels that carry blood away from your heart to other parts of your body. Arteries have thick, muscular walls that stretch when the heart pushes blood. Arteries **branch** into smaller and smaller tubes. Almost every artery carries blood with lots of oxygen.

The smallest kind of blood vessel is a capillary. Side-by-side, ten of these tiny blood vessels are barely as thick as one hair. Oxygen moves from the blood in your capillaries to your cells. Carbon dioxide and other wastes go in the other direction. They move from your cells to the blood in your capillaries. Capillaries join together to form your tiniest veins.

Veins are blood vessels that take blood from cells back to the heart. These tiny veins join many times to form larger and larger veins. Veins have valves. Valves are flaps that act like doors to keep blood flowing in one direction. Valves open to allow blood to flow to the heart. Valves close if the blood begins to flow away from the heart.

7. The topic of the above three paragraphs is "blood vessels." What is the central idea?

8. Analyze how arteries, capillaries, and veins are alike.

9. What is the meaning of "branch" in the context of the above passage?

10. What evidence in the text indicates that arteries and veins can be compared to a two-lane highway?

Summarize what the text says about what blood vessels do.

Adapted from: *Science: The Diamond Edition*. (2008). Glenview, IL: Scott Foresman Pearson, pp. 63–66.

Level 5

Biography

Jane Goodall, Goddess of the Apes

Jane Goodall is the most recognizable living scientist in the Western world. Her work with chimpanzees in Tanzania has been reported in books and movies. Her study of chimps happened despite her being a slight young woman without a formal education. This biography will explain how it happened.

Jane's mother, Vanne, introduced her to nature through walks in their back yard. She drew Jane's attention to the smallest of creatures, from insects to birds. A story from when Jane was eighteen months old suggests the scientist she would become. She discovered a bed of earthworms and hid them in her bedroom with some under her pillow. Her nanny ran to Vanne, reporting that Jane would not give them up. Vanne explained to Jane that the worms would die if she kept them in her room overnight because they needed soil. Amazingly, Jane understood and returned the worms to the garden. Her interest in nature continued to grow. Her first field study occurred when she was five years old. Her grandmother asked her to gather some eggs from the henhouse. Jane wanted to see how the hens laid the eggs. Four hours later a hen stood up and an egg came out. Jane returned to the house tired but pleased. As usual, her mother patiently listened to Jane's story. A few years later a neighbor's dog turned a light bulb on in her head when he taught Jane that animals have personalities and feelings of their

Level 5

own. Years later, she reflected that Rusty's lessons made her study of animals more insightful.

1. **Explain how events in Jane's childhood suggest the kind of work she would do as an adult.**
   Answer: She was interested in living things and learned that animals have feelings from her neighbor's dog. These events suggest that she would do something related to animals.
   Inference type: Support statements about a text

2. **What does the phrase "turned a light bulb on in her head" mean in the sentence toward the end of the last paragraph?**
   Answer: She had an insight/idea about animals, particularly Rusty; the metaphor is used to mean that she understood something for the first time.
   Inference Type: Understand the meaning of words/phrases

After high school she did not know what to do. Her family could not afford to send her to college, and her grades were only good in the subjects she liked. So, she did what many young women of the time did; she took secretarial courses. After working as a secretary for a few years she took a job at a company that made documentary films. She was charged with selecting the music for the films. The work was more interesting, and she took advantage of life in London by going to lectures, concerts, and having a social life. She was relatively content until she received a letter from an old school friend inviting her to visit her in Kenya, Africa. She quit her job and went to live with her family to save money. She worked long hours as a waitress and after 15 months had enough money for a ticket to Kenya. The sailing to Africa took two weeks and she loved every minute. On her way to her friend's farm she spied a giraffe by the roadside. At that moment she realized that she was really in Africa. After spending five months with her friend's family, she realized that she wanted to stay in Africa and work with animals. At a party she was told if she wanted to work with animals, she had to talk with Louis Leakey. So typical to Jane, she called the famous scientist and they arranged to meet.

They met at his office in the National Museum in Nairobi. He was impressed with her knowledge of Africa and animals, especially since she had no formal education. When she explained that she wanted to work with animals, he offered her a position as his assistant! He wanted to study the animal most closely related to humans. They agreed that the study of chimps, which share over 95% of their genetic material with humans, would be the key.

3. **What is a theme so far?**
   Answer: Jane loved animals; OR Jane worked hard to get what she wanted.
   Inference type: Determine the theme

4. **What is the author's point of view of Jane, and how does that affect how the biography is told?**
   Answer: The author believes Jane loves animals and hates them to be harmed. This view is why the

Level 5

Level 5

Social Studies

Level 5

Concept Questions

What is a cattle drive? (*3: a way to move a lot of cattle, moving cattle in a large group, herding cattle; 2: cowboys made them move, it was hard to do, it was the cowboy's job; 1: you see it in movies, driving cattle somewhere*)

_____

_____

_____ (3-2-1-0)

What is profit? (*3: making money, getting more money than you used; 2: people in business like it, it's important for a business; 1: A good thing, people talk about it all the time*)

_____

_____

_____ (3-2-1-0)

What is a stampede? (*3: a lot of animals or people moving fast, crowds rushing somewhere, a crowd that is out of control; 2: it can be dangerous, people can be hurt; 1: stamping hard*)

_____

_____

_____ (3-2-1-0)

What does it mean to enclose something? Answer: (*3: surround something, put a fence around something, not let everyone inside; 2: you can use wire or wood, people do it to their yards; 1: like closet*)

_____

_____

_____ (3-2-1-0)

Score: _____ /12 = _____%

_____ FAM (≥ 55%) _____ UNFAM

The Rise of Cattle Drives

While farmers were struggling to survive on the Great Plains, the cattle ranching industry was developing farther south. The first cows were brought to North America by the Spanish in the early 1600s. By the end of the Civil War, there were about 5 million cattle in Texas. They were a tough breed known as Texas longhorns.

In the 1860s, longhorns sold for about $4 each in Texas. But they were worth about $40 each in the growing cities of the East, where beef was scarce. Cattle ranchers realized they could make huge profits, but only if they could figure out a way to get their cattle across the country.

The solution was the cattle drive. On cattle drives, cowboys drove, or moved, huge herds of cattle north to the new railroad lines **extending** across the Great Plains. The cattle drives began in Texas and ended in towns along the railroad. From these towns, cattle were shipped by train to eastern cities.

Some of these towns, like Abilene, Kansas, became known as cow towns. In 1871 alone, about 700,000 longhorns trampled through the dirt streets of Abilene.

Level 5

1. The topic of the above paragraph is cattle drives. What is the central idea?
   Answer: Cattle drives moved herds of cattle to towns along the railroads.
   Inference Type: Determine the central idea

2. Analyze why cattle ranchers wanted to get their cattle to eastern cities.
   Answer: Cattle were worth more money in the east; OR they would make a huge profit.
   Inference Type: Explain why or how

3. Which text structure best explains how the author organized the above two paragraphs?
   _____*description of important features*
   _____*explanation of steps in a sequence*
   _____*account of cause and effect*
   _____*explanation of problem and solution*
   _____*comparison/contrast of two or more things*

   Give a reason from the text for your answer. For example, if you choose description, tell what is being described. If you choose sequence, list one or two steps. For cause and effect, state a cause or effect mentioned in the text. For problem and solution, tell what the problem is or describe the solution. For comparison, tell what is being compared or contrasted.
   Answer: Problem and Solution: The author describes how the problem of getting cattle across the country was solved.
   Inference Type: Identify text structure

   Note: This question has two separate answers: identification of structure and explanation of reason.

4. What is the meaning of "extending" in the context of the above passage?
   Answer: spreading; growing larger; expanding; getting longer
   Inference Type: Determine word meaning

5. What evidence in the text indicates that a cattle drive was only one part of getting the cattle to eastern markets?
   Answer: After the cattle drive, the cattle were shipped by train to eastern cities.
   Inference Type: Provide text evidence

Cowboy Life

In 1866, Charles Goodnight and his partner Oliver Loving drove their herd of 2,000 longhorns north from Texas to Colorado. This route soon became known as the Goodnight Loving Trail. "There were many hardships and dangers," wrote Charles Goodnight. But overall, he remembered his days on the trail as the happiest time of his life. "Most of the time we were solitary adventurers in a great land as fresh and new as a spring morning."

Cowboys were a diverse group. About a third of all cowboys were Mexican Americans or African Americans. Many were very young. An African American cowboy named Nat Love began working on cattle drives when he was just 15. Love later became famous for his cowboy skills. He wrote a book about his adventures on the cattle trail. Cowboys like Nat Love lived a hard, dangerous, and lonely life on the long cattle drives. They worked 16-hour days on horseback, seven days a week. At night, they took turns watching the herd.

Level 5

Level 5

6. **The topic of the above two paragraphs is "cowboy life." What is the central idea?**
   Answer: Cowboys lived a hard life; OR some cowboys became famous.
   Inference Type: Determine the central idea

7. **What was the point of view of Charles Goodnight regarding the cattle drives?**
   Answer: He knew it was hard and dangerous, but he was happy doing it; OR he thought it was an adventure; OR he enjoyed being in a fresh and new land.
   Inference Type: Determine point of view

8. **What is the meaning of "hard" in the context of the above passage?**
   Answer: Was difficult to do; took a lot of effort; was not easy; harsh.
   Inference Type: Determine word meaning

9. **What evidence in the text indicates that people were interested in the life of a cowboy?**
   Answer: Nat Love wrote a book about his life on a cattle drive OR Nat became famous for his cowboy skills.
   Inference Type: Provide text evidence

Cattle drives usually covered about 10 miles a day. The large herds moved along slowly, grazing as they walked. But longhorns were nervous animals, and there was the constant danger of a stampede. In a stampede, entire herds of longhorns took off running wildly. They could trample horses and people, or charge into rivers and drown. To try to keep the animals calm, cowboys would sing to them.

By the late 1880s, the cattle drives came to an end. One cause was the growing conflict between cattle ranchers and farmers on the Great Plains. To keep cattle off their farmland, homesteaders began fencing in their land. They used a new type of fence made of barbed wire, or twisted wire with sharp points. Barbed wire fences, which were cheap and easy to build, began enclosing the vast open plains. Expanding railroad lines also helped end the cattle drives. As new railroad lines reached into Texas, it was no longer necessary for ranchers to drive their cattle north.

Throughout the late 1800s, new railroad lines brought thousands of people to the West. Towns at the western end of railroad lines, such as Los Angeles, California, and Seattle, Washington, soon grew into important cities.

Taken from: *The United States* (2011). Glenview, IL: Scott Foresman Pearson. ISBN-13: 978-0-328-52028-2, pp. 550–552. Words = 567. Lexile = 970L

10. **Analyze why cattle drives came to an end.**
    Answer: Railroads came into Texas; OR farmers fenced in the land.
    Inference Type: Explain why or how

Level 5

Evaluating Performance by Inference Type

Determine central idea	_____ Q1	_____ Q6
Determine word meaning	_____ Q4	_____ Q8
Explain why/how	_____ Q2	_____ Q10
Provide text evidence	_____ Q5	_____ Q9
Identify text structure	_____ Q3	
Determine point of view	_____ Q7	

Summarize what the text says about a cowboy's job on cattle drives.

An acceptable text-based summary contains the following elements:

1. *An introductory statement of purpose.*
2. *Cowboys moved huge herds of cattle to railroad lines.*
3. *They faced hardships and dangers.*
4. *It was a lonely job.*
5. *They worked a 16-hour day.*
6. *They worked seven days a week.*
7. *They watched the herd at night.*
8. *They sang to the herd to keep them calm.*

Evaluating Summary Performance

Total elements included in student's summary = _____

Total possible elements included in summary = 8

Acceptable = 6

Level 5

Level 5

Science

Concept Questions

What does transportation mean? (*3: a way of moving somebody or something, a way of getting some place; 2: a car, my bicycle, it can cover a lot of ground; 1: across something, some animals can do it*)

_____

_____

_____ (3-2-1-0)

What is a system? Answer: (*3) An organized way of doing something, a method with steps in order, (2) it is complicated, it doesn't always work; (1) I have a system for cleaning my room*

_____

_____

_____ (3-2-1-0)

What are body cells? (*3: a basic unit of living things, something in the body that makes it work; 2: you can see them under a microscope; they are very small; 1: something good*)

_____

_____

_____ (3-2-1-0)

What is an artery? (*3: a vein, a type of blood vessel, a main route; 2: like a tube, it has branches, it's bad to cut it; 1: it's important for us, sometimes I hear it on the news*)

_____

_____

_____ (3-2-1-0)

Score: _____/12 = _____%

_____FAM (≥ 55%) _____UNFAM

The Body's Transportation System

The circulatory system is the body's transportation system. It moves food and oxygen to each cell and then takes away cells' wastes. The system includes the heart, blood, and blood vessels.

Blood

Your blood has several different parts. Each part has a different job. The biggest part of your blood is a straw-colored liquid called plasma. The cells in your body depend on the blood's plasma to carry food to them from the digestive system. Plasma also carries away the cells' wastes. Cells get their water from the plasma as well. Finally, plasma moves some chemicals from one part of the body to another. For example, adrenaline is a chemical made by glands in your lower back. Your blood carries adrenaline from these glands to your heart and muscle cells as a signal to be more active.

1. **Which text structure best explains how the author organized the above paragraph?**
   _____*description of important features*
   _____*explanation of steps in a sequence*
   _____*account of cause and effect*
   _____*explanation of problem and solution*
   _____*comparison/contrast of two or more things*

   Give a reason from the text for your answer. For example, if you choose description, tell what is being described. If you choose sequence, list one or two steps. For cause and effect, state a

Level 5

cause or effect mentioned in the text. For problem and solution, tell what the problem is or describe the solution. For comparison, tell what is being compared or contrasted.
Answer: Description: The author describes what plasma does.
Inference Type: Identify text structure

Note: This question has two separate answers: identification of structure and explanation of reason.

2. **Analyze why blood plasma is necessary to cells.**
   Answer: Plasma brings food to the cells AND/OR Plasma carries away wastes.
   Inference Type: Explain why or how

Red Blood Cells

Your cells need oxygen to get energy from food. The red blood cells carry oxygen to your body's cells. These cells are bright red when they are carrying oxygen. After they give the oxygen to the cells, their color turns a darker red.

White Blood Cells and Platelets

Different kinds of white blood cells work hard to protect your body against germs and other harmful things. Some white blood cells wrap around and break down germs, pieces of waste matter, dead cells, or cells that are carrying germs. Others make chemicals that kill germs. The number of white blood cells is always changing.

When the body needs to fight infection, it makes more white blood cells. Not all white blood cells are actually in the blood vessels. Some squirm their way between your body cells and attack germs there.

Platelets are pieces of cells that float in the blood. When a blood vessel is cut, platelets are there to stop the bleeding. They **clump** together and stick to the edges of the cut. They help form a clot.

3. **The topic of the above two paragraphs is "white blood cells and platelets." What is the central idea?**
   Answer: They work to protect your body; OR the author describes what they do.
   Inference Type: Determine the central idea

4. **What is the meaning of "clump" in the context of the above passage?**
   Answer: Pull together; combine; move close; form a mass.
   Inference Type: Determine word meaning

5. **Analyze how red blood cells and white blood cells have different jobs.**
   Answer: Red blood cells carry oxygen to cells; white blood cells protect against germs.
   Inference Type: Explain why or how

6. **What evidence in the text indicates that we would probably die without white blood cells?**
   Answer: Different kinds of white blood cells work hard to protect your body against germs and other harmful things.
   Inference Type: Provide text evidence

Level 5

Blood Vessels

The blood vessels can be thought of as highways your blood uses to move through your body. The three kinds of blood vessels are arteries, capillaries, and veins. Arteries are blood vessels that carry blood away from your heart to other parts of your body. Arteries have thick, muscular walls that stretch when the heart pushes blood. Arteries **branch** into smaller and smaller tubes. Almost every artery carries blood with lots of oxygen.

The smallest kind of blood vessel is a capillary. Side-by-side, ten of these tiny blood vessels are barely as thick as one hair. Oxygen moves from the blood in your capillaries to your cells. Carbon dioxide and other wastes go in the other direction. They move from your cells to the blood in your capillaries. Capillaries join together to form your tiniest veins.

Veins are blood vessels that take blood from cells back to the heart. These tiny veins join many times to form larger and larger veins. Veins have valves. Valves are flaps that act like doors to keep blood flowing in one direction. Valves open to allow blood to flow to the heart. Valves close if the blood begins to flow away from the heart.

Adapted from: *Science: The Diamond Edition.* (2008). Glenview, IL: Scott Foresman Pearson, pp. 63–66. Words = 524. Lexile = 850.

7. **The topic of the above three paragraphs is "blood vessels." What is the central idea?**
   Answer: There are three kinds of blood vessels, and they do different things.
   Inference Type: Determine the central idea

8. **Analyze how arteries, capillaries, and veins are alike.**
   Answer: They are all blood vessels; OR they all act like highways for moving blood; OR they all join together to form smaller or larger structures.
   Inference Type: Explain why or how

9. **What is the meaning of "branch" in the context of the above passage?**
   Answer: Split; divide; separate.
   Inference Type: Determine word meaning

10. **What evidence in the text indicates that arteries and veins can be compared to a two-lane highway?**
    Answer: Arteries carry blood away from the heart, and veins take blood back to the heart.
    Inference Type: Provide text evidence

Evaluating Performance by Inference Type

Determine central idea	____ Q3	____ Q7
Determine word meaning	____ Q4	____ Q9
Explain why/how	____ Q2	____ Q5 ____ Q8
Provide text evidence	____ Q6	____ Q10
Identify text structure	____ Q1	

Summarize what the text says about what blood vessels do.
An acceptable text-based summary contains the following elements:

1. *An introductory statement of purpose.*
2. *Blood vessels move blood through your body.*
3. *There are three kinds of blood vessels: arteries, capillaries and veins.*
4. *Arteries carry blood away from your heart.*

Level 5

Level 5

5. *Arteries carry blood with lots of oxygen.*
6. *Capillaries are the smallest vessels.*
7. *Oxygen moves from blood in capillaries to cells.*
8. *Carbon dioxide and wastes go from cells to capillaries.*
9. *Veins takes blood from cells back to the heart.*

Note: Students receive one point for each statement in their summary that matches the above statements in meaning.

Evaluating Summary Performance

Total elements included in student's summary = ____

Total possible elements included in summary = 8

Acceptable = 6

Level 5

Biography

The Legacy of Jim Thorpe

In 1950, at the age of 63 years, Jim Thorpe was named the Best Male Athlete of the Half Century by the nations' sportswriters. There was no one else who came even close. Jim was an unusually gifted athlete. His legacy was his ability to excel in many sports, including, baseball, football, and track.

Jim and his twin brother, Charlie, were born in 1887 in Oklahoma. Both of his parents, Hiram and Charlotte, were of Native American heritage. Hiram was half-Irish from his dad, thus the name Thorpe. Both parents could read and write, which was uncommon among Native Americans in the late 1800s, and wanted their boys to go to school.

1. **What details in the text suggest that the Thorpe family was unusual?**

Running, jumping, playing games, and learning to hunt were the center of the boys' life on the reservation. But, at age 6 years the boys entered school and had to live there. There was no transportation from the reservation to school. School life was vastly different from their life at home. The boys had to cut their hair and speak English. Jim hated the bells that told them what to do next. Life on the reservation was **free roaming**, and their days weren't structured around clocks. Jim ran away from the Sac and Fox Indian Agency School several times. The result was always the same; his father would punish him and take him back to school.

2. **Explain how Jim and Charlie's life before they went to school was different than their life in school.**

3. **What does the phrase "free roaming" mean in the sentence, "Life on the reservation was _free roaming_, and their day wasn't structured around clocks"?**

Finally, Hiram sent Jim to a school 300 miles away. Jim didn't tolerate the restricted life and ran away again. His father realized that he could not make his son stay at a school so Jim stayed at home and helped on the farm. His mother died two months later. Jim was devastated and withdrew from his work on the farm. Knowing that he would get a beating for not working, he ran away again, this time to Texas. He worked hard and at the age of 13 years earned a team of horses. He brought them back to his father, hoping to live there. Hiram agreed, but only if he attend the local public school. Jim agreed and spent two years at the school. However, his father remarried, and Jim felt uncomfortable at home. It was time for him to do something else. Hiram wrote a letter to the local Sac and Fox Agency expressing his desire for Jim to go to school. "I want him to go and make something of himself."

4. **What is a theme or central idea so far, and what details support that theme?**

Jim was accepted at Carlisle Indian Industrial School and enrolled at age 16. One day he observed that the track team's high-jumpers could not clear the 5'9" bar. Although he had never tried the high-jump before, he wanted to try. He cleared it easily, much to the astonishment of the team. Upon hearing of Jim's **feat**, Pop Warner, the track coach, declared Jim a part of the team. Although Jim enjoyed his success at track, he wanted most to be on the varsity football team. Pop Warner wasn't in favor of this because he didn't want to lose his track star, and Jim was still small (5'5") for the average college football player.

5. **What does the word "feat" mean in the sentence, "Upon hearing of Jim's feat, Pop Warner, the track coach, declared Jim a part of the team"?**

Jim begged the coach relentlessly, so finally Coach Warner gave Jim the football and asked him to run downfield. He expected the defensive players would tackle him and put an end to Jim's desire to play football. But, no one could tackle him. Coach Warner said, "Jim's performance at practice that afternoon was an exhibition of athletic talent that I had never before witnessed nor was I ever to again see anything similar which might compare to it."

Although Jim was named to the varsity football squad immediately, his first season was spent on the bench. Coach Warner believed that despite Jim's innate talent, he still had to learn the game of football. However, in the second season, Jim was the star from the beginning. Their record was 10-2-1. In addition to playing the games, they had to travel to each one. Unlike today, where schools have a mixed schedule of home games and away games, the schools that played Carlisle would only do so on their home field. They didn't want to play on "Indian turf."

6. **Describe how Coach Warner treated Jim when he was successful in the high-jump compared to when he was a first-year football player.**

7. **Explain the author's view of Jim Thorpe and how the descriptions in the text show how this point of view is developed.**

During the summers of 1910 and 1911, he went to North Carolina to play baseball. Pop Warner discouraged Jim from going, but Jim loved baseball and would be paid to play! When summer ended, he couldn't return to the schedule of school life. But, when Carlisle was not doing well in football in the fall, Pop Warner enticed Jim back for the football season by promising to help him train to make the Olympic team in 1912. Jim couldn't resist the idea of competing against the world's best athletes.

Jim competed in two events, the decathlon (ten events) and the pentathlon (five events). Both events included the javelin throw, which he'd only been throwing for three weeks. The gold medal was decided by points: one point for a win, two points for second, three points for third, etc., so the lower the score the better. The pentathlon was first, and Jim won two races, the long jump, and the discus throw. He placed third in the javelin throw. He'd won the gold medal! He had 10 days to rest before the decathlon, a three-day event. He won the high-jump, 100-meter hurdles, and the 1500-meter race. He came in second in the long jump, shotput, discus, and 400-meter run. He finished third in the pole vault and fourth in the javelin. Jim won by a large margin. When the king of Sweden awarded the gold medals to him, he said, "Sir, you are the greatest athlete in the world." His medals were only part of the reason that he was named the Male Athlete of the Half Century in 1950.

8. **Citing evidence in the text, why was Jim well suited to the pentathlon and the decathlon?**

9. **Explain how the paragraph on the Olympics continues to develop the author's point of view Jim Thorpe.**

10. **What is a theme of this biography, and which details provide evidence for your theme?**

Summarize the text.

_____

Social Studies

From Dynasty to Dynasty

The history of ancient Egypt is the history of each of its dynasties, a series of rulers from the same family or ethnic group. Historians group Egypt's dynasties into three major time periods, called kingdoms. The earliest major time period is called the Old Kingdom. Next comes the Middle Kingdom. The latest time period is called the New Kingdom. The gaps between the kingdoms were times of troubles such as wars, invasions, or weak rulers. These in-between periods were rare, for rule in most of ancient Egyptian history was **stable**.

Egypt Is Unified. According to legend, Egypt's first dynasty began when a king named Menes united Upper and Lower Egypt and built a city named Memphis near the present-day Cairo. From there, he ruled over the Two Lands. The unification of Egypt was the beginning of one of the most **stable** civilizations in history.

1. **What is the meaning of "stable" in the context of the above passage?**

All-Powerful Pharaohs. The pharaohs had absolute power, or complete control over their people. For help in making decisions, they could turn to their advisors or appeal to Ma'at, the goddess of truth but, in the end, whatever the pharaoh decided became law. For example, he decided when the fields would be planted, and at harvest time, he demanded crops from the workers in the fields.

Ancient Egyptians believed that their pharaohs were the earthly form of Horus, the falcon god. The pharaohs were god-kings. It was the pharaoh, Egyptians believed, who provided his people with the Nile's yearly floods and the harvests that followed.

2. **The topic of the above two paragraphs is "all-powerful pharaohs." What is the central idea?**

3. **What evidence in the text indicates that ancient Egyptians were probably afraid to go against or oppose the pharaoh?**

The Three Kingdoms

The Old Kingdom. The Old Kingdom was noted for its well-run system of government. The Old Kingdom pharaohs kept the peace and traded with Nubia, with only occasional conflicts. They sent merchants to the eastern coast of the Mediterranean to find timber that was used to make houses, boats, and furniture. Toward the end of the Old Kingdom, governors in the provinces began to **challenge** the power of the pharaohs' government. As a result, Egypt's unity crumbled, and the dynasties grew weak.

4. **What is the meaning of "challenge" in the context of the above passage?**

The Middle Kingdom. The early rulers of the Middle Kingdom restored order and reunited the country. Pharaohs spent the nation's wealth on public works instead of on wars. For example, they constructed buildings and irrigation projects. Egypt grew even richer. However, weaker and less able rulers followed and in time, they lost control of the country to foreign invaders.

The New Kingdom. Egyptian princes became strong enough to drive out the foreign invaders. This event marks the start of the New Kingdom. The first pharaohs of the New Kingdom wanted to build an empire and they created huge armies of foot soldiers, mounted warriors, and charioteers. Bronze swords and body armor made the Egyptians nearly unbeatable.

5. Which text structure best explains how the author organized the above passage titled "The Three Kingdoms"?

_____*description of important features* _____*explanation of steps in a sequence*
_____*account of cause and effect* _____*explanation of problem and solution*
_____*comparison/contrast of two or more things*

Give a reason from the text for your answer. For example, if you choose description, tell what is being described. If you choose sequence, list two steps. For cause and effect, state a cause or effect mentioned in the text. For problem and solution, tell what the problem is or describe the solution. For comparison, tell what is being compared or contrasted.

6. What evidence in the text indicates that New Kingdom pharaohs were interested in protecting their soldiers?

Rule During the New Kingdom

In 1504 B.C., a child named Thutmose III began his reign but, because of his youth, his stepmother was appointed regent. A regent is someone who rules for a child until the child is old enough to rule. His stepmother was Hatshepsut, who was not content to be regent. Hatshepsut had herself proclaimed pharaoh. She was Egypt's supreme ruler for about 15 years.

The Pharaoh Queen. Hatshepsut's reign was good for Egypt. She was a bold leader who is most known for creating a time of great peace and economic success. She encouraged trade with faraway places, sending a famous expedition to the land of Punt on the east coast of Africa. Egyptian traders returned with shiploads of ivory, leopard skins, and special trees used to make incense, a substance burned for its fragrance. When Thutmose grew up, Hatshepsut refused to yield the throne to him. After her death, Thutmose became pharaoh and destroyed all her statues. We don't know if Thutmose played a part in Hatshepsut's death.

Thutmose III Rules. Thutmose III became one of the greatest pharaohs of the New Kingdom. He led his army in wars against Syria and Phoenicia, in Southwest Asia. His troops advanced as far east as the Euphrates River and south into Nubia. Yet Thutmose was more than a conqueror. He was an educated man who loved to study plants and unlike most rulers of his time, he treated those he defeated with mercy.

Perseomedusa/Fotolia

7. The topic of the above three paragraphs is "rule during the New Kingdom." What is the central idea?

8. How did Hatshepsut's and Thutmose's points of view differ?

9. Analyze how Hatshepsut and Thutmose were alike.

10. Analyze why historians think Thutmose might have played a part in Hatshepsut's death.

Ancient Egypt <u>After</u> the New Kingdom. Toward the end of the New Kingdom, Egypt declined. Civil war left Egypt weak and poorly defended. In 332 B.C., long after the end of the New Kingdom, Egypt fell to the famous conqueror Alexander the Great of Macedonia.

Summarize what the text says about the accomplishments of the Three Kingdoms of Egypt.

Taken from *History of Our World*. Boston, MA: Pearson Prentice Hall. ISBN 0-13-203772-6, pp. 75–79.

Predicting Weather

Weather forecasting begins with looking at weather conditions all over the world. Meteorologists gather information about the factors that make up the weather: precipitation, temperature, wind speed, humidity, and air pressure. Then they use computers to analyze the information and make predictions.

Gathering Data

What tools do meteorologists use to gather weather information? Thermometers measure temperatures. Barometers measure air pressure, and anemometers measure wind speed. Simple rain gauges measure any precipitation that falls.

Knowing what is happening on Earth's surface isn't enough to make good weather forecasts. Meteorologists also gather information from above Earth. Scientists release weather balloons. The balloons gather information about Earth's weather from the troposphere. Another important tool, Doppler radar, uses radio waves to measure wind speed and precipitation. It also gives scientists information about the direction in which a storm is moving.

10. **Which text structure best explains how the author organized the above passage titled "Predicting Weather"?**

_____*description of important features* _____*explanation of steps in a sequence*

_____*account of cause and effect* _____*explanation of problem and solution*

_____*comparison/contrast of two or more things*

Give a reason from the text for your answer. For example, if you choose description, tell what is being described. If you choose sequence, list two steps. For cause and effect, state a cause or effect mentioned in the text. For problem and solution, tell what the problem is or describe the solution. For comparison, tell what is being compared or contrasted.

Summarize what the text says about how hurricanes form.

Science The Diamond Edition. Glenview, IL: Pearson Education. ISBN 13: 978-0-328-45595.9. pp. 336–339. Words = 684. Lexile = 880.

Level 6

Biography

Concept Questions

What does the word *legacy* mean? (*Answer: 3: tradition, gifted by someone who came before; 2: a gift your grandparents left to you; 1: to be known for something*)

_____

_____

_____ (3-2-1-0)

What does the word *restricted* mean? (*Answer: 3: to prevent from doing something, to be denied from something; 2: to be kept somewhere and not allowed out, to keep locked up, rules by your parents; 1: something really tight around something*)

_____

_____

_____ (3-2-1-0)

What does *free-roaming* mean? (*Answer: 3: the freedom to move around whenever or wherever one wishes; 2: to wander; 1: to take a trip*)

_____

_____

_____ (3-2-1-0)

What does the word *feat* mean? (not *feet*) (*Answer: accomplishment, something amazing; 2: running the fastest in a race, holding one's breath for a long time; 1: something you want*)

_____

_____

_____ (3-2-1-0)

Score: _____/12 = _____%

_____FAM (≥ 55%) _____ UNFAM

The Legacy of Jim Thorpe

In 1950, at the age of 63 years, Jim Thorpe was named the Best Male Athlete of the Half Century by the nations' sportswriters. There was no one else who came even close. Jim was an unusually gifted athlete. His legacy was his ability to excel in many sports, including, baseball, football, and track.

Jim and his twin brother, Charlie, were born in 1887 in Oklahoma. Both of his parents, Hiram and Charlotte, were of Native American heritage. Hiram was half-Irish from his dad, thus the name Thorpe. Both parents could read and write, which was uncommon among Native Americans in the late 1800s, and wanted their boys to go to school.

1. **What details in the text suggest that the Thorpe family was unusual?**
   Answer: The parents could read and write, which was unusual for Native Americans back then.
   <u>Inference type: Support statements about a text</u>

Running, jumping, playing games, and learning to hunt were the center of the boys' life on the reservation. But, at age 6 years the boys entered school and had to live there. There was no transportation from the reservation to school.

Level 6

Level 6

School life was vastly different from their life at home. The boys had to cut their hair and speak English. Jim hated the bells that told them what to do next. Life on the reservation was free roaming, and their days weren't structured around clocks. Jim ran away from the Sac and Fox Indian Agency School several times. The result was always the same; his father would punish him and take him back to school.

2. **Explain how Jim and Charlie's life before they went to school was different from their life in school.**
   Answer: At home they had no schedule and the boys were active outside most of the time. At school they had to speak English and their schedule was controlled by clocks/bells. (The correct answer should include one statement describing their reservation life and one describing life at school.)
   Inference type: Explain how or why

3. **What does the phrase "free roaming" mean in the sentence, "Life on the reservation was *free roaming*, and their day wasn't structured around clocks"?**
   Answer: Children were given freedom to do what they wanted all day and weren't held to certain time periods.
   Inference type: Understand the meaning of words/phrases

Finally, Hiram sent Jim to a school 300 miles away. Jim didn't <u>tolerate</u> the <u>restricted</u> life and ran away again. His father realized that he could not make his son stay at a school, so Jim stayed at home and helped on the farm. His mother died two months later. Jim was devastated and withdrew from his work on the farm. Knowing that he would get a beating for not working, he ran away again, this time to Texas. He worked hard and at the age of 13 years earned a team of horses. He brought them back to his father, hoping to live there. Hiram agreed, but only if he attend the local public school. Jim agreed and spent two years at the school. However, his father remarried, and Jim felt uncomfortable at home. It was time for him to do something else. Hiram wrote a letter to the local Sac and Fox Agency expressing his desire for Jim to go to school. "I want him to go and make something of himself."

4. **What is a theme or central idea so far, and what details support that theme?**
   Answer: The central idea so far is that Jim did not like the structure of school, but his father wanted him to get an education. This central idea was shown when the story said that Jim hated school and ran away from both schools. His father kept sending him back to school and finally wrote a letter asking them to accept Jim at the Sac and Fox Agency. In addition to giving the central idea, supporting evidence must be provided.
   Inference type: Determine the theme

Jim was accepted at Carlisle Indian Industrial School and enrolled at age 16. One day he observed that the track team's high-jumpers could not clear the 5'9" bar. Although he had never tried the high-jump before, he wanted to try. He cleared it easily, much to the astonishment of the team.

Level 6

Level 6

Upon hearing of Jim's **feat**, Pop Warner, the track coach, declared Jim a part of the team. Although Jim enjoyed his success at track, he wanted most to be on the varsity football team. Pop Warner wasn't in favor of this because he didn't want to lose his track star, and Jim was still small (5'5") for the average college football player.

5. **What does the word "feat" mean in the sentence, "Upon hearing of Jim's *feat*, Pop Warner, the track coach declared Jim a part of the team"?**
   Answer: Accomplishment or outstanding performance.
   <u>Inference type: Understand the meaning of words/phrases</u>

Jim begged the coach relentlessly, so finally Coach Warner gave Jim the football and asked him to run downfield. He expected the defensive players would tackle him and put an end to Jim's desire to play football. But, no one could tackle him. Coach Warner said, "Jim's performance at practice that afternoon was an exhibition of athletic talent that I had never before witnessed nor was I ever to again see anything similar which might compare to it."

Although Jim was named to the varsity football squad immediately, his first season was spent on the bench. Coach Warner believed that despite Jim's innate talent, he still had to learn the game of football. However, in the second season,

Jim was the star from the beginning. Their record was 10-2-1. In addition to playing the games, they had to travel to each one. Unlike today, where schools have a mixed schedule of home games and away games, the schools that played Carlisle would only do so on their home field. They didn't want to play on "Indian turf."

6. **Explain how Coach Warner's treatment of Jim differed when he was successful in the high-jump compared to when he was a first-year football player.**
   Answer: He immediately played Jim on the varsity track team, but he made him sit on the bench his first year on the football team. A comparison of when he was on the track team to when he was on the football team is required.
   <u>Inference type: Explain why/how</u>

7. **Explain the author's view of Jim Thorpe and how the descriptions show how this point of view is developed.**
   Answer: The author views Jim as a talented athlete who is persistent/doesn't give up. This is illustrated by Jim's talent at high-jumping and running and his persistence in how he keeps asking Pops to let him try football. OR The author has a positive or complimentary point of view of Jim because he describes all of his accomplishments. A point of view must be stated along with how that view is developed in the story.
   <u>Inference type: Determine point of view</u>

During the summers of 1910 and 1911, he went to North Carolina to play baseball. Pop Warner discouraged Jim from going, but Jim loved baseball and would be paid to play! When summer ended, he couldn't return to the schedule of school life. But, when Carlisle was not doing well in

Level 6

football in the fall, Pop Warner enticed Jim back for the football season by promising to help him train to make the Olympic team in 1912. Jim couldn't resist the idea of competing against the world's best athletes.

Jim competed in two events, the decathlon (ten events) and the pentathlon (five events). Both events included the javelin throw, which he'd only been throwing for three weeks. The gold medal was decided by points: one point for a win, two points for second, three points for third, etc., so the lower the score the better. The pentathlon was first, and Jim won two races, the long jump, and the discus throw. He placed third in the javelin throw. He'd won the gold medal! He had 10 days to rest before the decathlon, a three-day event. He won the high-jump, 100-meter hurdles, and the 1500-meter race. He came in second in the long jump, shotput, discus, and 400-meter run. He finished third in the pole vault and fourth in the javelin. Jim won by a large margin. When the king of Sweden awarded the gold medals to him, he said, "Sir, you are the greatest athlete in the world." His medals were only

part of the reason that he was named the Male Athlete of the Half Century in 1950.

Words = 996. Lexile = 930L

8. **Citing evidence in the text, why was Jim well suited to the pentathlon and the decathlon?**
   Answer: Because he was talented in many sports, not just one, and that is why he won those events.
   Inference type: Support statements about a text

9. **Explain how the paragraph on the Olympics continues to develop the author's point of view of Jim Thorpe.**
   Answer: It shows how talented Jim was in many sports and how hard he worked on the voyage.
   Inference type: Determine point of view

10. **What is a theme of this biography, and which details provide evidence for your theme?**
    Answer: That persistence and hard work are necessary along with innate talent to make a champion. The details are Jim's talent and his persistence toward his goals. His hard work is shown when he earned a team of horses at age 13. The theme must be given as well as supporting evidence from the text.
    Inference type: Determine the theme

Evaluating Inference Type

Support statements about a text	_____Q1	_____Q8
Understand the meaning of words/phrases	_____Q3	_____Q5
Explain why/how	_____Q2	_____Q6
Determine point of view	_____Q7	_____Q9
Determine the theme	_____Q4	_____Q10

Level 6

Summarize the text. The summary is scored by counting the number of story elements (setting, characterization, initiating event, episodes, and ending) that are included. A student only needs to include one statement within each category to earn credit for that category. Statements in bold were included in most summaries.

Summary

1. **Setting:** _____

    On an Indian reservation and in Indian schools _____

2. **Characterizations:** _____

    Jim Thorpe was a talented athlete and a hard worker. _____

    But he hated school. _____

    Hiram Thorpe, Jim's dad, wanted him to get an education. _____

3. **Initiating Event:** _____

    Jim kept running away from Indian schools because he didn't like the strict schedules. _____

    Jim's father kept sending him back. _____

    Finally, his father realized that he couldn't keep Jim at school. _____

4. **Episode #1:** _____

    Jim was accepted into Carlisle Indian School. _____

    Jim showed talent at the high-jump. _____

    Pops Warner, the track coach, made him a member of the team. _____

5. **Episode #2** _____

    Jim wanted to play football, but the coach didn't want him to. _____

    No one could tackle Jim, so he became part of the football team. _____

    The first year he sat on the bench. _____

    Later he became a star. _____

6. **Episode #3** _____

    Pops Warner promised he would help him train for the Olympics. _____

    Jim went to the Olympics in 1912 and **entered the pentathlon and the decathlon.** _____

    He won (two, several) gold medals. _____

7. **Ending** _____

    He was named the Male Athlete of the Half Century in 1950. _____

    Total elements included in summary = _____

    Total possible elements = 7

    Acceptable = 5

Level 6

Social Studies

From Dynasty to Dynasty

The history of ancient Egypt is the history of each of its dynasties, a series of rulers from the same family or ethnic group. Historians group Egypt's dynasties into three major time periods, called kingdoms. The earliest major time period is called the Old Kingdom. Next comes the Middle Kingdom. The latest time period is called the New Kingdom. The gaps between the kingdoms were times of troubles such as wars, invasions, or weak rulers. These in-between periods were rare, for rule in most of ancient Egyptian history was **stable**.

Egypt Is Unified. According to legend, Egypt's first dynasty began when a king named Menes united Upper and Lower Egypt and built a city named Memphis near the present-day Cairo. From there, he ruled over the Two Lands. The unification of Egypt was the beginning of one of the most **stable** civilizations in history.

1. **What is the meaning of "stable" in the context of the above passage?**
   Answer: Steady; secure; established; calm.
   <u>Inference Type: Determine word meaning</u>

All-Powerful <u>Pharaohs.</u> The pharaohs had absolute power, or complete control over their people. For help in making decisions, they could

Level 6

Level 6

turn to their advisors or appeal to Ma'at, the goddess of truth but, in the end, whatever the pharaoh decided became law. For example, he decided when the fields would be planted, and at harvest time, he demanded crops from the workers in the fields.

Ancient Egyptians believed that their pharaohs were the earthly form of Horus, the falcon god. The pharaohs were god-kings. It was the pharaoh, Egyptians believed, who provided his people with the Nile's yearly floods and the harvests that followed.

2. **The topic of the above two paragraphs is "all-powerful pharaohs." What is the central idea?**
   Answer: The pharaohs had absolute power over their people. OR Ancient Egyptians believed the pharaoh was a god. OR The pharaohs were god-kings.
   Inference Type: Determine the central idea

3. **What evidence in the text indicates that ancient Egyptians were probably afraid to go against or oppose the pharaoh?**
   Answer: They believed the pharaoh was a god OR They believed he controlled the yearly flood and the harvest.
   Inference Type: Provide text evidence

The Three Kingdoms

The Old Kingdom. The Old Kingdom was noted for its well-run system of government. The Old Kingdom pharaohs kept the peace and traded with Nubia, with only occasional conflicts. They sent merchants to the eastern coast of the Mediterranean to find timber that was used to make houses, boats, and furniture. Toward the end of the Old Kingdom, governors in the provinces began to **challenge** the power of the pharaohs' government. As a result, Egypt's unity crumbled, and the dynasties grew weak.

4. **What is the meaning of "challenge" in the context of the above passage?**
   Answer: Question; test; dispute; confront.
   Inference Type: Determine word meaning

The Middle Kingdom. The early rulers of the Middle Kingdom restored order and reunited the country. Pharaohs spent the nation's wealth on public works instead of on wars. For example, they constructed buildings and irrigation projects. Egypt grew even richer. However, weaker and less able rulers followed and in time, they lost control of the country to foreign invaders.

The New Kingdom. Egyptian princes became strong enough to drive out the foreign invaders. This event marks the start of the New Kingdom. The first pharaohs of the New Kingdom wanted to build an empire and they created huge armies of foot soldiers, mounted warriors, and charioteers. Bronze swords and body armor made the Egyptians nearly unbeatable.

Level 6

5. Which text structure best explains how the author organized the above passage titled "The Three Kingdoms"?
   _____*description of important features*
   _____*explanation of steps in a sequence*
   _____*account of cause and effect*
   _____*explanation of problem and solution*
   _____*comparison/contrast of two or more things*

   Give a reason from the text for your answer. For example, if you choose description, tell what is being described. If you choose sequence, list two steps. For cause and effect, state a cause or effect mentioned in the text. For problem and solution, tell what the problem is or describe the solution. For comparison, tell what is being compared or contrasted.
   Answer: Description: The author describes the Three Kingdoms. OR Comparison: The author compares the Three Kingdoms.
   Inference Type: Identify text structure

   Note: This question has two separate answers: identification of structure and explanation of reason.

6. What evidence in the text indicates that New Kingdom pharaohs were interested in protecting their soldiers?
   Answer: They gave them bronze swords and body armor.
   Inference Type: Provide text evidence

Rule During the New Kingdom

In 1504 B.C., a child named Thutmose III began his reign but, because of his youth, his stepmother was appointed regent. A regent is someone who rules for a child until the child is old enough to rule. His stepmother was Hatshepsut, who was not content to be regent. Hatshepsut had herself proclaimed <u>pharaoh</u>. She was Egypt's supreme ruler for about 15 years.

The Pharaoh Queen. Hatshepsut's reign was good for Egypt. She was a bold leader who is most known for creating a time of great peace and economic success. She encouraged trade with faraway places, sending a famous expedition to the land of Punt on the east coast of Africa. Egyptian traders returned with shiploads of ivory, leopard skins, and special trees used to make incense, a substance burned for its fragrance. When Thutmose grew up, Hatshepsut refused to yield the throne to him. After her death, Thutmose became <u>pharaoh</u> and destroyed all her statues. We don't know if Thutmose played a part in Hatshepsut's death.

Thutmose III Rules. Thutmose III became one of the greatest <u>pharaohs</u> of the New Kingdom. He led his army in wars against Syria and Phoenicia, in Southwest Asia. His troops advanced as far east as the Euphrates River and south into Nubia. Yet Thutmose was more than a <u>conqueror</u>. He was an educated man who loved to study plants and unlike most rulers of his time, he treated those he defeated with mercy.

Level 6

7. The topic of the above three paragraphs is "rule during the New Kingdom." What is the central idea?

   Answer: The rule of Hatshepsut and Thutmose III benefited Egypt; OR Hatshepsut and Thutmose III were great pharaohs; OR the author described the rules of Hatshepsut and Thutmose III.

   <u>Inference Type: Determine the central idea</u>

8. How did Hatshepsut's and Thutmose's points of view differ?

   Answer: Hatshepsut thought peace and economic success were most important; Thutmose believed in the importance of conquest.

   <u>Inference Type: Determine point of view</u>

9. Analyze how Hatshepsut and Thutmose were alike.

   Answer: They were both pharaohs; OR they both ruled in the New Kingdom; OR they both benefited Egypt.

   <u>Inference Type: Explain why or how</u>

10. Analyze why historians think Thutmose might have played a part in Hatshepsut's death.

    Answer: When he grew up, Hatshepsut refused to give up her throne; OR he destroyed her statues, which suggests he did not like her.

    <u>Inference Type: Explain why or how</u>

Ancient Egypt After the New Kingdom.

Toward the end of the New Kingdom, Egypt declined. Civil war left Egypt weak and poorly defended. In 332 B.C., long after the end of the New Kingdom, Egypt fell to the famous <u>conqueror</u> Alexander the Great of Macedonia.

Evaluating Performance by Inference Type

Determine central idea	____Q2	____Q7
Determine word meaning	____Q1	____Q4
Explain why/how	____Q9	____Q10
Provide text evidence	____Q3	____Q6
Identify text structure	____Q5	
Determine point of view	____Q8	

Summarize what the text says about the accomplishments of the Three Kingdoms of Egypt.

An acceptable text-based summary contains the following elements:

1. *An introductory statement of purpose.*
2. *The Old Kingdom had a well-run system of government.*
3. *The Old Kingdom was peaceful.*
4. *Old Kingdom pharaohs engaged in trade.*
5. *Middle Kingdom pharaohs built public works (or buildings and irrigation projects).*
6. *Egypt became rich during the Middle Kingdom.*
7. *New Kingdom pharaohs created huge armies.*
8. *Hatshepsut created peace.*
9. *Hatshepsut encouraged trade with foreign places.*
10. *Thutmose conquered new lands.*

Evaluating Summary Performance

Total elements included in student's summary = _____

Total possible elements included in summary = 10
Acceptable = 7

Taken from *History of Our World*. Boston, MA: Pearson Prentice Hall. ISBN 0-13-203772-6, pp. 75–79. Words = 752. Lexile = 970.

Level 6

Science

What Causes Weather?

Air Masses and Fronts

Weather is the condition of the atmosphere at a particular time and place. Air masses and fronts produce the weather around you. An air mass is a very large body of air that has a similar temperature and <u>humidity</u> throughout. An air mass forms when the same air stays over an area for days or even a week or more. The air mass gets its temperature and moisture characteristics from the area of Earth's surface over which it forms. For example, an air mass forming over a polar region would be cold.

1. **What evidence in the text indicates that Earth's surface affects air masses?**
   Answer: An air mass gets its temperature and moisture characteristics from Earth's surface.
   <u>Inference Type: Provide Text Evidence</u>

Air masses of different temperatures usually do not mix easily. Instead, a <u>boundary</u> forms between them. The <u>boundary</u> that forms between air masses is called a front. Meteorologists, scientists who study the weather, track the movements of air masses to predict weather conditions. What happens when fronts meet?

Cold Front. A mass of cold air runs into a mass of warm air, forcing the warm air above the cold air.

Level 6

Level 6

As the warm air rises, it cools and <u>condenses</u>. Clouds form, and heavy rain or snow may follow. Cold fronts move more quickly than warm fronts.

Warm Front. A mass of warm air runs into a mass of cooler air. The warm air is forced above the cooler air. As the warm air rises, it cools and <u>condenses</u>, forming clouds. Periods of steady rain or drizzle result.

2. **What is the meaning of "condenses" in the context of the above passage?**
   Answer: Changes into a liquid.
   <u>Inference Type: Determine Word Meaning</u>

Stationary Front. A warm air mass and a cold air mass meet but neither one moves. As the name implies, a **stationary** front does not move quickly. It can stay over an area for several days. The weather produced is similar to a warm front.

3. **The topic of the above section is "air masses and fronts." What is the central idea?**
   Answer: Air masses and fronts produce different kinds of weather.
   <u>Inference Type: Determine the central idea</u>

4. **What is the meaning of "stationary" in the context of the above passage?**
   Answer: Inactive; not moving; staying in one place.
   <u>Inference Type: Determine word meaning</u>

5. **Analyze how cold and warm fronts are similar.**
   Answer: In both, warm air rises and causes weather to change; OR in both, warm air rises, cools, and condenses.
   <u>Inference Type: Explain why or how</u>

6. **What evidence in the text indicates that weather in a stationary front might last for several days?**
   Answer: A stationary front does not move quickly; OR a stationary front can stay over an area for several days.
   <u>Inference Type: Provide text evidence</u>

Severe Weather

Thunderstorms. A thunderstorm is a small, intense storm that produces strong winds, heavy rain, lightning, and thunder. Thunderstorms occur all the time on Earth. They tend to happen more in spring and summer months, but they can pop up any time of the year.

Every thunderstorm has lightning, so all thunderstorms are dangerous. Every year lightning kills more people than tornadoes do. And the storm's heavy rain can cause flash flooding, which also is very dangerous.

Tornadoes. A tornado is a violent, funnel-shaped column of air that extends from a thunderstorm to the ground. The winds of a tornado can reach 512 kilometers an hour. They form very quickly from thunderstorms, so they are difficult to predict. The path of a tornado also can change quickly. That makes predicting their path difficult too. Tornadoes are always dangerous.

Level 6

activity was not known to whites, especially those in the cities where there were no temples. All that ceased when CBS produced a documentary in 1959 called *The Hate That Hate Produced*. The white newsman, Mike Wallace, explained the documentary as a "study of the rise of black racism ... of a call for black supremacy. ... Among a small but growing segment of the American Negro population." At that point there were at least 250,000 members of the Muslim community across the United States. Wallace warned not to underestimate the Muslims. Already they had started their own school, stores, restaurants, and department stores.

6. **What does the title of the documentary *The Hate That Hate Produced* mean, and how does the title explain why the black separatist movement began?**

7. **Analyze how the points of view of Malcolm X and Mike Wallace differed. How might that difference create suspense in the biography?**

As the movement became more widely known speeches by Malcolm X, who was a great orator, and Elijah Muhammad drew audiences of over 10,000 in large cities such as Chicago. Such crowds caused the police and FBI to pay close attention to this movement. The FBI attended his speeches and kept files of Malcolm's more radical statements waiting for an opportunity to arrest him.

Clearly Malcolm's beliefs ran counter to those espoused by Martin Luther King. Although their goals were the same, their methods couldn't have been more different. Whereas MLK preached non-violence and turning the other cheek, Malcolm preached "by any means necessary" to create equality and a better life for blacks. Malcolm became aware that as an aggressive black militant he was putting his life and that of his family at risk.

8. **Explain your point of view of Malcolm X so far and analyze how it has created suspense as you've read the biography.**

His faith in Elijah Muhammad was severely threatened when his mentor engaged in behavior forbidden by Islam. Malcolm decided to break from the Nation of Islam and establish a new mosque in New York. This mosque was open to all blacks independent of their religious or political beliefs. His new organization attracted many blacks who had been unwilling to give up practices forbidden by the Islamic Code, such as drinking.

Malcolm traveled to Africa to learn more about their governments. He was welcomed warmly by Muslims with lighter skin, which forced him to rethink his perspective on what it meant to be white. He learned that the descendants of the prophet Muhammad were black *and* white, and Muslims made no distinctions between the two. He met with ministers from lands with nonwhite populations who expressed concern at the plight of American blacks. Malcolm realized that the American black had great support from the world's nonwhite majority. His second trip to Africa led to new insights. A white ambassador told Malcolm he never noticed color in Africa, but instantly became conscious of it when he was in America. Malcolm concluded that racism was not innate in white people but was the result of a national culture that fostered it. Despite his change in attitude he remained convinced that only when black people achieved racial pride and confidence could they join with whites on an equal basis.

His return to the U.S. was marked with his new view that all whites weren't the enemy, only those who were racist. These statements, so unlike his previous philosophy, created quite an uproar. Now he invited everyone to attend meetings of the Muslim Mosque regardless of color. Although Malcolm's beliefs may have changed to be more inclusive, his earlier statements had been going on for so long that many blacks held to them. Riots broke out across the country and he was blamed for them.

9. Cite evidence in the text that Malcolm X was open to changing his opinion by listening to the opinions of others.

Elijah Muhammad became angry with Malcolm's statements that were not religion-based. Malcolm began receiving death threats. Wherever he went members of the Nation of Islam showed up. One night flaming gas bombs were tossed through his front window, setting fire to the house. He was frightened for his family and furious with members of the Nation of Islam whom he believed were behind the grievous act. Despite the threats he continued to preach what he believed. On February 21, 1965, he made a speech in Harlem and a man in the back created a ruse to distract people. A smoke bomb went off in the back and Malcolm's guards went there while three men in the front row rushed the stage, firing 16 bullets at Malcolm. He died that afternoon in a hospital.

Reactions to Malcolm's murder came from many countries as well as from black notables in the United States. Novelist James Baldwin called his death "a major setback for the Negro movement." Three black Muslims were charged with murder, but Elijah Muhammad denied that the Nation of Islam was responsible.

Other black leaders in America formed the Black Panthers whose goals were to serve poor families and defend the ghettos against police brutality. The leaders saw themselves as the heirs to Malcolm X. But the real heir, his daughter Attallah Shabazz, believed that these men misunderstood her father's message. She told the *Los Angeles Times* that those young men were "inspired by pieces of him instead of the entire man. They think 'by any means necessary' means with a gun, as opposed to with a book or getting an A in school." People continue to write to better understand the complexities of Malcolm X.

10. What is a central idea of this biography, and how has it been developed over the course of the text?

Summarize the text.

Social Studies

A Wave of Nativism

Increased immigration led to a wave of nativism. Nativists sought to preserve the United States for native-born American citizens.

Nativists argued that the new immigrants would not assimilate because their languages, religions, and customs were too different. They also charged that immigrants took jobs away from Americans. Nativists associated immigrants with violence, crime, and anarchy. An anarchist is a person who opposes all forms of government.

In 1917, Congress passed a law that denied entry to immigrants who could not read their own languages. Since education at the time was usually **restricted** to the wealthy, this law barred most of the world's poor people from immigrating to the United States.

1. What is the meaning of "restricted" in the context of the above passage?

2. The topic of the above paragraphs is "a wave of nativism." What is the central idea?

Asian Americans

On the West Coast, nativist feelings against Chinese immigrants ran high. Mobs drove Chinese from mining camps and cities and sometimes killed them. In 1882, Congress passed a law to **exclude** Chinese laborers from the United States. The Chinese Exclusion Act was the first law limiting immigration based on race. Employers on the West Coast and in Hawaii began hiring workers from other Asian countries, mainly the Philippines and Japan. The Chinese Extension Act was finally repealed in 1943.

More than 100,000 Japanese entered the United States in the early 1900s. Many of the newcomers were farmers. They settled on dry, barren land that Americans thought was useless. Through hard work, the Japanese made their farms profitable. Soon, they were producing a large percentage of southern California's fruits and vegetables.

3. What is the meaning of "exclude" in the context of the above passage?

A Gentlemen's Agreement

Prejudice against Asians was high. Unions and other groups put pressure on President Theodore Roosevelt to limit emigration from Japan. Because Roosevelt did not want to antagonize a growing naval power, he tried to soothe Japanese feelings.

In 1907, Roosevelt reached a "Gentlemen's Agreement" with Japan. Japan would stop any more workers from going to the United States. The United States, in exchange, would allow Japanese women to join their husbands who were already in the country.

Anti-Japanese feeling remained high. In 1913, California banned Asians who were not American citizens from owning land.

4. The topic of the above paragraphs is "a gentlemen's agreement." What is the central idea?

5. What evidence in the text indicates that Japan was upset about U.S. prejudice toward Asians?

6. What was Roosevelt's point of view regarding Japan?

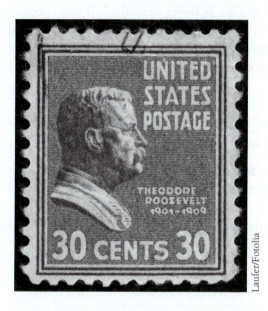

Mexican Americans

By 1900, about half a million Mexican Americans lived in the United States. Like African Americans, Mexican Americans often faced legal segregation. In 1910, the town of San Angelo, Texas, built new schools for its Anglo children. Mexican children were forced to go to separate, inferior schools. When Mexican children tried to attend one of the new schools, officials barred their way.

In 1910, revolution and famine swept Mexico. Thousands of Mexicans fled into the United States. They came from all levels of Mexican society. Many were poor farmers, but some came from middle-class and upper-class families.

At first, 90% of Mexican immigrants settled in the Southwest. In time, the migration spread to other parts of the country. People who could not find work in the Southwest began moving to the Midwest and the Rocky Mountain region.

Mexican immigrants often worked as field hands, built roads, or dug irrigation ditches. Some lived near the railroads they helped build. Still others worked in city factories under harsh conditions. They were paid less than Anglo workers and were denied skilled jobs.

Like other immigrants, Mexican Americans sought to preserve their language and culture. They created barrios, or ethnic Mexican American neighborhoods. Los Angeles was home to the nation's largest barrio. Its population almost tripled between 1910 and 1920.

7. Which text structure best explains how the author organized the above passage titled "Mexican Americans"?

_____*description of important features*_____ *explanation of steps in a sequence*
_____*account of cause and effect*_____ *explanation of problem and solution*
_____*comparison/contrast of two or more things*

Give a reason from the text for your answer. For example, if you choose description, tell what is being described. If you choose sequence, list two steps. For cause and effect, state a cause or effect mentioned in the text. For problem and solution, tell what the problem is or describe the solution. For comparison, tell what is being compared or contrasted.

8. Analyze why many Americans did not like immigrants.

9. What evidence in the text indicates that immigrants made positive contributions to the United States?

10. Analyze how the Congress of the United States unjustly discriminated against immigrants.

Summarize what the text says about how immigrants were mistreated.

America: History of Our Nation (2011). Boston: Prentice Hall Pearson. ISBN-13: 978-0-13-369951-7, pp. 626, 629, 663–664. Words = 562. Lexile = 920.

Science

What Is a Comet?

Comet Parts. Like planets and asteroids, comets are also members of the solar system. A comet is a lump of ice, frozen gas, and dust that orbits the Sun. Comets orbit the Sun in very long ellipses that often take them beyond the orbit of Pluto.

A comet has three parts. The core, or nucleus, is basically a dirty ice ball. It is made of water ice, frozen gas, and dust. The cloud of gas that surrounds the nucleus is called the coma. Stretching out from the coma is one or more tails. A stream of particles coming from the Sun pushes the tail or tails away from the center of the solar system.

Over time, the coma expands, and the tail stretches out into space. After rounding the Sun, the comet moves back into deep space and disappears from view.

Chris/Fotolia

1. The topic of the above paragraphs is "comet parts." What is the central idea?

2. What evidence in the text indicates that outer space is cold?

3. What evidence in the text indicates that a comet's tail faces away from the sun?

Ghostly Travelers. Comets travel in deep space where it is very cold. For most of their trip around the Sun, they are invisible. As a comet approaches the Sun, it begins to warm up. Some of the ice begins to melt. Gas and dust are released from the nucleus and spread out to form the coma. Soon the tail begins to form. Tails can stretch out for millions of kilometers.

From Earth, a comet looks like a ghostly patch in the sky. It suddenly appears one night as sunlight begins reflecting off it. Over time the comet expands, and the tail stretches out into space. After rounding the Sun, the comet moves back into deep space and disappears from view.

4. **The topic of the above two paragraphs is "comet travel." What is the central idea?**

5. **Analyze what happens to a comet's nucleus each time it orbits the Sun.**

Comets were formed billions of years ago when the solar system was young. After the Sun formed, gas and dust surrounding the new Sun formed into small pieces of ice, rock, and metal. These pieces eventually stuck together to form larger objects. The largest bodies became planets and moons. The smaller bodies became asteroids and comets.

6. **Analyze how comets are like planets, moons and asteroids.**

Predicting Comets. Scientists know that comets are coming days or months before they become visible to the **naked** eye. The comets appear in the sky right where scientists predict they will be. How do they do that?

7. **What is the meaning of "naked" in the context of the above passage?**

Most comets travel around the Sun many times before they melt or leave the solar system. British astronomer Sir Edmund Halley was the first person to predict a comet's return, in 1758. The comet was later named after him. Halley's Comet returns about every 76 years. It was last seen in 1986.

Old comets, ones that have passed by the Sun before, are easy to predict. Today, comet orbits are calculated by computers. To find new comets, astronomers take pictures of the same regions of the night sky several days apart. If one of the stars in the first picture is in a different place in the second picture, it could be a comet. Powerful telescopes are then **trained** on the object. Eventually, astronomers identify it as a comet or some other object, like an asteroid. If it is a comet, it will begin releasing gas as it nears the Sun.

8. **Which text structure best explains how the author organized the above passage titled "Predicting Comets"?**

_____*description of important features*_____ *explanation of steps in a sequence*
_____*account of cause and effect*_____ *explanation of problem and solution*
_____*comparison/contrast of two or more things*

Give a reason from the text for your answer. For example, if you choose description, tell what is being described. If you choose sequence, list two steps. For cause and effect, state a cause or effect mentioned in the text.

For problem and solution, tell what the problem is or describe the solution. For comparison, tell what is being compared or contrasted.

9. **Analyze how scientists differentiate a comet from an asteroid.**

10. **What is the meaning of "trained" in the context of the above passage?**

Amateur astronomers probe the depth of space using relatively inexpensive telescopes. They often form sky-watching groups. These dedicated individuals are sometimes the first to notice changes in the night sky. In fact, they have discovered many new comets.

Summarize what the text says about how comets became visible.

Taken from: *Earth Science: Concepts and Challenges* (2009). Boston: Pearson, pp. 430–431.

Level: Middle School

Biography

Concept Questions

What does the word *separatist* mean? (*3: a person who wishes to live separate from another group 2: choosing to be alone; 1: a person*)

_____

_____

_____ (3-2-1-0)

What is a racist? (*3: someone who believes one racial group is better than another; 2: the Ku Klux Klan; 1: think they're the best*)

_____

_____

_____ (3-2-1-0)

What does the word *supremacy* mean? (*3: to be the best; to have complete power over another; 2: a king or queen; 1: to get all A's*)

_____

_____

_____ (3-2-1-0)

What does the word *radical* mean? (*3: a reformist, someone who holds an extreme belief or a belief that few others hold; 2: MLK, Huey Newton, names a person or group that is recognized as being radical; 1: a math symbol*)

_____

_____

_____ (3-2-1-0)

_____ /12 = _____ %

_____ FAM (≥ 55%) _____ UNFAM

Malcolm X: The Development of a Separatist

Most United States citizens believe that for the country to succeed people of all races must accept and appreciate their differences and be able to live together peacefully. However, there have been people (and likely still are) who believed that the best course of action for the blacks in this country would be to separate themselves from whites. Blacks would set up their own banks, grocery stores, automobile dealerships, etc. Black families in the town or city would shop only at these businesses. This was the viewpoint of Malcolm X, who was born in 1925 and was murdered in 1965. How did Malcolm develop the belief that African Americans in the United States would benefit from living completely separate from whites? This biography will explain the events in his life that led to this viewpoint.

Malcolm was born as Malcolm Little in Nebraska, the son of a Baptist minister. His father was the president of a branch of the Universal Negro Improvement Association (UNIA). The association was started by a Jamaican man named Marcus Garvey who believed that black people would be better off separate from white people. When Malcolm's father went to UNIA meetings Malcolm often <u>accompanied</u>

Level: Middle School

him. He remembered seeing photographs of Marcus Garvey in a magnificent uniform leading a parade with huge crowds of blacks. Malcolm also recalled that his father adjourned his church's congregation with Garvey's rallying cry, "Up, you mighty race, you can accomplish what you want."

Malcolm was aware of the hazards of a black man in a white world from a young age. Several of his uncles were killed by white men. The actions of the Ku Klux Klan, a racist group that burned crosses and attacked black people, led Mr. Little to move his family to Michigan. However, the hostility toward his father's preaching of Garvey's <u>separatist</u> philosophy followed the family. When Malcolm was four years old, his home was set on fire, and the white firefighters simply watched it burn.

1. **What is a central idea of the paragraphs above, and how might it develop the plot of the story?**
   Answer: Malcolm learned as a child that racism existed, and the plot will be around how he developed into an adult and what views he will have; OR Malcolm heard ideas that blacks would be better off separate from whites when he was a child. It suggests that these ideas will continue to grow as he becomes an adult. The major idea must be supported by text evidence.
   <u>Inference Type: Determine a theme</u>

When he was six years old his father was killed by racists and thrown under a streetcar. His mother became unable to support eight children, so they were taken in as wards of the state. Because of the large family the siblings were sent to live with different families. Malcolm blamed the state for destroying his family. His behavior deteriorated and he was sent to a detention home in Michigan where he heard talk of "those nigg. . ." and the talk was hateful. The few black children in Albion, Michigan, heard adults talk about *nigg. . .s* as if the children weren't there. But in school Malcolm was popular, earned the best grades in eighth grade, and was elected the class president. Despite his academic success teachers didn't support his professional goals. "A lawyer," one teacher replied, "that's no realistic goal for a nigg. . ." Malcolm realized the racism inherent in this statement because lower achieving students were encouraged to become professionals. In later years he looked back on this part of his life and lamented that he tried very hard "to be white."

2. **Analyze how the events that Malcolm experienced as a child led to his philosophy that blacks would be better separated from whites.**
   Answer: He heard preachers talk about that philosophy and also experienced racism in his own life, so he had learned that he might be better off separated from whites.
   <u>Inference Type: Explain how or why</u>

Level: Middle School

3. **What does the phrase "he tried very hard to be white" mean, and how does it affect the tone of the biography so far?**
   Answer: It means that he tried to fit into the majority white culture where he lived. This phrase suggests an insecure adolescent trying to make his way with his peers, so it makes the tone sympathetic. The phrase must be explained along with its impact on the tone of the story.
   Inference Type: Understand the meaning of words/phrases

A visit to his half-sister's home in Roxbury, Massachusetts, introduced him to city life among blacks and he wanted to live there, rather than in Michigan. His sister, Ella, arranged the transfer to Roxbury and it was the beginning of Malcolm's exposure to the more sordid lives of pimps and gamblers. He was an impressionable young man who was enthralled with tales of drug peddling and armed robberies and he began to emulate them. At 18 years of age he stopped selling drugs and turned to armed robbery. A careless mistake led to his arrest and before he was 21, he was sentenced to 10 years in prison.

He was not a model prisoner, prone to outbursts of anger. Fortunately, one of his fellow prisoners encouraged Malcolm to use the prison library to improve his knowledge and vocabulary. He didn't know which words he needed to learn so he started by copying the first page of the dictionary. After copying all the A-words, he began the B-words and on and on it went until he copied the entire dictionary. Now he could pick up a book and understand what the book was saying. He was hooked on reading and he read every free moment in prison.

His brother wrote to him that he and several of his sisters had converted to a religion for blacks called the Nation of Islam and they were praying for his conversion too. He explained that its leader was Elijah Muhammad who preached that the black man's rightful place was at the top of society, a placed usurped by the blue-eyed white man. He preached of the need to overthrow the white man's world in North America. Malcolm began writing to Muhammad and immersed himself in black history. What he read supported Muhammad's theory of the evil white man. Malcolm soon realized that he needed to change his life, so he decided to give up his criminal past and work to build a united Black Muslim brotherhood. He said, "Islam gave me wings" and spent the rest of his prison term trying to convert other black prisoners.

4. **Analyze how learning to read affected the development of Malcolm's life in his final years in prison.**
   Answer: It hooked him into reading, which allowed him to learn more than he could before; OR it

Level: Middle School

provided him with a purpose and allowed him to read about the history of other blacks, which supported what Muhammad was preaching.
Inference Type: Explain how or why

Three years after being released from prison, he traveled to Chicago with members of the Muslim Temple to hear Elijah Muhammad. During the speech Malcolm thought of his father preaching Garvey's message. It was the same message, blacks must not integrate into white society, but build their own black nation. Malcolm was astonished and flattered when Muhammad told the audience of Malcolm's change from a life of crime to become a member of the Nation of Islam. Shortly thereafter he changed his name to Malcolm X. The X stood for his unknown African family name.

5. **Cite textual evidence that suggests that Elijah Muhammad was not unique in his viewpoint of how blacks should live.**
Answer: Marcus Garvey had been preaching the same thing, and this philosophy had been used in his father's sermons.
Inference Type: Support statements about a text

He began preaching that Christianity was a religion of the white man designed to make black people wish to be white. Malcolm's radical statements tripled the membership of the temple in Detroit in three months. By 1954 he was a full minister of a temple in Harlem. His name became synonymous

with power. Much of his activity was not known to whites, especially those in the cities where there were no temples. All that ceased when CBS produced a documentary in 1959 called *The Hate That Hate Produced.* The white newsman, Mike Wallace, explained the documentary as a "study of the rise of black racism . . . of a call for black supremacy. . . . Among a small but growing segment of the American Negro population." At that point there were at least 250,000 members of the Muslim community across the United States. Wallace warned not to underestimate the Muslims. Already they had started their own school, stores, restaurants, and department stores.

6. **What does the title of the documentary *The Hate That Hate Produced* mean, and how does the title explain why the black separatist movement began?**
Answer: It means that the hate that whites showed to blacks had produced the hate that blacks developed against whites and led them to the idea that they should separate from whites. The title must be explained as well as how it explained the black separatist movement.
Inference Type: Understand the meaning of words/phrases

7. **Analyze how the points of view of Malcolm X and Mike Wallace differed. How might that difference create suspense in the biography?**
Answer: Malcolm X's point of view was in favor of black separatism, but Mike Wallace warned the people watching the documentary about this point of view and implied that it would not be good for the

Level: Middle School

country. The differences created suspense as to which position most people would take. After analyzing the points of view the student must also explain how that difference created suspense in the story.
<u>Inference Type: Determine point of view</u>

As the movement became more widely known speeches by Malcolm X, who was a great orator, and Elijah Muhammad drew audiences of over 10,000 in large cities such as Chicago. Such crowds caused the police and FBI to pay close attention to this movement. The FBI attended his speeches and kept files of Malcolm's more radical statements waiting for an opportunity to arrest him.

Clearly Malcolm's beliefs ran counter to those espoused by Martin Luther King. Although their goals were the same, their methods couldn't have been more different. Whereas MLK preached non-violence and turning the other cheek, Malcolm preached "by any means necessary" to create equality and a better life for blacks. Malcolm became aware that as an aggressive black militant he was putting his life and that of his family at risk.

8. **Explain your point of view of Malcolm X so far and analyze how it has created suspense as you've read the biography.**
   Answers will vary, but there are two likely scenarios. One would be that the reader viewed Malcolm as an enemy of the country, so suspense might build as the reader reads of Malcolm's militancy. The other view is one who admires Malcolm and his beliefs,

so suspense might build as the story explains threats against him. The point of view must be stated along with how suspense was built.
<u>Inference Type: Determine point of view</u>

His faith in Elijah Muhammad was severely threatened when his mentor engaged in behavior forbidden by Islam. Malcolm decided to break from the Nation of Islam and established a new mosque in New York. This mosque was open to all blacks independent of their religious or political beliefs. His new organization attracted many blacks who had been unwilling to give up practices forbidden by the Islamic Code, such as drinking.

Malcolm traveled to Africa to learn more about their governments. He was welcomed warmly by Muslims with lighter skin, which forced him to rethink his perspective on what it meant to be white. He learned that the descendants of the prophet Muhammad were black **and** white, and Muslims made no distinctions between the two. He met with ministers from lands with nonwhite populations who expressed concern at the plight of American blacks. Malcolm realized that the American black had great support from the world's nonwhite majority. His second trip to Africa led to new insights. A white ambassador told Malcolm he

never noticed color in Africa, but instantly became conscious of it when he was in America. Malcolm concluded that racism was not innate in white people but was the result of a national culture that fostered it. Despite his change in attitude he remained convinced that only when black people achieved racial pride and confidence could they join with whites on an equal basis.

His return to the U.S. was marked with his new view that all whites weren't the enemy, only those who were racist. These statements, so unlike his previous philosophy, created quite an uproar. Now he invited everyone to attend meetings of the Muslim Mosque regardless of color. Although Malcolm's beliefs may have changed to be more inclusive, his earlier statements had been going on for so long that many blacks held to them. Riots broke out across the country and he was blamed for them.

9. **Cite evidence in the text that Malcolm X was open to changing his opinion by listening to the opinions of others.**
   Answer: When Malcolm went to Africa and learned about how the Muslims there viewed whites, he changed his view and opened his mosque to people of any color.
   Inference Type: Support statements about a text

Elijah Muhammad became angry with Malcolm's statements that were not religion-based. Malcolm began receiving death threats. Wherever he went

members of the Nation of Islam showed up. One night flaming gas bombs were tossed through his front window, setting fire to the house. He was frightened for his family and furious with members of the Nation of Islam whom he believed were behind the grievous act. Despite the threats he continued to preach what he believed. On February 21, 1965, he made a speech in Harlem and a man in the back created a ruse to distract people. A smoke bomb went off in the back and Malcolm's guards went there while three men in the front row rushed the stage, firing 16 bullets at Malcolm. He died that afternoon in a hospital.

Reactions to Malcolm's murder came from many countries as well as from black notables in the United States. Novelist James Baldwin called his death "a major setback for the Negro movement." Three black Muslims were charged with murder, but Elijah Muhammad denied that the Nation of Islam was responsible.

Other black leaders in America formed the Black Panthers whose goals were to serve poor families and defend the ghettos against police brutality. The leaders saw themselves as the heirs to Malcolm X. But the real heir, his daughter Attallah Shabazz, believed that these men misunderstood her father's message. She told the *Los Angeles Times* that those young men were "inspired by pieces of him instead of the entire man. They think 'by any means necessary' means with a gun, as opposed to with a book or getting an A in school." People continue to write to better understand the complexities of Malcolm X. Words = 1859. Lexile = 1080.

10. **What is a central idea or theme of this biography, and how has it been developed over the course of the text?**

    Answer: There are several possible themes. One is that being an aggressive person who preaches things that many people don't like can get you killed. It was developed from the beginning as the story explained how Malcolm developed his philosophy of black separatism and was further developed by the attacks on his home and family. Another theme is that people who preach something may change their ideas when they travel to other countries and listen to other opinions. This theme was developed as Malcolm preached against whites but changed his mind after going to Africa and listening to Muslims there. A theme of the story must be stated and how it was developed must be explained.

    Inference Type: Determine a theme

Evaluating Performance by Inference Type: Malcolm X

Support statements about a text	_____Q5_____Q9
Understand the meaning of words/phrases	_____Q3_____Q6
Explain how or why	_____Q2_____Q4
Determine point of view	_____Q7_____Q8
Determine the theme	_____Q1_____Q10

Summarize the text. The summary is scored by counting the number of story elements (setting, characterizations, initiating event, episodes, and ending) included. To receive credit the student only needs to include one statement within the story element category. The elements that are bolded were included in most summaries.

1. **Characterization:** _____
   - **Malcolm X learned as a young boy to believe that blacks would be better off separate from whites.** _____

2. **Initiating Event (s):** _____
   - **When he was four his house was burned, and no one helped.** _____
   - **Malcolm's uncles and/or father were killed by racists.** _____
   - His siblings were sent to separate homes because his mother couldn't care for all of them. _____

3. **Event 1:** _____
   - In eighth grade he was at the top of his class. _____
   - But **a teacher didn't think his goals to become a lawyer were realistic.** _____

4. **Event 2:** _____
   - **He went to live with his sister.** _____
   - He started selling drugs and began to rob people. _____
   - **He was caught robbing and was sent to prison.** _____

5. **Event 3:** _____
   - A prisoner told him to use the library to improve himself. _____
   - **He learned to read and read a lot.** _____
   - **His brother wrote to him about a religion, the Nation of Islam.** _____
   - He decided to dedicate his life to building a united black brotherhood. _____

6. **Event 5:** _____
   - When he got out of prison, he went to hear Muhammad preach. _____

Level: Middle School

- He started a temple and preached against Christianity. _____
- **He started a temple in New York and became well known.** _____
- He became powerful within the Nation of Islam. _____
- Malcolm started his own mosque. _____

Event 6: _____
- **He traveled to Africa to learn about their governments.** _____
- His meetings with leaders taught him to include whites who weren't racist. _____
- Although **his views changed**, his followers didn't. _____

Event 7: _____
- He started receiving death threats and his house was fire-bombed. _____
- **He was killed in Harlem** while giving a speech. _____

Ending: _____
- Some young people followed his philosophy (started the Black Panthers). _____
- His daughter said that the young followers misunderstood his message. _____

Total elements included in student's summary = _____

Number of possible elements = 9

Acceptable = 6

Level: Middle School

Social Studies

A Wave of Nativism

Concept Questions

What is nativism? (*3: favoring native-born individuals over newcomers or immigrants; 2: a belief about natives, feelings about people born in a certain country; 1: like a native*)

_____

_____

_____ (3-2-1-0)

What is anarchy? (*3: disorder, lawlessness, revolution, lack of government, rebellion, no rules; 2: riots and fighting, people do what they want; 1: like monarchy*)

_____

_____

_____ (3-2-1-0)

What does *antagonize* mean? (*3: provoke, upset, alienate, irritate; 2: people can't get along, bullies do it; leads to fighting; 1: like against*)

_____

_____

_____ (3-2-1-0)

What does *inferior* mean? (*3: lesser, lower, substandard, mediocre; not as good, second-rate; 2: people don't want something inferior, doesn't cost a lot, doesn't last very long; 1: like superior*)

_____

_____

_____ (3-2-1-0)

Score: _____ /12 = _____ %

_____ FAM (≥ 55%) _____ UNFAM

Increased immigration led to a wave of nativism. Nativists sought to preserve the United States for native-born American citizens.

Nativists argued that the new immigrants would not assimilate because their languages, religions, and customs were too different. They also charged that immigrants took jobs away from Americans. Nativists associated immigrants with violence, crime, and anarchy. An anarchist is a person who opposes all forms of government.

In 1917, Congress passed a law that denied entry to immigrants who could not read their own languages. Since education at the time was usually **restricted** to the wealthy, this law barred most of the world's poor people from immigrating to the United States.

1. **What is the meaning of "restricted" in the context of the above passage?**
   Answer: Limited, controlled, kept within boundaries, confined, only for certain people.
   Inference Type: Determine word meaning

2. **The topic of the above paragraphs is "a wave of nativism." What is the central idea?**
   Answer: Nativists were against immigrants; OR the author describes why nativists opposed immigration.
   Inference Type: Determine the central idea

Level: Middle School

Asian Americans

On the West Coast, <u>nativist</u> feelings against Chinese immigrants ran high. Mobs drove Chinese from mining camps and cities and sometimes killed them. In 1882, Congress passed a law to **exclude** Chinese laborers from the United States. The Chinese Exclusion Act was the first law limiting immigration based on race. Employers on the West Coast and in Hawaii began hiring workers from other Asian countries, mainly the Philippines and Japan. The Chinese Extension Act was finally repealed in 1943.

More than 100,000 Japanese entered the United States in the early 1900s. Many of the newcomers were farmers. They settled on dry, barren land that Americans thought was useless. Through hard work, the Japanese made their farms profitable. Soon, they were producing a large percentage of southern California's fruits and vegetables.

3. **What is the meaning of "exclude" in the context of the above passage?**
   Answer: Keep out, shut out, keep from entering, restrict, reject.
   <u>Inference Type: Determine word meaning</u>

A Gentlemen's Agreement

Prejudice against Asians was high. Unions and other groups put pressure on President Theodore Roosevelt to limit emigration from Japan. Because Roosevelt did not want to <u>antagonize</u> a growing naval power, he tried to soothe Japanese feelings.

In 1907, Roosevelt reached a "Gentlemen's Agreement" with Japan. Japan would stop any more workers from going to the United States. The United States, in exchange, would allow Japanese women to join their husbands who were already in the country.

Anti-Japanese feeling remained high. In 1913, California banned Asians who were not American citizens from owning land.

4. **The topic of the above paragraphs is "a gentlemen's agreement." What is the central idea?**
   Answer: Roosevelt and Japan made an agreement regarding Japanese immigration to the United States.
   <u>Inference Type: Determine the central idea</u>

5. **What evidence in the text indicates that Japan was upset about U.S. prejudice toward Asians?**
   Answer: Roosevelt tried to soothe Japanese feelings.
   <u>Inference Type: Provide text evidence</u>

6. **What was Roosevelt's point of view regarding Japan?**
   Answer: He did not want to anger Japan; OR he feared Japan's growing naval power; OR he feared Japan might use force against the United States.
   <u>Inference Type: Determine point of view</u>

Level: Middle School

Mexican Americans

By 1900, about half a million Mexican Americans lived in the United States. Like African Americans, Mexican Americans often faced legal segregation. In 1910, the town of San Angelo, Texas, built new schools for its Anglo children. Mexican children were forced to go to separate, inferior schools. When Mexican children tried to attend one of the new schools, officials barred their way.

In 1910, revolution and famine swept Mexico. Thousands of Mexicans fled into the United States. They came from all levels of Mexican society. Many were poor farmers, but some came from middle-class and upper-class families.

At first, 90% of Mexican immigrants settled in the Southwest. In time, the migration spread to other parts of the country. People who could not find work in the Southwest began moving to the Midwest and the Rocky Mountain region.

Mexican immigrants often worked as field hands, built roads, or dug irrigation ditches. Some lived near the railroads they helped build. Still others worked in city factories under harsh conditions. They were paid less than Anglo workers and were denied skilled jobs.

Like other immigrants, Mexican Americans sought to preserve their language and culture. They created barrios, or ethnic Mexican American neighborhoods. Los Angeles was home to the nation's largest barrio. Its population almost tripled between 1910 and 1920.

7. **Which text structure best explains how the author organized the above passage titled "Mexican Americans"?**
   _____*description of important features*
   _____*explanation of steps in a sequence*
   _____*account of cause and effect*
   _____*explanation of problem and solution*
   _____*comparison/contrast of two or more things*

Give a reason from the text for your answer. For example, if you choose description, tell what is being described. If you choose sequence, list two steps. For cause and effect, state a cause or effect mentioned in the text. For problem and solution, tell what the problem is or describe the solution. For comparison, tell what is being compared or contrasted.
Answer: Cause/Effect: The author describes the causes and effects of Mexican immigration. OR Description: The author describes why Mexican Americans immigrated and how they lived.
Inference Type: Identify text structure

Note: This question has two separate answers: identification of structure and explanation of reason.

8. **Analyze why many Americans did not like immigrants.**
   Answer: They took jobs away from native-born Americans; OR they were too different from native-born Americans; OR they were associated with anarchy and violence.
   Inference Type: Explain why or how

9. **What evidence in the text indicates that immigrants made positive contributions to the United States?**

   Answer: Japanese immigrants were producing a large percentage of California's fruits and vegetables; OR Japanese made dry, barren land profitable; OR Mexican immigrants often worked as field hands, built roads, dug irrigation ditches, or worked in city factories.

   Inference Type: Provide text evidence

10. **Analyze how the Congress of the United States unjustly discriminated against immigrants.**

    Answer: They passed laws that denied entry to immigrants who could not read; AND/OR they denied entry to Chinese laborers.

    Inference Type: Explain why or how

Evaluating Performance by Inference Type

Determine central idea	_____Q2	_____Q4
Determine word meaning	_____Q1	_____Q3
Explain why/how	_____Q8	_____Q10
Provide text evidence	_____Q5	_____Q9
Identify text structure	_____Q7	
Determine point of view	_____Q6	

Summarize what the text says about how immigrants were mistreated.

An acceptable text-based summary contains the following elements:

1. *An introductory statement of purpose.*
2. *Nativists associated immigrants with violence and anarchy.*
3. *Congress passed laws that denied entry to certain immigrants.*
4. *Immigrants were driven away from mining camps and cities.*
5. *Immigrants were killed.*
6. *In California Asians could not own land.*
7. *Mexican children were forced to attend inferior schools.*
8. *Mexicans worked at low-level jobs OR were denied skilled jobs.*
9. *Mexican immigrants were paid less than other workers.*

Evaluating Summary Performance

Total elements included in student's summary

= _____

Total possible elements included in summary = 9

Acceptable = 7

Taken from: *America: History of Our Nation* (2011). Boston: Prentice Hall Pearson. ISBN-13: 978-0-13-369951-7, pp. 626, 629, 663–664. Words = 562. Lexile = 920.

Level: Middle School

Science

Concept Questions

What is a comet? (*3: an object in the solar system, an object that travels around the sun, an object in the sky that is sometimes visible; 2: a comet has a long tail, Halley's comet keeps coming back, astronomers discover new ones; 1: I never saw one*)

_____

_____

_____ (3-2-1-0)

What is a particle? (*3: a small amount of something, a tiny piece of something, a small portion of matter; 2: some are so small you can't see them, if you look at rice, it is made of a lot of particles; 1: a part of something*)

_____

_____

_____ (3-2-1-0)

What is a nucleus? (*3: a central part of something; 2: a nut in a shell is like a nucleus, an atom has a nucleus; 1: is like nuclear*)

_____

_____

_____ (3-2-1-0)

What is an orbit? (*3: the path of a planet or other object in space; a revolution of an object in space; 2: goes round and round, planets have an orbit; 1: like an orb*)

_____

_____

_____ (3-2-1-0)

Score: _____/12 = _____%

_____ FAM (≥ 55%) _____ UNFAM

What Is a Comet?

Comet Parts. Like planets and <u>asteroids</u>, comets are also members of the solar system. A comet is

a lump of ice, frozen gas, and dust that orbits the Sun. Comets orbit the Sun in very long ellipses that often take them beyond the orbit of Pluto.

A comet has three parts. The core, or nucleus, is basically a dirty ice ball. It is made of water ice, frozen gas, and dust. The cloud of gas that surrounds the nucleus is called the coma. Stretching out from the coma is one or more tails. A stream of particles coming from the Sun pushes the tail or tails away from the center of the solar system.

Over time, the coma expands, and the tail stretches out into space. After rounding the Sun, the comet moves back into deep space and disappears from view.

1. **The topic of the above paragraphs is "comet parts." What is the central idea?**
   Answer: A comet has three parts: the core, coma, and tail.
   <u>Inference Type: Determine the central idea</u>

2. **What evidence in the text indicates that outer space is cold?**
   Answer: A comet is a lump of ice and frozen gas; OR a comet is a dirty ice ball; OR a comet is made of gas and water ice.
   <u>Inference Type: Provide text evidence</u>

3. **What evidence in the text indicates that a comet's tail faces away from the Sun?**
   Answer: A stream of particles coming from the Sun pushes the tail or tails away from the center of the solar system.
   <u>Inference Type: Provide text evidence</u>

Level: Middle School

Ghostly Travelers. Comets travel in deep space where it is very cold. For most of their trip around the Sun, they are invisible. As a comet approaches the Sun, it begins to warm up. Some of the ice begins to melt. Gas and dust are released from the nucleus and spread out to form the coma. Soon the tail begins to form. Tails can stretch out for millions of kilometers.

From Earth, a comet looks like a ghostly patch in the sky. It suddenly appears one night as sunlight begins reflecting off it. Over time the comet expands, and the tail stretches out into space. After rounding the Sun, the comet moves back into deep space and disappears from view.

4. **The topic of the above two paragraphs is "comet travel." What is the central idea?**
   Answer: Comets become visible when they approach the Sun.
   Inference Type: Determine the central idea

5. **Analyze what happens to a comet's nucleus each time it orbits the Sun.**
   Answer: It gets smaller as gas and dust are released.
   Inference Type: Explain why or how

Comets were formed billions of years ago when the solar system was young. After the Sun formed, gas and dust surrounding the new Sun formed into small pieces of ice, rock, and metal. These pieces eventually stuck together to form larger objects. The largest bodies became planets and moons. The smaller bodies became asteroids and comets.

6. **Analyze how comets are like planets, moons, and asteroids.**
   Answer: They were all formed from the same materials: ice, rock, and metal.
   Inference Type: Explain why or how

Predicting Comets. Scientists know that comets are coming days or months before they become visible to the **naked** eye. The comets appear in the sky right where scientists predict they will be. How do they do that?

7. **What is the meaning of "naked" in the context of the above passage?**
   Answer: Without glasses; without use of a telescope.
   Inference Type: Determine word meaning

Most comets travel around the Sun many times before they melt or leave the solar system. British astronomer Sir Edmund Halley was the first person to predict a comet's return, in 1758. The comet was later named after him. Halley's Comet returns about every 76 years. It was last seen in 1986.

Old comets, ones that have passed by the Sun before, are easy to predict. Today, comet orbits are calculated by computers. To find new comets, astronomers take pictures of the same regions of the night sky several days apart. If one of the stars in the first picture is in a different

2. **What is a major idea of the biography so far, and what text evidence supports your idea?**

3. **What is the author's point of view of O'Keeffe, and how is it shown so far?**

During the summer of 1915, O'Keeffe took classes at Teachers College of Columbia University in South Carolina where Arthur Dow, a specialist in Oriental Art, was teaching at the University. Dow's interest in non-European art helped O'Keeffe move away from the forms that she had found so restrictive in her previous studies. She said of him, "It was Arthur Dow who affected my start, who helped me to find something of my own." She realized that up to now she was painting as her teachers directed her rather than from her spirit; the only value of her education was teaching her the use of materials, charcoal, pen and ink, pencil, watercolors, pastels, and oils. However, *what* to paint must come from within, from her desire to paint something, not just be able to.

4. **Analyze the changes in O'Keeffe's reactions to her teachers' evaluations of her work and how they affected her development as an artist.**

When O'Keeffe went to Texas to teach, she made a handful of charcoal drawings, which she sent to a friend in New York. The friend, Anna Pollitzer, showed them to Alfred Stieglitz, a photographer and gallery owner. He was enthused with the vibrant energy of the work and asked to show them. So, without her knowledge, Georgia O'Keeffe had her first exhibition in 1916 at Stieglitz's *291 Gallery* in New York. It was one of the few times that O'Keeffe was not enraged that someone would take something of hers and display it without her permission. A review of her work in the *Christian Science Monitor* by Henry Tyrrell said that she "draws with unconscious naiveté what purports to be the innermost unfolding of a girl's being, like the germinating of a flower." Stieglitz was amazed that a woman expressed herself so frankly on paper. He believed her to represent all women when he said that, "Woman is at last on paper, expressing her relation to the Universe." Her career coincided with that of Freud, who touted a sexual interpretation of human behavior based on the client's relationship with his or her parents. People often interpreted O'Keeffe's work through the Freudian lens by describing her paintings in sexual terms. This infuriated her because she felt the sexual interpretation was a simple way to dismiss her paintings without serious analysis.

5. **What do the underlined words reveal about how others evaluated her work?**

6. **How did the time period in which O'Keeffe's paintings were first exhibited affect how art critics interpreted her work?**

During the spring of 1916 while she was in New York, she first met the man who had praised her drawings beyond anyone else. Alfred Stieglitz warmly welcomed her to the *291 Gallery* showing her works of other artists whom he supported. However, soon he overstepped his bounds and displayed some of O'Keeffe's works without her permission. She challenged him and he retorted that she had no right to deny the world to see her work. Over a lunch, Stieglitz used his powerful persuasion and flirtation to convince her to leave her paintings in the gallery. O'Keeffe demurred but she was playing her own game because she *wanted* to display in his gallery but also wanted his respect.

On May 2, 1916, Georgia's mother died from hemorrhaging in her lungs at the age of 52. Georgia was devastated and it affected her painting. Unable to produce anything that met her standards, she spent the summer grieving, climbing Mt. Elliot in

Virginia, and reading. Stieglitz's encouragement enabled her to begin painting again, producing over 40 works later that summer. During a camping trip, O'Keeffe found herself looking out of a tent at a distant light. Her emotional isolation and view to the outside were later represented in drawings, watercolors, and an oil painting. An image of the door to the outside became a recurrent theme in O'Keefe's art for many years.

Having no reason to stay in Virginia, she returned to the panhandle of Texas to teach. She was enamored of the empty open sky that seemed to go on forever. Forever curious about nature she spent a night in a canyon watching the moonrise. She returned to the same place at dawn to get a new perspective and watched the colors of the sky as black changed to blue to gray and eventually a white sky appeared. The perspective of open sky prompted a series of paintings, among them *Blue II* (1916).

7. Provide strong and thorough evidence that emotions affect what an artist is able to create.

It was during this time that Stieglitz wrote to O'Keeffe daily and sent her essays on modern art by critics. Her first solo exhibition, including the watercolors and charcoals of South Carolina, was presented at *291 Gallery*. The introduction of O'Keeffe to Stieglitz changed her professional and personal life. Alfred Stieglitz became a mentor to O'Keeffe and provided her with financial security by exhibiting her paintings in his gallery. It was through him that art lovers became aware of O'Keeffe's paintings.

During the winter of 1917–18 she contracted the Spanish influenza and had to take a leave of absence from teaching. Despite urging from Stieglitz to come to New York, she was too ill to travel that far and instead went to southeastern Texas. When she was well enough, she went to New York, but the journey tired her out and she fell ill again. The personal relationship between 54-year-old Stieglitz and 31-year-old O'Keeffe developed as he and his niece took care of her daily needs. The tender care that he provided her led to an intimacy that she had not expected. To the outside world, he provided her with an apartment in New York, but those in the art world knew that he was more than a mentor to her.

Stieglitz was the country's most famous photographer and wanted to photograph O'Keeffe in the nude. Once she was posing for him in his apartment when his wife came home. She was furious and gave him a choice, get rid of his model or move out of the house. Their marriage had not been a fulfilling one for either of them, so he happily left. Although his wife changed her mind and wanted him home, he did not return. Stieglitz photographed O'Keeffe in "his idealization of femininity—passive, beauty, illness, and tragedy." In addition to the psychosexual theories of the time, the nude photographs of O'Keeffe contributed to the sexual interpretation of her paintings, particularly, flowers.

8. What do the words in quotations in the paragraph above mean?

O'Keeffe's relationship with Stieglitz was complicated as she loved him and his intellect, and he provided financial security as well as her entry into the art world. On the other hand, she sought to be alone so she could paint. The struggle between independence and dependence challenged her friendships as well as her relationship with Stieglitz. They enjoyed a wonderful summer in 1918 at his mother's summer home on Lake George, New York. At the end of the summer, he promised that he would find funds from wealthy friends to support her for a year. This gave her freedom to paint without worry of where she would live and whether or what she would eat. Although she recognized that Stieglitz would never give her children, something she had wanted, he could provide her an entryway for her career.

Stieglitz took advantage of the 1920s mentality, of racketeering and clandestine parties. In this milieu, he showed 145 black and white prints previously unseen. Included within them were photos of O'Keeffe partially or fully nude, although her face was obscured. While he was reveling in the positive reviews, O'Keeffe was deeply ashamed by the reviewers' implication that she was Stieglitz's mistress. It promoted the belief that being his mistress was why he promoted her work, not because she was a great artist. Again, he had overstepped his boundaries by using photos of her without her knowledge. The view of women as sexual beings led some in the art world to dismiss the paintings by women. Despite these general beliefs, in 1921, at the age of 34 years, three of O'Keeffe's paintings were on display at the Pennsylvania Academy of Fine Arts. This did not occur without a fight as to whether or not any woman's paintings would be in evidence. Stieglitz said, "Take it or leave it. They'll be no show without her." This statement provides an example of how much Stieglitz promoted O'Keeffe's work and the lengths that he took to provide her an audience. Without his support, her paintings might have languished in obscurity.

9. **What is the author's point of view toward Stieglitz, and what text evidence shows it?**

Her life would be a constant struggle between wanting and needing to be alone but at the same time seeking caring relationships. One of her problems was that although she wanted relationships, she would tire of people very quickly, which confused both her lovers and her friends.

In 1949, at the age of 62, she was elected to the prestigious National Institute of Arts and Letters, but not without several male artists attempting to prevent her admission.

10. **Determine the theme of this story and explain in detail how it has developed in the biography.**

"Where I was born and where and how I lived is unimportant," wrote 90-year-old Georgia O'Keeffe in her autobiography published in 1976. The book, titled simply *Georgia O'Keeffe*, includes examples of her many paintings. Perhaps she was trying to tell us to look at her paintings and learn about her life from them. She continued to speak to us, "It is what I have done with where I have been that should be of interest." Her paintings are a testament to her life and the varied locations in which she lived. She spent the last many years living and painting in New Mexico and the subjects of her paintings were frequently images of the desert. Her eyesight was failing in 1972 so she had to give up painting; she died in 1986 at the age of 99 years.

Summarize the text.

Social Studies

America Adjusts to Peace

The end of World War I produced an unstable international order. The loss of territory and the harsh reparations **imposed** by the Allies encouraged a strong desire for revenge in Germany. Meanwhile, Lenin's Soviet Russia threatened revolution throughout the industrial world. In the United States, the horrors of the war along with widespread fear of communists and radicals led Americans to question their political, if not their economic, role in the world.

1. **What is the meaning of "imposed" in the context of the above passage?**

World War I produced significant economic, social, political, and cultural changes in America and throughout the world. This led to important, occasionally painful, adjustments.

Flu Epidemic Grips the Nation

The movement from war to peace would have been difficult even in the best of times. But the end of 1918 and 1919 were not the best of times. In September 1918, an unusually deadly form of the influenza, or flu, virus appeared. Research in recent years shows that the 1918 influenza virus was originally a bird flu that **mutated** to spread to humans. Many historians now believe that the virus originated in the United States, then traveled around the world. Once the virus began, it spread like a wildfire and killed millions worldwide like a predator feasting on its prey. The great influenza pandemic, coming on the heels of the Great War, gave a sense of doom and dread to people around the globe.

National Archives and Records Administration

Street car conductor in Seattle not allowing passengers aboard without a mask. 1918.

Level: High School

When Georgia was 13, she was taken to a boarding school run by Dominican nuns. Her first assignment in the art studio was to draw a white plaster cast of a baby's hand. She drew it very small with dark lines; she liked it and enjoyed doing it. However, the teacher chastised her dark lines and told her the hand was too small. Fighting back tears, Georgia vowed she would never draw small again. The next year brought a new art teacher who taught her to look carefully at details. Although Georgia didn't like the teacher, she acknowledged in her autobiography that, "it was certainly the first time my attention was drawn to the outline and color of any growing thing with the idea of drawing or painting it." This provided O'Keeffe an important lesson, as later in life she would be known for her paintings of flowers.

1. **Cite two sources of textual evidence to support the inference that Georgia O'Keeffe's art was affected by memories and experiences from before she was 16 years old.**
   Answer: Her early memories of color were represented in her paintings as an adult; her experiences from the boarding school made her draw only large things; her experience in the boarding school taught her to pay attention to detail in living things.
   Inference Type: Support statements about a text

Despite her family's financial troubles, her parents decided that after high school graduation in 1905, she should attend the Art Institute of Chicago, a prestigious art school then and now. A year later she went to study at the Art Students League of New York where William Merritt Chase, an early impressionist, was her teacher. A fellow student, Eugene Speicher, remarked that it didn't matter how well O'Keeffe painted, she would end up teaching art in a girls' school, but <u>he</u> would become a famous painter. This attitude was common among male artists at the time, and women did not have the same opportunities as men.

2. **What is a major idea of the biography so far, and what text evidence supports your idea?**
   Answer: That it was difficult for a woman to become an artist. The evidence is that her fellow male students didn't believe that women could become artists. Other evidence is that the story tells of female art teachers when she was in middle school, but a male art teacher at the college level. The major idea must be supported by text evidence.
   Inference Type: Determine a theme

3. **What is the author's point of view of O'Keeffe, and how is it shown so far?**
   Answer: That she was not naturally gifted in painting but was gifted with a keen sense of observation. The text describes that she was not a child prodigy. However, she had an unusual sense of color even as a very young child and remembered the patterns and color of a quilt and had vivid memories of nature from her childhood. The student must give a point of view and how it is shown in the text to receive credit.
   Inference Type: Determine point of view

Level: High School

During the summer of 1915, O'Keeffe took classes at Teachers College of Columbia University in South Carolina where Arthur Dow, a specialist in Oriental Art, was teaching at the University. Dow's interest in non-European art helped O'Keeffe move away from the forms that she had found so restrictive in her previous studies. She said of him, "It was Arthur Dow who affected my start, who helped me to find something of my own." She realized that up to now she was painting as her teachers directed her rather than from her spirit; the only value of her education was teaching her the use of materials, charcoal, pen and ink, pencil, watercolors, pastels, and oils. However, *what* to paint must come from within, from her desire to paint something, not just be able to.

4. **Analyze the changes in O'Keeffe's reactions to her teachers' evaluations of her work and how they affected her development as an artist.**
   Answer: In the beginning she reacted personally to her teachers' evaluations, so she painted to please the teachers; but after studying with Dow, she learned that she had to paint from her desire to express something, not simply be able to paint.
   Inference Type: Explain why/how

When O'Keeffe went to Texas to teach, she made a handful of charcoal drawings, which she sent to a friend in New York. The friend, Anna Pollitzer, showed them to Alfred Stieglitz, a photographer and gallery owner. He was enthused with the vibrant energy of the work and asked to show them. So, without her knowledge, Georgia O'Keeffe had her first exhibition in 1916 at Stieglitz's *291 Gallery* in New York. It was one of the few times that O'Keeffe was not enraged that someone would take something of hers and display it without her permission. A review of her work in the *Christian Science Monitor* by Henry Tyrrell said that she "draws with unconscious naiveté what purports to be the innermost unfolding of a girl's being, like the germinating of a flower." Stieglitz was amazed that a woman expressed herself so frankly on paper. He believed her to represent all women when he said that, "Woman is at last on paper, expressing her relation to the Universe." Her career coincided with that of Freud, who touted a sexual interpretation of human behavior based on the client's relationship with his or her parents. People often interpreted O'Keeffe's work through the Freudian lens by describing her paintings in sexual terms. This infuriated her because she felt the sexual interpretation was a simple way to dismiss her paintings without serious analysis.

5. **What do the underlined words reveal about how others evaluated her work?**
   Answer: Her work was seen as an expression of her developing self (innermost unfolding; germinating of a flower) without concern for how others would judge it.

Level: High School

6. **How did the time period in which O'Keeffe's paintings were first exhibited affect how art critics interpreted her work?**

   Answer: Her early paintings occurred when the world was affected by the writings of Freud, who wrote extensively on sexual interests of adults that were expressed in indirect ways. A work of art gives an indirect message, so it could be interpreted sexually.

   Inference Type: Explain why/how

During the spring of 1916 while she was in New York, she first met the man who had praised her drawings beyond anyone else. Alfred Stieglitz warmly welcomed her to the *291 Gallery* showing her works of other artists whom he supported. However, soon he overstepped his bounds and displayed some of O'Keeffe's works without her permission. She challenged him and he retorted that she had no right to deny the world to see her work. Over a lunch, Stieglitz used his powerful persuasion and flirtation to convince her to leave her paintings in the gallery. O'Keeffe demurred but she was playing her own game because she *wanted* to display in his gallery but also wanted his respect.

On May 2, 1916, Georgia's mother died from hemorrhaging in her lungs at the age of 52. Georgia was devastated, and it affected her painting. Unable to produce anything that met her standards, she spent the summer grieving, climbing Mt. Elliot in Virginia, and reading. Stieglitz's encouragement enabled her to begin painting again, producing over 40 works later that summer. During a camping trip, O'Keeffe found herself looking out of a tent at a distant light. Her emotional isolation and view to the outside were later represented in drawings, watercolors, and an oil painting. An image of the door to the outside became a recurrent theme in O'Keefe's art for many years.

Having no reason to stay in Virginia, she returned to the panhandle of Texas to teach. She was enamored of the empty open sky that seemed to go on forever. Forever curious about nature she spent a night in a canyon watching the moonrise. She returned to the same place at dawn to get a new perspective and watched the colors of the sky as black changed to blue to gray and eventually a white sky appeared. The perspective of open sky prompted a series of paintings, among them *Blue II* (1916).

7. **Provide strong and thorough evidence that emotions affect what an artist is able to create.**

   Answer: After her mother died, O'Keeffe was unable to paint because of her grief; OR her love of the open sky led her to spend a night in a canyon watching the moon rise and again watching at dawn; AND these images led to a series of paintings (e.g., Blue II).

   Inference type: Support statements about a text

Level: High School

It was during this time that Stieglitz wrote to O'Keeffe daily and sent her essays on modern art by critics. Her first solo exhibition, including the watercolors and charcoals of South Carolina, was presented at *291 Gallery*. The introduction of O'Keeffe to Stieglitz changed her professional and personal life. Alfred Stieglitz became a mentor to O'Keeffe and provided her with financial security by exhibiting her paintings in his gallery. It was through him that art lovers became aware of O'Keeffe's paintings.

During the winter of 1917–18 she contracted the Spanish influenza and had to take a leave of absence from teaching. Despite urging from Stieglitz to come to New York, she was too ill to travel that far and instead went to southeastern Texas. When she was well enough, she went to New York, but the journey tired her out and she fell ill again. The personal relationship between 54-year-old Stieglitz and 31-year-old O'Keeffe developed as he and his niece took care of her daily needs. The tender care that he provided her led to an intimacy that she had not expected. To the outside world, he provided her with an apartment in New York, but those in the art world knew that he was more than a mentor to her.

Stieglitz was the country's most famous photographer and wanted to photograph O'Keeffe in the nude. Once she was posing for him in his apartment when his wife came home. She was furious and gave him a choice, get rid of his model or move out of the house. Their marriage had not been a fulfilling one for either of them, so he happily left. Although his wife changed her mind and wanted him home, he did not return.

Stieglitz photographed O'Keeffe in "his idealization of femininity—passive, beauty, illness, and tragedy." In addition to the psychosexual theories of the time, the nude photographs of O'Keeffe contributed to the sexual interpretation of her paintings, particularly, flowers.

8. **What do the words in quotations in the paragraph above mean?**
   Answer: That Stieglitz's photographs of O'Keeffe represented his idealization of women who he perceived were beautiful and passive, but also tragic. She represented "woman" to him.
   Inference Type: Understand the meaning of words/phrases

O'Keeffe's relationship with Stieglitz was complicated as she loved him and his intellect, and he provided financial security as well as her entry into the art world. On the other hand, she sought to be alone, so she could paint. The struggle between independence and dependence challenged

Level: High School

was originally a bird flu that **mutated** to spread to humans. Many historians now believe that the virus originated in the United States, then traveled around the world. Once the virus began, it spread like a wildfire and killed millions worldwide like a predator feasting on its prey. The great influenza pandemic, coming on the heels of the Great War, gave a sense of doom and dread to people around the globe.

2. **Which text structure best explains how the author organized the above passage titled "Flu Epidemic Grips the Nation"?**
   _____*description of important features*
   _____*explanation of steps in a sequence*
   _____*account of cause and effect*
   _____*explanation of problem and solution*
   _____*comparison/contrast of two or more things*

   Give a reason from the text for your answer. For example, if you choose description, tell what is being described. If you choose sequence, list two steps. For cause and effect, state a cause or effect mentioned in the text. For problem and solution, tell what the problem is or describe the solution. For comparison, tell what is being compared or contrasted.
   Answer: Description: The author describes the flu epidemic. OR Cause and effect: The author explains the cause of the flu epidemic and/or its effects on people.
   Inference Type: Identify text structure

   Note: This question has two separate answers: identification of structure and explanation of reason.

3. **What is the meaning of "mutated" in the context of the above passage?**
   Answer: Changed, transformed, altered.
   Inference Type: Determine word meaning

Women and African Americans Confront New Realities

Women and African Americans made significant advances during the war. However, the end of the war also spelled the end of wartime economic opportunities for both groups. A postwar recession, or economic slowdown, created a competitive job market. By 1920, there were fewer women in the workforce than there had been in 1910.

In northern industrial cities, African American workers vied with returning soldiers for jobs and housing. During the hot summer of 1919, race riots erupted in cities throughout the country. The worst, in Chicago, was triggered by the drowning of a young black man by whites and went on for 13 days. In 1921, violence erupted in Tulsa, Oklahoma, when armed African American men, many of them returning veterans, tried to protect a young black man from lynching. By the time the Tulsa race riots were over, at least 10 whites and 26 African Americans were dead. In one African American neighborhood, white rioters burned 35 city blocks to the ground.

4. **Analyze why economic advances made by women and African Americans during the war did not continue.**
   Answer: There was a postwar recession, which led to fewer jobs; AND/OR returning soldiers competed for jobs.
   Inference Type: Explain why or how

Level: High School

determi
found u
Diagnos

Piloting

The pil
that we
words (
"jump,"
to mod
through
ued to
assessed

The
dents fr
fall of 2
fore, no
the stud
permiss
from or
was nee

Of t
were m
65% wl
and 0.7

Analys

A descr
In this

1. Ar
   the
   tex
   rea
   de
   on
   the
   nc
   ad

Table

Mean
S.D.
N

2. W
   re
   th
   or
   th
   gr
   si

Inflation Leads to Labor Unrest

During the war, inflation, or rising prices, had been held in check. After the conflict, Americans rushed to buy consumer goods rather than war bonds. The scarcity of these goods, coupled with widespread demand, caused inflation. During the war, the price of corn, wheat, cotton, cattle, and other agricultural goods had risen, encouraged by the president's policies. After the war, prices fell sharply, making it difficult for farmers to pay their mortgages or buy what they needed for the next growing season. This began a long period of tough times for farmers.

5. **Analyze what caused inflation after the war.**
   Answer: People wanted to buy goods that were scarce, so prices went up.
   <u>Inference Type: Explain why or how</u>

Industrial workers also felt the pain of inflation when their wages did not buy as much as they had during the war. In 1919, more than 4 million workers, or 20% of the workforce, went on strike at one time or another. Demanding rewards for their wartime patriotism, workers struck for higher wages and shorter workdays. In Boston, even the police force struck. The workers won some of the strikes, but they lost far more. When some strikes turned violent, the pro-management press blamed the presence of radicals among the strike leaders.

6. **The topic of the above two paragraphs is "inflation." What is the central idea?**
   Answer: Inflation resulted in difficult times and labor unrest.
   <u>Inference Type: Determine the central idea</u>

7. **What was the postwar point of view of the industrial workers?**
   Answer: They believed they should be rewarded for their patriotism during the war; AND/OR they believed they should make more money; AND/OR they believed they should work fewer hours.
   <u>Inference Type: Determine point of view</u>

The Red Scare

The reaction against labor was partly spurred by a wave of fear of radicals and communists. Revolutionary activity abroad, coupled with strikes across the United States, prompted the first American Red Scare, a wave of widespread fear of those thought to be plotting revolution within the United States. Real revolutionary activity inside America gave substance to the scare. Authorities discovered bombs mailed to important industrialists and government officials. Suspected anarchists, members of a radical political movement, exploded bombs in cities across America.

results suggest that as students' decoding skills increase across reading levels, they can figure out progressively more words than they recognize automatically.

Correlational analyses were also conducted to examine the relationships between the percentages of correct words read automatically, total percentage correct, and words correct per minute (WCPM) in stories. At each instructional level, the correlation between the percentage of words recognized automatically on the word list and WCPM in stories was slightly higher than the same analysis using only the total percentage of words read correctly on the word list. This result suggests that words read automatically predict rate and accuracy of word reading in text. The analysis of the Reading by Analogy Test is found in Section 5.

DEVELOPMENT AND ANALYSIS OF THE PRIOR-KNOWLEDGE ASSESSMENTS

Identification of Concepts

We chose the concepts for the conceptual-questions task based on the implicit comprehension questions. Chrystal (1991) found that concepts chosen because of their relationship to implicit questions correlated more highly with comprehension than did concepts not chosen for that purpose. Therefore, in developing *QRI* concepts, the authors and two master's degree students in reading independently chose concepts necessary to understand implicit questions on each passage. For example, consider the first-grade passage "The Bear and the Rabbit." The last question is a difficult one for many young readers: "Why did the bear and the rabbit become friends?" We felt that in order to answer that question, using the clues in the passage, children needed to know that one reason why people become friends is shared interests (in this case, their love of music). Thus, we chose the concept question "What makes a friend?" After the four of us independently chose concepts, we met to examine the consistency of our selections. We were pleased to discover that in over 90% of the cases, we chose the same concepts. Often our wording was different, so we negotiated what we thought would be the best wording, and final decisions were made after piloting.

Analyses of Correlations Between Prior Knowledge and Other Test Components

1. **Is knowledge or general reading ability more predictive of comprehension?** Previous editions of the *QRI* addressed this question, and specific details of the analyses can be found in the fourth and fifth editions. An analysis of this question on materials in grade 4 through upper middle school found that the prior-knowledge assessment correlated significantly with a measure of comprehension on 12 of the 14 passages. On the six middle school texts, prior knowledge was the best predictor of one or more comprehension measures. Similar results were found using high school materials.

   In summary, prior knowledge of concepts contained in passages correlated significantly with passage comprehension more frequently than did a general measure of reading achievement. This finding illustrates the value of measuring conceptual knowledge in reading assessment.

2. **How much prior knowledge is enough?** We conducted discriminant function analyses on all passages that showed significant correlations between the total concept scores and the total comprehension score to determine which concept score best discriminated instructional-level comprehension (70%+) from frustration-level comprehension (< 70%). The concept score that best predicted the cutoff score was obtained from the classification function coefficients. The average concept score across the passages was 55% (range 40–66%, with 70%

between 50% and 60%). Therefore, we used 55% of the points on the concept measure as the criterion for familiar.

DEVELOPMENT OF THE MEASURES OF COMPREHENSION: LEVEL-DIAGNOSTIC MATERIALS

We use three measures of comprehension:

- a retelling measure of what the student remembers from the passage;
- explicit questions (those for which the answer is stated explicitly in the passage); and
- implicit questions (for which an inference must be made to answer the question).

We include both the retelling and question measures of comprehension, because research has indicated that the two are measuring some different components of comprehension.

The authors designed the questions. Those from narrative texts were designed around the goal of the main character (protagonist), which is the focus around which all other information is interpreted. Therefore, in all narratives, one question asks for the goal of the protagonist. The other questions were designed to tap important information the student uses to make a coherent representation of the text. That is, a detail was questioned if it was an important detail in the story, but not if it was unimportant. In expository text of third-grade readability and above, the first question always asks for the implicit main idea of the passage. Again, the other questions were written to tap understanding of important information contained in the exposition. In each case the authors read each passage and questions and categorized the questions into explicit/implicit categories. If the authors disagreed on whether an answer was explicitly or implicitly stated in the passage, the question was rewritten or dropped.

At the high school level, a different procedure was used. We gave the texts to high school teachers of the relevant content (e.g., History teachers read the history texts), and asked them to underline the segments of text they thought were important for students to remember. Then they were asked to reread the texts and underline (in a different color) the segments that they thought students would remember after one reading. If a segment of text was underlined by 50% or more of the teachers, it was put on the high school retelling sheet. If over 20% of students recalled a segment that the teachers had not marked, it was added. Although this did not occur frequently, there were details that over 20% of students remembered that teachers did not believe were important. Thus, the retelling sheets were a combination of teachers' judgments of important propositions and students' memory of text.

Analyses of the Measures of Comprehension on Level-Diagnostic Passages

1. **What is the relationship between explicit and implicit comprehension?** Because there are only four or five explicit questions and zero, two, four, or five implicit questions per passage, depending on the level of the passages, any conclusion about a child's ability to answer these types of questions based on the administration of *a single passage* is not recommended. Based on the standard error of measurement on explicit and implicit questions on two passages (eight of each type of question), if a student answered three to four explicit questions and only one or no implicit questions correctly on *two or more passages at his or her instructional level in familiar text,* then the difference is of diagnostic significance. This figure was determined by considering the standard error of measurement of these questions. The standard error of measurement of the difference between two scores is roughly equal to the square root of the sum of the squared standard errors of both tests (Thorndike et al., 1991).

2. **Is comprehension different in narrative and expository text?** Table 13.2 presents the means and standard deviations for proportion of correct scores on conceptual knowledge, retelling, comprehension, and total comprehension (when look-backs were counted) on narrative and expository texts as a function of readability levels in fourth grade through high school. Differences between the retelling of narrative and expository texts were found only at the fourth-grade and upper middle school levels. Retelling was quite low at the fifth- and sixth-grade levels and again at the high school level. The only comprehension difference based on questions between narrative and expository texts was found at the upper middle school level.

It should be noted that students answered many more questions when allowed to look back in the text.

Table 13.2 Means and Standard Deviations for Proportion of Correct Scores on Conceptual Knowledge, Retelling, Comprehension, and Total Comprehension on Narrative and Expository Texts as a Function of Readability Level

Readability Level	Conceptual Knowledge	Retelling	Comp	Total Comp
Fourth (*n* = 12)				
Narrative	.56 (.26)	.26 (.12)*	.55 (.08)	.67 (.08)
Expository	.63 (.26)	.18 (.07)	.58 (.18)	.50 (.23)
Fifth (*n* = 14)				
Narrative	.57 (.29)	.19 (.13)	.72 (.10)	.81 (.10)
Expository	.62 (.42)*	.18 (.11)	.81 (.40)	.91 (.11)
Sixth (*n* = 32)				
Narrative	.77 (.18)*	.14 (.08)	.68 (.17)	.94 (.09)
Expository	.68 (.23)	.17 (.09)	.67 (.18)	.86 (.24)
Upper Middle School (*n* = 46)				
Narrative	.75 (.23)	.28 (.16)*	.84 (.17)*	.97 (.05)
Expository	.71 (.20)	.13 (.97)	.66 (.18)	.95 (.08)
High School (*n* = 12)				
Social Studies	.47 (.25)	.09 (.11)	.43 (.25)	.85 (.14)
Science	.41 (.21)	.11 (.11)	.28 (.11)*	.75 (.14)

Note: * = A significant difference between narrative and expository text (*p* < .05) was found on that dependent variable.

Analysis of Look-Back Data   Table 13.3 presents the means and standard deviations of comprehension assessed with and without look-backs. It shows that students with a reading instructional level at third grade or higher can answer more questions when allowed to look back. In general, students were better able to increase their explicit comprehension because the answers to the questions were stated directly in the text and were complex details that taxed memory. We believe that allowing students reading at the third-grade level and above the opportunity to look back in text provides the examiner with useful information to separate problems in comprehension versus problems with memory of what was read.

We examined whether the comprehension or total comprehension scores (i.e., with look-backs) were more often correlated with standardized measures of reading comprehension by comparing the correlations between Terra Nova Standard Scores or Percentile Ranks and comprehension scores with and without look-backs. The results varied by grade level. At grades 4 through upper middle school correlations were more often significant when comprehension was measured without look-backs rather

Table 13.3 Means and Standard Deviation of Comprehension with and without Look-Backs

Passage	Level	n	Comprehension Scores	
			Without Look-Backs	With Look-Backs
"A Special Birthday for Rosa"	3	25	.82 (.08)	.89 (.18)
"Tomie dePaola"	4	76	.47 (.22)	.68 (.12)
"Early Railroads"	4	22	.52 (.21)	.67 (.18)
"Plant Structures for Survival"	4	20	.37 (.20)	.55 (.23)
"Patricia McKissack"	5	52	.59 (.18)	.70 (.19)
"Farming on the Great Plains"	5	17	.60 (.16)	.89 (.16)
"How Does Your Body Take in Oxygen?"	5	14	.70 (.25)	.88 (.22)
"The Early Life of Lois Lowry"	6	33	.69 (.17)	.95 (.08)
"Temperature and Humidity"	6	27	.54 (.24)	.69 (.29)
"Clouds and Precipitation"	6	19	.66 (.17)	.91 (.16)
"Building Pyramids"	6	32	.79 (.19)	.89 (.13)
"The Lifeline of the Nile"	6	29	.70 (.17)	.93 (.09)
"Immigration—Part 1"	MS	11	.77 (.26)	.98 (.04)
"Immigration—Part 2"	MS	11	.80 (.13)	1.00 (.00)
"Life Cycles of Stars—Part 1"	MS	18	.58 (.23)	.92 (.11)
"Life Cycles of Stars—Part 2"	MS	13	.58 (.19)	.92 (.09)

than with look-backs. Therefore, we recommend that the comprehension score *without* look-backs be used to estimate instructional reading level at these levels. In contrast, the standardized test scores of students reading the high school passages significantly correlated with comprehension including look-backs more frequently than without them. Therefore, we conclude that comprehension *with* look-backs should be the score to use to determine the instructional level on the high school texts on the *QRI-7*.

DEVELOPMENT OF THE THINK-ALOUD PROCEDURE

The *QRI-3* introduced the think-aloud procedure (TAL) at the high school level, and the *QRI-4* extended the think-aloud procedure into middle school. A middle school level passage, "The Mining Boom," was used to model different types of think-alouds, those that indicate understanding and those that do not. Figure 8.1, in Section 8, provides a list of the types of think-alouds within these two categories. After observing the modeling, the students read one 423-word section of an expository text without thinking aloud, and the next 417-word section of text while thinking aloud.

The location of the stop points (marked as //) that indicated it was time to think aloud varied depended on the complexity of the text and our judgment of where a think-aloud might facilitate comprehension. We include stops after the statements of main ideas and after groups of sentences that support main ideas. For example, on an upper middle school social studies text, a // was placed after six sentences that describe the main idea of a paragraph. Later, a // was placed between two paragraphs where the first introduced a new topic and the second expanded on the topic.

Details of the think-aloud studies can be found in the *QRI-3, QRI-4 or QRI-5* and in Caldwell and Leslie (2010). The TAL procedure was used with middle school students reading material at their instructional level. Students reading the sixth-grade text recalled more if they thought aloud, but students reading the eighth-grade text recalled less if they thought aloud. Despite this inexplicable result, the type of clauses

their growth. These data suggest that reading acquisition is a developmental process that is sensitive to different instructional methods. The students' abilities can be assessed by the *QRI,* and relevant instructional decisions can be made.

Issues of Reliability of an Informal Reading Inventory

Interrater Reliability.   Standard 2.7 of the *Standards for Educational and Psychological Testing* (2014) indicates that when subjective judgment enters into test scoring, evidence should be provided on both interrater consistency in scoring and within examinee consistency over repeated measures. We examined the reliability of judges' scores on total percentage of miscues, percentage of meaning-change miscues, prior-knowledge concept score, total explicit comprehension score and total implicit comprehension score, and recall. All examiners had the same scoring manual to judge these scores. However, our expert scorers ($n = 3$) were reading teachers or specialists who had master's degrees. Thus, our reliability estimates compare persons without extensive training by the test developers to those with training by the test developers. It should be noted that the experts did not receive their master's degrees from the program of either test author, but one test author trained the experts in the scoring.

Estimates of the inter-scorer reliability of the conceptual knowledge questions found agreement on 299 of the 304 concepts sampled, for a 98% agreement. Estimates of inter-scorer reliability of total miscues, acceptable miscues, and explicit and implicit comprehension were assessed by examining data from 122 readings. These data were gathered across all readability levels and both types of text. Of the 122 readings, 49 were conducted orally. Thus, the estimate of reliability for total miscues and acceptable miscues is based on 49 observations. The estimates of inter-scorer reliability were found using Cronbach's alpha (Cronbach, 1951). Alpha reliability estimates were .99 for total miscues, .99 for meaning-change miscues, .98 for explicit comprehension, and .98 for implicit comprehension. These reliability estimates are higher than those reported by Benjamin, et al., (2013), but similar to those reported by Dickens & Meisinger (2017) and Morris et al. (2011) indicating a high degree of consistency between scorers. Thus, an examiner should be able to score the *QRI* reliably without extensive training.

A reliability study (Bernstein, J., 2004) using oral reading data from the National Assessment of Adult Literacy found that different raters were able to reliably score Total Accuracy (.96) and Total Acceptability (.96). In addition, each rater was examined on the same recording twice. The mean intra-rater reliability for Total Accuracy was .97 and for Total Acceptability was .95. The raters all had undergraduate degrees, all had taught for a minimum of two years, and many had advanced degrees in education or linguistics. The raters received an instruction manual that explained all aspects of the study followed by an interactive training session conducted by phone.

Internal Consistency Reliability.   This form of reliability examines how reliable the score is as an estimate of the true score. For example, when we measure total comprehension, how reliable is the score as an estimate of the student's true comprehension score?

The standard error of measurement of the comprehension score was estimated through an analysis of variance with items (1–5; 1–6; 1–8; 1–10) as the within-subject factor and subjects as the between-subjects factor. Crocker and Algina (1986) recommended the use of the standard error of measurement rather than a correlational estimate of reliability for tests where there is reduced variability in the student's performance. Remember that a correlation is based, in part, on variability. In our case, we did not give harder passages to students who scored as frustrated on easier material, and so we reduced variability. Thus, a traditional correlational measure of reliability would not accurately reflect the reliability of the scores. Similarly, because the alpha coefficient is based on variability, it is subject to the same restrictions. Crocker and

Algina (1986, p. 196) illustrated that the standard error of a criterion-referenced test can be very low (such as .001), indicating a highly reliable score; yet the reliability, expressed as a generalizability coefficient, could be very low (.00). This happens when there is no variability in the data. Because we have restricted variability, we chose to use the standard error of measurement. The formula for determining the standard error of measurement from analysis of variance data is:

$$\text{Standard error of measurement} = \sqrt{\dfrac{\dfrac{MS_i - MS_r}{n_p} + MS_r}{n_i}}$$

where MS_i = mean square for items
MS_r = mean square residual
n_i = number of items
n_p = number of persons

Table 13.6 presents the mean, standard deviation, and standard error of measurement (SEM) of the proportion correct comprehension score for all passages. Consider the highest SEM for an eight-item test, .18 for "Wool: From Sheep to You." A student with a score of 75% has a true score between 57% and 93%, 68% of the time. Because of the relatively large SEMs on any single passage, we recommend that an examiner

Table 13.6 Means and Standard Deviations and Standard Errors of Measurement of Proportion Correct Comprehension Scores for Level-Diagnostic Passages on the *QRI-6*

Passage Level and Name	Mean	SD	n	SEM
Pre-Primer				
"I Can"	.71	.18	23	.20
"I See"	.95	.13	23	.18
"Just Like Mom"	.82	.17	69	.21
"Lost and Found"	.90	.12	83	.13
"Lost and Found"*	.74	.24	36	.19
"Spring and Fall"	.70	.16	56	.20
"Spring and Fall"*	.60	.19	41	.22
"People at Work"	.30	.20	28	.20
Primer				
"A Night in the City"	.70	.28	14	.21
"Fox and Mouse"	.76	.30	51	.14
"Fox and Mouse"*	.63	.22	48	.19
"The Pig Who Learned to Read"	.75	.28	65	.19
"The Pig Who Learned to Read"*	.61	.32	50	.20
"Who Lives Near Lakes?"	.67	.19	12	.19
"Living and Not Living"	.58	.17	25	.21
First				
"The Surprise"	.86	.14	25	.14
"Marva Finds a Friend"	.86	.14	94	.14
"Marva Finds a Friend"*	.64	.18	72	.18
"The Bear and the Rabbit"	.76	.27	57	.18
"The Bear and the Rabbit"*	.54	.36	67	.21
"Air"	.55	.27	18	.19

(continued)

Table 13.6 (*Continued*)

Passage Level and Name	Mean	SD	*n*	SEM
"The Brain and the Five Senses"	.78	.16	8	.17
"The Brain and the Five Senses"*	.47	.16	13	.17
Second				
"The Lucky Cricket"	.81	.10	78	.14
"The Lucky Cricket"*	.58	.20	82	.17
"The Family's First Trip"	.81	.18	32	.14
"Father's New Game"	.80	.12	74	.13
"Father's New Game"*	.49	.19	91	.17
"Whales and Fish"	.68	.18	17	.17
"Seasons"	.50	.22	13	.17
Third				
"A Special Birthday for Rosa"	.86	.13	72	.12
"A Special Birthday for Rosa"*	.57	.19	73	.17
"A New Friend from Europe"	.83	.24	25	.17
"The Friend"	.60	.20	25	.17
"Cats: Lions and Tigers in Your House"	.69	.21	20	.16
"Where Do People Live?"	.47	.30	20	.16
"Wool: From Sheep to You"	.45	.19	14	.18
Fourth				
"Amelia Earhart"	.64	.16	18	.18
"Amelia Earhart"*	.51	.20	43	.17
"Tomie dePaola"	.61	.21	34	.16
"Tomie dePaola"*	.46	.26	108	.23
"Early Railroads"	.52	.22	22	.17
"Plant Structures for Survival"	.37	.17	20	.17
Fifth				
"Margaret Mead"	.66	.18	23	.16
"Patricia McKissack"	.65	.22	17	.16
"Patricia McKissack"*	.59	.20	52	.17
"Farming on the Great Plains"	.60	.23	17	.17
"How Does Your Body Take in Oxygen?"	.71	.20	14	.14
Sixth				
"Abraham Lincoln"	.75	.17	20	.16
"The Early Life of Lois Lowry"	.69	.17	33	.12
"The Early Life of Lois Lowry"*	.35	.19	18	.14
"The Lifeline of the Nile"	.71	.14	22	.16
"Building Pyramids"	.79	.19	32	.14
"Temperature and Humidity"	.55	.22	23	.16
"Clouds and Precipitation"	.67	.20	17	.16
Upper Middle School				
Literature				
"Jaime Escalante"	.67	.24	49	.22
Social Studies				

(*continued*)

Table 13.6 *(Continued)*

Passage Level and Name	Mean	SD	*n*	SEM
"Immigration—Part 1"	.77	.26	11	.11
"Immigration—Part 2"	.80	.13	11	.14
Science				
"Life Cycles of Stars—Part 1"	.58	.14	18	.16
"Life Cycles of Stars—Part 2"	.54	.18	13	.16
High School				
Social Studies				
"World War I—Part 1"	.37	.24	35	.14
"World War I—Part 2"	.42	.26	27	.14
Science				
"Characteristics of Viruses—Part 1"	.29	.18	35	.14
"Characteristics of Viruses—Part 2"	.29	.19	30	.14

*You will note that we have presented separate standard error of measurement (SEM) estimates for mean scores in the instructional-level range and in the frustration-level range for narrative text through sixth grade. According to Standard 2.14 from the *Standards for Educational and Psychological Testing*, "When possible and appropriate standard errors of measurement should be reported at several score levels unless there is evidence that the standard error is constant across score levels" (2014, p. 46). The data presented indicate that when comprehension scores fall within the instructional-level range, the SEM is usually smaller than when scores fall in the frustration-level range.

give passages of the same type (such as narrative or expository) with which the student is familiar when attempting to estimate true score. When the examiner uses two passages the percentage correct is determined from 16 to 20 items depending on the grade level of the material. The standard error is based on 16 items and is reduced substantially. When we pooled data from children who read two third-grade stories, the SEM for 16 items was .10. Thus, a child with a total score of 75% has a true score that lies between 65% and 85%, 68% of the time; this is a much more reliable estimate of true score than their separate SEMs of .14 and .14 based on eight items.

Cautions in Interpretation

Because of the relatively large SEMs on any single passage, we recommend that an examiner give Level-Diagnostic passages of the same type (such as narrative or expository) with which the student is familiar when attempting to estimate true score. For similar reasons, we cannot recommend that users interpret scores for explicit and implicit comprehension on a single passage. First, these subtests do not contain enough items to be reliable indicators of the children's true scores in these areas if only one passage is used. Even when the examiner uses two passages, and the total number of explicit items from both passages is compared to the total number of implicit items from both passages, large differences are needed for reliable diagnostic conclusions. When we pooled explicit items from two third-grade stories, we obtained a SEM of .13; the standard error for implicit items was .14. The standard error of the *difference* between these two is .20. (The formula is SEM_{diff} = the square root of the sum of the two squared SEMs.)

Thus, only if a student received scores of 75% to 100% correct on explicit questions and 0% to 25% correct on implicit questions can we be 95% sure that these scores do not overlap. If a student receives explicit and implicit scores that differ by as much as 50% on two or more passages, then an interpretation that a student is better in answering one type of question than the other is more reliable.

Table 13.7 presents the mean and standard deviation of proportion correct on the Inference-Diagnostic measures of comprehension and includes the standard error of measurement and alpha reliability measures.

Table 13.7 Mean, Standard Deviation, Standard Error of Measurement of Comprehension Scores, and Alpha Reliability on Inference-Diagnostic Materials

	Mean	SD	N	SEM	Alpha
Fourth					
Biography: Cynthia Rylant	.36	.28	7	.20	.62
Social Studies: Linking East and West	.29	.20	31	.14	.62
Science: How Do Organisms Compete for Resources	.45	.30	8	.14	.80
Fifth					
Biography: Jane Goodall	.30	.24	13	.17	.60
Social Studies: The Rise of Cattle Drives			< 6		
Science: The Body's Transportation System	.46	.25	6	.16	.71
Sixth					
Biography: Jim Thorpe	.65	.27	30	.18	.58
Social Studies: From Dynasty to Dynasty	.54	.25	22	.16	.67
Science: What Causes Weather			< 6		
Upper Middle School					
Biography: Malcolm X	.42	.40	25	.18	.83
Social Studies: A Wave of Nativism	.39	.24	39	.15	.66
Science: What Is a Comet?			< 6		

Test-Retest and Alternate Form Reliability

In a study of a summer reading program in the state of Michigan, researchers examined whether student scores on the *QRI-3* were reliable over time. Positive and significant test-retest reliability was reported in Paris et al. (2002).

Alternate-Form Reliability (Consistency) of Placement Decisions. If the major purpose is to determine an instructional level, then it is important to have consistency in that level. Thus, the reliability issue becomes: "If I find an instructional level of fifth grade on this test, would I find an instructional level of fifth grade if I gave the test tomorrow or next week?" This type of reliability is called *test-retest reliability*, the consistency of test results over time or conditions. As many test developers have learned, there is a problem in giving the same test over two time periods in order to assess test-retest reliability, because the student may learn something in the first administration that changes his or her score on the second administration.

An alternative method of estimating level reliability is to examine performance on two passages similar in design; this method is called *alternate-form reliability* (*Standards*, 2014, p. 37). In the *QRI-6*, this means that we would examine performance on two similar passage types (such as narratives or familiar expository). If performance on these indicates the same instructional level, we have evidence for alternate-form reliability.

To obtain the best estimate of alternate-form reliability of level, we examined the reliability of the total comprehension score to estimate instructional level across passages of the same type. The procedure used to estimate alternate-form reliability was Livingston's (1972) K^2. This index reflects the magnitude of the discrepancy of misclassification in judging the reliability of the decision. In our case, the question is:

"How close are the two comprehension scores to the cutoff of 70% for instructional level?" The formula for K^2 may be found in Crocker and Algina (1986, p. 203).

The data on the Level-Diagnostic primer through third passages indicated that of the 149 students who read two passages at the same level of readability, 88% scored at instructional level in comprehension on the new story as well as a previous one in the *QRI*. When we analyzed by readability level, at the pre-primer level the new stories were written to be easier than the previously easiest story, "Just Like Mom." And as expected, the new stories "I Can" and "I See" were easier than "Just Like Mom," but were similar to each other. "I Can" is a bit easier to read accurately, and "I See" is easier to retell and answer comprehension questions. At the primer level the two stories matched 100% of the time, at the first-grade level matches occurred 91% of the time, at the second-grade level matches occurred 84% of the time, and at the third-grade level, matches occurred 79% of the time.

The reliabilities of our instructional-level decisions at all other levels based on comprehension scores were all above .80; 75% were greater than or equal to .90. In addition, we examined whether the same instructional level would be indicated using the comprehension scores on each passage. Across the readability levels, 75% to 81% of the time the same instructional level would be found on both passages (specifically, at fourth, 80%; fifth, 75%; sixth, 77%; and upper middle school, 81% of the time).

Because all reading assessment involves interpretation (Afflerbach, 2012) we have offered evidence to indicate the appropriate and inappropriate uses and interpretations of the *QRI*. There are additional misuses that we wish to address. The *QRI* is not a high-stakes test and *should not* be used by itself to decide upon promotions to a higher grade. We also acknowledge that the instructional levels found should not be used to restrict students' access to harder material. If a student is very interested in a topic, he or she will persist in reading it, unlike many content textbooks. We hope that you will find our reliability and validity data helpful.

Appendix

Videos for Extra Practice (Pearson eText)

DIRECTIONS

Note: The interactive resources in this section are available via the Pearson eText.

This section provides videos of full-length *QRI* sessions for six different students that you can use to practice scoring and interpreting assessment results. Each session is accompanied by blank versions of the examiner protocols that you can print and use to practice scoring. On the next page you will find links to examiner protocols for each session that have been scored by the authors so you can compare your results.

We also recommend filling out a Student Summary Form for each session as part of your practice. Author-scored versions of the summary form are included on pages 526–527.

Pearson eText Teacher Resource: Blank Student Summary Form

Roberto—Grade 1

Pearson eText

Video Example A.1:
Roberto's Word Lists

Pearson eText

Teacher Resource: Roberto Blank Word Lists for Scoring

Pearson eText

Video Example A.2:
Roberto's Passages

Pearson eText

Teacher Resource: Roberto Blank Passages for Scoring

Sophia—Grade 1

Pearson eText

Video Example A.3:
Sophia's Word Lists

Pearson eText

Teacher Resource: Sophia
Blank Word Lists for Scoring

Pearson eText

Video Example A.4:
Sophia's Passages

Pearson eText

Teacher Resource: Sophia
Blank Passages for Scoring

Ailyn—Grade 2

Pearson eText

Video Example A.5:
Ailyn's Word Lists

Pearson eText

Teacher Resource: Ailyn
Blank Word Lists for Scoring

Pearson eText

Video Example A.6:
Ailyn's Passages

Pearson eText

Teacher Resource: Ailyn
Blank Passages for Scoring

Nicolas—Grade 3

Pearson eText

Video Example A.7:
Nicolas's Word Lists

Pearson eText

Teacher Resource: Nicolas
Blank Word Lists for Scoring

Pearson eText

Video Example A.8:
Nicolas's Passages

Pearson eText

Teacher Resource: Nicolas
Blank Passages for Scoring

Calvin—Grade 3

Pearson eText

Video Example A.9:
Calvin's Word Lists

Pearson eText

Teacher Resource: Calvin
Blank Word Lists for Scoring

Pearson eText

Video Example A.10:
Calvin's Passages

Pearson eText

Teacher Resource: Calvin
Blank Passages for Scoring

Vann—Grade 3

Pearson eText

Video Example A.11:
Vann's Passage

Pearson eText

Teacher Resource: Vann
Blank Passage for Scoring

Author-Scored Protocols

DIRECTIONS

This section provides links to author-scored protocols for the practice videos found in the previous section. Use these resources to check your work.

Roberto—Grade 1

Pearson eText Teacher Resource: Roberto's Scored Word Lists

Roberto's Scored Passages

Roberto's Student Summary Form

Sophia—Grade 1

Pearson eText Teacher Resource: Sophia's Scored Word Lists

Sophia's Scored Passages

Sophia's Student Summary Form

Ailyn—Grade 2

Pearson eText Teacher Resource: Ailyn's Scored Word Lists

Ailyn's Scored Passages

Ailyn's Student Summary Form

Nicolas—Grade 3

Pearson eText Teacher Resource: Nicolas's Scored Word Lists

Nicolas's Scored Passages

Nicolas's Student Summary Form

Calvin—Grade 3

Pearson eText Teacher Resource: Calvin's Scored Word Lists

Calvin's Scored Passages

Calvin's Student Summary Form

Vann—Grade 3

Pearson eText Teacher Resource: Vann's Scored Passages

Vann's Student Summary Form

References

An asterisk (*) marks a sample of published studies that used the **QRI** to describe reading behavior, to compare different assessment measures, and/or to document growth in reading.

Afflerbach, P. (2012). *Understanding and using reading assessment, K–12*. Newark, DE: International Reading Association.

American Educational Research Association, American Psychological Association, and National Council on Measurement in Education. (2014). *Standards for educational and psychological testing*. Washington, DC: American Educational Research Association.

Anderson, L. W., & Krathwohl, D. (2001). *A taxonomy for learning, teaching, and assessing: A revision of Bloom's taxonomy of educational objectives*. New York, NY: Addison Wesley Longman.

Applegate, M. D., Quinn, K. B., & Applegate, A. (2002). Levels of thinking required by comprehension questions in informal reading inventories. *The Reading Teacher, 56*, 174–180.

Beck, I. L. (2006). *Making sense of phonics: The hows and whys*. New York, NY: Guilford Press.

Benjamin, R. G., Schwanenflugel, P. J., Meisinger, E. B., Groff, C., Kuhn, M., & Steiner, L. (2013). A spectrographically grounded scale for evaluating reading expressiveness. *Reading Research Quarterly, 48*(2), 105–133.

Bernstein, J. (2004). Oral reading reliability study, personal communication, August, 2004.

Betts, F. (1946). *Foundations of reading instruction*. New York, NY: American Book.

Bloom, B., & Krathwohl, D. (1956). *Taxonomy of educational objectives: The classification of educational goals*. New York, NY: Longmans Green.

*Braasch, J. L. G., Goldman, S. R., & Wiley, J. (2013). The influence of text and reader characteristics on learning from refutations in science texts. *Journal of Educational Psychology, 105*, 561–578.

Brown, R., Pressley, M., Van Meter, P., & Schuder, T. (1996). A quasi-experimental validation of transactional strategies instruction and low-achieving second-grade readers. *Journal of Educational Psychology, 88*, 18–37.

Caccamise, D., Friend, A., Littrell-Baez, M. K., & Kintsch, E. (2015). Constructivist theory as a framework for instruction and assessment of reading comprehension (pp. 81–103). In S. R. Parris & K. Headley (Eds.), *Comprehension instruction: Research-based best practices* (3rd ed.). New York, NY: Guilford.

Caldwell, J., & Leslie, L. (2010). Thinking aloud in expository text. *Journal of Literacy Research, 42*(3), 308–340.

Caldwell, J., & Leslie, L. (2009; 2013). *Intervention strategies to follow informal reading inventory assessment: So, what do I do now?* (3rd ed.). Boston, MA: Pearson.

Catts, H. W. (2018). The simple view of reading: Advancements and false impressions. *Remedial and Special Education, 59*(5), 317–323.

*Chrystal, C. (1991). *Assessing prior knowledge across cultures*. Unpublished doctoral dissertation, Marquette University.

Ciardiello, A. V. (1998). Did you ask a good question today? Alternative cognitive and metacognitive strategies. *Journal of Adolescent and Adult Literacy, 42*, 210–219.

Coleman, D., & Pimentel, S. (2011). *Publisher's criteria for the common core standards in English language arts and literacy: Grades 3–12*. Retrieved March 13, 2012, from www.corestandards.org, p. 1.

Conrad, N. J. (2008). From reading to spelling and spelling to reading: Transfer goes both ways. *Journal of Educational Psychology, 100*, 869–878.

Cordova, J. R., Sinatra, G. M., & Jones, S. H. (2014), Confidence in prior knowledge, self-efficacy, interest and prior knowledge: Influences on conceptual change. *Contemporary Educational Psychology, 39*, 164–174.

Council of Chief State School Officers (CCSSO) & National Governors Association (NGA). Common Core State Standards for English language arts and literacy in history/social studies, science, and technical subjects. Retrieved September 28, 2010, from www.corestandards.org

Crocker, L., & Algina, J. (1986). *Introduction to classical and modern test theory*. New York, NY: Holt, Rinehart and Winston.

Cronbach, L. J. (1951). Coefficient alpha and the internal structure of tests. *Psychometrika, 16*, 297–334.

Cunningham, J. W., Spadorcia, S. A., Erickson, K. A., Koppenhaver, D. A., Sturm, J. M., & Yoder, D. E. (2005). Investigating the instructional supportiveness of leveled text. *Reading Research Quarterly, 40*, 410–427.

Davis, F. B. (1968). Research in comprehension in reading. *Reading Research Quarterly, 3*, 499–545.

Davis, F. B. (1972). Psychometric research on comprehension in reading. *Reading Research Quarterly, 7*, 628–678.

*Dickens, R. H., & Meisinger, E. B. (2017). Examining the effects of reading modality and passage genre on reading comprehension in middle school students. *Reading Psychology, 38*, 321–347.

Ehri, L. C. (1992). Reconceptualizing the development of sight word reading and its relationship to recoding. In P. B. Gough, L. C. Ehri, & R. Treiman (Eds.), *Reading acquisition* (pp. 107–143). Mahwah, NJ: Lawrence Erlbaum Associates.

Ehri, L.C. (2014). Orthographic mapping in the acquisition of sight word reading, spelling memory and vocabulary learning. *Scientific Studies of Reading, 18*(1), 5–21.

Ferretti, R. P., & De La Paz, S. (2011). On the comprehension and production of written texts: Instructional activities that support content-area literacy. In R. E. O'Connor & P. F. Vadasy (Eds.), *Handbook of reading interventions* (pp. 326–412). New York, NY: Guilford Press.

Fisher, D., & Frey, N. (2014). Close reading as an intervention for struggling middle school readers. *Journal of Adolescent and Adult Literacy, 57*, 367–376.

Fisher, D., Frey, N., & Lapp, D. (2012). *Text complexity: Raising rigor in reading.* Newark, DE: International Reading Association.

Fountas, I. C., & Pinnell, G. S. (2006). *The Fountas & Pinnell leveled book list, K–8.* Portsmouth, NH: Heinemann.

Fry, E. (1998). The most common phonograms. *The Reading Teacher, 51*, 620–622.

Fuchs, L. S., Fuchs, D., Hosp, M. K., & Jenkins, J. R. (2001). Oral reading fluency as an indicator of reading competence: A theoretical and historical analysis. *Scientific Studies of Reading, 5*, 239–256.

Gaskins, I., Downer, M., & the teachers of Benchmark School. (1997). *The Benchmark word identification/vocabulary development program.* Media, PA: Benchmark Press.

Gavelek, J., & Bresnahan, P. (2009) Ways of meaning-making: Sociocultural perspectives on reading comprehension. In S. E. Israel & G. G. Duffy (Eds.), *Handbook of research on reading comprehension*, (pp. 140–176). New York, NY: Routledge.

*Glass, S. (1989). *The effect of prior knowledge on reading miscues and comprehension of narrative text.* Unpublished master's thesis, Marquette University.

Good, R. H., & Kaminski, R. A. (2002). *Dynamic indicators of basic early literacy skills* (6th ed.). Eugene, OR: Institute for the Development of Educational Achievement. Retrieved November 30, 2014, from https://dibels.uoregon.edu

Goodman, K. S. (1965). A linguistic study of cues and miscues in reading. *Elementary English, 42*, 639–643.

Goodman, K. S. (1967). Reading: A psycholinguistic guessing game. In H. Singer & R. B. Ruddell (Eds.), *Theoretical models and processes of reading* (pp. 497–503). Newark, DE: International Reading Association.

Goswami, U. (1986). Children's use of analogy in learning to read: A developmental study. *Journal of Experimental Child Psychology, 42*, 73–83.

Gough, P. B., Hoover, W. A., & Peterson, C. L. (1996). Some observations on a simple view of reading. In J. V. Oakhill & C. Cornoldi (Eds.), *Reading comprehension difficulties: Processes and intervention* (pp. 1–13). Mahwah, NJ: Lawrence Erlbaum.

Gough, P. B., & Tunmer, W. E. (1986). Decoding, reading and reading disability. *Remedial and Special Education, 7*, 6–10.

Graesser, A. C., Ozuru, Y., & Sullins, J. (2010). What is a good question? In M. G. McKeown, & L. Kucan (Eds.), *Bringing reading research to life* (pp. 112–141). New York, NY: Guilford Press.

Graesser, A. C., & Person, N. K. (1994). Question asking during tutoring. *American Educational Research Journal, 31*, 104–137.

Hall, K. M., Markham, J. C., & Culatta, B. (2005). The development of the early expository comprehension assessment (EECA): A look at reliability. *Communication Disorders Quarterly, 26*, 195–206.

Harris, A. J., & Sipay, E. (1990). *How to increase reading ability: A guide to developmental and remedial methods* (8th ed.). New York, NY: Longman.

Helsel, L., & Greenberg, D. (2007). Helping struggling writers to succeed: A self-regulated strategy instruction program. *The Reading Teacher, 60*, 752–760.

Hiebert, E. H. (2013). Supporting students' movement up the staircase of text complexity. *The Reading Teacher, 66*, 459–469.

Hiebert, E. H., & Mesmer, H. A. (2013). Upping the ante of text complexity in the Common Core Standards: Examining its potential impact on young readers. *Educational Researcher, 42*, 44–51.

Hinchman, K. A., & Moore, D. W. (2013). Close reading: A cautionary interpretation. *Journal of Adolescent and Adult Literacy, 56*, 441–450.

Hoover, W. A., & Tunmer, W. E. (2018). The simple view of reading: Three assessments of its adequacy. *Remedial and Special Education, 39*(5), 304–312.

*Hua, A. N., & Keenan, J. M. (2014). The role of text memory in inferencing and in comprehension deficits. *Scientific Studies of Reading, 18*, 415–431.

Johns, J., & Johns, B. (2016). *Basic reading inventory K–12 and early literacy assessments.* Dubuque, IA: Kendall Hunt.

Johnson, A. M., Ozogult, G., & Reisslein, M. (2014). Supporting multimedia learning with visual signaling and animated pedagogical agent: moderating effects of prior knowledge. *Journal of Computer Assisted Learning*, 1–19.

Kame'enui, E. J., & Simmons, D.C. (2001). Introduction to this special issue: The DNA of reading fluency. *Scientific Studies of Reading, 5*, 203–210.

Kessler, B. & Treiman, R. (2001). Relationships between sounds and letters in English monosyllables. *Journal of Memory and Language, 44*, 592–617.

Kim, Y., Petscher, Y., Schatschneider, C., & Foorman, B. (2010). Does growth rate in oral reading fluency matter in predicting comprehension achievement? *Journal of Educational Psychology, 102*, 652–667.

Kintsch, W., & van Dijk, T. A. (1978). Towards a model of text comprehension and production. *Psychological Review, 5*, 363–394.

Klauda, S. L., & Guthrie, J. T. (2008). Relationships of three components of reading fluency to reading comprehension. *Journal of Educational Psychology, 100*, 310–321.

Klingner, J. K., Morrison, A., & Eppolito, A. (2011). Metacognition to improve reading comprehension. In R. E. O'Connor & P. D. Vadasy (Eds.), *Handbook of reading interventions* (pp. 220–254). New York, NY: Guilford Press.

Klingner, J. K., & Vaughn, S. (2004). Strategies for struggling second-language readers. In T. L. Jetton & J. A. Dole (Eds.), *Adolescent literacy research and practice* (pp. 183–209). New York, NY: Guilford Press.

Kraall, A., Koornneef, A.W., Saab, N., & van den Broek, P. (2017). Processing of expository and narrative texts by low- and high-comprehending children. *Reading and Writing*, 1–14, https://doi.org/10.1007/s11145-017-9789-2

Kuhn, M. R., Schwanenflugel, P. J., & Meisinger, E. B. (2010). Aligning theory and assessment of reading fluency: Automaticity, prosody, and definitions of fluency. *Reading Research Quarterly, 45*, 230–251.

Language and Reading Research Consortium (2015). Learning to read: Shall we keep things simple? *Reading Research Quarterly, 50*(2), 151–169.

La Russo, M., Kim, H. Y., Selman, R., Uccelli, P., Dawson, T., Jones, S., Donovan, S., & Snow, C. (2016). Contributions of academic language, perspective taking, and complex reasoning to deep reading comprehension. *Journal of Research of Educational Effectiveness, 9*(2), 201–222.

*Leslie, L., & Allen, L. (1999). Factors that predict success in an early intervention project. *Reading Research Quarterly, 34*, 404–424.

Leslie, L. & Caldwell, J. (1995). *Qualitative Reading Inventory-II*. New York, NY: Harper Row.

Leslie, L., & Caldwell, J. (2001). *Qualitative Reading Inventory-3*. New York, NY: Longman.

Leslie, L., & Caldwell, J. (2006). *Qualitative Reading Inventory-4*. Boston, MA: Allyn & Bacon.

Leslie, L., & Caldwell, J. (2009). Formal and informal measures of reading comprehension. In S. E. Israel & G. G. Duffy (Eds.), *Handbook of research on reading comprehension* (pp. 403–427). New York, NY: Routledge.

Leslie, L., & Caldwell, J. (2015). *Content area reading assessment: A formative measure of the Common Core State Standards*. Boston, MA: Pearson.

Leslie, L. & Caldwell, J. (2017). Assessments of reading comprehension: Challenges and directions. In S. Israel (Ed.), *Handbook of Research on Reading Comprehension*. (2nd ed.). New York: Guilford Press.

*Leslie, L., & Calhoon, A. (1995). Factors affecting children's reading of rimes: Reading ability, word frequency, and rime-neighborhood size. *Journal of Educational Psychology, 87*(4), 576–586.

*Leslie, L., & Cooper, J. (1993). Assessing the predictive validity of prior-knowledge assessment. In D. J. Leu & C. K. Kinzer (Eds.), *Examining central issues in literacy research, theory and practice* (pp. 93–100). Chicago, IL: National Reading Conference.

Lipson, M. Y. (1983). The influence of religious affiliation on children's memory for test information. *Reading Research Quarterly, 18*, 448–457.

Livingston, S. A. (1972). Criterion-referenced applications of classical test theory. *Journal of Educational Measurement, 9*, 13–26.

McCallum, R. S., Sharp, S., Bell, S. S., & George, T. (2004). Silent versus oral reading comprehension and efficiency. *Psychology in the Schools, 41*, 241–246.

*McCarthy, P. (1999). *The effects of balanced literacy instructional training: A longitudinal study of reading performance in the primary grades*. Unpublished doctoral dissertation, Marquette University.

McGee, L. M., Kim, H., Nelson, K. S., & Fried, M.D. (2015). Change over time in first graders' strategic use of information at point of difficulty in reading. *Reading Research Quarterly, 50*(3), 263–291.

McKenna, M. C., & Picard, M. C. (2006–2007). Revisiting the role of miscue analysis in effective teaching. *The Reading Teacher, 60*, 378–380.

McMaster, K. L., Espin, C. A., & van den Broek, P. (2014). Making connections: Linking cognitive psychology and intervention research to improve comprehension of struggling readers. *Learning Disabilities Research and Practice, 29* (1), 17–24.

McMaster, K. L., van den Broek, P., Espin, C. A., White, M. J., Rapp, D. N., Kendeou, P., et al., (2012). Making the right connections: Differential effects of reading intervention for subgroups of comprehenders. *Learning and Individual Differences, 22*, 100–111.

*Menon, S., & Hiebert, E. F. (2005). A comparison of first graders' reading with little books or literature-based anthologies. *Reading Research Quarterly, 40*, 12–38.

MetaMetrics. (2013). Retrieved August 24, 2013, from www.metametrics.com

Miles, K.P., Rubin, G.B., & Gonzalez-Frey, S. (2018). Rethinking sight words. *The Reading Teacher, 71*(6), 715–726.

Miller, J., & Schwanenflugel, P. J. (2008). A longitudinal study of the development of reading prosody as a dimension of oral reading fluency in early elementary school children. *Reading Research Quarterly, 43*, 336–354.

Moos, D. C., & Azevedo, R. (2008). Self-regulated learning with hypermedia: The role of prior domain knowledge. *Contemporary Educational Psychology, 33*, 270–298.

Morris, D. (2014). *Morris Informal Reading Inventory*. New York, NY: Guilford Press.

*Morris, D., Bloodgood, J. W., Perney, J., Frey, E. M., Kucan, L., Trathen, W., Ward, D., & Schlagel, R. (2011). Validating craft knowledge: An empirical examination of elementary-grade students' performance on an informal reading inventory. *The Elementary School Journal, 12*, 205–233.

Morsy, L., Kieffer, M., & Snow, C. E. (2010). *Measure for measure: A critical consumers' guide to reading comprehension assessments for adolescents*. New York, NY: Carnegie Corporation of New York. Retrieved December 8, 2010, from www.carnegie.org

Mosenthal, P. (1996). Understanding the strategies of document literacy and their condition of use. *Journal of Educational Psychology, 88*, 314–332.

National Reading Panel (2000). *Report of the National Reading Panel: Teaching children to read: An evidence-based assessment of the scientific research literature on reading and its implications for instruction*. Rockville, MD: NICHD Clearinghouse.

Nicholson, T., Lillas, C., & Rzoska, M. A. (1988). Have we been misled by miscues? *The Reading Teacher, 42,* 6–10.

Paris, S. G., Carpenter, R. D., Paris, A. H., & Hamilton, E. E. (2005). Spurious and general correlates of children's reading comprehension. In S. G. Paris & S. Stahl (Eds.), *Children's reading comprehension and assessment* (pp. 131–160). Mahwah, NJ: Erlbaum.

Paris, S. G., Pearson, P. D., Carpenter, R. D., Siebenthal, S., & Laier, B. (2002). *Evaluation of the Michigan Literacy Project Progress Profile (MLPP). Final Report Year 1.* Lansing, MI: Department of Education.

Pellegrino, J. S., Chudowsky, N., & Glaser, R. (2001). *Knowing what students know: The design of educational assessment.* Washington, DC: National Academy of Science.

Perin, D. (2007). Best practices in teaching writing to adolescents. In S. Graham, C. A. MacArthur, & J. Fitzgerald (Eds.), *Best practices in writing instruction* (pp. 242–264). New York, NY: Guilford Press.

Pinnell, G. S., Pikulski, J. J., Wixson, K. K., Campbell, J. R., Gough, P. B., & Beatty, A. S. (1995). *Listening to children read loud.* Washington, DC: U.S. Department of Education, National Center for Education Statistics.

Pressley, M., & Afflerbach, P. (1995). *Verbal protocols in reading: The nature of constructively responsive reading.* Mahwah, NJ: Lawrence Erlbaum Associates.

Prior, S. M., Fenwick, K. D., Saunders, K. S., Ouellette, R., O'Quinn, C., & Harvey, S. (2011). Comprehension after oral and silent reading: Does grade level matter? *Learning Research and Instruction, 50,* 183–194.

Raphael, T. E. (1982). Question-answering strategies for children. *The Reading Teacher, 36,* 186–190.

Raphael, T. E. (1986). Teaching question-answer relationships, revisited. *The Reading Teacher, 39,* 516–522.

Rapp, D. N., van den Broek, P., McMaster, K. L., Kendeou, P., & Espin, C. A. (2007). Higher-order comprehension processes in struggling readers: A perspective for research and intervention. *Scientific Studies of Reading, 11,* 289–312.

Rasinski, T., Rikli, A., & Johnson, S. (2009). Reading fluency: More than automaticity? More than a concern for the primary grades? *Literacy Research and Instruction, 48,* 350–361.

Recht, D. R., & Leslie, L. (1988). The effects of prior knowledge on good and poor readers' memory for text. *Journal of Educational Psychology, 80,* 16–20.

Reed, D. K., & Vaughn, S. (2012) Retell as an indicator of reading comprehension. *Scientific Studies of Reading, 16,* 187–217.

*Regner, M. (1992). Predicting growth in reading in regular and special education. Unpublished doctoral dissertation, Marquette University.

Roe, B., & Burns, P.C. (2010). *Informal reading inventory: Pre-primer through twelfth grade.* (8th ed.). Belmont, CA: Wadsworth Cengage Learning.

Roelle, J., Lehmkuhl, N., Beyer, M. U., & Berthold, K. (2014). The role of specificity, targeted learning activities, and prior knowledge for effects of relevance of instruction. *Journal of Educational Psychology, 107,* (3), 705–723.

Rodgers, E., D'Agostino, J. V., Harmey, S. J., Kelly, R. H., & Brownfield, K. (2016). Examining the nature of scaffolding in an early literacy intervention. *Reading Research Quarterly, 51*(3), 345–360.

Romero, F., Paris, S. G., & Brem, S. K. (2005). Children's comprehension and local-to-global recall of narrative and expository texts. *Current Issues in Education, 8,* 25.

Samuelstuen, M. S., & Bråten, I. (2005). Decoding, knowledge, and strategies of comprehension of expository text. *Scandinavian Journal of Psychology, 46,* 107–117.

Seidenberg, M. S., & McClelland, J. L. (1989). A distributed developmental model of word recognition and naming. *Psychological Review, 96*(4), 523–568.

Shanahan, C. (2009). Disciplinary comprehension. In S. E. Israel & G. G. Duffy (Eds.), *Handbook of research on reading comprehension* (pp. 240–261). New York, NY: Routledge.

Shanahan, C., Shanahan, T., & Misischia, C. (2011). Analysis of three readers in three disciplines: History, mathematics and chemistry. *Journal of Literacy Research, 43,* 394–430.

Snow, C. E. (2018). Simple and not-so-simple views of reading. *Remedial and Special Education, 39*(5), 313–316.

Stahl, S. A. (2006). Understanding shifts in reading and its instruction. In K. A. Dougherty Stahl & M. McKenna (Eds.), *Reading research at work: Foundations of effective practice* (pp. 45–75). New York, NY: Guilford Press.

Stahl, S. A., & Hiebert, E. H. (2005). The "word factors": A problem for reading comprehension. In S. G. Paris & S. A. Stahl (Eds.), *Children's reading comprehension and assessment* (pp. 161–186). Mahwah, NJ: Lawrence Erlbaum Associates.

Stanovich, K. E. (1993–1994). Romance and reality: Distinguished educator series. *The Reading Teacher, 47,* 280–291.

Stanovich, K. E. (2004). Matthew effects in reading: Some consequences of individual differences in the acquisition of literacy. In R. B. Ruddell & N. J. Unrau (Eds.), *Theoretical models and processes of reading* (5th ed., pp. 454–516). Newark, DE: International Reading Association.

Steffenson, M. S., Joag-Dev, C., & Anderson, R. C. (1979). A cross-cultural perspective on reading comprehension. *Reading Research Quarterly, 15,* 10–29.

Stenner, A. J., Burdick, H., Sanford, E., & Burdick, D. S. (2006). How accurate are Lexile text measures? *Journal of Applied Measurement, 7,* 302–322.

*Sutherland, H., & Neill, P. (2012). English language learners: A study of the effects of a summer enrichment program on language proficiency, reading self-concept, and value of reading. *The Educational Collaborative, 3,* 1–21.

Taboada, A., & Guthrie, J. T. (2006). Contributions of student questioning and prior knowledge to construction of knowledge from reading informational text. *Journal of Literacy Research, 38,* 1–35.

*Taft, M. L., & Leslie, L. (1985). The effects of prior knowledge and oral reading accuracy on miscues and comprehension. *Journal of Reading Behavior, 17,* 163–179.

Thorndike, R. M., Cunningham, G. K., Thorndike, R. L., & Hagen, E. P. (1991). *Measurement and evaluation in psychology and education* (5th ed.). New York, NY: Macmillan.

Tilstra, J., McMaster, K., van den Broek, P., Kendeou, P., & Rapp, D. (2009). Simple but complex: Components of the simple view of reading across grade levels. *Journal of Research in Reading, 32*(4), 383–401.

Trabasso, T., & Magliano, J. P. (1996). Conscious understanding during reading. *Discourse Processes, 21,* 255–287.

Tunmer, W. E., & Nicholson, T. (2011). The development and teaching of word recognition skill. In M. L. Kamil, P. D. Pearson, E. B. Moje, & P. P. Afflerbach (Eds.), *Handbook of reading research.* New York, NY: Routledge.

*Valencia, S. W., & Buly, M. R. (2004). Behind test scores: What struggling readers really need. *The Reading Teacher, 57*(6), 520–531.

Valencia, S. W., Smith, A. T., Reece, A. M., Li, M., Wixson, K., & Newman, H. (2010). Oral reading fluency assessment: Issues of construct, criterion, and consequential validity. *Reading Research Quarterly, 45,* 270–291.

van Kesteren, M., Rijpkema, M., Ruiter, D. J., Morris, R., & Fernandez, G. (2014). Building on prior knowledge: Schema-dependent encoding processes relate to academic performance. *Journal of Cognitive Neuroscience, 26*(10), 2250–2261.

Vellutino, F. R., Tunmer, W. E., Jaccard, J. J., & Chen, R. (2007). Components of reading ability: Multivariate evidence for a convergent skills model of reading development. *Scientific Studies of Reading, 11*(1), 3–32.

Willingham, D. T. (2006). How knowledge helps. *American Educator, 30,* 30–37.

Woods, M. L., & Moe, A. J. (2014). *Analytical reading inventory comprehensive standards-based assessment of all students including gifted and remedial.* (10th ed.). New York, NY: Pearson.

*Yeh, Y. F., McTigue, E. M., & Joshi, R. M. (2012). Moving from explicit to implicit: A case study of improving inferential comprehension. *Literacy Research and Instruction, 51,* 125–142.

Zeno, S. M., Ivens, S. H., Millard, R. T., & Duvvuri, R. (1995). *The educator's word frequency guide.* Brewster, NY: Touchstone Applied Science Associates, Inc.

Index

A

"A New Friend from Europe,"
214–216, 227–230
"A Night in the City," 137–140, 150
"A Special Birthday for Rosa,"
210–211, 220–222
"A Wave of Nativism," 456–458,
469–473
"Abraham Lincoln," 277, 284–286
"Air," 170, 181–182
"Amelia Earhart," 240, 244–246
"America Adjusts to Peace,"
481–483, 495–499
Automatic word recognition, 40
Automaticity of oral reading, 14
evaluating, 55–57
recognition, 42

B

"The Bear and the Rabbit," 167–169,
178–180
Bloom's taxonomy, 19
"The Body's Transportation System"
(Science), 415–417, 425–429
"The Brain and Five Senses," 171,
183–184
"Building Pyramids," 280, 296–300

C

"Cats: Lions and Tigers in Your
House," 217, 231–233
CBM (curriculum-based measures), 14
CCSS (Common Core State
Standards), 20, 21
"Clouds and Precipitation,"
282–283, 305–309
Comprehension
automaticity and, 14–15
content knowledge, 16
fluency and, 14–15
inferential, 3
interactive strategies, 22–23
listening comprehension, 60
literal, 3
look-backs, 21–22, 68–69
oral reading, 11–13
prosody and, 14–15
questions, 19–21, 59–62
reading fluency and, 2
retelling and summarization,
17–18, 57–60, 62–68
silent reading comprehension, 2
text structure, 16–17
thinking aloud, 22–23

verbal proficiency and, 2
word recognition, 10–11
Content Area Reading Assessment
(CARA), 21
Content knowledge, comprehension
and, 16
CVCE (consonant vowel/
consonant/e pattern), 11
"Cynthia Rylant: The Development
of an Author" (Biography),
390–391, 398–401

D

Decoding, 1–2
sounding out, 10
Dialect speakers, 52
Duration, prosody and, 14

E

"The Early Life of Lois Lowry," 278,
287–292
"Early Railroads," 242, 250–252
eText videos, 522–525
Explicit questions, 60–62
Expository passages
instructional reading level, 36
question stems, 21
reading levels and, 34–35
retelling, 66–68

F

"The Family's First Trip," 185,
195–197
"Farming on the Great Plains," 258,
268–271
"Father's New Game," 190–192,
201–203
Fluency, 3, 14–15
Fountas and Pinnell system, 5
"Fox and Mouse," 141–144, 152–153
"The Friend," 212–213, 224–226
"From Dynasty to Dynasty" (Social
Studies), 433–435, 444–449
Frustration reading level, 33

G

Graphophonic (graphic) cue
system, 12

H

Harris-Jacobson Readability Levels
QRI-7, 7
Hiebert's qualitative components, 5
High School Passages

"America Adjusts to Peace" (Social
Studies), 481–483, 495–499
"Characteristics of Viruses—Parts
1 & 2," (Science) 351–355,
385–395
"The Kingdoms of Life" (Science),
484–486, 499–502
"The Life of Georgia O'Keeffe:
The Artist and the Woman"
(Biography), 477–480, 487–495
"World War I—Parts 1 & 2," (Social
Studies) 345–350, 372–384
"How Do Organisms Compete for
Resources?" (Science), 395–397,
406–409
"How Does Your Body Take in
Oxygen?" (Science) 259,
272–275

I

"I Can," 104–109, 125–126
"I See," 110–114, 127–128
"Immigration—Parts 1 & 2,"
312–315, 326–334
Implicit questions, 60–62
Independent reading level, 33
Inference-Diagnostic passages, 6, 19
evaluations, 385–388
versus Level-Diagnostic passages,
381–382
mode of reading, 382
purpose, 380–381
questions, 381–384
selecting, 382
Inferential comprehension, 3
Insertions, 50
Instructional reading level, 33
determining, 35–38
expository text, 36
narrative text, 36
order of administration, 35–36
passage level
scores, 36–37
passages, 36
Total Acceptability, 36
Total Accuracy, 36
word lists, 36
IRI (informal reading inventory)
assessment, 3–4

J

"Jaime Escalenté: Teacher
Extraordinaire" (Literature),
310–311, 320–325

"Jane Goodall, Goddess of the Apes" (Biography), 410–411, 418–421
"Just Like Mom," 115–119, 129–130

K

"The Kingdoms of Life," 484–486, 499–502

L

"The Legacy of Jim Thorpe" (Biography), 430–432, 439–443
Level-Diagnostic passages, 6, 18
versus Inference-Diagnostic passages, 381–382
Level 1 Passages
  "Air," 170, 181–182
  "The Bear and the Rabbit," 167–169, 178–180
  "The Brain and Five Senses," 171, 183–184
  "Marva Finds a Friend," 164–169, 175–177
  "The Surprise," 160–163, 172–174
Level 2 Passages
  "The Family's First Trip," 185, 195–197
  "Father's New Game," 190–192, 201–203
  "The Lucky Cricket," 186–189, 199–200
  "Seasons," 191, 207–209
  "Whales and Fish," 193, 204–206
Level 3 Passages
  "A New Friend from Europe," 214–216, 227–230
  "A Special Birthday for Rosa," 210–211, 220–222
  "Cats: Lions and Tigers in Your House," 217, 231–233
  "The Friend," 212–213, 224–226
  "Where Do People Live?" 218, 234–236
  "Wool: From Sheep to You," 219, 237–239
Level 4 Passages
  "Amelia Earhart," 240, 244–246
  "Cynthia Rylant: The Development of an Author" (Biography), 390–391, 398–401
  "Early Railroads," 242, 250–252
  "How Do Organisms Compete for Resources?" (Science), 395–397, 406–409
  "Linking East and West" (Social Studies), 392–394, 402–405
  "Plant Structures for Survival," 243, 253–255
  "Tomie dePaola," 241, 247–249

Level 5 Passages
  "The Body's Transportation System" (Science), 415–417, 425–429
  "Farming on the Great Plains," 258, 268–271
  "How Does Your Body Take in Oxygen?" 259, 272–275
  "Jane Goodall, Goddess of the Apes" (Biography), 410–411, 418–421
  "Margaret Mead," 256, 260–262
  "Patricia McKissack," 257, 263–267
  "The Rise of Cattle Drives" (Social Studies), 412–414, 422–425
Level 6 Passages
  "Abraham Lincoln," 277, 284–286
  "Building Pyramids," 280, 296–300
  "Clouds and Precipitation," 282–283, 305–309
  "The Early Life of Lois Lowry" (Biography), 278, 287–292
  "From Dynasty to Dynasty" (Social Studies), 433–435, 444–449
  "The Legacy of Jim Thorpe" (Biography), 430–432, 439–443
  "The Lifeline of the Nile," 279, 293–296
  "Temperature and Humidity," 281, 391–304
  "What Causes Weather" (Science), 436–438, 448–451
Lexile scales, 4–5, 7–8
"Life Cycles of Stars—Part 1," 316–317, 335–338
"Life Cycles of Stars—Part 2," 318–319, 339–343
"The Life of Georgia O'Keeffe: The Artist and the Woman," 477–480, 487–495
"The Lifeline of the Nile," 279, 293–295
"Linking East and West" (Social Studies), 392–394, 402–405
Literal comprehension, 3
"Living and Not Living," 146, 155–156
Look-backs, 27
  comprehension and, 21–22
  comprehension assessment, 68–69
"Lost and Found," 123, 133–134
Low-frequency words, 45
"The Lucky Cricket," 186–189, 198–200

M

"Malcom X: The Development of a Separatist" (Biography), 452–455, 462–469
"Margaret Mead," 256, 260–262

"Marva Finds a Friend," 164–166, 175–177
Mean of Seven Readability Formula Estimates, 8
Meaning change miscues, 50, 54
Middle School Passages. *See also* Upper Middle School Passages
  "Malcom X: The Development of a Separatist" (Biography), 452–455, 462–469
  "A Wave of Nativism" (Social Studies), 456–458, 469–473
  "What Is a Comet?" (Science), 459–461, 474–476
Miscue analysis (oral reading), 12–13, 49–56

N

Narrative passages, 21, 34–36, 63–65

O

Omissions, 48, 50
Oral language, 1
Oral reading
  automaticity evaluation, 55–57
  miscue analysis, 12–13, 49–56
Oral Reading Prosody Scale, 15
ORF (oral reading fluency), 14

P

"Patricia McKissack," 257, 263–267
Pauses, prosody and, 14
Pearson eText videos, 538–543
"People at Work," 120–122, 131–132
Phonograms, 41
"The Pig Who Learned to Read," 145–147, 154–155
Pitch, prosody and, 14
"Plant Structures for Survival," 243, 253–255
PP2/3 (pre-primer 2/3), 11
PP1 (pre-primer 1) list, 10–11
Pre-Primer 1 passages
  "I Can," 104–109, 125–126
  "I See," 110–114, 127–128
Pre-Primer 2 passages
  "Just Like Mom," 115–119, 129–130
  "People at Work," 120–122, 131–132
Pre-Primer 3 passages
  "Lost and Found," 123, 133–134
  "Spring and Fall," 124, 135–136
Primer passages
  "A Night in the City," 137–140, 150
  "Fox and Mouse," 141–144, 152–153
  "Living and Not Living," 149, 158–159

"The Pig Who Learned to Read,"
    145–147, 154–155
"Who Lives Near Lakes?" 148,
    156–157
Prosody, 14–15, 26–27, 58

Q
Question types, 19–21, 27, 60–62

R
Readability formulas, 4–7
Reading by analogy, 10–11, 41,
    45–47
Reading growth assessment, 27–28,
    87–88
Reading levels, 33–35, 61
Reading Recovery, 5
Retelling and summarization, 17–18,
    63–68
Reversals, 50
"The Rise of Cattle Drives" (Social
    Studies), 412–414, 422–425

S
"Seasons," 194, 207–209
Semantic acceptability, 53
Semantic cues, 12
SFI (standard frequency index),
    10–11, 48
Sight vocabulary, 38, 56
Signal words, readability formulas, 4
Silent reading comprehension, 2, 57
Sounding out (decoding), 10
Spelling patterns, 41
"Spring and Fall," 124, 135–136
Substitutions, 49, 50
"The Surprise," 160–163, 172–174
SVR (Simple View of Reading), 1–2
    higher-order comprehension, 2
Syntactic acceptability, 54–55
Syntactic cue system, 12

T
Technical development *(QRI-7)*
    alternate-form reliability, 520–521
    educational assessment, 511
    Inference Diagnostic materials,
        510–511
    informal reading inventory, 511–519
    interpretation, 519–520
    Level-Diagnostic materials, 507–509

measures of comprehension,
    507–511
piloting materials, 504–506,
    505–506
prior-knowledge assessments,
    506–507
test-retest reliability, 520–521
think-aloud procedure, 509–510
"Temperature and Humidity," 280,
    301–304
Text structure knowledge
    assessment and, 3
    comprehension and, 16–17
Think-alouds, 70–71
    commands, understanding
        and, 71
    examples, 73–78
    modeling, 71–73
"Tomie dePaola," 241, 247–249
Total Acceptability, 36
    oral reading and, 11–12
    miscues, 53–55
    semantic acceptability, 53
    syntactic acceptability, 54–55
Total Accuracy, 36
    oral reading and, 11–12
    miscues, 51–53

U
Upper Middle School Passages.
    See also Middle School Passages
    "Immigration—Parts 1 & 2,"
        312–315, 326–334
    "Jaime Escalenté: Teacher
        Extraordinaire" (Literature),
        306–307, 324–329
    "Life Cycles of Stars—Parts 1 & 2,"
        316–319, 335–343

V
Verbal proficiency, comprehension
    and, 2
Vocabulary and/or content
    knowledge, 3
Vowel patterns, 41
Vowel pronunciation, 10

W–Z
WCPM (words correct per minute),
    15, 27, 57
"Whales and Fish," 193, 204–206

"What Causes Weather" (Science),
    436–438, 448–451
"What Is a Comet?" 459–461,
    474–476
"Where Do People Live?" 218,
    234–236
"Who Lives Near Lakes?" 148,
    156–157
"Wool: From Sheep to You," 219,
    237–239
Word difficulty
    readability formulas, 4
Word identification. *See* word
    recognition/identification
Word lists
    accuracy, 42
    additional uses, 47
    analysis, 47–48
    automaticity, 42
    development, 47–48
    identification estimate, 39–40
    letter-sound matching knowledge
        estimate, 41
    passage administration starting
        point, 40
    procedures for administering, 41–43
    purposes for administering, 39–41
    recognition automaticity, 40
    recognition estimate, 39–40
    scores, 43–45
    vowel pattern knowledge estimate,
        41
Word recognition/identification,
    1–2, 10–11
    assessment and, 3, 10
    automatic word recognition, 40
    context in, 12
    frequency of occurrence, 10
    isolation *versus* context, 41
    phonograms, 41
    reading by analogy, 10–11, 41
    SFI (standard frequency index), 10
    sight vocabulary, 40
    spelling patterns, 41
    Total Acceptability, 53–55
    Total Accuracy, 51–53
    vowel patterns, 41
    word list administration, 39–40
"World War I—Parts 1 & 2," 345–
    350, 372–384
WPM (word-per-minute) score, 57